PUBLIC SPEAKING
AS A
LIBERAL ART

Public Speaking as a Liberal Art

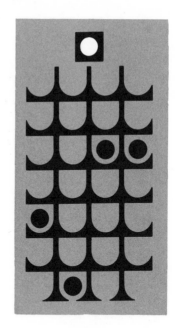

THIRD EDITION

JOHN F. WILSON
*Herbert H. Lehman College of
the City University of New York*

CARROLL C. ARNOLD
The Pennsylvania State University

Allyn and Bacon, Inc.
Boston · London · Sydney

LIBRARY OF CONGRESS CATALOG CARD NUMBER: 73–88387

ISBN: 0-205-04299-6

Third printing . . . May, 1975

PRINTED IN THE UNITED STATES OF AMERICA

Contents

Preface

This third edition of *Public Speaking as a Liberal Art* reasserts our belief that speech is best studied when students pursue the subject in search of knowledge and experience that can enlarge the range of personal freedom. In communication, as elsewhere, there is freedom of choice only if the chooser knows the options he has and the discriminations he needs to make in the situations in which he finds himself. And there is freedom of choice only if he knows what attitudes are relevant to varying situations and what "excellence" consists of within them. It is to widen students' grounds for choice in communication that we undertake to set before them a record of how public speech has been thought of and reflective rather than prescriptive discussions of the decisions that affect command of self and environment where communication is relatively formal.

In this edition we treat public speaking more broadly than in earlier editions. In keeping with the democratized, informalized nature of today's public speech and in accord with recent developments in the study of rhetoric, we have defined public speaking as any continuing utterance that occurs in a rhetorical situation functioning as a system specially dependent on a single communicator.

We have rewritten all but a few, small portions of the book. We have approached the history of rhetorical theory as a series of attempts to solve problems that persist in all oral communication: problems of invention, disposition, style, delivery, and *memoria*. Those who have used former editions of this book will find the two introductory chapters reorganized in major ways. Within the chapters on style and delivery, materials have been significantly rearranged. Throughout, new material has been added, especially concerning the nature of rhetorical situations, *memoria*, nonverbal communication, and the settings in which public speech occurs. More extensive use has also been made of conceptions originating in Stephen E. Toulmin's *The Uses of Argument.*

We wish to invite students who read this edition to consider the evidence, reflect, and come to decisions of their own. If they do, we believe they will function with better judgment and better effect in practical public speech.

For assistance in preparing this edition we express our thanks to: Bie Arnold, Professor Mary W. Graham, J. C. Robertson, III, and Jane P. Rose, who helped in preparing the manuscript; Professor Anthony J. Mulac, University of California at Santa Barbara, who provided unusually valuable criticism; Sheryl Avruch, Editor, Allyn and Bacon, Inc., who gave valuable editorial assistance, Wayne A. Barcomb, Director of the College Division, Allyn and Bacon, Inc., who instigated this project originally, Frank Ruggirello, Associate Editor, and Allen Workman, Editor, also of Allyn and Bacon, Inc., who gave helpful advice and encouragement.

John F. Wilson
Carroll C. Arnold

CHAPTER
1

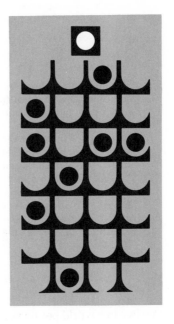

The Art of
Public Speaking

We ought, therefore, to think of the art of discourse just as we think of the other arts, and not to form opposite judgments about similar things, nor show ourselves intolerant toward that power, which, of all the faculties which belong to the nature of man, is the source of most of our blessings. For in the other powers which we possess . . . we are in no respect superior to other living creatures; nay, we are inferior to many in swiftness and in strength and in other resources; but, because there has been implanted in us the power to persuade each other and to make clear to each other whatever we desire, not only have we escaped the life of the wild beasts, but we have come together and founded cities and made laws and invented arts; and generally speaking, there is no institution devised by man which the power of speech has not helped us to establish.

Isocrates, "Antidosis"[1]

We live in a world permeated by the spoken word. Nonverbal communication is often substituted for verbal as in agitation, communicating through sit-ins, button-wearing, fist waving, posters, and the like, but in practical affairs the spoken word still remains our most basic medium. Millions are spent to create and maintain *vocal* contact with deep-sea divers, airplane pilots, and astronauts. One study of clerks, secretaries, technicians, and engineers in a large research and development laboratory found the staff actually spent about 35 percent of all working time in face-to-face talk with others, though when asked to estimate their communicative and other activities they *underestimated* their talking time by about 40 percent and *overestimated* their reading-writing time by about the same amount![2] Few organizations seem able to exist without "meetings"; committees abound, and lectures and discussions dominate in educational experience and in religious experience.

Over 96 percent of the families in the United States own television sets which operate in some homes for as many as 60 hours a week.[3] Those who watch television are bombarded with "little speeches" in advertising, are entertained by watching others talk on "talk shows" and in interviews, are informed by news reports which are in reality public speeches, and learn the

1. Reprinted by permission of the publishers and the Loeb Classical Library from Isocrates, "Antidosis," trans. by George Norlin in *Isocrates* (Cambridge, Mass.: Harvard University Press, 1956), II, p. 327.
2. E. T. Klemmer and F. W. Synder, "Measurement of Time Spent Communicating," *The Journal of Communication,* XX (June 1972), 142–158.
3. Joan Ganz Cooney, "Sesame Opens Doors to Knowledge," *New York Times,* Jan. 12, 1970, p. 61C.

2

state of politics by watching political conventions which consist largely of keynote, nominating, acceptance, and other sorts of formal speeches. They hear and see political commentaries, debates, discussions, and spot announcements for and by candidates. Meanwhile, ecology groups and boy scout troops send members singly and in teams from door to door to sell ideas and projects and to solicit funds.

It is said that oratory is dead. If by "oratory" is meant a kind of formal, stylized, inflated communication, we hope it is dead. But ordinary, consecutive, oral communication is by no means dead or out of fashion. In a multitude of forms public speech is with us now more than ever. The easier it is for citizens to move about, the more they meet and make talks to one another. Each step in democratizing the media that carry speech increases the numbers of public speakers who use them and the numbers of audiences spoken to. Public speaking has taken a new cast, it is true. It is less ritualistic and less formal than it once was, but people increasingly are required to "take a few minutes to report," to "sell ideas," to "raise the problem," to "speak to this point," and to engage large and small audiences in countless other *public* ways.

One can learn something useful about this sort of speech merely by asking what the term "public" really means when it is used today. Why, indeed, do people even try to make distinctions between "public" and "private" speech? One explanation is that everyone *feels* about conversation differently from the way he or she *feels* about speaking "in public." Yet the number of people present does not fully account for these different feelings. No one would say, "Speech is public if seven people hear it but private when six or fewer are involved." One thing the different feelings reflect is that sometimes a single individual gets the responsibility for creating and maintaining interpersonal relations through speech with "a public," or audience, which expects that individual to "carry on." In other situations the burden for maintaining communicative relationships through speech acts is distributed, shared. A major difference between public speech and private speech is that in the settings we call *public*, responsibility for maintaining communicative relationships becomes focused upon individuals for varying periods of time. In private speech the location of this responsibility is unpredictable, and often its assumption is entirely voluntary.

Now, a further meaning of the distinction between public and private speech emerges. If someone is given responsibility for maintaining communication over a period of time, someone else assumes the role of relatively quiet listener. As there is a responsible speaker, there is also an audience (at least a listener) who acquiesces in the arrangement of responsibilities. There is a communicator and a "public," an audience. That public or audience may be one person or many persons, but the public or audience we mean when we refer to "public speaking" is really just those people-who-will-listen, acquiescing in a speaker's attempt to create a communicative, human relationship through speech acts for some never-quite-predictable length of time.

If we ask once more whether there is much of this kind of public speaking in our lives, we shall have to answer that it goes on more widely than was suggested even by the first paragraph of this chapter. A secretary tells her boss just what supplies are in the office inventory and what must be bought. An athletic scout returns from scouting a future opponent and tells their game strategies to the head coach, or to two or three coaches, or to the coaches and the entire team. A committee member tells the committee the facts he was asked to collect. You summarize the causes for a stock market boom for your economics professor, or for your classmates. A teacher talks briefly or at length to a class. It is all public speaking, for someone has responsibility for maintaining mutually rewarding communicative experience with an audience that acquiesces in the arrangement for a not-always-predictable period of time. This is the public speaking about which this book is written.

MISCONCEPTIONS ABOUT SPEAKING

As there are misconceptions about how speech becomes "public," there are misconceptions of what speaking and developing skill in speaking involve. Some of the misconceptions are understandable because the very ways we learn speech discourage us from thinking systematically about this unique ability which only human beings seem to have. We learn to speak from those around us: from parents, friends, teachers, social and religious leaders, movie and television personalities. The learning is largely unselfconscious. Naturally enough, we then take our speech habits for granted until events force us to see that our talk does not attain our goals. Then comes the sense that "communication has broken down," and that sense is not rare. A Louis Harris poll recently indicated that 32 percent of a cross section of 26 million Americans between the ages of 15 and 21 had trouble communicating with parents, and 74 percent of these people thought the communicative problems stemmed from both sides.[4]

Without suggesting that they account for all or even most "breakdowns" in speech communication, we want to point to six, too common misconceptions about how oral communication works. No doubt some of them account for an unknown number of failures in social and familial communication, but any *one* of them can prevent you from becoming as effective as possible in public speech.

First, there is the idea that effectiveness in oral communication cannot be learned, that it is inherited or just "rubs off on you," or fails to. Unquestionably a "good" environment encourages socially effective speech behavior.

---

4. Anon., "Change, Yes—Upheaval, No," *Life*, LXX (Jan. 8, 1971), 22.

But it is equally true that few people who seriously study and practice speech as a communicative art fail to improve whatever skills they began with. Educators and corporation executives have tested for the effects of speech training as rigorously as they have known how, and concluded that able people become abler communicators in consequence of studying the nature and methods of speaking.[5] And the testimony of those who have taken the study of speech seriously plus the evident improvement of speaking in speech classes confirm that whatever may have been inherited or "rubbed off" can be refined by thoughtful, informed study and practice.

A second and ancient misconception is that if you have anything to say, you needn't worry about how to say it. Allegedly, good content will assure its effective presentation. The idea is old, and it dies hard. Yet everyone has experienced professorial lectures poorly organized, delivered with blurred articulation and inadequate volume, or directed to trees and windows. These experiences amply refute the content-is-enough notion. To be effective, communicators must have learned somewhere that speaking is *behaving in relation to other people* and that the behaving must show that the speaker is thinking about his listeners as well as about content.

Equally unfounded is a third misconception: that content is *not* important in oral communication. The folk saying, "It isn't what you say, it's how you say it," conceals a grain of truth in a bushel of falsehood. Experimentation and experience make it clear that when manner is discernible above content, suspicion rather than conviction follows. So-called dynamic salesmen and commentators are less trusted than "conversational" ones. Students easily distinguish "showmen" from "real teachers." The playwright Arthur Miller wrote his American tragedy *Death of a Salesman* in part to dramatize the human inadequacy of the doctrine that method is all. "How you say it" is important in speaking, but manner alone does not for long protect the absence of matter.

A fourth misconception has particularly to do with courses in speech communication and especially with public speaking courses. It is that a course in speech is primarily concerned with the management of body and voice, with how to move about a lectern and speak in seductive tones. Specialists in communication do teach effective vocal behavior and devote considerable attention to nonverbal communication. But study of the whole act of speaking effectively to others usually is primarily concerned with preparing ideas for public reception. Ideas need to be reinforced by voice and gesture, but these are incidental, not central, matters in creating effective communication for any public. The point is obvious to those who have explored the nature of

---

5. There is relatively little published research on this point, but our "product" has never been more rigorously tested than when we have taught public speaking for industrial firms and other private organizations. One of our universities has for several years maintained a flourishing in-service training program in speech communication for school systems and their teachers, which supervisors and teachers agree enhances the work of even experienced teachers.

public communication, but the conception that studying speech is studying delivery is still found to be widely held when college and university students are interviewed *before* entering speech courses. As you begin the course of study developed in this book, you should expect to give attention to your delivery, but only as support for concepts and feelings.

A fifth misconception is that speaking to an audience, especially a large one, is something like acting. The view is that a speaker plays a role, becoming someone other than himself. Yet, in contrast to an actor, a speaker rarely dares project personality traits other than his own. Why? Because as a speaker he is expected by his listeners to communicate his *own* thoughts and feelings, not those of someone else. He will be held tomorrow for all the meanings he communicated yesterday; to be consistent, he had better be himself on both occasions. More important, every speaker operates in what his listeners expect to be a genuine, personal relationship; he is expected to talk in and concerning reality—using his own resources. Of course, in very formal situations special lighting and platform decorations—even makeup and television cameras—are not unknown. We see them, for example, at conventions, in telecasts, and the like, but if they are competent, speakers must show they could have succeeded without such aids.

As his audience and his situation define him, a speaker must be himself because the responses at issue are primarily utilitarian, not aesthetic. Even when listening to be entertained, audiences meet their speakers in *their* own worlds, in *their* time, expecting to retain their awareness of real problems, real things, and real happenings.

The sixth and final misconception we shall consider is the notion that communicators behave the same way when they read aloud as when they speak extemporaneously. This is not the case. Public speaking differs from oral reading in the purpose of the presentation, the process of preparation, and the material presented. Unless an oral reader is reading his own composition, he acts as an interpreter of someone else's ideas. In preparation he must discover the real author's intellectual and emotional meanings and transmit these to his audience. This requires a different imaginative capacity from that required of public speakers, especially those who speak extemporaneously. In addition, the two manners of speaking involve different processes of selectivity. An oral reader has had the ideas and words selected for him; he must select the speech behaviors that will convey the meanings of another person. But a public speaker selects his own ideas and all the symbols for those ideas; then he chooses how to behave to convey his own meanings.

A reader's purpose may or may not be rhetorical. He may read to provide information, to instruct, to persuade, or to entertain his audience. His purposes, like those of the public speaker, may then be distinctly utilitarian, aimed at useful, practical ends. On the other hand, his purpose may be largely aesthetic; he may seek a response to the beauty of his material. A good public speaker seldom invites primarily aesthetic responses. While he may evoke feelings and engender emotional response, his aim is to focus attention upon the specific, personalized meanings he has conceived as peculiarly suited to a specific audience and situation.

Those who read their speeches usually do so because they have not had time to gain command of their ideas or because they lack confidence in their control over them, or because any deviation from plan or wording could have serious public consequences, as in diplomacy. Before the advent of disc and tape recording, speakers also memorized or read for a reason that no longer applies: to assure accurate reproduction of their speeches in print. With modern means of recording this concern is no longer very important; nonetheless, in some settings such as dedications, anniversaries, commencements, and important state occasions, tradition still prompts speakers to write out and read their messages. In ordinary circumstances, it is debatable whether reading or memorizing serves the cause of effective communication.

SPEECH AS A LIBERAL STUDY

In our view, to be "liberally educated" is to be personally and socially effective, and being able to interact purposefully with other people through speaking and listening is a significant part of being "personally and socially effective." This is our basic meaning in calling public speaking a liberal art. It is an art of achieving effective, constructive human relationships in situations where one bears responsibility for sustaining interpersonal relationships through speech. Looked at in this way, the ultimate end of studying public speaking is to achieve social understanding—of one's self and of others.

The Freeing of Self

At its best the tradition of the liberal arts has been to emphasize studies which free people to achieve all they are capable of within the constraints of human powers and the world they live in. And from this point of view mastering an "art" is making one's self free to do what can be done without constraint by ignorance of what the possibilities are. Attaining such freedom comes not only from Socrates' injunction, "Know thyself," but from another injunction: "Know others!" In the study of any communicative art the injunctions mean: Understand how *you* and *others* act and react when engaged in reaching and influencing one another through your unique powers to behave symbolically and to understand symbolic behavior. Applied to the art of public speaking, mastery of the art demands understanding of how we and those we address in consecutive, oral discourse act and react symbolically. One cannot have even basic understanding of these matters without acquaintance with theories people have had and have now about this kind of experience and how it is rendered personally and socially constructive.

The Study as a Search

An advantage of approaching the study of speech as a search for social and artistic understanding is that one learns to discriminate among possibilities. The numerous options one has in creating messages are discussed in Chapters 3, 4, 5, and 6, and the alternatives one has in structuring thinking and speech are treated in Chapter 8. Discriminating among the speech practices others use well and not so well is the special concern of the final chapter of this book. We hope this emphasis on the full array of your options will help to free your thought and behavior from the constraints of mere habit. We hope to stimulate you to sift your rhetorical options, combine them in fresh ways that are distinctively appropriate to rhetorical situations, and so increase your personal and social potentialities now and for the future.

A further advantage of conducting study of speech as a search is that it lets one see the interconnections of ideas, actions, and processes. The psychology of audiences can be seen as the real reason for communicating a set of ideas in one way rather than other sets of ideas in other ways, yet the *ways* are the content of an *art,* while the ideas may be those of science, literature, history, or some other "discipline." Liberally oriented, studying speaking can become a study of how knowledge, *in general,* is rendered *humanly* significant in situations.

Wisely conducted, the study of speaking can and should correlate with other liberal studies. In deciding what to say in speeches, you will need to draw upon other subjects such as history, government, and literature. In deciding how to speak reasonably and systematically, you will need to call upon your experience with practices in thinking, acquired through study of philosophy, the physical sciences, and mathematics. You may assimilate what you learned in literature, English composition, linguistics, and foreign languages as you select verbal symbols to convey your messages. The process of voicing your thoughts may make you see special meanings in physics, music, or acoustical engineering. The management of your body to reinforce your ideas may prompt you to bring to bear knowledge acquired in biology, physiology, physical education, and dance. The art of speaking is an eclectic art, the resources of which are as varied as man's shared knowledge.

The Appreciation of the Best

A liberal approach to speaking or any other subject involves one in striving to understand and to produce the best, even though what the "best" is is not fully known or attainable. In speech, as in other human enterprises, some theories, some achievements, some works have emerged as the nearest approximations to the "best" so far known. They can be sorted out from the ordinary; thus liberal study is necessarily linked but not chained to the past. If what we have inherited as models and standards is not looked to at all, we can only repeat the mistakes of the past and lose its achievements. Hence, in this book we have tried to draw lessons from the thinkers whose thoughts seem to "stand up" best and from examples of speaking that has "stood out" even in a long view. In the chapters to follow we have tried to discriminate among theories, advice, and examples in the belief that some have "proved best" over the long run. And, naturally enough, some seemingly "best" ideas turn out to be ancient and some exceedingly modern.

Experiments in Adjustment

In a sense all liberal study makes acquisition of techniques and skills subsidiary to acquiring a philosophy of doing—acquiring premises from which we can think fruitfully in specific, even unique, situations. The point is that we do not become personally and socially effective by following recipes. We have to adjust ourselves *knowingly* to whatever environments we enter. This does not mean that in studying speech we should study *about* it but not *do* it. We learn in very important ways by experimenting, but if speaking experiments are made for their own sakes, we shall only learn recipes for specific kinds of oral interactions. We shall gain no rationales and principles that apply to communication generally. What we need from experiments with public speaking are generalizations, guidelines, that cover *more* situations than the one experimented with. Then, understanding of socially effective speech can grow until we can adjust creatively to situations never met before.

The Perspective

This, then, is the perspective in which we propose that you view your study of public speaking. We urge you to make your goal the exercise of free intellect in making informed communicative choices, in discriminating among the values your alternatives have, and in recognizing that all you do in speaking draws upon what you know, what you are, what your auditors know, what they are, and everything knowable about the situation in which you speak. To approach study and practice of speech in this manner can enlarge your freedom as a person and will enable you to make practice into application of artistic principles rather than rehearsal of techniques.

In the hope that you will want to study and practice in these ways, we shall provide in the pages that follow advice you will need to make free, discriminating, communicative choices.   But we shall not prescribe what you should talk about or what courses of action you should follow; we shall suggest possibilities.   From choosing a subject to talk about, through choosing supportive ideas, to deciding on words and actions, you will be invited to inform yourself of your options and then to act in the freedom of that wide knowledge.   To encourage you to notice the intertwined character of human knowledge, we shall often draw parallels between speech and other subjects of study.   In examples and models we shall try to illustrate how dependent effective speaking is on the resources of other subject matters.   And as a way of inviting you to see the wide range of alternatives over which communicators exercise judgment even as they act, we shall suggest exercise materials which we hope will invite your reflection as well as your action.

Specific Concerns

What will you achieve if you study public speaking in the spirit we have suggested?   We hope, an inclusive and especially practical understanding of a major segment of your present and future communicative life.   We shall be concerned with speaking in which one person — perhaps you — has special responsibilities for creating communication that has impact upon other people. He or she has responsibilities for *creating* something — a "work," and one hopes an artistic work.   As with any other created thing — a painting, a musical score, a poem, an essay — someone purposefully *selects* what he will work with, gives it distinctive form or shape, and releases it in a particular manner calculated to influence others.   Significant works of art do not happen by setting monkeys to work on typewriters, canvases, or clavichords; significant works of art come into being when an artist, both skilled and sensitive, successfully matches idea, medium, and purpose, utilizing all relevant resources to endow ideas with just the qualities his purpose requires.   This is precisely the achievement of the ideal speaker.   He is an artist, a good one if he understands enough about the world in which he lives to distinguish a significant from an insignificant idea, if he understands the full range of resources and limitations embodied in his medium — human speech — and if he can bring those resources to bear upon his ideas and hence endow them with the qualities his social purposes require.   Practice without understanding will never bring him to this achievement except by sheer, unrepeatable accident. This is the sense in which we choose to call public speaking an art.   Disciplined study helps one to apply such principles, and such experience will, at the least, produce knowledge of self and of others; at best it will produce the sensitivity and skill essential to artistic use of speech in formal communication. This is the breadth of awareness to which you are invited, because it is so eminently practical in rhetorical situations.

THE RHETORICAL SITUATION

If audiences and the situations in which speakers meet them were less complex than they are, it would be less important than it is to study speaking in the reflective, liberal spirit we have just discussed. But all speaking relationships are difficult to understand in a comprehensive way. Every speaker's basic problem is to analyze and respond strategically to the situation and the social system in which he finds himself.

The basic elements of a rhetorical situation include: an audience, a particular occasion, a body of available ideas constituting possible speech materials, the speaker himself, and the conditions under which he and the auditors meet. The interplay of these elements and some ways of analyzing them and adapting to them have been helpfully clarified by Lloyd F. Bitzer, in an analysis of what he calls a "rhetorical situation." To help you conceptualize the role and function of a speaker, we shall adapt some of Bitzer's perceptions and combine them with ideas that come from a way of thinking about dynamic forces which is usually referred to as "systems analysis."

Professor Bitzer says that a "rhetorical situation" is "a complex of persons, events, objects, and relations presenting an actual or potential exigence" that can be modified by "creation of discourse which changes reality through the mediation of thought and action."[6] Bitzer defines "rhetoric" as communication that is "pragmatic; it comes into being for the sake of something beyond itself; it functions ultimately to produce action or change in the world; it performs some task." Thinking of speakers who address audiences of one or many, we could restate these observations as follows. A speaker enters a "system" that was originally governed by the desires of people (the audience) who were influenced by objects (their past and present surroundings which comprise a speech occasion), but because of pressures somewhere in this "system" there is some willingness on the listeners' parts to allow their views to be changed if appropriate speech can be created and adequately presented to them.

In a sense every speaker "intrudes" into waiting "systems" of this sort. But each speaker comes out of his *own* "system" of experience and desiring and enters someone else's. If that speaker wants to produce "action or change" in the waiting system, the job is to let loose speech forces that will cause listeners to conceive *differently* of themselves and the objects, events, and relations with which they associate themselves. If the speaker succeeds in altering this rhetorical situation, it means that the listeners no longer see themselves in quite their old ways; the systems of which they are parts will now seem at least a little different than before. If this kind of change occurs,

---

6. Lloyd F. Bitzer, "The Rhetorical Situation," *Philosophy and Rhetoric,* I (Jan. 1968), 1–14.

the speaker has achieved the goal of changing his listeners' world by altering their thoughts about it.

At first this way of thinking about speakers and audiences seems unnecessarily abstract; but if you will reflect on it, you are apt to see that what Professor Bitzer is saying in effect is that rhetorical speakers are always engaged in trying to change *patterns of perception and belief* about the "worlds" their listeners perceive. It is not so much people, as people's perceptions of the forces around them, that speakers seek to change.

To put this view of speech in focus, let us begin with a definition of public speech that grows out of all we have said in this chapter. *Public speech is that form of speech which is relatively uninterrupted and in which the communicator recreates his own ideas and symbolizes them in order to elicit primarily utilitarian responses from an audience which already has a somewhat changeable conception of their relations to the world and the specific situation in which they believe they find themselves.* Into these conceptions of their relations to the world and a specific situation steps a speaker. What are the patterns of relationship which that speaker can *work with?* They can be diagrammed thus:

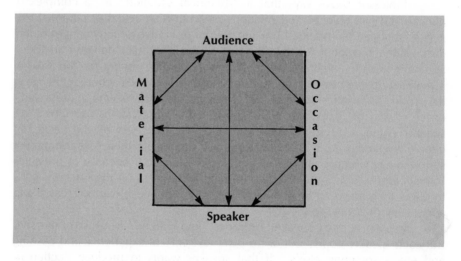

The *audience* in the diagram represents all who comprise the speaker's immediate "public." The *occasion* is the specific set of circumstances (psychological as well as physical) under which speaker and audience meet. *Material* is whatever the speaker knows about himself, the audience, his subject, and the occasion. When you, as speaker, enter such a rhetorical situation, all of the relationships suggested by the double-headed arrows in the diagram are yours to use and alter in the interests of eliciting the responses you need from the audience which now shares this situation or system with you. If you are related to the audience as chairman to group members, you can use your "position" as something authorizing you to speak now *unless*

the relation of audience to occasion is one that decrees that this is a time for conversation, not formal speaking. Even so, it is possible that your idea ("material") is *so* important to the audience that it can overwhelm the pre-conceptions of what the occasion calls for and, upon attention being called to your thought, dominate the situation as an idea that authorizes consecutive discourse from you, just now. Different balances of the forces within a rhetorical situation could, of course, produce quite the opposite conclusion: that this is *not* a rhetorical situation for *you* at all. You might have to conclude that the occasion so authorizes *conversation* just now that you must not try to engage in *public* speech.

The diagram gives you, as it were, the compass points of a situation, points by which you can calculate whether the situation is a *rhetorical* one inviting public speech and, if so, to what situational factors you must adapt in order to succeed in creating the changes you want in that situation. The diagram suggests these questions which you ought to review in your mind as a preliminary to giving final shape to any message you decide to loose into the intellectual-psychological system you must enter in order to communicate:

1. What is my relationship to the audience?
2. What is the audience's relationship to me?
3. What is the relationship between the audience and the occasion?
4. What effect does the occasion, the particular circumstance in which the speech is to be delivered, have upon the audience?
5. What influence does the audience exert upon my material, upon what I have to say?
6. What is the relationship of my speech content, my material, to the audience?
7. What is my relationship to my material? What do I as a person bring to my material to determine its final substance and form?
8. What effect does my material (my subject choice, the facts, opinions, and illustrations) have upon me as a person?
9. What is my connection with the occasion?
10. What is the effect of the occasion upon me as a speaker?
11. What influence does the occasion have upon my materials, upon what I intend to say?
12. What does the content of my speech do to modify the nature of the occasion?

In some situations some of these questions will be more important than others. Sometimes the best answers you can give yourself will be merely educated guesses. But in all cases you will need to calculate the probable answers to as many of these questions as possible if you are to understand *yourself* in relation to the rhetorical situation of which you plan to become an influential part.

In summary of this introductory chapter these concepts deserve restatement. We believe that the study of speech is a broad, man-centered inquiry and that study of public speech is a significant branch of that whole. Public speech, as we have defined it, is relatively uninterrupted speech which seeks utilitarian responses from a listener or listeners who have granted a speaker the right to continuous communication with them. We conceive the study of public speech as study of sustained social interaction, a study best approached with the liberal attitude that seeks understanding and principles first and techniques secondarily. We suggest that understanding public speech begins with conceptualizing the dynamics of rhetorical situations as communicative systems into which speakers enter in hope of accomplishing change. This conception draws attention to the interrelationships of audience, occasion, speech materials, and speaker. These, public speakers always have to modify to achieve the effects they desire. Skillful, informed modification of these relationships is art in the creative senses of that term.

In the remainder of this book we shall invite you to look at speaking in public largely as a process of satisfying the demands of audience, content, self, and occasion, in order to alter rhetorical situations. After a brief survey of matters particularly important to your first experiments with public speech we shall examine successively five constellations of problems all speakers must resolve in designing communications that will fit rhetorical situations. We shall first examine the problems associated with rhetorical *invention,* considering the nature of audiences and the means by which ideas for speeches may be discovered and sifted. Next we shall consider the *disposition* of materials selected for inclusion in a speech—the principles according to which they may be assembled and structured. Our third and fourth considerations will concern the symbolization of ideas—*style,* and *delivery* of the finished speech. What ancient writers called *memoria* or command of the entire speech as planned and composed will be discussed at various points in the chapters that follow, since many of the decisions that speakers make during discovery, disposition, and symbolization of ideas have direct bearing on ability to retain command over plans until delivery is completed. In considering each of these five major aspects of public speaking we shall seek to determine what demands you must meet and the reasons they must be met if you are to be understood as you intend in the situations you enter.

In our final chapter we shall consider how a critic of the art looks at public speech. There, we shall treat speech as a critical object and explore practical methods of general and classroom speech criticism.

EXERCISES

Written

1. Keep a diary on two or three hours of your normal activities, noting all the occasions on which you found people, including yourself, speaking to others in relatively uninterrupted fashion and with the aim of altering listeners' perceptions of their relationships to people, ideas, and things having significance for them.

2. Write a criticism of the definition of public speech given in this chapter on page 12. Support, expand, refute, or delete elements of the definition, but give reasons for each change you make.
3. After viewing a movie, television, or live theatre performance, list the major things you observed the actors doing which were (a) similar to and (b) different from the things you have observed in the practices of public speakers you consider superior.
4. In anticipation of your first speech in your class, choose a subject you hope to speak on and analyze the class as a rhetorical situation for your speech, answering the twelve questions posed on page 13 as far as is possible. (Or form a group with four or five other members of the class and construct a general analysis of the class as a "system" in which rhetoric is going to occur.) Write a paragraph or two explaining what advantages and disadvantages you (or each member of your discussion group) will have in speaking in this rhetorical situation.

Oral

1. Make a short talk in which you describe a specific rhetorical situation and point out aspects of it to which you might have been insensitive had you not attended this class and read this chapter.
2. Report to your classmates how many "public speeches" (as defined in this chapter) you have given in the last 24 hours. Indicate where you were most and least successful and why.
3. Observe a public speaker (student, teacher, television personality, or any other) and report on his strengths and weaknesses in adapting to the rhetorical situation.

CHAPTER
2

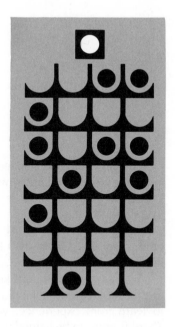

First
Considerations

One day in your class a speech will be assigned to you. A time for the speech will be set. You will know when you are expected to appear and make a talk. When the announcement is made, questions will begin to crowd your brain. "What shall I talk about?" "What must I do to carry off the assignment successfully?" "How can I avoid saying things that have been said a dozen times before?" "How shall I start to prepare?" "How can I avoid being too nervous to talk at all?"

Ideally, you should know all the theoretical and practical knowledge in this book before making a speech; but in order to have ample opportunity to learn from experience, your experiments in speaking must begin early. There is more to be gained than lost from this. Each opportunity to speak will allow you to explore your own nature and capacities as a communicator and to study others as they listen and react to what you say. And you can learn enough quickly to make useful *experiments* in public speech, as we shall try to show in this chapter.

Your development as a fully informed speaker will be gradual. As your study, understanding, and control develop, you will become increasingly able to meet higher standards and solve more difficult problems in com- munication. But first experiences can be profitable ones, too. So that this can be true, we ask you to study the elemental observations in this chapter before your first classroom speech. These "first considerations" are relevant to all your speaking, but they have special value at the beginning of a course in public speech.

In the following pages we shall deal with six topics you need to think about before addressing any audience. The topics are: listening, basic pro- cedures in speech preparation, readying a first speech assignment, kinds of delivery, stage fright, and oral rehearsal.

LISTENING

Wherever we talk in order to communicate, there are listeners. They are reasons for the talk. So some basic facts about listening and about listening as a student of speechmaking are "first considerations."

There are at least three ways in which listening especially concerns you as a student in a speech class: (1) you are going to be listened to, so you need to think about how people listen; (2) you are going to listen to colleagues, both as a consumer of their knowledge and as an evaluator of their skills in communication; (3) by studying your own listening habits and those of others you can learn to listen more effectively outside the speech class—in lecture halls, before television sets, and among friends. Here, then, are some basic facts and suggestions about listening.

People can listen most profitably when they know what they are listening *for*. Are you listening to gain information? To absorb material you will later be tested on? Or are you listening to be entertained? Are you listening as a critic, to assess the speaker's thinking or other communicative skills? The list could go on, but the point is that unless you can decide your *primary* purpose in listening, you will be unable to focus your attention efficiently.

You or any other listener must have decided the primary purpose for listening in order to discover which items in a speech demand closest attention. What we attend to depends on what we listen *for*. When we listen to weigh arguments, we pay less attention to style unless the speaker's language begins to confuse us. When we listen to be entertained, we pay little attention to arguments and a good deal to language because we know much of the amusement may come from the ways language is used. As listeners, all of us *select* what we want to hear, take note of, and absorb. That means that even in first speeches you will need to think out how you will get your listeners to select for special attention what *you* think is most important in your speech. And as a listener, even to first speeches, you can experiment with disciplining your own listening habits by making your listening purposes clear to yourself.

Comprehensive listening is hard work. Perhaps that is why most of us listen so inefficiently. Efficient listening requires disciplining the senses of hearing and seeing. The attorney Louis Nizer says, "So complete is this concentration that at the end of a court day in which I have only listened, I find myself wringing wet despite a calm and casual manner."[1] You know, too, that listening closely to even two or three lectures in a day is tiring. What does this imply for first speeches? Several things.

You need to plan what you say so that you make listening as easy as possible without sacrificing the worth of your thoughts or your purpose for speaking. Here are some stragetic considerations. Listeners' attention wanders easily. A dog's bark, a flickering light, a noisy radiator can steal attention away from you unless you, yourself, are ready and able to compete by emphatic activity, voice, or interjected ideas. But it is much more usual for beginning speakers to *give away* attention. They do it by treating all points as though they were of equal importance, by not having planned "high points" in their speeches, by talking monotonously—vocally and physically. These "giveaways" can almost always be avoided if a speaker thinks carefully

---

1. *My Life in Court* (New York: Doubleday, 1961), pp. 297–298.

about *holding* attention as he or she prepares a talk. All your plans for a first speech ought to be given a special inspection to determine whether there are better ways of holding listeners' attention without sacrificing content or purpose.

And in training yourself as a listener during first speeches you ought to keep in mind some of the things that interfere most with people's listening. They are such things as allowing one's self to daydream—to think of private affairs, allowing speech to pass by unnoticed. Another common interference with effective listening is allowing biases or preferences to lead you to construct so many counterarguments in imagination that what is said goes unattended to. If you are to learn to listen better and if your listening is to allow you to respond helpfully to other speakers in your class, these two internal distractions are the ones you have to guard most against: daydreaming and making so many mental challenges you fail to take in most of what is said.

But it is fair to ask, "Do I have any duty as a listener?" It is surely not senseless to say, "It's the speaker's duty to *make* me listen." We suggest that in a speech class and in at least some other places there is a special rule —the Golden Rule. When you are in the role of speaker, you will want others to listen to you so they can make constructive suggestions for your improvement. You will hope they listen carefully to *what* you say and to *how you say. it.* To improve, you need their *informed* reactions on both points. And if this sort of listening is desirable for you, you ought to be willing to listen to others in the same ways—with conscious effort to take in as much as possible of what is happening when others speak. Outside the classroom, of course, you are the only listener to whom you can prescribe "duties." On the other hand, a liberally educated citizen ought to recognize that if he does not listen cooperatively to both content and method, he will simply not know "what was going on" in the speaking offered him.

Your speech classroom can be a listening laboratory for you in two other ways. You can increase your ability to take in different types of speech organization because many different speech structures will be offered you. And you can take inventory of the kinds of nonverbal behaviors that are signals of attention and inattention. To attain the first goal, notice the different ways you have to take notes in order to get a quick record of your colleagues' differently constructed talks. How do you need to think differently when one speaker gives you evidence and *then* his conclusion but another announces his conclusion and *then* argues for it? College lectures come in these and other forms; so do essays and books. You can train yourself to "process" different forms of information as you listen in a speech class. Observing the nonverbal signs of attention and inattention as you observe other speakers' speaking can be very valuable to you, when you speak. A good question to ask as you prepare for a first speech is: "How will I *know* when I am succeeding or when the audience is slipping away?" If you can answer the question, you can adjust to what you see while speaking. And you can get the data for answering the question by watching yourself and your colleagues as listeners.

It is worth repeating that the main goal of listening in a speech class is to discover how method in oral communication affects the intelligibility and impact of content. You will serve yourself and your colleagues best, and they will serve you best, if you all listen to each other purposefully and with self-discipline in order that each may be as useful as possible to others *as natural but alert respondents*. There is at least as much to be learned from alert listeners of good will and candor as from speech textbooks and speech teachers. Your key question in classroom listening is: *"Why* did what was said affect me and the other listeners as it did?"* Every answer you can defensibly make to that question will add to your understanding of speaking and listening, and in the process of answering you will acquire new general information about the nature and resources of oral communication.

BASIC PROCEDURES IN SPEECH PREPARATION

Preparing any speech is above all a matter of exercising judgment. In judging what to do and what not to do, your intellectual behavior needs to be specially guided by what you know of the nature and frailties of human thought, the conventions of communication, and the nature of listening. We shall consider the consequences of these determining factors on speech preparation in later chapters, but certain procedures related to them need mention here.

Subjects and Goals

Before you can make any extended comments effectively you must know your goal and what needs to be said to accomplish it. Goals and what to say are interrelated. In classroom speaking it does not matter a great deal whether you first decide to talk about drug abuse and then decide to try for the goal of making the extent of the problem clear, or settle first that you will try to make a problem clear and then choose drug abuse as the problem. Outside the classroom, however, subjects are often "assigned," in the sense that people are invited to speak on specified topics or they decide they *must* speak to a specific topic. In general, then, setting one's goal for speaking is the initial task when a speech is to be made, though it may not always be so in a classroom.

Determining the Response

Given a subject, you must decide what sort of response you may legitimately seek from your particular audience. For example, you must determine whether to inform, inquire, reinforce, persuade, or entertain. This decision made, you must next determine what central idea is to dominate your information, inquiry, reinforcement, persuasion, or entertainment. Let us briefly examine how and why each of these decisions must be made.

You should think of classroom speaking as real communication rather than as an unrealistic exercise. Suppose you decide to speak to your colleagues about the dramatic club to which you belong. As soon as you decide this, you have to decide what sort of response you want to elicit from the class. Should you inform them of something they do not know about the club's purposes and activities and seek the response, "Yes, I understand"? Or should you review and amplify some club project they have heard of, you may approach the giving of information in other ways by seeking the response, "Yes, I understand better (or more fully)"? Or should you persuade the group to attend a coming production by the club, thus trying for the response, "Yes, we ought to go" or "Yes, that seems worthwhile"? Should you inquire with the class, raising some question about the proper functions of groups like the drama club, trying to excite the response, "We ought to think more about that" or "We ought to discuss this issue"? Or should you reinforce something your audience already believes and try to get them to strengthen their affirmations, responding with "Yes, drama *is* an important cultural influence on this campus"? Should you simply amuse the audience with satire or irony or amusing things you have experienced with the club, seeking smiles, laughter, and "That's funny" as your responses? These are your normal options in preparing any speech. A subject may be treated in many ways; how *you* should treat your subject depends first on how you want your listeners to react.

The five purposes which we have just reviewed need not be mutually exclusive in your speech. You may inform in order to persuade or reinforce. You may persuade in order to get a group to inquire. You may entertain as you inform. But despite such intermixing and overlapping of the five primary purposes, one purpose must dominate and the others must be subordinate, providing a substructure upon which the dominant purpose rests. The reason is as simple as it is inexorable: neither you nor your listeners can think clearly about any subject unless you plainly understand the chief reason for thinking about it at all.

Choosing Your Subject

As we said earlier, the group that asks you to speak may specify your subject and purpose. But a class assignment may simply say, "Talk to us about anything you want to." When you must decide upon a subject, there are several guidelines you should follow.

1. First is your own experience. It is unwise to choose a subject about which you know absolutely nothing. Experience, however, is not the whole

answer. We think of the student who had much experience with turtles. He was a turtle expert. He spoke first on diamond-back turtles. The class was fascinated with his breadth of knowledge, enthusiasm, and thoroughness. Experience served him well. The second time, he chose to talk about snapping turtles. He was still interested in turtles and he was still experienced, but the audience had heard enough of turtles and turned its attention elsewhere. In this case experience and personal interest did not serve.

We also think of the students who, told to consider their personal experiences in arriving at subject choices, gave speeches on "my summer job as a milkman" and "my days as a lifeguard." Their subjects were not well received, though they had experience and enthusiasm. What they had to say was trite and familiar, incapable of stimulating their audiences to think.

2. Prior knowledge is a second factor to be considered. If you do not know your subject, you must learn before you have earned the right to take your listeners' time. Remember, 5 minutes spent before an audience of twenty people consumes 100 minutes of the world's time. Therefore, you will need to decide upon a subject you already know a great deal about or about which you can know a great deal before your speaking engagement.

3. The availability of material becomes a third determinant in choosing a subject. Don't choose speech subjects without making a preliminary survey of the resources for obtaining the information you will need. We will mention possible sources of speech materials on page 26 and will discuss them further in Chapter 4. Unless you make a preliminary inventory you may find that there is just not enough material to warrant a speech.

4. The audience will also have a bearing upon your choice. Age, sex, expectations, knowledge, and socioeconomic level may rule out some subjects which otherwise seem excellent. We treat these matters more fully in Chapter 3.

5. A fifth determinant in your choice ought to be the speech situation with its inherent limitations: what will have gone on before, the time of day, the setting, and so on. And in the classroom some subjects will be inappropriate because of the assignment, the time allowed, and listeners' special expectations.

6. Time, just mentioned, makes it important for you to consider the complexity of subjects and whether each possibility can be narrowed or broadened to suit the agreed-upon time. You may find some subjects too simple to occupy the minutes profitably and others incapable of being "cut down" and remaining meaningful.

7. Lastly, subjects ought to challenge the audience and the speaker. Something ought to be gained by both. There ought to be "news." Brain stretching and creative cogitation ought to be products of good subjects. Puerile and parochial subjects do not encourage that kind of thinking.

Sometimes it is not the subject area which is responsible for a poor choice but your selection of the aspect to be treated. The merit of a speech often has to do with how you approach and treat a subject rather than with the subject itself.

Given the general topic, drama, for your first speech, your real business in finding a subject begins with deciding what kind of response you want from your audience and with determining how you can narrow this topic down to a specific subject for a particular talk with a clear purpose that can be accomplished in the time you will have. If you can reduce the topic, drama, to a subject like, "Off-Broadway theatre during the late 1960's," you can turn at once to deciding whether you want to inform, inquire, persuade, or amuse your listeners. On the other hand, if you have come no farther than, "Recent Off-Broadway drama," you still have decisions to make concerning what period "recent" covers. And that decision, again, is going to be significantly guided by what kind of *response* you want to seek. If you want to inform about recent history, you must decide *how much* history you want to inform about. If you want to persuade listeners that recent Off-Broadway drama has certain characteristics, you must decide *which parts* of *what* recent history support your persuasive goal. You will have the same experience with any speech subject. As you shape it to manageable *and purposeful* dimensions, the crucial, defining question is: What response do you want from your listeners?

Locating Your Central Idea

If you are assigned a "report," or choose to give one, your task becomes to inform. If the assignment, or your choice, brings you one step farther so you can say what specific subject it is you will report on, your purpose and your subject are decided. When you have arrived at this stage, your next task is to locate a central idea, a proposition or thesis or subject sentence upon which to structure what you will say. In framing this core idea it is helpful to think of it as the hub of a wheel from which supporting spokes extend, as the roof of a pavilion which is supported by pillars, or as the apex of a pyramid supported by blocks of specific information which substantiate the epitomizing statement.

Any praiseworthy speech has a central idea or proposition to which the audience's attention is directed and for which a specific response is sought. Detailed ideas, reasons, or assertions may form primary points in the general framework of your speech; but you must subordinate details to a central subject sentence. Once your subject and purpose are known, your task invariably becomes to decide upon that statement which will express pointedly the encompassing thought to which all that you will say ultimately refers. Once this is determined, you are ready to search for lesser ideas and special material which will amplify, substantiate, and vivify the central thought in ways that will evoke the response you earlier identified from your listeners.

To sum up: sometimes you must choose your own subject; sometimes it is assigned; sometimes you must locate a narrower, more specific subject within a topic or subject area. Always you must define the responses you seek from listeners; always you must formulate a central idea that epitomizes the content of what you say; always you must locate the subordinate ideas that give meaning to your central thought. We emphasize conscious identification of desired responses, and conscious and precise formulation of central ideas, because of the nature of man. All listeners look for "the point of it all" in what they hear. Their demand must be met.

Phrasing Your Subject Sentence

Listeners welcome some ingenuity in the framing of central ideas and statements of purpose. "I shall inform you this morning . . ." or "Let me instruct you . . ." or "It is my purpose tonight to persuade you that . . ." can suggest lack of regard for the mentality of an audience. If your intentions are stated so bluntly, your listeners may also back away feeling you have come to manipulate them. To say, "This morning I will explain the four ways pulp is processed," fulfills the formal requirements of a good subject sentence, but it is rather bald. The purpose stands out obtrusively and is tritely phrased. It is an excellent, clear statement for you to carry *in your head,* but your intention can be *communicated* more deftly and more interestingly. It would be better to *say,* "The paper in my hand is the product of one of four ways that pulp is produced." Without being flashy or at all unclear, a subject sentence that is baldly put to guide the speaker can usually be altered in actual communication to catch the listener's interest.

A listener not only wants to be interested by the ways speakers express their purposes; he also wants to be able to detect speakers' rhetorical purposes in the words of the subject sentences. He can get a clue to purpose from both the contents and the grammatical forms of subject sentences. Assertions are usually used for speeches of information and entertainment. Questions usually indicate that the purpose is inquiry. Propositions are reserved for persuasive speeches of various kinds. Suppose a speaker's subject is community theatre in the United States. For each of the usual rhetorical purposes his subject sentence might be worded in the following ways:

Informing: The history of the community theatre movement in the United States clearly reveals its purpose and nature.
Persuasion: The federal government ought to subsidize the community theatre movement.
Inquiry: Ought the federal government to subsidize the community theatre movement?
Reinforcement: The community theatre movement in the United States is a worthwhile institution which enriches the lives of many people.
Entertaining: The community theatre movement is too bizarre for words.

Note that each of these sentences does three things: (1) reveals the subject of

25

the speech, (2) states the central idea clearly, and (3) plainly implies the kind of response sought.

Good subject sentences are phrased so that a single idea emerges clearly and unambiguously. They are framed in uncomplicated and uncluttered fashion. They do not focus thought on only *part* of what is to be said and they express but a single idea. Beware of compound statements — sentences containing "and" or "but." Conjunctions are often signals that two main ideas are present. Avoid such sentences as "The Bessemer steel process is important, because planes are made of steel" and "The Scottish poets ought to be studied, and the poems of Sir Walter Scott ought to be analyzed by all who study British literature." The first narrows to a specific heading. The second contains more than a single idea.

Supporting the Central Idea

Let us suppose you have completed the initial steps of finding a subject, determining your purpose, narrowing your subject, and framing your subject sentence. You must now discover varied and interesting materials to clarify, to add detail to, or to prove and reinforce your theme. You must, in short, discover (1) facts; (2) testimony; (3) examples, whether long or short, real or hypothetical; (4) stories; (5) statistics; (6) comparisons, contrasts, and analogies; and (7) definitions for the purpose of proving or amplifying your subject sentence. At a later point in this book we shall explain these forms of support and amplification fully. (See pages 124–135.) For now, it is enough to point out that you must find such materials and that you must structure them as simply as possible into a coordinated, organically unified whole that becomes a speech. In your first attempts to discover and arrange materials, it will be well to concentrate upon a clear, simple main theme rather than upon an elaborate and complicated structure of points and supporting material. It will also be wise to locate a number of pieces of support and from these select a half dozen of the best for arrangement in clear, connected order. Once you have delivered one or two simple speeches consisting of one or two main points adequately supported or clarified, you will see that a longer speech is but a series of simple units, each developed individually and orginally, and juxtaposed so as to form a larger, more elaborate, more complicated whole.

Your first classroom speech will be easiest if it consists of only a single point which might well be a segment of a longer speech. Your specific procedure may be as follows:

PREPARING A FIRST ASSIGNMENT

1. First, select from a subject area of interest to you and your audience a relatively simple, single idea which you can clarify for your audience or which you wish them

to accept. Sometimes you can arrive at such an idea by making a rough plan for a longer speech and then selecting from it one main point for development.

2. Once this idea has been selected, phrase it accurately in a single subject sentence.
3. Concentrate on a single, simple method of development — a structural pattern. Explain or persuade, for example, by arranging your materials in chronological, spatial, effect-to-cause, or problem-solution order.
4. Draw upon several sources other than personal experience for material to amplify or support your idea.
5. Carefully plan even this short speech; prepare an outline though it may consist of only six or eight items.
6. Make each of these items bear upon your subject sentence. Show the audience that each item does clarify or support your subject sentence.
7. In delivering this single point and its amplifying or supporting material, make each item stand out clearly.
8. A final test of the speech will be an affirmative answer to one of two questions: "Does my audience understand the subject better now that I have spoken?" or "Does the audience more nearly accept the idea I have been proposing?"

A simple outline will serve in planning this first speech. To illustrate how you might locate and outline a single point appropriate for a brief talk, let us imagine that you think a major speech might be given on the subject sentence: "We need to support mental health organizations better than we do." If you ask yourself what would be the main headings of such a speech the following could occur to you:

I. Anxiety is a disturbing phenomenon.
II. Anxiety is widespread in our society.
III. Mental health organizations help people to reduce their anxieties.
IV. Mental health organizations deserve more help than we give them.

Any of these four points could be used as a central idea for a shorter speech, although the fourth is least promising because it depends for support on the other three. If you chose the first of these points for a one-point speech, you would need to prepare a simple outline or plan of its development. It might look like this:

Subject Sentence: *Anxiety is a disturbing phenomenon.*[2]

Supporting Material:

Example, brief	1. A recent article in *Time* tells the story of a woman's unwarranted anxiety over the fate of her handicapped son.
Fact	2. The anxiety response is often characterized as objectless, therefore frustrating.
Definition, Testimony	3. A group of prominent psychologists, including Harold Basowitz and Roy Grinker, define anxiety as ". . . the conscious and reportable experience of in-

---

2. This sample outline was prepared by John K. Thorne. Used by permission.

	tense dread and foreboding, conceptualized as internally derived and unrelated to any external threat."
Comparison	4. Anxiety produces a result like that experienced in marching in place when we only raise the dust around us.
Quotation	5. An old saying is that "Anxiety and worry, not work, tire one out."

A comparable plan for a one-point speech amplifying a proverb might well look like this:

Subject Sentence: *"A bird in hand is worth two in the bush" is widely applicable in our day.*[3]

Supporting Material:

Restatement of Central Idea	1. Aesop related this concept in stronger language in *The Fisher and the Little Fish:* "A little thing in hand is worth more than a great thing in prospect."
Fact	2. Great expectations may easily become only false hopes, since the future is unpredictable.
Fact	3. Psychologically, when one continually gambles on the prospect of a "great thing" and loses, he may develop complexes and may become mentally unbalanced.
Example, brief	4. A young girl may physically decay as a result of waiting for "a great thing in prospect."
Example, brief	5. The value of a "bird in hand" is exemplified by local policy in football: going for the sure extra point rather than gambling on the two-point conversion.
Example, extended	6. It is better to have a date with a local coed for a big week end than to have no date at all. (Tell story.)

Neither of these sample outlines indicates what would be said in opening and closing.   Neither indicates whether the talk will or should have a title.   Obviously a finished outline of your talk ought to indicate what you will probably say in introduction and conclusion.   And if the circumstances are going to be formal enough so someone else will introduce you to the audience, it might help both chairman and audience if you chose a title for even this short talk.   But at present our concern is chiefly with how one amplifies or proves a main point, hence the illustrative outlines show only the "body" of each speech, and the bits of supporting material are labeled to show the kinds of support these speakers used.   Notice the variety of those types of support; variety enlivens communication.

---

3. This sample outline was prepared by James Hamasaki.   Used by permission.

MODES OF DELIVERY

There are four general ways people deliver consecutive talk: *impromptu, extemporaneously,* by *reading* it, and from *memory.* Your first classroom talks are most likely to be presented extemporaneously; possibly some will be given impromptu. These methods of delivery are the ones that best promote development of conversational quality in speaking—the quality preferred far above others in our society. We shall discuss *impromptu* and *extemporaneous* delivery briefly here, then return to the general subject of delivery in Chapter 10.

You may be among the many who confuse impromptu speaking with extemporaneous speaking. As the terms are used in the study of communication, they do not refer to the same processes. The *impromptu* manner of presentation is one in which you make no formal preparation until a few minutes (at most) before you begin to talk. The most preparation you have time for will be opportunity to jot down a few words. Impromptu speaking is spur-of-the-moment activity. It is not a way of speaking from which you will *learn* much about the art of public speech, but it is a kind of speaking that demands you *put quickly to use* all you know about speaking in public. Except as an exercise in self-command and in emergencies, speaking impromptu is almost never a satisfactory way of speaking if one has had any forewarning at all. On the other hand, it is *the* way you must speak if you are a member of a committee and find it important to make moderately extensive remarks on points of discussion as they arise.

In *extemporaneous* speaking, as we use the term, you will have had time to think out what to say and will have planned with considerable care. You will probably have outlined your plan and also rehearsed orally. Finally, you will present your thoughts publicly with or without notes to guide you. In this kind of delivery you can be at your best, as a person and as a communicator. You have freedom to adjust to the speech situation, you can be spontaneous in language, and most important, you can deal with your listeners directly—*converse* with them.

You may or may not be allowed to use notes for classroom extemporaneous speeches. If you use notes, they should be unobtrusive and kept to a minimum. Do not call attention to them. On the other hand, it is best not to try to hide them in the palm of your hand or under your sleeve. Few in the audience will expect you to memorize troublesome sets of statistics or long quotations. It is natural to read them. But few listeners will feel you are direct and in control of your ideas if your eyes are constantly on your notes. Whether you do or do not take notes with you when you are going to talk continuously for a bit of time, the less you have to refer to them the better. The reason? Listeners want to be shown you are thinking of *them,* not of pieces of paper.

Wherever you speak in public, and especially in the classroom, you ought to keep yourself free of preset wordings and mechanical physical movement. If you freeze fast your ideas and words during preparation, you may finally talk with precision but you are apt to be rigid in ideas, language, and action. Then, you simply cannot *interact* with those who listen; and yet, oral communication never is fully communicative unless speakers show their alertness to the listeners as people and listeners respond openly to speakers. This is what a famous teacher of speech, J. A. Winans, meant when he coined the phrase, "vivid realization of the idea at the moment of utterance" and made it the key idea in his educational revolt against elocutionary speaking. His point is crucial. No listener—including *you*—enjoys listening unless there is clear evidence that whoever he is listening to is thinking, "realizing," his ideas *as he says them.* Speaking extemporaneously allows speakers their best compromise between the cold mashed potatoes a rigidly learned talk is apt to become in the final presentation and the haphazard mix of thoughts impromptu speaking so commonly produces. For classroom speaking and for much outside speaking you *can* prepare, rehearse to set your line of thought firmly in mind, and still *re-create* those thoughts as "real talk" vividly, spontaneously, and directly realized *for listeners* as the thoughts are uttered. This kind of directness with cogency is entirely possible for you in public speech, and your speech class is precisely the place to develop your particular extemporaneous style. Not all extemporaneous speaking looks exactly the same.

Many lecturers and some legislators and lawyers appear to their audiences to speak impromptu when in reality they have made extensive preparation during years of authoritative investigation, experience, and practice. Those who seem to speak impromptu when they are really speaking extemporaneously are commonly people who engage in formal speaking almost daily, so that practice sessions are not a necessity for them. If you lack such experience and practice, you must conduct a specific investigation to enrich each utterance and must gain command over each particular set of ideas by rehearsing them in special, oral practice sessions. But you need not be less spontaneous in public speech because of that.

By urging you to practice and develop skill in extemporaneous presentation of public speech we are not disparaging all reading and memorizing in public settings for speech. Some people read aloud very well, and some can memorize material and recite it so their listeners never know that it is memorized. In Chapter 10 we shall discuss reading in some detail. (See pages 268–274.) We are saying that the beginner is more likely to achieve conversationality in his speaking if he speaks extemporaneously. This mode allows not only careful, thorough preparation but audience adaptation and spontaneous regeneration of ideas when the speech is given. We discuss oral rehearsal for extemporaneous speaking in a later section of this chapter. (See pages 33–34.)

STAGE FRIGHT

Although not everyone will admit it, most beginning (and very many experienced) speakers are apprehensive about facing audiences, especially for the first time. If you are worried about how your audience will react, rest assured that your concern is normal. After all, in facing even classmates you are taking a risk. You hope they will respond favorably or at least sympathetically. Chances are that they will, but you are not quite sure. This doubt, felt by most good speakers in some degree, produces tension and anxiety. How to ease such feelings and adjust optimally to an audience becomes a special problem.

At the outset, you ought to remind yourself that the real causes of stage fright are psychological. For the most part *attitude* is at the bottom of the matter. Lack of self-confidence results in fear. Insecurity stems from the uncertainties of the situation. Literally, you become afraid if you feel you may lose control of the audience. Or, you may be apprehensive about your mastery of what you are going to say. Then you are apt to experience fear because you feel you are not perfect. Or, you may experience fear because you are anxious about how well your voice and body will function, or whether you will choose the right words. The mere fact that you are separated from the listeners in a formal situation may be responsible for feelings of insecurity and aloneness. For some people, wishes to avoid such situations, to flee from them, have caused them to make such serious excuses that they have not had to speak at all. Thus they have reinforced their fears by preserving the causes.

The fear which causes anxiety about speaking results in physiological changes. Some who undergo these changes think they are organically ill, that they may have some sort of secretion imbalance or other fundamental disorder. What actually happens is that the flow of epinephrine (adrenaline) accompanying anxiety and fear sets off additional changes. Blood pressure, rate of respiration, and nerve conductivity increase. More blood sugar, furnishing energy, enters the system. More thyroxine may be secreted, speeding the burning of blood sugar. More oxygen is taken into the blood. More poisons are removed from your system. As a result of these changes, fatigue probably lessens, and you may experience the kind of increase in strength that frequently accompanies the release of tensions during anger. These bodily changes may interest you, but they are not the causes of fear.

How can you reduce fear and, subsequently, the tensions which afflict you? The solutions to this problem can be discovered only by going back to causes to see what can be done to remove them.

First, realize that everyone else at some time or other experiences the same apprehensions you do. The most any speaker can do is to guess how an audience will react, then calmly calculate how best to promote the responses he seeks and to meet the demands an audience makes. Insights to human behavior come with experience, but they are always less than perfect. Realize this fact, but make educated guesses on how you can best adapt to your particular audience in order to get them to react as you wish them to. They are human beings like you. They may vary in age, interest, and creed, but they are similar to you in more ways than you probably realize. We know it is easy to say, "Feel at one with the audience," "Know that they will be more uncomfortable than you are if you don't succeed," "Remember that they are faced with the same problems, the same fears, and the same reactions to fear as you are." All of this is to say, "Get yourself in the right frame of mind." But determining to adopt an attitude conducive to a feeling does not necessarily guarantee that you will have the feeling you seek. Yet you must make first tries; you can gain composure by repeatedly making speeches in the face of varying conditions. One of the functions of a speech class is to give you these kinds of experiences. Striving for realistic attitudes, coupled with such practice as you gain in classrooms and elsewhere, can teach you how to make natural insecurity a positive asset.

Thorough preparation, once the calculated guesses have been made, ought to be your natural "counter" to a sense of uncertainty about speaking. Apprehension ought to motivate you to pay close, careful attention to your pattern of organization, to your supporting and amplifying materials, to phrases of greatest importance, and to potentially troublesome spots in your whole plan. If fear of speaking can cause you to prepare carefully, it has provided its own best antidote.

Proper attitudes, practice, and preparation ought to be any sensible person's response to the risks we all sense in formal communication. But the wish to communicate is a still more powerful protection against unease. If you *want* to speak, you have won half the battle in most instances. If you have more than enough to say and are determined to make the audience understand or accept your point of view, you will have come a long way toward releasing your tensions into meaningful, constructive actions which will contribute to the accomplishment of your goals. If your desire to communicate is strong enough, you will forget to worry about your hands or feet or what they are doing. This is not to say that you will forget you have a voice and body which you must control. It is to say that if you bend all efforts toward gaining specific audience responses, you will have your best opportunity to accomplish what you set out to do. You will be like a swimmer in a race who, once he has hit the water, lets nothing divert his attention until he reaches the finish line. All distractions will be swept aside or ignored. With proper practice, you can substitute controlled gestures for wasted motion. Wordings will become economical, because your mind will be filled with the business of communicating that which you know securely. You will say just enough and no more to elicit the reactions you seek. Losing yourself in your speech without losing your self-control will cause you to forget fears.

Natural insecurity about formal speaking can also be countered by being sure that what you will say is worthy of you, of the time spent in preparation, and of your audience's time. Confidence on these matters allays fear; misgivings about them generate fear. Only by choosing wisely and carefully what you will say can you hope to approach a speech situation with confidence. If you feel that what you are going to say isn't worth much to you or your audience; if you feel that your ideas are shabby, that you have settled for words that are dull or imprecise, or that your speech is just something to get over, of course you will be afraid, and you deserve to be!

REHEARSAL AND ATTITUDES TOWARD SPEAKING

Oral rehearsal for extemporaneous delivery can assure you of mastery of your plan, remembrance of the succession of points in it, and confidence in your skills in delivery. The problem in extemporaneous speaking is to transfer your plan to your mind and become thoroughly familiar with its sequence of ideas. Specific choices of words will, and ought to, vary from one rehearsal to another. This will give you a large stock of verbal resources from which you can choose at will as you present your structured ideas in your meeting with listeners. But *how* you rehearse makes a difference. If you rehearse for extemporaneous speaking wisely, rehearsal becomes a route to confidence. The suggestions outlined below will help you. Following them can give you considerable reassurance, clarity of mind, and even serenity when you go to talk to your audience.[4]

1. Read through your written plan, fixing your mind on the succession of main points. Re-read it, this time concentrating not only on the main points but on the details supporting each.
2. Still referring to your outline, speak through the speech in whatever words happen to come. Talk out loud, not under your breath. You will find it helps to stand up and face an imaginary audience. Try out gestures as you verbalize. Get through the whole speech. If you bungle a part, go right on to the end without stopping to straighten out the troublesome section. Come back to that when you have finished running through the entire speech.
3. Without using your outline or any memoranda except those notes you will use on the platform, stand up and speak through the speech as before. If you can find a patient listener or group of listeners, so much the better.
4. When you can get through your total speech fairly well, time yourself and adjust the speech to the time allotted for your actual presentation. Such an adjustment may call for omissions or condensations, or it may call for additions or expansions of points. It is important to acquire a sense of time on the platform and develop the habit of keeping within time limits.

4. The material that follows is adapted from *Manual for Public Speaking, I,* p. 22, by H. A. Wichelns and others (1932) and *Manual for an Elementary Course* by H. A. Wichelns, G. B. Muchmore, and others, p. 19. Used by permission.

5. In the moments before speaking keep the plan of your speech uppermost in your mind; review it. This is the most constructive outlet for tensions.
6. During preparation and just before speaking renew your desire to share a worthwhile message with others. Remind yourself that the experience before you is not a "performance" but an opportunity. You have earned that opportunity through the knowledge you have acquired and your position as a respected human being in a communicating society.
7. Recall that your auditors are persons not very different from yourself, that they want you to succeed.
8. Don't expect to avoid all tension. Some tension is good for you. Properly channeled, tension can serve you positively by increasing your alertness and your available supply of energy.
9. As a general rule, avoid last-minute changes in your speech, especially during your maiden efforts. Don't add to uneasiness by entertaining misgivings about choices already made. Adapt to the moment and to other speakers but do not make changes that undermine the overall plan you established in your mind by systematic rehearsal.

Oral rehearsal is insurance. Fluent discourse demands it. Speakers are often tempted to omit this important stage of speech preparation because of self-consciousness or because they are unwilling to take time for it. It is significant, however, that from ancient times to the present even the busiest of public figures who became known for effective speech have found the time to rehearse for major speeches. They have known what you should learn if you do not already know it: control over self and control over content are imperative when what you say is important, and both kinds of control are established through such oral rehearsal as we have described.

AN OVERVIEW OF PREPARATION

In the foregoing pages we have emphasized the things a speaker ought to consider in preparing for a simple assignment requiring that he speak publicly. In concluding we shall summarize the sequence of preparatory steps serious speakers have found it important to follow. Ordinarily you will need to do the following things in getting ready to speak to an audience:

1. Considering the nature of your audience and the occasion, decide what response you seek concerning the topic you have decided or been assigned to talk about.
2. Narrow or expand your topic until you have located the specific subject that will fit your capacities, your goal, and the requirements of the situation.
3. Wed your rhetorical purpose and your central idea in a clear-cut statement expressing unambiguously the coverage of what you will say and your reason for saying it.
4. Gather the variety of materials that will most strongly and interestingly amplify or support what is expressed in your subject sentence.

5. Organize these materials into a structure which can be shown clearly and systematically in outline form.
6. Consider what kinds of language will best interrelate your materials to form a *whole* that interestingly asserts the basic message contained in your subject sentence.
7. If it is at all possible, prepare yourself to present your talk extemporaneously, so you can speak in an organized, informed way, yet spontaneously and adaptively.
8. As insurance for your plan and against stage fright, rehearse your speech orally to gain full control of the pattern of your ideas, alternative wordings, timing, and confident self-control.

By listing preparatory steps as we have, we do not mean you must invariably proceed in exactly the way our summary suggests. For example, a speaker asked to talk about his recent experiences as a member of a rehabilitation project in Peru need not pause very long over step 4, but he may have more trouble than some others with the narrowing and focusing processes of steps 1 and 2. A speaker assigned to make a report on the budget has step 1 settled for him, as is most of the work of steps 2 and 4. The speaker who has been in Peru may find his most difficult problem is to sift out irrelevant knowledge to accomplish step 5. The speaker giving the budget report may find that there are standard forms for budget reports that accomplish most of step 5 for him. On the other hand, when you decide to talk to your colleagues on a topic you have only recently learned about, you will probably need to devote about the same amount of attention to each of the eight steps listed. But if a committee in your class should ask you to report on the history of the National Association for the Advancement of Colored People, you would find that most of the considerations implied by steps 1, 2, and 3 were suggested in the way the assignment was given. However, to be sure you understood the assignment clearly, it would still be useful to run through the first three steps quickly in your mind.

We have tried to summarize the normal preparatory procedures for *any* speaking in which you will bear special responsibility for creating and sustaining human interaction through speech. What needs to be done at each stage may vary from speaking assignment to speaking assignment, but *each of these speech problems must be settled somehow.* Whether some have been taken care of by an "assignment" or by your own experience or by your listeners' expectations is something *you* must decide. That is your freedom and burden as a communicator.

In this chapter we have touched on matters you need to consider before speaking in a speech class (or elsewhere) for the first time. We hope to have suggested that getting ready to present a more or less formal talk involves more than following some routine set of prescriptions for how to win friends and influence people. We have tried to imply that planning a speech is a matter of modifying your private informational impulses so that they will be accommodated to listeners who make their own kinds of demands on speakers. We have argued that you will learn most in a speech classroom if you treat it as a laboratory for experiments in both speaking and listening. Treating your speech class thus, you can develop listening habits that will teach you about oral communication and speaking habits that will enable you to be conversationally direct and flexible in extemporaneous speaking. If the prospect of speaking extemporaneously troubles you psychologically, we have tried to show you that stage fright is not to be exorcised by any tactics except those that recognize fear of oral communication as a matter of attitudes. And careful preparation—neither too rigid nor too casual—seems the best available antidote for uncertainty about and fear of speaking in formal and semiformal circumstances. What "careful preparation" involves, we have reviewed and summarized.

EXERCISES

Written

1. Write down five simple, single ideas which you think would be good ones for development in a speech of 2–3 minutes.
2. Select a subject area. Frame a subject sentence for each of the rhetorical purposes: informing, persuading, inquiring, reinforcing, and entertaining.
3. Listen carefully to a speech by one of your classmates. Take notes in outline form on what he is saying. Following the speech, compare your outline with the one the speaker used. Check to see (a) how accurately you noted what was said, and (b) how much you missed noting.

Oral

1. Deliver a 3-minute speech in which you develop a single point which could be one of several main points in a longer speech. In developing your point use at least three different kinds of supporting material. In preparation, prepare a simple outline like that found on pages 27–28.
2. Prepare and deliver a brief speech on a proverb of your own choosing. Select at least five items to support its truth or falsity. In preparation devise a simple outline like that on page 28.

CHAPTER
3

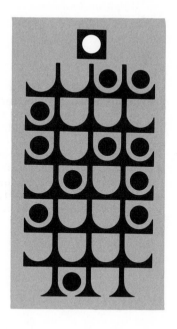

Understanding
Audiences

When he can thus give a satisfactory account of the kind of man that is amenable to any particular kind of argument, and is further able to recognize in practice the kind of thing he was discussing when it occurs before his eyes, and can fit his speech and method of persuasion to it, when he has learned all this he must learn when to speak and when to be silent, when is the moment for brevity, when for an appeal to pity or fear and all the things he has learned. Then, and not until then, has the art of speaking been well and fully acquired. But whenever any one who falls short of this in speaking, teaching or writing, boasts that he is an expert, we shall be right not to believe him.[1]

Plato, *Phaedrus*

No one will attain the knowledge Plato demands in the quotation above. Anyone completely able "to handle arguments according to the rules of art, as far as their nature allows them to be subjected to art" would have to be one of Plato's "philosopher kings." The ideal is a good one, but we practical men and women can scarcely hope for more than to work in the direction of the ideal. We shall never know *all*—either about the things we speak of or the people to whom we speak. That should depress no one. After all, we use speech as much to share and to learn as we use it to "prove" or "convince." Plato's challenge can push us toward trying to know as much as possible about what we tell others, about the people we talk to, and about ourselves as speakers and listeners. The ideal can be a healthy pressure toward fuller realization of what potentials we have.

This chapter will not teach you "the nature of the soul" (human psychology, we would say, today). We hope simply to move you a little farther toward full understanding of yourself and your future listeners. We shall remind you of a good many things you already know but too seldom put to artistic use when you talk or listen, and perhaps we shall be able to bring you a few new thoughts.

---

1. Plato, *Phaedrus*, pp. 271–272. As translated by G. M. A. Grube, *Plato's Thought* (Boston: Beacon Press, 1958), p. 214.

It helps listeners and readers if speakers and writers begin with familiar ideas. We want to begin this chapter that way. We ask you to think again about some things you doubtless know about interpersonal relationships you experience when you talk to others and they talk with you.

Observing Responses

Whenever you speak meaningfully with someone, you expect to observe responses. You speak because you want to be heard, understood, and reacted to. So you watch your listeners and try to "read" what they feed back to you. This everyone knows, but it is easy to forget how different this human relationship involving direct "feedback" is from the relations most writers experience. Poets, novelists, composers of epigrams, many scientists, and others concentrate on the timelessness, the universal significance, or the beauty of what they write. Instead of depending on immediate responses they often try to reach beyond their surroundings, even to other cultures and times. But when any of us communicate through *speech,* we depend on the responses of immediate listeners, now. Those responses tell us how to continue. Even if you try to influence a large and distant audience through radio or television, you would prefer to have some immediately present "studio audience" so you could watch for signs telling what kind of human relationship you were creating.

The importance of communicative "feedback" is widely recognized. We have said nothing new. What we want to call your attention to especially is that we all *need* "feedback" information; we depend on *it* in order to monitor our *own* talk. We all forget this from time to time, yet every speaking situation is in fact a test of our abilities to discover and use the information "sent" to us by *particular* listeners in a *particular* place and time.

Speech is a process, yes. But it is also a personal relationship attempted by someone, with someone. This is so even when we are only thinking about speaking to someone; we are then thinking about relating to someone and about that someone's probable responses. One of the things that makes speech unique as experience is that our "success" depends on immediate reactions of others. Do not be fooled by the fact that when you speak on the telephone, over radio, or on television you cannot see and fully interact with your listeners. You *know* they are there. If you are at all alert to what you are doing, you imagine them as real people with whom you are trying to establish personal bonds. However far removed in space, your immediate listener is the only one through whom you can "measure" your influence and adjust your efforts.

Within a speaker, it does not matter that speech is sometimes preserved for later consumption by people who will listen to recordings, see video tapes, or read printed texts. Experimental evidence and the testimony of broadcasters and other speakers agree that speech communication actually deteriorates when speakers have no "live" (real or imagined) audiences to "read" and adjust to. All evidence reinforces two propositions:

1. Because we are human we need human "feedback," if we are "normal";
2. Speakers who know how to "read" listeners and adapt to them find that visible listeners enhance communicative effectiveness.

Egocentrism as an Influence

It is not easy, though, to adjust speech to what one learns from listeners. For one thing, we are all rather egocentric. That gets in the way of our adaptations to listeners. Self-love whispers that listeners *ought* to attend to what we say, or that "just being myself" *ought* to be sufficient. Or we tell ourselves, "They *ought* to listen and understand because I'm telling them how *I* thought it out." Sometimes the thought runs: *"I* will tell them what they *need* to hear." Then, if we discover "they" didn't listen as we hoped, we complete the self-delusion by saying, "Well, that's their loss; the stuff was there. They could have understood if they had tried." What we overlook in all this is that if we speak egocentrically, we talk chiefly to and for ourselves. We use no new thoughts about the people "out there." We talk in *privately* pleasing ways, which may not be clear or interesting to others. So, listeners tire of us.

Egocentrism is not entirely defeating, of course. We would speak to one another very little if our desires to express and to influence did not impel us. And if anyone is more tiresome to hear than an egocentric, it is a speaker who talks chiefly to say what we already know or what he thinks we want to hear. We then wonder whether the speaker has no personal thoughts. The problem posed in speaking privately or publicly is: How are we to balance egoism and social acquiescence to form orally influential messages?

Adjusting to Listeners' Preferences

What effective conversationalists and formal speakers seem to accomplish is to act on the premise that not even their own egos can be well served unless *listeners'* preferences and expectations are accommodated. To do this takes conscious, careful thinking—in advance of and during speaking. But anyone can make the adjustment *if* he will think seriously about what communicating with a particular group of listeners does and does not require of him. Here is an example of one student's efforts in this direction.

A student of landscape architecture whom we shall call Dick Barnes was recently in a basic course in speech taught by one of your authors. Barnes was not especially effective orally, but he recognized that in his chosen profession he had to be able to reduce abstract and often technical concepts of landscape architecture to terms and images nonspecialists could understand and think with. He, his instructor, and the class struck a bargain. It was that Dick would talk regularly about landscape architecture, another student of architecture in the class would report on whether what Dick said was "professionally sound," and the class would write down anything that confused or bored them as Dick talked. In conferences the instructor tried to help Dick think up ways of getting around obscurities and causes of apathy among listeners. Twice Dick tried to explain architectural concepts; both times his colleague said he was "sound," but his other listeners said things like, "I couldn't get it," or "You told me more than I wanted to hear about that." Dick and the instructor tried to rethink his strategies, and they concluded that Dick had not translated his concepts into images his listeners could "see" and he had not associated his ideas with values about which they had feelings. Dick decided that next time he would "concentrate on the visuals." His third try worked. He was "sound," but he turned his subject, "The values in open spaces," into seeable, feelable realities. Here is a bit of what he said:

> Consider the area behind the Dairy Building. It's small, but it's a pleasing area to walk through. You can walk through it and have different experiences each time because of the very different kinds of plantings—shrubbery, flowers, trees. It's an enjoyable place to be. But so is the Mall. It has a canopy. You see it walking through. Half way up, ahead of you, the trees arch together. You are "inside" yet you're out-of-doors. And there at the center of the arch's end you see Pattee Library, with its straight columns. It completes the enclosing of the area. You feel "inside," but you know you're outside and free. These are things a landscape architect means when he says outdoor spaces have "value" or can be given "values." He's saying he tries to put things into outdoor space in such ways that you will say it's interesting to be there or that you like to be there. The value he's talking about is your good feeling; that's what he tries to create with his shapings and plantings.

There was no weakening of the architectural concepts "space" and "value." Barnes simply illustrated their reality by transporting his listeners to campus spots they all knew well enough to picture in their minds. Then he made them feel the values he spoke of as his words directed their eyes and movements—in imagination. In these ways the speaker's and listeners' egocentric inclinations were balanced. Barnes *willed* that listeners *should* sense what "values" are to an architect, but he transformed the professional concept into experienced sensations. That is what his listeners had been demanding of him. Without in any degree becoming a sycophant, he accommodated his own *and* the listeners' wishes. And there was communication!

Another general and familiar fact about listeners is that they don't always make it easy for speakers to adjust to their demands. They aren't always as open about their requirements as Dick Barnes's classmates were. Each of us has played the role of polite but evasive listener, actually engrossed in private thought.   Each of us has missed points in a college lecture, heard only half a newscast item, and mixed up a set of directions because of self-indulgent daydreaming.   That is the way listeners are.   Notice the partly pertinent, partly irrelevant thoughts a juror recalls having had as a prosecuting attorney began to speak:

> As he faced us head-on, I noticed how weary he seemed and how arched his eyebrows were behind his glasses.   His dogged determination had kept the case moving against the defendants for almost four months; this morning he suffered from laryngitis.   I recalled my hostility toward him during the long days of jury selection.   Now I listened intently.[2]

No doubt the juror "listened intently," but he was not thinking of the prosecutor's *ideas* in those seconds when he was reflecting on the lawyer's health, eyebrows, apparent weariness, and earlier behavior.   But let every speaker take note and remember: this juror was listening as people really do listen.   His attention was drifting in and out of the flow of ideas which the speaker was *steadily* creating through words and action.

The simple but important implication is that speakers dare not presume that their listeners will or even can give unbroken attention.   When you speak, you must plan adaptations to the ways listeners behave—to their tendencies to "drift in and out," to their fascination with tangential details, to the necessity of pressing them to focus on what is important, and above all to their insistence that their whole listening experience is supposed to be a highly personal encounter with *you*.   To be effective you need to be continually gathering listeners *back:* directing, redirecting, recapturing, and disciplining those wandering minds "out there."   In the moments of talk we have quoted, Dick Barnes probably had better control over his listeners' experiences than the prosecutor had over Mr. Chester's.   Why?   Because Dick more precisely directed his hearers' thoughts to imagined actions and sensations which they could only interpret as Dick wished.

The paragraphs above have said little you did not know before.   But we suspect that in communicating orally you have probably not made full use of these bits of common knowledge about how people listen.   We hope to have pulled to the forefront of your mind the facts that "feedback" from immediate listeners is *there* and you need to *use* it; that egocentricity can, but need not, blind you to what you can do to adapt effectively to equally egocentric listeners; that adapting to an audience need not be "surrender" of one's own concepts; and that listening is an errant process requiring all speakers to work with the full resources of art to control it.

The remainder of this chapter deals with aspects of speaking situations

---

2. Giraud Chester, *The Ninth Juror* (New York: Random House, 1970), p. 104.   Mr. Chester, once a teacher of speech and broadcasting and now a broadcasting executive, wrote this interesting book to recount his experience as a juror in a criminal case in New York City.

you may not have thought about before and with special forces that control listeners' willingness to participate in spoken communication. Some of what we shall say will continue to be familiar except in application, but we hope from time to time to give you new information that you can use in practical ways.

SPEECHES AND SITUATIONS

For a great many years it was customary to say that in formal or informal speaking a speaker should analyze his subject, his audience, the occasion, and his own relation to all of these. The speaker, we used to say, must adapt himself and his speech to all he learned through analyzing these elements in any speech situation. In 1968, Lloyd F. Bitzer published an award-winning essay in which he suggested a somewhat different way of thinking about speech situations, or "rhetorical situations" as he called them. His way of thinking is so useful that we shall borrow heavily from his "Rhetorical Situation"[3] in later chapters of this book.

We shall try to explain Mr. Bitzer's concept as practically as possible. Suppose you are to speak to a group of people. When you begin to talk, certain specific people will be "out there." They will be in some specific place or places—in a classroom, in a circle on the grass, in an auditorium, in their homes listening to the radio or listening and watching you on television. Whoever they are and wherever they are, they will have a unique notion about themselves. They will be aware that you are treating them as an "audience." As you begin to talk, they will begin to think of themselves as parts of a collection of other people who are sharing in or "stuck with" what you are saying. They will begin to respond to what you say, but they will also be responding to *all the other forces that conspired to constitute them parts of your "audience."* They will not respond just to you; they will respond to all their past relationships to you and what you represent for them, to all other known objects and persons associated with you and the circumstances in which they are meeting you, and to their sense of the others whom they know or imagine are also parts of your "audience." Professor Bitzer's point is that rhetorical speech happens within a whole complex of conditioning factors and that it is wiser to think of speech as a message inserted into "sets of conditions" or an intellectual "system" than to think of it merely as statements directed to specific persons. The people "out there," Bitzer thinks, are as much conditioned by past and present events as by anything we might say about their ages, sexes, educational

3. Lloyd F. Bitzer, "The Rhetorical Situation," *Philosophy and Rhetoric,* I (Jan. 1968), 1–14. The essay received the James A. Winans Award for Distinguished Scholarship in Rhetoric and Public Address in 1968.

levels, etc. What happens is that a speaker and some listeners try to have a human relationship *within* a whole set of conditions, a "situation," that envelops them all and imposes opportunities and restrictions on all of them.

Entering a Talk Situation

If you think about speaking publicly in this way, you will not think of yourself as addressing an "audience" as much as you will think of yourself as *entering* a *situation* in which other people and you are conditioned by time, place, occasion, past history, and expectations that certain kinds of changes are supposed to take place as the result of your coming together. Bitzer stresses another important point: influenced by all these forces, the people in the situation may or may *not* think their situation needs some *talk*. There are situations in which money or clothes or something else, but not *talk*, can solve the "exigence" or urgent needs of the situation. But if the forces that created the situation have created an "exigence" or urgency that can be helped by talk of some sort, then obviously *you* can enter the situation with some prospects of making it change. There will also be situations in which the need is for some talk from *you* and not from someone else. On the other hand, there will be situations within which you will first have to create a need for *talk* from *you*—make room for yourself within the conditions that constitute the speech situation. For example, a political speaker at a nonpolitical picnic will need to give those attending some reasons for becoming serious and political before he can safely launch a discussion of political issues.

If you think of yourself as "entering" speech situations, your key questions become something like the following. For what and for whom are they *ready* in this situation? If the situation doesn't already invite *me* to change it by talk, can I reconstruct it so it *will* accept *me* and my *talk*? What is the *need* that talk must fill here? Can *my* talk fill it? If not, how must I change my talk or how must I change the situation to make it ready for my talk? Asking questions of these sorts will tell you whether you have two tasks or one: to change the situation in some way (by what you say or otherwise) and *then* to insert the talk you had in mind, or simply to enter a situation that is already "set" to receive *your* influence through *talk*.

We can illustrate this situationality of speech from a common classroom circumstance. If your class has been studying how information can best be given orally, and if the assignment for a series of talks is, "Give a five-minute informative speech," all your listeners will be conditioned by their study and by the assignment. If you now give a talk that entertains or argues more than it informs, some listeners (not *just* your instructor) will be perplexed by what you are saying and why. Some will wonder: "Doesn't he know he was to inform us?" "Is he deliberately violating the assignment, or doesn't he know what he's doing?" "How's the instructor going to react to this?" It is no sin to do the unexpected or the unassigned, but it is communicatively inefficient unless one's disregard of a situation's readinesses is explained in ways that will actually alter the situation and make it ready for the "unexpected." The general fact is that when an audience has been conditioned to hear one kind of thing and then hears something else, it spends much time thinking about how its expectations are being violated. Altering or ignoring situationally defined constraints has to be done very carefully, if at all.

When an Assignment Is Imposed

It is sometimes possible, desirable, or even necessary to insert unexpected issues and ideas into speech situations. But when something about past experience or planning has created a situation that imposes a widely recognized "assignment," a change is difficult to accomplish. Two recent incidents will illustrate when speech situations can be altered and when they cannot.

One of your authors recently taught a speech class where there occurred a group discussion in which several students expressed great concern about preserving wildlife in the United States. A few days after, there was a series of speeches, several of which also dealt with ecology. Discussions following those speeches produced many remarks sweepingly critical of disturbers of Nature. Criticism was showered on various groups from industries to hunters. At this point a biology major decided privately that the climate of opinion was becoming too one-sided and, since wildlife management was one of his special interests, he decided to "straighten things out" by making a speech in favor of regulated hunting of female deer. It happened that doe hunting was then being criticized by some conservationists. What had happened in the class and what was being printed in newspapers and being broadcast all generated a situation in which another speech on ecology could have influence. But a speech endorsing hunting would have to be worked out with care for a bias against hunting had developed in the class and was being fed from outside it. The biology major adapted so skillfully to this situation that he changed some attitudes.

He began his speech by recalling earlier talk about "management," "protecting the balance," "caring about Nature," and the like. Then he said:

> I want you to think some more about "balance." I want you to think about how we are to keep the deer of this state in balance with the space and food we are willing to allow them. I'd like you to think whether you want to protect healthy deer or sick and scrawny ones, whether you want more deer killed on highways, and whether you have any sympathy for the human beings who run the farms of our rural areas. Let me tell you about the balancing problems that affect the lives of deer.

He went on to show that natural reproductive processes would cause deer in his state to overpopulate available wild land every two years unless a certain number of does were regularly eliminated.   Fewer than the required number had been killed in past years, he said.   The present imbalance was justification for extending the annual doe season.   Several listeners' reactions were well expressed by one student who said, afterward: "Now you've got me almost embarrassed.   I don't hunt; I don't even like the idea.   But the way you put it, it seems like I *ought* to take up hunting deer if not enough other people do.   Really, I don't feel too comfortable!"

The incident illustrates that where the forces creating a speech situation have only shaped *opinions,* an astute speaker can usually change the constraints or restrictions of the situation by taking time to discover what there is in the opinion-making background that can be used to justify *other* directions of thought.   The biology major seized upon the ways in which "balance" had been installed in his listeners' minds as a "proper" concept, and he artistically made his thoughts about doe hunting suitable for the situation by linking all of his potentially unacceptable or irrelevant ideas to that agreed-upon, positive value.

Violating of the Assignment

But sometimes situations evolve or are created so that they dictate "assignments" to speakers.   "Assignments" are much harder to change than evolved opinions.   For example, academic ceremonies tend to dictate that education be talked about.   Sometimes a speaker is so important that he can deviate from such an "assignment," but these circumstances are rare.   Sir Winston Churchill was once invited to speak at a convocation at Westminster College in Missouri.   The situation certainly prescribed talk about education, but Sir Winston gave his famous "Iron Curtain" speech describing cold war tensions. Apparently no one worried about his violating the dictates of an academic occasion, but not many speakers have his fame to give them freedom to re-create speech situations at will.   A far more representative event happened in 1971 at a national conference of officers of college and university women's associations.

This conference's planning committee invited a well-known newswoman to be the conference's keynote speaker.   Since student governments were becoming more and more coeducational, the women's associations needed to redefine their functions, so the 1971 conference was to be devoted to exploring new areas of service for the women's groups.   We do not know exactly what the conference's planners told their keynote speaker, but the call for the conference and the published titles of the workshops were so written as to make clear what the conference's problem was.   And the planners had scheduled things in hopes that the keynote speech would contain starting-off ideas about what the women's associations ought to be doing.

The keynote speaker spoke interestingly of problems and gratifications experienced by professional women, especially journalists.   Nothing was said about university women's associations. The conference leaders were deeply upset, and audible murmurs developed during the speech—apparently indicating that listeners were perplexed or losing interest. The speech was an excellent one for this speaker to make, but this was not the situation for it. The publicity and planning had announced something different would happen. Moreover, the conference itself "got off to a very slow start" according to one of the planners, for the program's success depended on the keynote speaker to provide the workshops with "starting points." Perhaps the planners had created a speech situation the speaker could not fill, or had failed to brief her on the created situation, or perhaps the speaker had not investigated the situation as she should have. In any case, the "assignment" was violated; the speaker suffered, the audience became uneasy, and conference plans went awry. The "assignments" of situations cannot be ignored with safety.[4]

Something of the last sort is what happens in a classroom when expected patterns of speaking are violated. If a nationally known newswoman cannot alter the assignment from an all-woman audience without upsetting her hearers, it is unlikely a student in a classroom can do it. Not to try to persuade when everyone expects persuasion is like making a solemn after-dinner speech on a convivial occasion—the maladjustment to the speech situation must be specially justified if attempted at all.

The practical meaning of what we have said so far is that whenever you engage in serious talk—formal or informal—you will be wise to analyze carefully what your speech situation *invites, allows,* and *discourages.* It is important to think about audiences as individuals and as groups of listeners, but it is important to look *first* behind the listeners to discover what forces have conditioned them for this occasion and what readinesses and unreadinesses have been specially generated within them. It is important to remember that not every situation with people in it calls for *talk.* And not every situation calls for talk from *you.* Nonrhetorical situations like this seldom exist in speech classrooms, but they arise elsewhere. So, the first question you ought to ask is: "Can *speech* from *me* do anything here?" If the answer is "Yes," your next task will be to study the situation more deeply and make as much use of its readinesses as possible. To adapt thoroughly, you will need still more specific knowledge about audiences in general and about the particular audience that exists within the situation you will enter.

CONCEPTUALIZING AUDITORS AS POTENTIAL LISTENERS

Audience is a common word, yet we often think unclearly about what it means. Some conceive of an audience as a mass of faceless beings who

---

4. During the next year, one of the disappointed planners was wise enough to invite the newswoman to give the *same* speech to a campus gathering of women students. This time the occasion was announced as a speech and discussion on "Women in Professional Life." This time the same speaker, with substantially the same speech, was eminently successful. So was the entire meeting.

present an impressionable surface on which speakers may make imprints at will. Some imagine that groups of listeners respond automatically to specific appeals or techniques. You cannot safely hold either of these views when thinking about creating oral communication.

An audience listening to speech is not faceless or will-less. Neither is it a collection of conditioned animals whose responses are mindlessly automatic. An audience is made up of individuals, each intent on his own and his group's life and happiness, each preferring pursuit of those private interests to any other activity. Though each of us tends to conform in some as yet unknown degree to the pressures of the rhetorical situations we are in, listeners seldom surrender their individualities to the group. Thus two important things to remember are: *listeners are individuals,* and *listeners do not have to listen unless they want to.* You need only examine your own behavior as a listener to see the truth of these propositions.

In the Classroom

You have undoubtedly sat in a class in history. Sometimes you were genuinely part of the classroom situation, sometimes not. Sometimes you gave active, "I'm-anxious-to-learn" attention to almost everything going on. At other times you found nothing of interest to you, so you allowed your thoughts to wander and scarcely knew what was going on around you. Once in a while, perhaps, something literally seized your attention and you became completely a part of the communicative situation, letting the attitudes and behaviors of others influence you considerably. But in all these experiences *you* retained a great deal of control over what you would admit into your consciousness and over the ways you would respond to what you admitted. Though you were among many, you were no speaker's puppet. You were somewhat affected by those around you, but you and each of your classmates tended overwhelmingly to grant or withhold participation according to your own interests, ideas, attitudes, and desires.

Outside the Classroom

Of course, a classroom situation is not universally representative of how we listen. Some people insist that the situations in which religious revivals and political rallies occur, create "mass effects" and transport people out of themselves. That there is a special phenomenon called "crowd psychology" is a notion that has existed in our culture since the late nineteenth century, but there is no empirical evidence in support of it and much evidence that calls it into question. The British social psychologist, J. A. C. Brown, concluded a general study of opinion and attitude change thus:

... it would appear that the main lesson to be drawn from our present study of propaganda is how very resistant people are to messages that fail to fit their own picture of the world and their own objective circumstances, how they deliberately (if unconsciously) seek out only those views which agree with their own.[5]

Brown's conclusion is general, based on restudying data concerning religious conversion, "mass hysteria," brainwashing, and the like. Even here, where presumably the most psychologically powerful forces are loosed, Brown finds individuality more impressive than conformism. He finds that dramatic outbursts within audiences or in more private situations turn out to be expressions of preexisting strong beliefs and feelings, now released because they are confirmed and encouraged by factors in the situation, not as instances of any social "contagion" within a "herd."[6]

You will be wise to think of your listeners as aggregations of *individuals* who have *some* tendency to behave as their situations encourage them to behave but who have an even greater disposition to remain themselves in a firm, individualistic sense. But you cannot motivate every member of your audience independently of every other; therefore your thought about listeners needs always to follow what has been the counsel of rhetorical theorists for centuries: make your plans and conduct yourself *according to what your listeners have in common* — as individuals and as participants in a speech situation of which you and they are parts.

In this kind of audience-situation analysis you begin with a great advantage. One thing you have in common with all your listeners is your humanity. Your hearers are people; you can depend on and use the general characteristics of human beings as bases for adapting to them. Let us look at some of those predictable facts about human beings. All will give you practical opportunities to secure and hold attention and to shape attitudes.

GETTING ATTENTION

A great German zoologist wrote, "The outside world — the world perceived by the senses — is the source of all that a form of life is and does, thinks and feels."[7] One way to describe a speaker's job is to say his task is to direct what listeners

---

5. *Techniques of Persuasion: From Propaganda to Brainwashing* (Baltimore: Penguin Books, 1963), p. 309. The term "propaganda" is used by Brown to apply to "any scheme of propagating a doctrine or practice *or for influencing the emotional attitudes of others.*" (p. 12. Brown's italics.)
6. The classic experiments on group pressure and individual judgments were conducted by S. E. Asch. They showed that college students regularly gave wrong judgments about the lengths of lines when a majority of the group of eight took what were in fact wrong positions. When these experiments are cited as evidence that people overwhelmingly conform to the behaviors of those around them, it is often forgotten that *if just one other group member agreed on a judgment,* most of Asch's subjects held out for their own *right* judgments about the lines. Furthermore, there is no evidence that convictions about *values* are as easy to "upset" as perceptions of the lengths of lines. See Bernard Berelson and Gary A. Steiner, *Human Behavior: An Inventory of Scientific Findings* (New York: Harcourt, Brace & World, Inc., 1964), pp. 335–336.
7. Wolfgang von Buddenbrock, *The Senses,* trans. Frank Gaynor (Ann Arbor: The University of Michigan Press, 1958), p. 12.

take into themselves and how they form themselves by so doing. It is generally agreed that (1) the nature of the stimuli that impinge on us, (2) our expectations as they have been built up from our previous experience, and (3) what we want and need or don't want and need are the factors that determine what we choose to attend to in the world outside our private beings.[8] Out of these generalizations about human beings' selective attention we can build some "rules of thumb" for adapting to people when we speak to them.

Whatever yields strong sense experience is likely to be selected for attention by listeners. What does that have to do with how one should speak? Images induced by words and actions enable listeners to "see," "hear," "feel"; imagistic language stimulates vicarious perceptions and therefrom responses. If reminded by vivid words, for example, we sense once more the "blue-grey glint" of a desert sky we once saw or the zigzag outline of yesterday's flash of lightning.

We also expect to find intelligible *relations* among stimuli. Therefore, we search for similarities and differences among things we hear about. We try to connect the likenesses or dissimilarities with what we have experienced before. In this way we also test how the things we hear are likely to affect us; we judge the future by comparing what we are *told* will happen with what we *know* happened in past circumstances. For such varied reasons things brought "near to us" through words or delivery are especially likely to be selected for our attention.

Of the "needs, desires, wishes, interests" of listeners we shall say more later, but a point to be made immediately is that if you will supply your hearers with the kinds of behaviors, images, and senses of relationship that create "live" stimuli, that relate closely to those hearers' experiences, you will be *directing* their attention and so controlling what they do and do not respond to.

The Task of Control

Speakers often misjudge the nature of this task of controlling attention. They suppose the important thing is to *secure* attention. But this is easy. Usually you have only to move about in some way—generate any kind of change—and you will draw attention. Introductory gimmicks, so beloved by exhibitionistic speakers, are really seldom necessary. They seldom fail because it is so very easy to secure attention. To *hold* and to *direct* attention are what speakers should spend their effort on in speech. Some useful strategies have just been mentioned, and we shall offer others throughout this book. Meanwhile, it is worth noting here how attention is commonly *lost* in speaking.

Let ideas remain remote from listeners' experience, loose some atten-

---

8. Berelson and Steiner, *Human Behavior,* p. 100.

tion-grabbing stimuli that are irrelevant to your message's real purpose, or weaken the sensory qualities of what you say, and you will begin losing a hearing. This is why wordy or vague observations, dullness of expression, themes or arguments that are ill adapted to the situation need to be avoided. They tell listeners there is nothing *for them* in your stimuli. The audience then searches for more immediately interesting activity. Irrelevancies such as graceless utterance, awkwardness of manner, and even what an audience takes to be unusual clothing can also interfere. These distracting stimuli can be psychologically stronger than the stimuli of what is said, and so pull attention away from your important ideas.

It is unobtrusiveness and "fitness" of manner, plus proof that your concerns are those of your listeners, that will hold attention. These earn for you the right to work with your listeners' perceptions. The rest is a matter of *directing* thoughts and feelings along lines that are consistent with your communicative purpose. And for this you need to understand some things about listeners' readiness to believe or change.

LISTENERS' READINESS TO BELIEVE OR CHANGE

Many experiments and other inquiries have been made in efforts to determine just what controls people's willingness to adopt beliefs and to change attitudes. Some findings are uniform enough to yield generalizations that speakers can use. For other questions, systematic research has given no clear answers. In the next few pages we shall have to draw on both scientific evidence and common sense in order to present judgments about human listeners.

Gratifying Biological Needs

We can begin with the basic fact that *biologically* we are mammals and have bodily and organic needs generally found among mammals. We want gratifications for hunger, for thirst, for our need for oxygen, and for our sexual drives, and we want to preserve ourselves from injury, punishment, and other physical discomfort. But being human, we also exercise conscious and unconscious preferences in many of these matters. For example, we seek gratifications for our physical needs, but we are also capable of deferring or even suppressing some of those needs when we want something else still more. All of us have put off eating in order to meet a friend, and audiences have even been known to endure cold and wet in order to hear speakers.

So, if you want to hold and direct listeners' attention, one rough "rule" is to show them that you can help them toward gratification of some biological needs. Unless they want something else still more, they are likely to listen to you at least until they begin to doubt the promise you hold out or to suspect that following your invitations will force them to give up goals and needs they prefer even more strongly. Whenever you can link your thoughts even indirectly to physical needs of your listeners you ought to do so, for it will almost surely increase the prospects of your being heard with favor.

Sex

Sex is both a biological and a social condition that makes differences in listeners' readiness to believe and change. As a speaker you ought to accommodate what you say to these differences. It is easy to overemphasize the interests, motivations, and persuasibility that allegedly differentiate men from women, but experimental evidence argues firmly that the sexes do respond somewhat differently to communication. According to most of the research that has been done, women are somewhat more persuasible than men. But there is also some evidence that this may not be true when the persuader is a woman speaker. In addition, Thomas M. Scheidel found indications that college women "retain less from persuasive communications than do men."[9] It is unsafe to generalize about this last point, but you can lose nothing by trying to make all your persuasion as inviting as possible for *both* men and women. And if you are male, it will be wise to assume that the males in your audience will be harder to persuade than the women. If you are a woman, you ought to expect more difficulties with women than with men. Unfortunately we simply do not know how sex differences affect the processes of informing, entertaining, and other nonpersuasive kinds of communication.

Age

Age, too, seems to affect listeners' attitudes and their general responses to communication. To generalize across situations about any age group is precarious, and there is not much research on the relation of age to judgments except in reference to specific subjects. However, the studies that have been made tend to confirm the general allegations of traditional lore in rhetoric and literature: the young are more persuasible than their elders and the elderly cautious; the young, middle-aged, and the old tend to give closest attention to different aspects of ideas and issues. What is scientifically known suggests that in speaking you can safely follow the implicit guidelines of Aristotle, unless you know something special about a situation or audience that indicates otherwise. None of the observations we are about to paraphrase from Aristotle has been disproved and many have been confirmed sociologically.

---

9. "Sex and Persuasibility," *Speech Monographs,* XXX (Nov. 1963), 353–358.

Aristotle tried to address himself, as few modern psychological studies have, to "the proper means of adapting both speech and speaker to a given audience." He sought rhetorically applicable generalizations about the young, "men in their prime," and the elderly. Below is a quick summary of his observations, and if you take the trouble to compare them to the results of public opinion polls which report opinions by age groupings, you will be struck by the modernity of what he said.

In youth "men have strong desires, and whatever they desire they are prone to do. Of the bodily desires the one they let govern them most is the sexual; here they lack self-control. They are shifting and unsteady in their desires. . . ." They are "quick to anger, and apt to give way to it," and they are "fond of honor" but even "fonder of victory." Money means relatively little to them "for they have not yet learned what the want of it means." They are not cynical; rather, they are trustful "for as yet they have not been often deceived." Being quick to hope, and living much in anticipation, "they are easily deceived." Though brave and spirited, they are also shy. Being idealistic, "in their actions they prefer honor to expediency" and are dogmatic. "All their mistakes are on the side of intensity and excess. . . ."

In middle life, Aristotle thought, people "will be neither excessively confident . . . nor yet too timid; they will be both confident and cautious. They will neither trust everyone nor distrust everyone; rather they will judge the case by the facts. Their rule of life will be neither honor alone, nor expediency alone. . . ." They will temper valor with self-control, and they will be neither parsimonious nor prodigal with their possessions. Generally, "all the valuable qualities which youth and age divide between them are joined in the prime of life."

The aged have characteristics opposed to those of the young. Thus, "they err by an extreme moderation" and are "positive about nothing" for they have lived long and been disappointed much. They tend to be cynical and "put the worst construction on everything"; they are suspicious, and sometimes small-minded. They "aspire to nothing great or exalted, but crave the mere necessities and comforts of existence." They are constantly apprehensive and "live their lives with too much regard for the expedient and too little for honor." What other people think means little to them, for they "live in memory rather than in anticipation."

Aristotle concluded: "Now the hearer is always receptive when a speech is adapted to his own character and reflects it. Thus we can readily see the proper means of adapting both speech and speaker to a given audience."[10]

In these descriptions you can find useful generalizations about how the reactions and interests of age groups are apt to differ across situations and

---

10. From *The Rhetoric of Aristotle*, translated and edited by Lane Cooper, pp. 132–137, bk. II, chaps. 12–14. Copyright 1932, renewed 1960 by Lane Cooper. Reprinted by permission of Appleton-Century-Crofts, Educational Division, Meredith Corporation.

subjects. A speaker cannot, of course, always gratify the idealism of youth and the caution of age with the same argument, nor can he depend on it that he has *no* cautious youths and *no* radical elderly persons in an audience. But more often than most speakers realize, ideas are at once honorable (satisfying idealists) and expedient (satisfying the cautious). For example, every discussion of Medicare or Social Security contains opportunities for development of the humanitarian, economic, and security-assuring aspects of the subject. If you discuss such subjects you are easily capable of emphasizing the humanitarian aspects if there are relatively young people in your audience. To do so would trouble no one else. But if you have reason to think there are elderly or just generally conservative listeners in the audience also, you are equally capable of giving emphasis to the practicalities of your subject. That would upset no one either. The point is not that speakers should address only one age group in a mixed audience; it is that they should include something *for* each prominent group.

Intelligence

Intelligence is another attribute everyone has in some degree, so any speaker needs to take note of it as an aspect of his listeners' condition. What we call intelligence is normally expressed as a measure of a variety of capacities: verbal comprehension, ability to handle numbers, spatial perception, ability to remember, reasoning power, fluency with words, and perceptual speed.[11] If your listeners are supposed to have "high intelligence," this does not mean they are high in *all* these capacities or that they have them in equal degrees; it simply alleges that they are high in this *set* of abilities. Notice how important "language skills" are in this set of factors embodying what we call "intelligence." A useful generalization is embedded there. Given the kinds of capacities composing "intelligence," you will be safe in surmising that the higher your listeners' "intelligence," the better able they will be to understand spoken messages, to interpret them, and to evaluate them. The lower their measured "intelligence," the harder these tasks will be, and the more help they will need from *you.*

At first glance, what we know about relations between general intelligence and responses to communication seems confusing. Summarizing the evidence as of 1967, one pair of authors said:

> . . . it is as plausible to assert that the factor of intelligence is positively correlated with persuasibility as it is to assert a negative correlation, or even no correlation. On the one hand, the more intelligent a person, the better able he is to comprehend the issues. The less intelligent person, because of his limited comprehension, is less susceptible to persuasion on complex issues. On the

---

11. Berelson and Steiner, *Human Behavior,* pp. 212–215.

other hand, the more intelligent a person, the greater his critical ability, and the less he is influenced by persuasion. There is literature in support of the null, the positive, and the negative relationship.[12]

For a practical speaker this seems discouraging; but if you will study the statement carefully, you can extract some good advice. The *higher* the intelligence of your listeners, the more readily you can expect them to understand what you say, *but* the quicker they will be to criticize you if you make what they take to be mistakes. Your safe course with highly intelligent listeners, then, is to be careful to justify and qualify your data and your claims. However, if there are people of limited intelligence among your listeners, you will need to worry about being especially clear and explicit in order to help them to comprehend what you say. To these generalizations another can be added: Regardless of intelligence levels, people who have little or no initial knowledge of what is said to them are likely to accept what they hear *first* about that subject.

If you are to make use of such practical generalizations, you will need to reflect in advance on the levels of intelligence that will be represented among your listeners. And you will need to consider what they already know about your subject. If they know your subject well, be careful to leave no doubt about *your* full command of it. Being vague, imprecise, or inconsistent among people who know a subject is a good way to be "put down" as a communicator. But if you are clear, plainly well informed, and unpretentious, you will have good reason to expect that both the gifted and the ungifted will comprehend you and find you believable.

Strength of Attitudes

Strength of attitudes already held by listeners is another quality to try to estimate in audiences. All listeners have *some* attitudes toward most things you can speak of, and you need to think about what those attitudes will be in each speaking situation. B. E. Lane and D. O. Sears have made a succinct statement of what you will be up against in this connection:

> People who differ from you will tend to distort your views. When you differ slightly from your friends, they will think you agree with them. Your enemies will think you disagree with them more than you actually do. Both tendencies will weaken your capacity to influence them in the way you wish to.[13]

This kind of predictable situation implies that speakers ought to reflect carefully on whether the various segments of their audiences will be friendly, indifferent, or hostile to ideas that need to be presented. If you can discover

---

12. Ralph L. Rosnow and Edward J. Robinson, *Experiments in Persuasion* (New York: Academic Press, 1967), p. 198.
13. *Public Opinion* (Englewood Cliffs, N.J.: Prentice-Hall, Inc., 1964), p. 51.

which attitudes prevail strongly among your hearers, Lane and Sears's state-ment suggests what kinds of *misunderstandings* you need to guard against. You can then gauge more closely what you can reasonably expect to accom-plish.   A careful student of human communication has said,

> One of the best established findings in social psychology is that individuals who have well-established attitudes and beliefs act so as to maintain them; the more extreme the attitudes, the more difficult they are to change.[14]

From the data about the roles strong attitudes play in regulating re-sponses at least two clear guidelines for speaking can be inferred.   One is: The more firmly your listeners hold a view, the easier it will be for you to strengthen or vitalize that view, but the *less* change *from* that view you should ask for.   Even hostile listeners' opinions can be changed a *little* if you proceed cautiously and with respect for attitudes already held, but if you ask for im-mediate, major changes, you are apt to be rejected.   On the other hand, if what you need to say confirms attitudes your listeners hold, merely to restate those views somewhat freshly can intensify the opinions already held.   An-other useful guideline is: If you believe certain attitudes are *lightly* held by your listeners, you are safe in asking for large changes and for full acceptance of your ideas on those points.   When attitudes are lightly held, accepting new views is often easier for a listener than "splitting hairs" about the matter.[15]

What we have just said means that you will need to make the best estimates you can of how closely your ideas and those of your listeners con-form to each other.   If there are likely to be significant differences between your ideas and theirs, your next question will be how *strongly* the hearers' different positions are held.   If those positions are strongly held, you will need to seek small, step-by-step changes in the listeners' views—provided you have to touch on the point of difference at all.   If the listeners are neutral or indifferent to the ideas you must develop, you will probably lose little by asking for completely new or even "turn-around" judgments.   If the hearers already agree with you, your task is simply to make the agreed-upon views more highly valued by adding reasons for them or by making them seem more important than ever.

Commitment

Commitment to ideas deserves some special attention even though in the section just above we have treated some aspects of this topic.   Whether people

---

14. Gary Cronkhite, *Persuasion: Speech and Behavioral Change* (Indianapolis: The Bobbs-Merrill Company, Inc., 1969), p. 139.

15. Listeners' "involvement" with ideas can be deep even though they hold "moderate" views.   "Moderation" should not be confused with holding views lightly for listeners *can* be strongly involved with their "moderation." For general discussion see Carolyn Sherif, Muzafer Sherif, and Roger Nebergall, *Attitude and Attitude Change: The Social Judgment-Involvement Approach* (Philadelphia: W. B. Saunders Company, 1965).   A particularly inclusive experiment generally confirming what we have said above is C. David Mortensen and Kenneth K. Sereno, "The Influence of Ego-Involvement and Discrepancy on Perceptions of Communication," *Speech Monographs*, XXXVII (June 1970), 127–134.

who have *acted* on behalf of an idea *then* hold the idea more firmly than people who simply believe it intellectually has been probed in a number of empirical studies. Despite the research effort, we still do not know *how much* difference acts of prior commitment make *under what circumstances.* The situation is much like that with respect to what differences age may make. Apparently to make a speech or write an essay on a subject can cause a person to hold more firmly to the views supported in the writing or speaking. It is helpful to know this, but most of the research on the point has taken place in laboratories and on specialized topics, so we cannot generalize very far concerning what difference it will make if some of your listeners have contributed money or time to a political party or taken part in a demonstration for or against something you want to discuss. At least one general inference seems possible, however: If just making a speech or writing an essay can fix opinions more firmly in people's heads, we should probably expect that if our listeners have joined organizations, given money, marched, and done other major acts relative to a position, they will have *strong* commitments to those ideas.

On this reasoning it seems that you ought to find out whenever you can whether your listeners have *acted* toward any ideas you intend to speak about. If some have, you can lose nothing by assuming that their acts are evidence of firm, fixed views. Use those views if you can. If you can't use them, avoid arousing those beliefs against you, and ask for minimal changes of opinion on anything closely associated with ideas the listeners' previous acts show commitment to.

Another kind of commitment is often disregarded by inexperienced speakers simply because it isn't very important in classrooms but is so commonplace everywhere else that it is overlooked. It is the commitment that merely *coming* to listen expresses. In your classroom your listeners are there as much because they have to be as because they are breathlessly waiting to hear you speak. In a class the presence of an audience expresses no special commitment to you or any other speaker, but in most out-of-class speech situations things are different. Consider yourself. It takes at least curiosity to get you out of your apartment or dormitory and into a meeting where someone talks publicly. It expresses some kind of commitment to some set of ideas for you to be in the meeting at all. It even expresses a kind of commitment in favor of a speaker when you turn your head on campus to listen more closely to someone else. The basic point is that when listeners listen *voluntarily,* their effort is an expression of a favorable commitment to the person who speaks—unless we know that the listeners' real purpose in listening or attending a meeting is to scoff or oppose. And there are, of course, speech situations in which desire for information or desire for reasons to believe is what brings listeners into the situation. Very many rallies, seminars, lecture-discussions, teach-ins, and the like are in fact meetings where listeners come *to commit* themselves toward speakers and their subjects. Wherever this occurs, the speaker has a great advantage, for he has clear signs that there are favorable commitments he can work with. But he also has great responsibilities. *Not* to be informative, convincing, impressive, or inspiring according to the listeners' expectations will violate their commitments and make them strongly negative toward the offending speaker.

What we have just said emphasizes the challenge of classroom speaking. The presence of listeners in a class is not a sign of commitment in favor of those who speak. But it could *become* so. The acid test of classroom speaking is: Can you establish a climate of opinion in which your colleagues actually try to "make class" just to hear you? We have seen this achieved. It is the ultimate compliment to a speaker who is serious about his or her communication.

Obviously audience analysis is essential to effective public speech. Before speaking you will need to discover as much as you can about the factors already affecting your listeners' readiness to understand, believe, and change. Thinking carefully about what kinds of listeners you will have unearths the special problems and the ready-made advantages you will have when you enter the speech situation. When you know these things, your next step in informed preparation is to explore what resources are at your disposal for using the needs, dispositions, and commitments the listeners will present to you. One set of resources grows out of the fact that listeners are almost always receptive to certain *kinds* of rhetoric. If you know these options and how to use them, you are that much farther along toward a strategy for achieving your goals when speaking to listeners.

AUDIENCES' READINESS FOR RHETORIC

Stereotypes.   There are those who prefer not to admit, or who admit and deplore, that all of us simplify the world in order to get along in it—and especially to talk and hear about it. Fortunately or not, everyone thinks by means of stereotypes much of the time. One cannot understand the humanity of audiences if he disregards this truth. Listeners are constantly perceiving and responding to what they hear by referring new perceptions to the simplifying categorizations they have elsewhere acquired.

We have said that it is difficult to change preconceptions. But it can be done if you make skillful use of beliefs and ways of thinking your listeners *already have*. The character of much commonplace belief and thinking was described a good many years ago by Walter Lippmann in his famous chapter, "Stereotypes":

> For the most part, we do not first see, and then define; we define first and then see. In the great blooming, buzzing confusion of the outer world we pick out what our culture has defined for us, and we tend to perceive that which we have picked out in the form stereotyped for us by our culture.[16]

---

16. Walter Lippmann, *Public Opinion* (New York: Harcourt, Brace, 1922), p. 81.

Thus we can talk of "cowboys" and communicate a total image of a certain type of man, or we can talk of "freedom," knowing that at least some dimensions of a very complicated idea will arise in listeners' minds. We *must* talk to each other on the basis of the values, "facts," and patterns of experience we share. These are, after all, primary materials with which we all think.

In approaching any group of listeners you need to reflect carefully on how they are used to thinking about and used to defining any subject you want to discuss. The biology major whose speech on deer hunting we reported did precisely this. Consequently he not only received an understanding hearing; he changed opinions. He remembered that his classmates had been led by earlier discussion to simplify an entire group of ecological problems by defining them all as "maintaining balance." Though almost none of his listeners was initially concerned about the deer herd in his state, the speaker was able to make *his* problem significant because he made it a *balance* problem. He could have done the same thing, by the same strategy, if he had been talking about fishing, oil depletion, waterways, or any of a dozen other topics. The listeners' simplification of ecological issues was there to be used; adapting to this stereotypical perception allowed the listeners to see a specific set of natural forces in a way for which they felt they had a "rule" of judgment: balance the forces. They could even be taught that ecological problems are more *complex* than they knew by being invited to apply their stereotype to a specific case. And they learned!

Dramatization

Dramatization—always interesting—can sometimes be achieved by using simplifications analogically. In the early part of his famous "I Have a Dream" speech, Dr. Martin Luther King did this. He said:

> In a sense we've come to our nation's capitol to cash a check. When the architects of our republic wrote the magnificent words of the Constitution and the Declaration of Independence, they were signing a promissory note to which every American was to fall heir. This note was a promise that all men—yes black men as well as white men—would be guaranteed the unalienable rights of life, liberty, and the pursuit of happiness.
>
>   It is obvious today that America has defaulted on this promissory note insofar as her citizens of color are concerned.[17]

Dr. King was using a metaphorical analogy, of course, but the strength of it lay in the fact that most people can readily think of obligations in *financial* terms. By reducing the complicated matter of blacks' demands for just rights to a simpler, unchallengeable issue of right and wrong, Dr. King gave greater clarity to his thought and drew to the support of his position the hard force of a

---

17. Excerpted from a recording made as the speech was broadcast from Washington, D.C., August 28, 1963.

familiar cultural "rule": You pay your debts and back your checks or you are a "defaulter."

Comparable options are always open to you. In whatever cultural simplifications your listeners carry with them there are starting points for clear, influential communication. Use such ideas if you can. You will be likely to be both understood and trusted. What is required is that you fit *your* concept to the terms and "rules" of thought your hearers have already formulated and which guide their thinking and judgment in ordinary cases.

The prestige of acknowledged *authorities* gives ideas added weight with almost everyone. The authority must be one whom listeners approve as a source on *this* topic, but if this is the case, listeners' opinions and attitudes can be altered where you can show that *both* you and the admired authorities agree. Experiments have supported this proposition with striking uniformity, though with one significant qualification. It is possible for a speaker to be so authoritative in his own right that citing an "outside" authority adds nothing more to his influence. Even then, using respected authorities does little harm unless it becomes tiresome; it simply adds nothing more to the authoritative speaker's credibility. A safe, overall generalization to follow is: Audiences will respond favorably to ideas supported by authorities they have already learned to respect on the subject in question.[18]

What are the practical applications of this universal tendency to accept without much question the judgments of previously favored authorities? Are you speaking to engineers or other students of science? Show them the system you are explaining rests on physical laws they know and trust, and you will probably renew their attention and secure their belief. Would you address a group of businessmen? Make it clear that your proposals have support in the business world. If you know that your listeners will have a wide variety of intellectual and personal interests, search for the community and cultural experiences they have in common, then consider what opinion leaders, symbols, and institutions those experiences have raised to the level of authority. Identify your thought with the voices of the leaders and institutions of your listeners' social and private creeds. To reach listeners' minds and influence their behavior you need to discover and use their favorite sources of authority to illumine and justify whatever new thoughts you offer.

Familiarity and Novelty.   For reasons that probably lie very deep within us, we all tend to reject, even fear, that which is alien to our experience; yet certain levels of novelty attract us. In greater or lesser degree we are all timidly bound to the familiar and adventurously drawn toward the unknown. Thus, while it is true to say that speakers must discover and use their listeners' stereotypes and authorities, it is equally true to say speakers must offer their hearers "news." We all demand that the new and the old be blended in the ideas and language of effective speech.

---

18. An excellent summary of the experimental evidence on this matter (which remains at some points inconclusive) appears in Gary Cronkhite, *Persuasion: Speech and Behavioral Change,* pp. 186–191.

Whatever is familiar (especially if it appears in a strange setting) or whatever seems strange (especially if it appears in a familiar setting) can crowd almost everything else out of our perceptions. You do not notice the flawless playing of sixty musicians when the sixty-first player blows a discordant note. You do not pay much attention to twenty cars in a parking lot or to twenty different hats; but your eye unerringly picks out your car or the hat similar to yours. These dual tendencies of the mind, to embrace the familiar and inspect the new, afford a speaker many opportunities to command thought by mingling elements of the new and old.

Parables are, of course, the classic examples of how one can secure acceptance for a new thought by embedding it in stories about well-known activities or familiar kinds of persons. Likewise, one can see in the King James version of "The Sermon on the Mount" the attention-compelling power of the new linked to the familiar—especially when what is familiar has the prestige of authority. In this sermon Jesus introduced several sections of new instruction with the words: "Ye have heard that it was said by them of old time. . . ." In these two clauses Jesus was able to reassure His audience that the new thoughts would only extend and amplify what was already accepted on the authority of the lawgivers. When Abraham Lincoln wanted to convey his fears about the spread of slavery, he expressed his disturbing view in a familiar figure: "A house divided against itself cannot stand." Parables, references to old and familiar law, and Lincoln's metaphor illustrate some of the means by which speakers may supply the needed reassurance of the familiar while introducing ideas that are essentially new or strange.

Though too much that is unusual disturbs listeners, they still expect any worthwhile experience to contain some novel elements. Aristotle expressed it in his *Rhetoric:*

> Words are like men; as we feel a difference between people from afar and our fellow townsmen, so it is with our feeling for language. And hence it is well to give the ordinary idiom an air of remoteness; the hearers are struck by what is out of the way, and like what strikes them.[19]

He was speaking of style, but the unexpected idea, like the unexpected or out-of-the-way word, has power to catch and hold attention.

The speaker who uses—as he must—man's curiosity about the new and his affection for the old should also remember that people do not usually look deeply into what is new nor contemplate the familiar. They tire easily, especially when listening. The key to holding their attention through the means we have just been discussing is that *it is the shift from the familiar to the unfamiliar and back again that pleases and holds the mind.* It is change that controls attention. The speaker who remembers this important generalization will see to it that his listener has, at every possible point, something familiar to which he

---

19. From *The Rhetoric of Aristotle*, translated and edited by Lane Cooper, p. 185, bk. III, chap. 2. Copyright 1932, renewed 1960 by Lane Cooper. Reprinted by permission of Appleton-Century-Crofts, Educational Division, Meredith Corporation.

can cling for assurance and something new which will give him a sense of learning and, possibly, adventure.   Too much of the old bores; too much of the new baffles.

Treating ideas in ways that conform to listeners' definitions and stereotypes, associating ideas with already favored institutions and authorities, alternating and combining the new and the familiar are ways of making use of listeners' constant readiness to respond to certain especially common rhetorical patterns.   These patterns are universally available as useful resources in speaking.   There are also some *qualities* you can give speech to make it more *interesting* to listeners.

SPECIAL RESOURCES IN IDEAS AND LANGUAGE

Because listeners and listening are as we have described them in this and earlier chapters, there are certain qualities in ideas and the ways they are expressed which make speech especially engaging and interesting.   We have already considered the facts that proximity, familiarity, and novelty are features of talk for which listeners are particularly ready, but when we turn to qualities that can be *built into* thoughts and language, additional resources emerge.   What are sometimes called "factors of attention" are naturally present in some ideas and sometimes they can be *given* to speech by the ways you handle yourself, select your ideas, and choose your language.   Below is a brief statement of what each of these qualities is (including again proximity, familiarity, and novelty), accompanied by a reminder of the general reason that quality is likely to control or direct attention and by quick examples of the qualities.

Resource	Basis of Influence
1. *Activity:* actual movement suggested by the idea or by verbal imagery or by activity displayed in speaking. You draw a sweeping curve on the blackboard, or you say, "He *scurried* out of his hiding place."	Noticeable *change* or movement always tends to attract attention; real or imagistic movement creates the sense of change; a speaker's movement *is* change.
2. *Proximity:* showing things as near in time or space to the listener, or as near to one another (actually or figuratively). You draw two shapes close to one another, or you say, "Such a person could be sitting next to you on the bus."	Adjacency is among the simplest relationships to perceive, and adjacency to a listener (real or imagined) implies the listener is or could be directly involved.

3. *Realism or vividness:* pictorial or other sensory qualities introduced by imagistic language or action or physical illustration. You say, "I was covered with *black, sticky mud,*" or point to where the mud covered you, or you bring some mud and show what it is really like.

Learning through the senses, directly or vicariously, is the basic experience by which knowledge is gained and survival defended.

4. *Familiarity and novelty:* association of ideas with what listeners know, or presentation of what was either unknown or never perceived in the way proposed. You compare governmental budgeting to family budgeting, or the family budget to regulating the international balance of payments.

All humans prize and attend to what they have experienced before; they also enjoy or are curious about experience that is new.

5. *Conflict and suspense:* showing either animate or inanimate things in opposition to one another or in competition with one another, the details or the outcome being in either case uncertain in some degree. You inject the image of a contest between science and the environment, or you say, "This is a *race* between ideas and fear," or you inject a "fight image" or illustration.

Opposition is the most obvious of differences, hence easily perceived. When active clash or competition is present, *change* and the *unknown* are both present to draw human attention.

6. *Vitality:* associating ideas or objects with matters of direct concern to the lives of people—especially the lives of listeners. You relate a financial topic to listeners' own purchasing and saving, or you make listeners see *their* future lives depend on the science-environment contest.

Personal interests and purposes are prime reasons for granting attention; what seems to touch life itself has special significance for all.

7. *Specificity:* presentation of precise detail. You say, "spreading oak" instead of "tree," or you show a model or mock-up instead of just describing, or you give descriptions for which listeners can fill in details, as Dick Barnes did with campus scenes (see pages 40–42).

The more concrete or specific any concept, the more easily it is acquired by humans—provided the detail doesn't obscure the nature or meaning of the *whole*.

8. *Intensity:* the force of any aspect of communication—of voice, movement, or energy of language. Wide

Within certain limits too complicated to explain here, the strength of impact of any stimulus tends to vary with the in-

variations in intensity levels are possible in speech: of sound, of physical energy, of vividness or color in language. You increase loudness for emphasis, move to lean toward listeners, or point, or you say with deliberateness, "This next point is the most important one," or you say, "The floor was littered with garbage" instead of "covered with debris," thus getting greater intensity through greater specificity.

tensity of the stimulus; also, noticeable *changes* in stimuli and *contrasts* between intensities of stimuli draw attention to the *dissimilarities* and to *change.*

9. *Humor:* introduction of exaggeration, incongruity, irony, word play, unexpected turns of thought or phrase. Left-handed people have been discussed as a minority denied civil liberties and "equal rights." You might talk about playing basketball as though the game were warfare, or call football "agitation of a bag of wind."

The nature of response to humor is not fully understood, but the attractions of the *novel* or unexpected and satisfactions derived from safely regaining reality—the *familiar*—after having expectations built up, then reversed, appear to be involved.

We hope you will see from the lists above that the general qualities for which you must strive in speech are not qualities invented by pedagogues or impractical theorists. Our speech needs these qualities because human beings' psychological characteristics are as they are. It is because people attend to some kinds of qualities more readily than to others that speech must symbolically represent activity, proximity, realism, familiarity and novelty, conflict and suspense, vitality, specificity, intensity, and humor. Those are the features of ideas, behaviors, and things we all attend to most readily.

It is all too easy to make a superficial interpretation of what we have just said. Just any adaptation to the interests of listeners will not serve your speech, nor will just any active image or bit of suspensive development. Your job is to understand your listeners as human beings and then to understand the rhetorical resources people's natures give us as speakers. It is then possible to fit together the particular complex of materials and methods that can win and hold human attention in a particular time and place on *your* subject and in the interests of *your* goals.

The broad, over-arching question in rhetorical invention is: Given the range of what I might say and how I might say it, what content and what methods fit my audience's humanity, its special conditioning by the speech situation, the capacities my listeners have, their readiness to believe and change beliefs, and their readiness for particular rhetorical methods that give special powers to ideas? The question is complex. Nor can the answers to it be wholly scientific.

If we knew precisely what commands the attention of, let us say, a man of thirty who holds a law degree and is attending a Chamber of Commerce luncheon, speaking would be more nearly a science than an art. But we do not know all the ways that the above conditions can singly or in combination influence a given man's responses to a particular message. We have, instead, crude generalizations. Even with these rough tools, however, a diligent speaker can refine his command over the minds of his listeners. If he remembers to use the tools he has and makes the inquiries he ought to make, he will recognize at least some of the existing opportunities and limitations. As Plato implied in the passage quoted at the head of this chapter, it is by discovering the natures of hearers, by experience in bringing different messages to differing audiences, and by imaginatively adapting content to human nature that speakers ultimately achieve artistic, insightful social control.

More specific solutions to more specific problems begin to emerge as we turn from the nature of audiences to the kinds of ideas and feelings that speakers have to adapt to audiences. Ideas and feelings are pliable, but only to a degree. Force is not weakness; each must be treated as it is. Language is easier to *talk* about than music or principles of painting. Because ideas and feelings in some degree control what speakers can do with them, speakers need to understand more about invention than just the nature of audiences and basic ways of commanding listeners' attention. In the next three chapters we shall concentrate on the problems of discovering and sifting speech material.

EXERCISES

Written

1. Write a careful description of some specific audience with which you are familiar (fraternal group, political or other club, religious congregation, or other) giving special consideration to the following:
   a. Chief biological wants and needs, if any, that affect this audience;
   b. Chief social wants and needs, if any, that affect this audience;
   c. Favorite sanctions and authorities of this audience;
   d. Any special characteristics of age, sex, expectation, knowledge, and socio-economic level that all speakers addressing this audience should take into account. In what ways?
2. You are to prepare a short speech using the central idea: "Television should be used as a major resource in general education." Outline the major points you might make in such a speech if it were to be given to audience *a* below; then outline the major points you might try to make if the speech were for audience *b* below. Justify any differences there may be in the two outlines.
   a. An audience of twenty college students aged seventeen to twenty-two, made up of ten men and ten women, assembled for an informal class on study habits orga-

nized for students whose academic records do not "meet the potentialities indicated by standardized aptitude-test results."

b. An audience of twenty college students aged nineteen to twenty-two, all cadet teachers in an elementary school attending one of a series of weekly seminars. The seminar topic for this meeting is "Motivation." There are eighteen women and two men in the group.

3. Using the text or a recording of any speech, identify the points at which the speaker seems to have adapted content for the specific purpose of suiting it to one or another of the audience characteristics discussed in this chapter. Identify and evaluate the effectiveness with which he took advantage of special resources in ideas and speech.

Oral

1. With four or five classmates, work out through discussion an outlined description of your speech class as a rhetorical situation for the next group of talks to be given in your class. Use the subpoints of Written Exercise 1 above as headings for your descriptive outline. *Optional:* As an exercise in completing a group assignment and in reporting, assign parts of your completed outline to each member of your group and have each report that part of the group's findings to the class.

2. Give an expository speech on one of the following subjects: stereotypes, the psychological process called suggestion, the psychological process called conditioned response, the social (or ethical or other) values of college students today, the expectations of audiences assembled at modern ceremonial occasions, the unique expectations of audiences that have power to determine policy or legislate, theories of crowd behavior, authority as a source of persuasion.

3. Prepare and deliver an oral report on the methods of audience analysis and adaptation used by a trial lawyer, preacher, or political speaker you have observed or read about.

4. Prepare and deliver a talk on some aspect of audience research, advertising or market research, or the relation of market research to industrial design.

CHAPTER
4

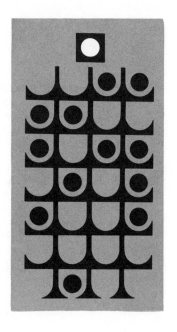

Invention:
Basic Processes

I would not be hurried by any love of system, by any exaggeration of instincts, to underrate the Book. We all know, that, as the human body can be nourished on any food, though it were boiled grass and the broth of shoes, so the human mind can be fed by any knowledge. And great and heroic men have existed, who had almost no other information than by the printed page. I only would say, that it needs a strong head to bear that diet. One must be an inventor to read well. . . . When the mind is braced by labor and invention, the page of whatever book we read becomes luminous with manifold allusion. Every sentence is doubly significant, and the sense of our author is as broad as the world. We then see, what is always true, that, as the seer's hour of vision is short and rare among heavy days and months, so is its record, perchance, the least part of his volume.[1]

Ralph Waldo Emerson, "The American Scholar"

There are five kinds of *problems* that anyone who speaks always contends with either consciously or by accident. They are the problems of "inventing" what to say in a speech situation, of "shaping" into some intelligible form what is said, of choosing and refining the language to be used in communicating, of presenting (delivering, in speech) one's thoughts, and of remembering one's preconceived plans well enough so the message gets presented as intended. With this chapter we begin a series of discussions in which we hope to help you solve each of these inescapable kinds of problems. (The last-named problem—remembering and commanding one's plans, *memoria*—will be considered in several connections especially in chapters on arrangement and delivery.)

The first problem faced by anyone who speaks seriously is *what* to say. Your problem as a student in a speech class is somewhat different from what it will be elsewhere. Outside classrooms most of us speak because someone invites us to say something about what we are well acquainted with. Or, we find ourselves in situations where we want to talk about something that

---

1. *The Works of Ralph Waldo Emerson* (Boston: The Jefferson Press, n.d.), IV, p. 67. Originally delivered as a speech to the Phi Beta Kappa Society, Cambridge, Massachusetts, August 31, 1837.

comes up and about which we have ideas or feelings we want to express. Outside classrooms, invitations, situations, and our own knowledge tend to tell us what to talk about. Subjects tend to *choose us* more often than we freely choose subjects.

But as a student in a class, you will have unique freedom to choose subjects to talk about. This gives you both opportunities and difficulties; so, since your classroom needs are immediate, we shall focus the next few paragraphs on choosing subjects for practice speeches.

CHOOSING SUBJECTS

A good speech subject—for a class or anyone else—ought to be timely and significant in the view of the listeners. It ought also to be appropriate to *you* as the person who will try to create a human relationship with a particular audience. And, of course, you should be able to say what you need to say about the subject within the time that will be allowed.

To list requirements for a speech subject in this way gives the "tests" of a suitable subject, but it does not help you to *locate* subjects that will satisfy you, meet the demands of classroom situations, and tailor what you attempt to your own capacities. Let us try a different way of discovering how inviting, suitable subjects can be discovered.

To find a subject which can interest you and also have significance for your listeners, let your mind run freely over all kinds of subject matters. Suspend your doubts and critical inclinations temporarily. Just try to see what is interesting in the world about you and within you. The next paragraph illustrates how the process sometimes called "brainstorming" can work. The subjects and subject areas discovered are printed in brackets following the stimulus that brought them to mind.

It happens that this paragraph was originally written in the spring, in a motel apartment. That fact will affect the thoughts that come to mind [the power of suggestion; hotel-motel-hostelry operations]. The highway is visible from the window [mass transportation problems, highway construction, auto and truck licensing, highway safety, scenic routes]. Across the highway is a row of shrubs [horticulture, landscaping, plant breeding, land use, plant pathology]. The storm windows are still on the motel [insulating materials and properties, maintenance industries, glass making, fabricating for the construction industries, custom building vs. prefabrication]. A school bus passes [the topic of education calls up too many possibilities to enumerate]. The typewriter is before me [mechanisms of communication, the publishing industry, business machines, automation]. A bookshelf is at my side. On it stands *The Ugly American* [foreign policy, diplomacy, the responsibility of the press], a murder mystery [escapist reading, paperbacks, censorship], Chaim Perelman's *Traité de L'Argumentation* [foreign language study, foreign travel, methods of persuasion, the study of philosophy, the relative merits of different academic subjects].

Twelve minutes passed while this little "brainstorming" experiment took place and the results were typed out. By the most conservative count thirty-two different, discussable subjects and general speech topics were discovered and typed. If this had been your brainstorming, you could almost surely locate something to talk interestingly about within these thirty-two topics. If there is no prospect here — and we doubt it — do your own brainstorming for ideas, wherever you happen to be right now. Look up from this page and let your thoughts run freely, jotting down each idea that occurs to you. Or, try a different tack. Walk along library shelves noting book titles. Scrutinize any group of people, animals, machines, plants. Or take any class of things as your starting point and begin enumerating members of that class. Try *vehicles, buildings, clothing, inventions,* or *authors* as a start. The fund of potential speech subjects is virtually inexhaustible if you let your mind run freely in one direction after another. But keep some record of the often strange, often familiar ideas free-wheeling thought grinds out. If you don't use anything from these notes this time, keep them anyway. Some idea there could help you decide on a subject for some future occasion — even as an idea with which to start a conversation.

Once you have a list of *available* subjects, reactivate your critical powers and judge the results. Cull the list for timely, significant themes that interest *you*. Do not ask, yet, whether a subject is manageable, and don't worry about whether your audience will be interested. If a subject is timely and interests you, there may be a way to trim or expand it to make it manageable. Your immediate problem is to draw from random lists of ideas those that are potentially timely and potentially *significant for you*. In this and succeeding chapters we shall try to help you fit such ideas to specific kinds of speech situations.

To be a live option, a subject need not be patently within your present knowledge and preparation. It need only be one you can and want to learn more about than your audience already knows. Given that much, it is probably within your power to command some phase of the subject and to make it vital for your listeners. We cannot tell you which option to choose from any list you invent; you are the only one who knows what you are willing to try to do as a communicator. However, we warn you against two enfeebling practices: dawdling and choosing overworked subjects.

One mistake many speakers make is to dawdle over choosing a specific subject and purpose. A colleague of ours who studied diaries of more than a thousand college students in speech classes found that a consistent difference between good speakers and poor speakers was that the good speakers chose subjects for speeches carefully but swiftly and then stuck with their choices. Most of their available time went into preparation. Poor speakers consistently reported that they spent days trying to settle on acceptable subjects. We do not know just how indecisiveness is related to poor speaking, but the evidence is clear that good speakers choose subjects promptly and stick with them; poor speakers do not. If indecisiveness is your problem, it could be useful to keep a simple chart of the hours you spend on each phase of speech preparation: choosing a subject, locating your specific purpose, searching for further ideas, outlining, rehearsing. Perhaps if you see in graphic form where you actually spend your time, you will be able to use time more efficiently by setting deadlines for the various tasks.

A second practice that endangers success in speaking is choosing only subjects that are already known to listeners. Listeners want *news,* and speakers need challenges if they are to do their best. If you choose subjects already familiar to everyone, both you and your listeners will end by being indifferent. A shopworn subject will disappoint your partners in a speech class and will prove a poor way to develop your ability as a speaker. You cannot learn what your own powers really are until you test them against a task that demands skill and creativity.

CLASSROOMS AS SPEECH SITUATIONS

There is a cliché in modern education which runs that classroom life is necessarily artificial. To the contrary, we contend that a speech class can be an ideal life situation in which to *practice* human communication. You are unlikely ever to find another situation so generous to people seeking communicative contact with others. First, you can learn about your audience rather easily. Naturally, your listeners change, grow in understanding, and develop special needs and yearnings as the result of their shared experiences, but they also learn more about you as a speaker. They alter their expectations accordingly, and that makes communication easier for you. Everybody, including you, shares in all these developments; so there can be rare, mutual understanding between speaker and audience in a classroom. But most fundamentally, a speech class is filled with live *people* jointly bent on exercising their humanness fully. All alike, they seek encouragement to make the class a real community—a vibrant communicative, learning "system."

An inhuman way to view the rhetorical situation in a speech class is to see it as a communicative "system" populated by "captives" to be talked *at.* A humane view would show a speech class as a place where people yearn to function as fully conscious human beings eager to function that way with *you* whenever you extend yourself toward them as a person conscious of their natures, needs, and preferences. Do note that simply "expressing myself" does *not* give due regard to the natures, needs, and preferences of others. The issue for you, your colleagues, and your instructor is a sharp one: Are you going to treat your classroom as a haven for soliloquies, or will you all contribute toward creating a situation where "communication presupposes other minds"?[2] This is partly your instructor's choice, of course, but it is especially yours. Every time you choose a subject to talk about, every time you choose an idea for inclusion in a talk, every time you arrange thoughts for communication, you will extend communication *toward* your colleagues or take a step backward *from* them.

What are your listeners really like generally? An eminent psychologist described them. He was writing about all of us:

> . . . people want a good opinion of themselves both in their own eyes and in those of others. Self-respect and popular esteem are active needs. If a man is deprived of them he becomes anxious, tense, and restless. . . . Abilities are rarely useless, and to be able to exercise one's wits may be a means of self-respect and general esteem.[3]

Mr. Thomson's observations imply this question for you as a speaker: Will you consider *others'* opinions of themselves, *their* self-respect, and allow *them* the exercise of wits they want and need to exercise? Your answer determines whether you will make your classroom a real or an artificial communicative system.

DISCOVERING LINES OF THOUGHT

When you have found a subject about which you can say something significant for both you and your colleagues, your next problems in invention will be to find out what you *might* say, then to choose what you *ought* to say to this audience in its particular situation. A systematic search for ideas is preferable to an impulsive one, as we shall presently show. So the question becomes: How shall I work my mind when searching for ideas worth talking about in connection with my subject?

A very old system for guiding creative thought about communicating was detailed by Aristotle in his *Topics* and his *Rhetoric,* and in later books on rhetoric. Simplified, this procedure can direct your thoughts toward ideas suitable for any speaking situation.

On many occasions speakers want to give *advice*. When an audience has to decide on a course of action, advice is needed. The basic question for both speaker and listener is: What shall be done or left undone? In the language we are using in this book, this kind of situation can be called one that invites *persuasion about a proposition of policy*. It is a situation in which

---

2. Henry W. Johnstone, Jr., *The Problem of the Self* (University Park, Pa.: The Pennsylvania State University Press, 1970), p. 131.
3. Robert Thomson, *The Psychology of Thinking* (Baltimore: Penguin Books, 1959), p. 155.

any speaker's central idea is almost certain to contain the words "should" or "ought to" or their equivalents. Central ideas might run: "The United States ought to establish normal diplomatic relations with the People's Republic of China," or "Regional government should replace municipal and county governments in metropolitan areas," or "You should vote for John P. Findley."

If a speaker sees that he will be entering a situation of this sort, he can narrow his field of research and thinking. It should be immediately clear that ideas having to do with the expediency of the alternative courses of action are the ones that will be most negotiable. These are ideas that have to do with rewards and costs in the future and with the prospects of happiness for those who are going to take an action or refuse to take it.

So, a useful shortcut in research and thinking has been discovered. When your situation invites a speech on a central idea concerning the *future behavior* of your listeners, most of your initial preparation time ought to be spent finding facts and lines of thought that say something about the consequences of the actions (and inactions) among which your listeners are to choose. Simply by recognizing that you are going to talk about "should's" and "ought's," you isolate a particular type of material your speech must include.

A second class of situations in which we speak are those in which audiences function as "judges" rather than as deciders of future action. In discussing these circumstances Aristotle talked almost entirely of judgments at law, but we require a broader view. Audiences have to or want to render judgments about facts and events in many different situations. Every speech to inform is such a case. Most of what one says in a speech of inquiry deals with what the facts are, though when solutions are being considered, the situation becomes concerned with policies and future actions. All persuasion about propositions of fact succeeds or fails according to the judgments of fact finally rendered by the listeners. So, if your central idea must focus on what something is, or whether it exists, you will be asking your listeners to function as judges of accuracy, truth, propriety, or legality. The most significant point about any such situation is that your listeners will have to interpret the facts or events in light of some "code" or set of standards. The code may be the law of the land, the theory of probabilities, the standards of historical research, the canons of artistic excellence, personal standards for distinguishing truth from error, or others. Whatever the code, your judging listeners will especially need two kinds of knowledge: (1) knowledge about the facts or events they are to judge, and (2) knowledge about the codes or standards they are to use in weighing the facts or events. Once more, simply thinking about what your listeners will be asked to *do* quickly reveals the main kinds of ideas you will need to give them.

To restate this guide: If in informing, inquiring, or persuading you are going to ask for judgments, you will need ideas that define and clarify whatever is to be judged and the standards to be used in judging. You may need other information too, but these two kinds of content are certain to be crucial for you and for your listeners.

Ancient Romans had a special interest in legal argument. This led them to notice that three subordinate kinds of information about facts have special usefulness when listeners make judgments of the sort we are now considering. These kinds of information are: (1) information about whether there really *are* relevant facts to talk about; (2) information about *what* facts are worth talking about; and (3) information about how acknowledged facts are to be *interpreted* in the light of whatever criteria apply to them. Knowing that these are the kinds of information you will need further narrows your hunt for ideas. If you understand this, you will know what it is most important to find out for this kind of speech. When you know whether these are *your* important questions for a given speech situation, you will have settled the major things you need to know about your subject in order to communicate what others will want to know about it.

There are also speaking situations in which the main exigence or need is to have old beliefs strengthened, to have familiar beliefs made more firm, to have convictions deepened, or to have old knowledge rendered amusing or diverting. In such situations new judgments and new courses of action are usually neither sought nor very much wanted. Commencement exercises are such situations. So are many worship services, service club meetings, fellowship meetings, banquets, and political rallies. Those who attend commencements accept the worth of education; worshippers accept the greatness of their deity; fellowship groups accept the worth of being together and wish their association to be strengthened by being made more enjoyable. Whoever prepares to speak to such audiences must locate the kinds of ideas that deepen, enrich, magnify, or even exaggerate the listeners' current knowledge. The chief end of the worship service may be to strengthen faith that already exists; the chief end of the club dinner may be not calorie intake, but some magnification of the joys of friendship.

Ancient advice on what lines of thought to use in situations like this is still practical. Look for ideas that connect your subject with such well-known virtues as justice, courage, moderation, grandeur, liberality, gentleness, prudence, or with the *opposites* of similar values held by the audience. Whatever has such virtues becomes impressive and admirable to an audience, and whatever lacks them or is inconsistent with them becomes the object of ridicule or disdain and disgust. A like method entertains. Lightheartedly done, assigning virtues and their opposites where they do *not* belong is a standard way of rendering subjects amusing. Listen carefully to the next comedian or satirist you hear.

When you are going to enter a situation of this sort, your preparation ought to begin with a hunt for the virtues possessed by whatever it is that you and your audience are committed to, and for the nonvirtues possessed by what you and your audience disapprove or think absurd. Except for incidental use, you will not need ideas that deal with what an expedient action is or with the existence and legitimacy of facts and events.

Let us imagine now that you have to "think up" a speech. Let us suppose you are a psychology major and you are standing in the foyer of your college or university library. A friend hails you: "I just saw Professor James in the Psych Department. He says there's a meeting of underclassmen Friday afternoon at the Student Union. Some of the academic departments have been asked to pick upperclass majors to talk at the meeting about their departments. The Psych Department wants you to speak for them. So get in that library and hit the books; you've got to work up a speech."

You know the general speech assignment and have at least a notion of the situation. As you stand in the library foyer, your problem is not whether to go in the library and begin reading. Your first problem is *to think about how to collect lines of thought* for this talk. Not every idea connected with academic majors in psychology is appropriate for a talk to underclassmen, so it would be foolish to collect ideas at random. If you search your mind casually, you will find some pertinent ideas but many others that are so nebulous you, yourself, can't formulate them clearly. You need a plan by which to identify just those kinds of thoughts that will prove negotiable between you and an all-underclass audience of people who haven't chosen majors yet. What we have been saying on pages 72–73 furnishes some help for proceeding.

Though your friend didn't say so, the Psychology Department probably hopes you will tell the underclassmen what kinds of psychology courses are open to them and what requirements govern those who major in that department. Since other departments are to be represented at your meeting, the gathering evidently is not organized as a recruiting session for any particular department. Still, you ought to make studying psychology seem inviting.

As soon as you know these facts about your assignment and the situation, you have roughly defined procedures for preparing your talk: (1) you do *not* need to hunt up much material on such long-range matters as whether psychology majors have better professional opportunities than other majors; (2) you *do* need to get facts about specific courses and the regulations governing the psychology major, because your listeners will want to pass some sort of judgment on what this major *is;* (3) you *do* need to find out the standards by which underclassmen and other people measure the desirability of a course of study—their standards of "desirability" will form the "codes" by which the facts you present will be judged. With these judgments made we have the crucial diagnosis of your speech situation: It is one in which the listeners will function primarily as "judges" of information weighed against their own "standards." Settling that much puts you in a position to begin "inventing" speech material efficiently.

On the basis of these decisions, you need stand indecisively in the library foyer no longer. Take two immediate actions: (1) obtain information about psychology as it is taught in your college; (2) find out how underclass-men distinguish "good" from "not-so-good" in thinking about academic subjects. If you enter the library, you will want to read the college announce-ment or catalogue; if you don't go in, you will be wise either to set off for the Psychology Department's offices or to conduct some interviews to see what standards (codes) underclassmen use when they make judgments about the attractiveness of courses and subjects. Any other actions on your part will probably be irrelevant to your speech preparation.

These are the general ways you can point thinking and research in potentially useful directions. Ask what you want your listeners to *do:* Decide about courses of action, make judgments about facts or events, acquire stronger or lighter attitudes toward something of which they already are aware? Go after the kinds of information and lines of thought associated with the kind of response you want from your listeners.

The ways of thinking we have so far discussed suggest only broad classes of speech materials that speakers need in different proportions, de-pending on the kinds of speech situations those speakers enter. There are also more specific ways of searching out useful lines of thought for communica-tion.

For centuries, Western thinkers used systematic ways of discovering what *could* be said about subjects. This is why they paid so much attention to "rhetorical invention." Unfortunately, from the Middle Ages—and especially from the eighteenth century—to the middle of the twentieth century prevailing Western theories of how man thinks were unfriendly to the notion that people need to search for what to *say* in ways that are different from the ways they search when looking for new knowledge without regard to par-ticular speech situations.

We are going to describe for you some very old ways of searching for "sayables." We do not do this simply to drag in some historical lore. We do it because experiments and classroom experience in the last dozen years clearly show these procedures *work;* they make speakers better equipped to do their jobs.

For a good many centuries scholars argued that people talk on a fairly limited number of themes, that they vary the *treatments* of basic ideas but not the basic ideas themselves. You need not hear or read many speeches or essays to see that these thinkers were right. We all discuss the same general types of ideas over and over. This is not a sign of laziness; it is the natural result of the kinds of things people feel they need talk to each other about. We all discuss and argue chiefly about human affairs, and the ways you can think about human affairs are limited within any culture. The result is that we can actually predict in advance many of the categories of thought any talker will use if we know what his situation calls for.

When you read the excerpt below, notice first its date; it is 1951! It is from a speech probably made before you were born. Notice also the subject:

foreign policy. Specific issues about foreign policy change all the time, but as this speech illustrates, the *kinds* of issues foreign policy problems always bring up remain the same across decades, generations, even centuries. If you know recent history you know that when this speech was made "The Korean War" was going on, there was a "cold war" in Europe, the United States was not much involved with Southeast Asia, relations with continental China were vastly different from today, and dozens of other factors distinguished foreign policy problems of 1951 from those of the 1970's. And, yet, the *ways* Professor Carleton proposed in 1951 to build a speech on foreign policy remain precisely the ways to build a policy speech today. Why? Because the *"lines* of thought" one *always* needs for policy speeches are standard in our culture. The details change; the lines of thought and inquiry do not. Use exactly Professor Carleton's lines of thought, insert new data, and you can build a sensible speech on contemporary American policy toward African nations, toward monopoly, toward world peace, or toward the smallest country you ever heard of. You would change the words and the data, but the *directions* in which your mind needs to go to discover what to say are precisely Professor Carleton's directions. Even if you chose not to speak of all his themes, you would still need to *think* of all to be sure you omitted nothing crucial.

Read the passage, now, noticing the *kinds* of ideas Carleton identifies as necessary to establish a comprehensive case for an *expedient* foreign policy. Talking about "Effective Speech in a Democracy," Carleton said at one point:

> Will you permit me to illustrate my point by demonstrating for a moment how I would construct a speech on current American foreign policy? It so happens that I favor the following foreign policy: In the countries of Asia and Europe where the non-Communists are in control, I would, where conditions indicated, put the United States squarely behind a policy of social democracy or even democratic socialism as a way of combating Communism; and in the countries where the Communists are in control, I would play upon the nationalistic tendencies everywhere evident in Communist governments and Communist parties, to attempt to divide Communist countries from each other on national grounds and thereby contribute to the restoration of a multiple balancing-of-power system, a system which would prevent the Communists from acting together in a Communist front and threatening to upset the balance of power. For if we can remove the Communist threat to the balance of power we can remove the real cause of another great war.
>
> In order to present effectively my point of view on the importance of playing wise social politics, it seems to me that I would have to show how and why conditions in Europe and Asia are converging to produce collectivist movements there and why laissez-faire capitalism there is not feasible [1]; also I would have to show the difference between totalitarian socialism and democratic socialism [2] and examine the reasons why I believe America's backing of social-democracy and even democratic socialism in Europe and Asia would check Communism and serve America's national interests [3]. In order for me

to present effectively my belief that nationalism within Communist countries and parties could be used to divide Communism and restore a multiple balance-of-power system, I would have to examine in some detail the degree to which Communist revolutions and movements are in fact nationalistic in aim, method, and development [4], and actually point out the specific grounds of possible national conflict between specific Communist countries [5].

However, even when I had done all this my intellectual task would not be completed. I would have to point out why other courses in foreign policy would not serve America's national interests as well as the policy I favored [6]. This would involve my examining the reasons why political isolation would not work today; why a policy of mere military containment of Communism through the United Nations would not be enough and would not work permanently [7]; and why if it worked it would be the hard way to do something that could be done with less possibility of war and fewer long-time sacrifices [8]; why a policy of mere military containment of Communism by the United States alone — a policy of American imperialism — would be even less workable and less desirable than a policy of military containment through the United Nations [9]. In short, in order to carry intellectual conviction on so large and controversial a question, it seems to me I would have to construct a speech that analyzed critically all courses — those I oppose as well as those I favor [10].[4]

Professor Carleton is a political scientist. It probably never occurred to him to say, "I have now outlined the standard 'themes' or 'rhetorical topics' for speeches and essays on public policy," but he did it. Let us see.

Here are the standard lines of thought that Carleton says a good policy speech ought to develop. *Feasibility* — how and why a thing can or cannot work: note the remarks just preceding [1]. (Bracketed numbers refer to the quotation from Professor Carleton's speech.) *Similarities and dissimilarities:* see the statement that differences would have to be defined, in the clause before [2]. *Causality* would have to be established before anyone would think Carleton's policy would in fact "serve America's national interests" [3]. *Degree* must be discussed if Carleton is to show there is enough nationalism in Communist systems to allow his plan to work [4]. And the *existence* of circumstances that make national conflicts likely must be treated [5]. Another set of *similarities and differences* ought to be treated [6]; and to explain these, a new set of *causalities* would have to be discussed [7]. Incidentally, a comparison of the *potency* or power of alternative policies to bring *desirable* results would have to be treated [8]. Then, Carleton finds he would need to consider a further set of *similarities and differences* among the *desirable* and *feasible* features of several policies [9]. All these specific lines of thought would need to be discussed, says Carleton, in order that his speech might have the kind of *substance* or quality ("carry intellectual conviction") he would want it to have [10].

Professor Carleton actually touched most of the topics or themes that

4. William G. Carleton, "Effective Speech in a Democracy," *Vital Speeches of the Day*, XVII (June 15, 1951), 540–544. Reprinted by permission of the publisher and author.

people normally develop in any speech about popular affairs. A tolerably complete list of such topics is this:

A. Attributes commonly discussed:
1. *Existence* or nonexistence of things.
2. *Degree* or quantity of things, forces, etc.
3. *Spatial* attributes, including adjacency, distribution, place.
4. Attributes of *time.*
5. *Motion* or activity.
6. *Form,* either physical or abstract.
7. *Substance:* physical, abstract, or psychophysical.
8. *Capacity to change,* including predictability.
9. *Potency:* power or energy, including capacity to further or hinder anything.
10. *Desirability* in terms of rewards or punishments.
11. *Feasibility:* workability or practicability.

B. Basic relationships commonly asserted or argued:
1. *Causality:* the relation of causes to effects, effects to causes, effects to effects, adequacy of causes, etc.
2. *Correlation:* coexistence or coordination of things, forces, etc.
3. *Genus-species* relationships.
4. *Similarity or dissimilarity.*
5. *Possibility or impossibility.*

A speaker seldom develops all of these topics in any particular situation, nor is every imaginable thought suggested as soon as one asks whether he needs to talk about one or another of these eleven attributes and five relationships. Nonetheless, this simple list of topics can be easily mastered and used to generate ideas for possible use in *any* speech. Here is an illustration of how, with these sixteen suggestive terms or "topics" before you, you could canvass what you could say about a subject.

Suppose you are preparing a speech on how space science has affected industries in the United States. If you do your inventing as we propose, your first step will be to consider what kind of rhetorical situation you will step into. Assume for now that you have asked such questions about the situation as we suggested in Chapter 3 and that you have further found that it is chiefly *information* that your audience will need at the time you meet them. You'll be asking your listeners chiefly to *interpret and judge facts;* you'll not be asking them to choose among courses of action or to adopt evaluative attitudes toward something (except incidentally). From this observation you will know that you especially need two kinds of materials: (1) facts about the impact of the space age, and (2) standards of judgment for your listeners to apply in judging the truth and significance of those facts. At this point you can turn to the checklist of attributes and relations we have provided and use them to "pull out" facts and standards you have in your head about space exploration and industry.

First, try *existence.* Will you need any facts showing the existence of, say, the space age? Not unless yours is a primitive audience. But what about the existence of a "space industry" or of "space markets"? Asking this question could remind you that it may be worthwhile to show your audience that a space industry does *exist* within the general business system we call industry. That kind of information could be useful to your audience. You might have thought of the same item without asking yourself about *existence*, but to ask the question increases the probability that this useful idea will come to your mind.

Continuing your canvass you might ask: Will I need to talk about the *degree* or quantity of anything? Unquestionably. You will want your listeners to know how much of industry is now space industry. How much of our industrial output depends on government's space program. Similar lines of thought will occur to you if you pause over *degree*. What about *time*—the order in which the space industries emerged? This theme may prove important in developing some details, but it will probably not be a major topic in your speech unless you decide to stress something like the rapidity or slowness with which space enterprises have developed. The theme of *motion* or activity does not suggest much material to be included in your speech. Were you explaining how a space shot is accomplished, you would want to include information about preparatory, launching, and orbital movements, but you probably will have little need to discuss such procedures in the situation we are imagining.

Form ought to suggest that you can discuss such matters as whether space industries have grown up independently or inside other types of organizations. *Substance* (the essential nature of things) seems unlikely to suggest much information you will need, unless you choose to discuss the importance of research in space science, opportunities for industrial growth, or perhaps kinds of work in space industries. *Capacity to change* suggests an important idea: whether space industries are stable or change rapidly as scientific technology advances. And the topic, *potency,* ought to suggest that you need to know what spurs and slows an industry's capacity to compete in production of space goods.

The *desirability* and *feasibility* of various industrial practices will also need to be touched—not because your audience must approve any courses of action but because they should understand why practices in production, financing, and organization had to change as space industries developed and changed.

When you turn to common relationships for suggestions, your judgment will tell you that information about *genus-species* relationships will be relatively unimportant to you—except when you distinguish space and nonspace industries from one another. Otherwise, you will seldom classify or define things in this talk. But *causes* and *effects* will certainly have to be discussed. For example, what were the effects of our space industries' having grown large and then declined *(degree)?* What *causes* space industries to be so volatile and speculative as places to invest money? What are the *effects* of the industries' dependence on governmental expenditures? You should also know enough to discuss the *similarities* and *dissimilarities* between space and traditional industries. And to try another likely topic, whether there is any reliable *correlation* between the amount of research done by a space industry and the industry's growth or profit is a correlative matter you will probably need to talk about.

These are examples of the directions in which thought and research can be guided by reviewing sixteen familiar themes for discussion. The values of this kind of autosuggestive review will be evident in your speech. Your examination of your own knowledge is likely to be thorough, fruitful, and relevant to the business of discovering what is discussable. Reviewing a checklist of possible topics for development assures that you will not overlook either significant information lodged in your own mind or significant topics for detailed research.

From the time of Aristotle to the days of Francis Bacon it was periodically proposed that the way of searching for ideas which we have just described was the only feasible way a speaker could attain any assurance that he had properly reviewed his own knowledge of his subject. Bacon put it:

> . . . a faculty of wise interrogating is half of knowledge. For Plato says well, "whosoever seeks a thing, knows that which he seeks for in a general notion; else how shall he know it when he has found it?" . . . The same places [topics] therefore which will help us to shake out the folds of the intellect within us, and to draw forth the knowledge stored within, will also help us to gain knowledge from without; so that if a man of learning and experience were before us, we should know how to question him wisely and to the purpose; and in like manner how to peruse with advantage . . . books and parts of books which may best instruct us concerning what we seek.[5]

We first proposed this scheme of "cuing words" in 1963. There was then no experimental evidence that using such a list was worthwhile for speakers. There were psychological reasons for thinking the process should be helpful. Recent experiments with college-aged students of speech have shown that with brief instruction in using the cues on page 79 (plus synonyms for those terms) students were able to "think up" at least 10 percent more ideas for a speech on an "uninteresting" topic than their peers using no "cue words." Using an "interesting" topic, the students using the cues produced an average of 17 percent more ideas in a given amount of time.[6] A later, unpublished experiment using *groups* of students rather than individuals produced similar results: groups using the cues (plus synonyms) were able to "think up" markedly more solutions to an ecological problem than paired groups working without the cues. After an interval of time, the students in-

5. *De augmentis scientiarum*, V, p. 3, *Works*, IV, p. 423.
6. William F. Nelson, "*Topoi:* Functional in Recall," *Speech Monographs*, XXXVII (June 1970), 121–126.

volved in the experiment reviewed *all* solutions developed in the classes. They concluded that the cued groups' solutions tended to be more "acceptable" than the rest of the proposed solutions.[7]   Using different cues from those presented in this book, other research has tended to support the notion that when speakers have "standard themes" at hand to remind them of what *can* be said, the speakers are likely to think more readily of what *needs* to be said in a specific communicative situation.[8]

It is also consistent with what is known about how people think to suppose that recalling standard "lines of thought" will help us locate "sayables" about a subject.   "The solution to a complex problem is generally approached via several increasingly specific considerations," write Berelson and Steiner in summarizing what is known of creative thinking and problem solving.   These authors enumerate the stages of such thought as, "starting with a general scanning of the class of possible approaches [examining the speech situation and predicting the kinds of decisions required of listeners], moving to a selection of one or more 'functional solutions' [determining the broad *kinds* of material needed], and then narrowing to one or more of these in specific, operational solutions [deciding what *specific* themes or topics need to be developed]."[9]

The procedures we have just proposed can also assist you in planning the development of individual points within a speech.   For example, if you see that you must distinguish between the effects of sales taxes and income taxes, the checklist we have provided might help.   It might remind you that one way of making this distinction is to emphasize that income and sales taxes are different *species* of taxation and, therefore, exert their influence (*causal* effects) in different ways.   Noting this would direct your search for detailed materials toward examples, comparisons and contrasts, formal definitions, and other data that are particularly helpful in describing the *natures* of things.

Finally, the cuing system we have offered can suggest what you need most to find out in reading and interviewing when preparing for speaking. If reviewing a cue makes you say, "I don't know whether I need to say anything about that," you can study other materials or talk to knowledgeable authorities to discover whether communicators other than you think discussion of that topic is important, why, and under what circumstances.

---

7. This experiment was done at the University of Nebraska, Lincoln, using chiefly students registered in a business administration curriculum.   Professors John L. Petelle and William F. Nelson conducted the experiment.

8. Dominic A. Infante, "The *Eide Topoi* and Cognitive Structure: Predictors of Attitude and a Paradigm of Invention," paper presented at the annual convention of the Speech Communication Association, San Francisco, Calif., December 29, 1971.

9. Bernard Berelson and Gary A. Steiner, *Human Behavior, An Inventory of Scientific Findings* (New York: Harcourt, Brace & World, Inc., 1964), p. 202.

RESEARCH

Systems of classifying speech situations and systems for suggesting discussable themes do not of themselves provide information. They stimulate recall of things previously learned and they direct your research. Inventional schemes such as we have been discussing show you what to look for. Once you have by these means decided what *kinds* of information you need, routine research for speaking begins. Concerning this research we shall repeat some advice familiar to you, because all of us need reminding that some ways of digging for information are more practical than others. We shall also mention some sources you need to know, but nothing short of personally investigating the research facilities of the library available to you can equip you to prepare speeches adequately.

Books are among the very best places to go for information, but they are not the only wells of knowledge. We have already pointed out that *you* are a valuable source of information. Perhaps instead of talking about research for speeches, we ought to speak of "recovery, inquiry, and research for speeches." In preparing to speak, ask yourself: What have I already read about this subject, or this point? What have I heard in conversation, in lectures, on radio or television? What have I seen firsthand or in photographs? Such questions often stir the memory. Any expectant speaker ought to explore his memory and check his notebooks as an early step in research.

Other people are excellent resources. What photographer is not happy to answer questions about photography? What traveller is not all too pleased to reminisce about what he has seen? What professional man is unwilling to talk about the problems and accomplishments of his profession? We all know people who would be happy to supply information; yet, just as we often forget to probe our own minds, we neglect convenient, willing resource persons.

Public officials, teachers, businessmen and businesswomen, and others are often overlooked as sources of valuable information. One must be careful about seeking assistance from such persons because of the heavy demands on their time, but even the busiest people are frequently willing to grant limited aid to those who know what they want and are able to draw out needed information efficiently. The busier these people are, the more likely they are to have responsible aides and researchers who can provide you with factual information even more readily than their principals. We recall a speech student who wanted to cite a statement the president of her university had made in an unpublished address. She went to the president's personal aide, hoping to see the president. She did not need to see him. The aide was able to produce within minutes a mimeographed copy of the speech the student needed; he was also able to give her a quick review of the occasion and audience for the speech. She had the key information needed for her speech —

and at no trouble to the president. Congressmen and other officers have staff members specifically assigned to care for requests for service from their constituents—and this includes supplying documentary information. Many major corporations maintain public information departments whose business it is to supply data to people interested in their operations. To draw on such resources you need chiefly a very clear idea of what it is you want, and knowledge—from prior research—of who is most likely to know what you want to know. Carefully planned, prearranged interviews or clear and precise letters are the usual ways of securing help from busy people. Such interviewing and correspondence ought to be a normal part of an effective speaker's preparation.

Personal investigation is another neglected avenue of research. We would think ill of a person who, after urging us to read Hemingway's *For Whom the Bell Tolls,* turned out to have only seen the movie. What then, of speakers who deplore the low level of television programming without having checked the full program listings and explored the viewing options open to their particular audiences? To take other examples, you are fortunate if you have never been subjected to speeches on juvenile delinquency by speakers who had never visited a youth court, a settlement house, or even talked with young people of the kinds they discuss. One need not be an ex-convict to speak of prisons or a parent to discuss children, but to neglect obvious and convenient opportunities for firsthand inquiry is to miss vital and immediately relevant information.

Do not overlook your friends as resources. Discuss with them ideas you think of presenting to an audience. At the least you will have a test of how these thoughts "go over"; at best you may come away from such conversation with new information or new directions in which to look for information.

Unless you already know your subject very well, it is best to begin research by looking at general books, survey articles, and encyclopedic articles. These will give you background material into which specialized data can later be fitted. For example, before you look for detailed information about the classical Greek theatre or Greek scientific theories, or Greek politics, you ought to read some brief, general, authoritative essay or book on ancient Greek society. Edith Hamilton's *The Greek Way* is a readily available, short book of this sort. Or an encyclopedia article on Greek art (or science, or politics) might suit. Remember, too, that there are excellent specialized encyclopedias. On any topic concerning social psychology, the *Handbook of Social Psychology,* edited by Gardner Lindzey and Elliot Aronson, is almost sure to have an excellent essay. Many other fields have similar encyclopedias and handbooks; philosophy, biological sciences, theology, and social work are just a few. Your object in reading such works should be twofold: (1) to get an overview of the topic, and (2) to secure leads to other, more detailed information. Of course, a third possibility is that you will discover nothing useful under the heading you check; in that case you have probably saved much time you might otherwise have spent combing individual books and essays on a useless topic that at first seemed promising.

General source materials usually do not contain the detailed information you will ultimately need if you want to establish, say, the precise *degree* or the *desirability* of something. But when you search general works, you hope you will be led toward specific kinds of information that will complete your understanding. Let us illustrate with examples.

At best, your general work—an encyclopedia article or general book—will tell you where to go next for specialized information. If your speech subject concerned advertising in the United States, you might consult some source like the *Columbia Encyclopedia*. There, under "advertising," you would learn that advertising is commonly thought of in several different ways: with reference to who sponsors it (retailers, wholesalers, etc.), according to the medium of communication used (newspapers, radio, TV, etc.), according to the audience addressed (consumer, dealer, national audience, etc.). You would also learn that advertising practices have been changing over the years and that, now, advertising *agencies* handle most large corporations' advertising programs. The article will also give you the names of leading trade journals of this industry: *Advertising Age, Printer's Ink, Advertising Agency,* and *Tide*. These are sources to which you will need to go for more specific information on advertising today. You should know, too, however, that such standard indexes as *The Readers' Guide to Periodical Literature* and the *International Index to Periodicals* will give you additional leads to articles on advertising in *general* journals. The point is that for almost any topic you want to talk about, there is a general, survey essay *that you can understand* in some encyclopedia or book for general readers. Find it, and you will have a good start on your research and, often, the same general source will give you guidance on where to turn next.

But research does not always go as smoothly as our first example suggests. Here is the actual experience of the author of this chapter, just before writing these sentences. He entered his university's main library saying to himself, "I shall pretend I want to make a talk on some aspect of *libel*." Going directly to the reference section of the library, he chose the first encyclopedia which met his eye: *The Encyclopedia Americana, International Edition*. Under "libel" he found a well-written, clear article that defined libel, distinguished it from "slander," discussed what constitutes "publishing" a libel, and explained exceptions to the general rule. An excellent, understandable essay—but no directions at all as to where to turn next! So, he tried the most famed of encyclopedias, *The Encyclopaedia Britannica*. There he found a longer, more technical essay. It covered substantially the same topics that were treated in the *Encyclopedia Americana*, but some of the technicalities were beyond your author's understanding. To the *Britannica* article was appended a bibliography telling where to go to find the most authoritative histories of libel law in the United States, Great Britain, and Scotland. All titles sounded too technical for any but an expert to consult. Thinking that you would have been discouraged at this point, your author decided to change his attack and consult the other invaluable resource every library has—the card catalogue of books held. Under the heading, "libel," were cards for more than fifty full-length books. Their publication dates ranged from 1906 to 1972. Legal interpretations change, so obviously only the more recent books would give information suitable to an up-to-date talk; hence all books published before 1950 were ignored. We cite the titles of some of the post-1950 books because we want to make an important point about *choosing* what to read in getting information for a speech. Some post-1950 titles were:

Clark Gavin, *Foul, False, and Infamous: Famous Libel and Slander Cases of History* (1950).
Charles Angoff, *The Book of Libel* (1966).
Paul P. Ashley, *Say It Safely* (1969), 4th edition.
Clifton C. Lawhorne, *Defamation and Public Officials: The Evolving Law of Libel* (1971).
Robert H. Phelps, *Libel: Rights, Risks, and Responsibilities* (1966).
George P. Rice, *Law for the Public Speaker* (1958).

Confronted by titles such as these, the practical question for a speaker doing research for a speech is, "What book is most likely to give me the comprehensive material I need at the start of my research?"

Anyone who reflected for even one minute on the information printed on the catalogue cards for the above six books should choose Ashley's *Say It Safely*. These are the reasons. The book was in its fourth edition in 1969, though it was first published in 1956. Someone thinks it's worth buying! It is published by The University of Washington Press, Seattle, Washington. University presses are careful about their reputations and would be unlikely to publish a book that discussed laws carelessly. Such a press might, however, publish a very technical book. But this title is casual, communicating that it may be a book a layman could read understandingly. For the other books there are reasonable grounds for not making them *first* reading materials: Gavin's, Lawhorne's, and Rice's books are obviously specialized; they might be useful later but not just now. The titles of Angoff's and Phelps's books are ambiguous; they may or may not be useful just now. Of the six books, *Say It Safely* seems most likely to give modern information in layman's terms. Your author decided to ask for *Say It Safely* first. His reasoning, and some luck, paid off. The book turned out to be written by an attorney as a "manual for journalists and speakers." Its chapter headings touched most of the topics mentioned in the encyclopedia essays, but it also specially treated libelous broadcasts and pictures. It contained specific examples of kinds of statements, pictures, and the like which would or would not be libelous; best of all, it *interpreted* all the legal decisions it cited. Clearly this was an ideal special source to read if one were working up a speech for a general audience on the subject of libel.

We recount this little experience, made as much like yours as possible, because through it we can illustrate the nature of *efficient* library research. From start to finish the experiment took forty minutes; the author had scanned two essays, begun a bibliography, and had in hand for examination an excellent book for the next step in research. Many books that were "poor bets" had been eliminated from the search simply by reading and *thinking about* the information given on library catalogue cards. In all this, the *general* nature of the imagined speech was the key standard of judgment in deciding what was a "good bet" and what was not. You can work by precisely the same patterns, keep the same commonsense questions in your mind. Sometimes your research will be as swift as ours; almost always it will be far less time-wasting than if you *randomly* wander among indexes to periodicals and card catalogues. Unless you have time to "just fish," proceed in businesslike fashion. Use the resources of your library as they were meant to be used. And use your own mind constantly.

As a talk takes shape there will be times when exact bits of information — statistics, authoritative estimates, dates, facts about topography or design or authorship — are needed to fill small gaps in what one plans to say. What was the area of some battlefield, the height of a building, the probable authorship of the "letters of 'Junius,'" the date of President John F. Kennedy's assassination, a dramatic case of libel tried in the United States? When this is the class of information you require, it is time to explore some of the many volumes of classified data: *The World Almanac; The Statistical Abstract; Facts on File;* the specialized encyclopedias; compendiums of statements like *Bartlett's Quotations;* and other specialized sources like Gavin's *Foul, False, and Infamous: Famous Libel and Slander Cases in History,* Jane's *Ships of the World* or *Aircraft of the World.* These are sources of isolated, classified facts. Your reading in them will, of course, be far more selective than in any of the general works.

There is another resource in almost every college and public library which students and faculty members too seldom use. On the library staff is probably someone designated "reference librarian," often with a staff of assistants. These people are hired to help *you* solve research problems, find useful information, and conquer the many indexes and other research facilities of the library. Overwhelmingly they *want* to help you, but they have to be asked — asked clearly so they can understand your needs precisely. Appeal to these people when the routines we have described don't work; they are experts on aids to research.

In all exploratory activities connected with preparing speeches, you should never forget that the purpose of it all is to extract what is necessary to create a *communication that will serve as your personalized way of getting a particular set of responses* from a specific audience that is going to meet with you on a specific occasion at a specific time. One does not assemble a speech; he collects specific kinds of raw materials out of which he can mold a personal message — a unique composition. Research for speaking properly ends whenever you have collected most of the raw materials for weaving together an original, informed communication that will serve a specific purpose with the audience that will hear it.

In all research an important but somewhat technical matter is: How should you *record* information you find by reflecting, conversing with others, and reading? Speaker after speaker compounds his difficulties by jotting research information randomly on page after page of notebook paper. If he paused to think how he was going to use that information, he would adopt very different methods of note-taking.

Whoever does research for speaking will ultimately have to weave together the materials discovered. Doing this is clumsy business if you have to turn notebook pages back and forth to rediscover what you have collected. Suppose you are going to talk about cancer and you wonder whether you should discuss *types* of cancer. If all your notes are scattered through a notebook or on sheets of paper and are ordered as you found them in thought, interviews, and reading, your information about types of cancer will be thoroughly mixed in with other kinds of information — about causes, methods of control, tests for, and so on. Your recovery task would be simple if all your notes were on individual slips of paper or cards, each labeled according to the subject covered. You could then in a few moments shuffle the cards marked "Cancer — Kinds" out of your full pack of notes, examine what you have, and decide clearly what to do with that *set* of information.

There are many satisfactory ways of recording information for convenient use during speech composition. This is one:

Humor — Kinds

Donald J. Gray, "The Uses of Victorian Laughter," *Victorian Studies,* X (Dec. 1966), 175–176.

". . . nonsense does not end in laughter. And its laughter is the product of devices and habits. . . . The laughter of nonsense is not a surprised recognition of the savagery of nature or the brutality of man. It is rather . . . laughter of release, a happy acceptance of the chance to look at something trivial or profound, pointless or terrifying, without thinking about it."

(Donald J. Gray: Assoc. Prof., English, Indiana University. Specialist on Victorian poetry and humor.)

What you need from any record of information is very clear: The record should be complete enough so you needn't make a second trip to the original source; it must give you an accurate representation of what you found; it must allow items of information to be separated, sorted, and compared in any conceivably useful way. As far as we know, only recording individual units of information on individual slips of paper meets the last requirement. So, we say: Note separate bits of information on separate note slips and put the complete reference to your source on all slips (or work out some code system for identifying exact sources). It's tedious, but it saves steps! We know from experience the extra steps we've taken in consequence of sloppy note-taking.

Thus far in this chapter we have been dealing with stages of preparation that precede the actual composition of a message to be spoken. We have suggested a simple series of topics and questions that can direct thought toward the types of information you need. These topics and questions can efficiently guide explorations of your own mind and your explorations of the minds of others and of the world of print. We have pointed out that different kinds of source materials are needed at different stages of preparation and that they must be studied in ways appropriate to their natures and to what you need to draw from them. Finally, we have observed that it is laborious and confusing to record the results of research in any way that does not allow you to sort and compare related pieces of information easily. But a speaker is more than a bibliographer or research clerk. He investigates in order that he may compose and deliver personalized speech that will do what it needs to do in a particular situation.

HUMANIZING IDEAS

Let us go back to a supposition we made earlier. You are to speak to underclassmen about the psychology program at your college. Suppose you have picked the brains of professors and underclassmen and have read generally and specifically on your subject. Your pockets may bulge with notes inscribed on labeled, three-by-five cards. You still have no speech. Your raw materials still must be molded into a communication from one human being to a particular group of other human beings.

The gist of your intended talk may be clear in your mind: "The psychology major here makes sense; it offers a course of study that helps a person understand himself and other people." To crystallize in such a way what your thought and research "add up to" is the first, indispensable step toward composing a meaningful communication. But because you will be giving a talk, you have also to fit yourself and your materials to the *situation* into which you will step. The position to which your thought and research have so far led you is yours, but does it fit the situation you will enter? You have no cause to give up your own positions, no matter what audience you address or under what circumstances you meet them. But whether it is sensible to *present* your ideas in *exactly* the form that appeals to *you* is quite a different matter. You are not the one who is going to receive this communication. Nor will the listeners hear you in circumstances like those under which you worked out your own positions.

Your listeners will be people who have lived different lives, whose knowledge differs from yours and from each other's, who have all the general and special susceptibilities discussed in Chapter 3. And they, not you, are going to be the final judges of whether the study of psychology is justifiable, compelling, inviting. They are going to make these judgments at a time when other people are "talking up" other studies offered in your college. The whole tenor of the meeting will be one that says to your listeners: "Look over all your opportunities for study. Don't decide quickly or thoughtlessly on any concentration of courses." Your job, then, is to prepare a communication that will clarify the study of psychology and its benefits in ways appropriate to all the conditioning factors embodied within the speech situation of which you will become a part.

Accommodating to Audiences

No matter what seems compelling to you, you dare not use *only* your own personal judgments of adequacy, clarity, or persuasiveness in rhetorical communication. No communicator is completely free, but because they always face particular listeners in specific situations, speakers are less free than essayists, poets, or writers of imaginative prose literature. An essay, a poem, a novel, or a scientific paper can be composed as an expression of private feelings and can be published on a take-it-or-leave-it basis. But no speaker dares treat his listeners thus. He must meet and deal with listeners in a particular time, place, and set of circumstances. If the listeners are unready for him and his ideas he must create readiness. No speaker can retire to the bookshelf to wait until his audience falls into a mood to seek out what he has to say.

Today, as in the past, there are some people who contend that extensive accommodation to the demands of audiences and situations is somehow incompatible with personal integrity. The challenge goes like this: How can you sort, pare, rearrange, and perhaps even suppress things you know or think you know and still be faithful to yourself and to your audience? People who ask this kind of question are rightly impatient with answers that say only, "You have to do these things in order to win over audiences." The challengers properly ask, "Are there not men it is demeaning to please?"

The authors of this book think such challenges and responses misconstrue the nature of human communication. In the first place the challenges we have just described imply that integrity and candor require *publication* of everything you know or feel about a subject. It is implied that we should all say everything we think we know, exactly as we think we know it, in every situation. It is also implied that all simplification is misrepresentation. The challenges further presuppose that there is but one faithful version of a discussable subject. As to this last assumption, the facts are that in human affairs almost no version of anything is perfectly true in the sense of being complete and universal. Physicists and mathematicians have learned that perfect truth for all conceivable cases is rare even in their areas of study. In human affairs, the situation is as a committee of scholars put it when summarizing the deliberations of two conferences on rhetoric and rhetorical discourse:

> Issues in the arts, in politics, in social organization, are not apodictically [incontestably] resolvable, and the pretense that they are is a major cause of contemporary social and educational unrest. It was argued, especially at the Wingspread Conference, that to encourage expectations of "scientific" or apodictic determinations in problem areas where such determinations are by nature unattainable will foster disillusionment and distrust of the institutions encouraging so unattainable a hope.[10]

A subject worth *discussing* is susceptible to various understandings, else we would not discuss it—we would *know* the "answer" and *demonstrate* it! Discussable, arguable subjects are therefore susceptible to various presentations, all valid from some points of view though not equally complete. For example, both of the following propositions are in some senses true: By studying psychology one comes to understand his fellows. By studying psychology one comes to understand more about himself. Believing *both,* a prospective speaker might justly reason: "I have only five minutes to talk. Either I can treat both benefits superficially or I can treat one of them carefully. To show that I really know what I'm talking about, it's better to be thorough than superficial. I'll treat one benefit only. Which? Most people are especially interested in themselves, and this audience will be focused, by the situation, on *their* well-being. It is therefore wiser, in this case, to stress how psychology helps one to understand himself. In some other situation there may be opportunity to talk about the social insights to be gained from studying psychology."

This soliloquy fairly presents some of the accommodations speakers must make in order to communicate effectively and with integrity. Part of what this speaker thinks is going to be suppressed, not to misrepresent anything but so he can properly represent a *portion* of his perceptions. He would surely serve his listeners less well if he attempted more or gave them a discussion less pertinent to interests engendered in them by the character of the speech situation.

Subtle Adaptive Decisions

Adaptation is not, of course, always just a matter of simplification and partition. There are more subtle adaptive decisions that speakers have to make. One of the most famous examples in literature is found in the story of St. Paul's sermon on Mars Hill in Athens. As it is told in the book of Acts in the Christian New Testament, Paul came on a missionary journey to Athens,

---

10. Lloyd F. Bitzer and Edwin Black, eds., *The Prospect of Rhetoric* (Englewood Cliffs, N.J.: Prentice-Hall, Inc., 1971), p. 243. The excerpt comes from the "Conclusion" of this report of the National Developmental Project on Rhetoric, 1970.

Greece. There he became upset at the many idols he saw in the city, and he argued strongly in synagogues and on the streets against idol-worship. However, there was in Athens a group of philosophers and religious thinkers who held regular discussions in an open meeting place called the Areopagus at the top of Mars Hill, overlooking the city. One day these men invited Paul to come to speak with them. The rest of the account, including a summary of what Paul said, runs this way in the Revised Standard Version:

> And they took hold of him and brought him to the Areopagus, saying, "May we know what this new teaching is which you present? For you bring some strange things to our ears; we wish to know therefore what these things mean." Now all the Athenians and the foreigners who lived there spent their time in nothing except telling or hearing something new.
>
> So Paul, standing in the middle of the Areopagus, said: "Men of Athens, I perceive that in every way you are very religious. For as I passed along, and observed the objects of your worship, I found also an altar with this inscription, 'To an unknown god.' What therefore you worship as unknown, this I proclaim to you. The God who made the world and everything in it, being Lord of heaven and earth, does not live in shrines made by man, nor is he served by human hands, as though he needed anything, since he himself gives to all men life and breath and everything. And he made from one every nation of men to live on all the face of the earth, having determined allotted periods and the boundaries of their habitation, that they should seek God, in the hope that they might feel after him and find him. Yet he is not far from each one of us, for
>
> 'In him we live and move and have our being';
> as even some of your poets have said, 'For we are indeed his offspring.'
>
> "Being then God's offspring, we ought not to think that the Deity is like gold, or silver, or stone, a representation by the art and imagination of man. The times of ignorance God overlooked, but now he commands all men everywhere to repent, because he has fixed a day on which he will judge the world in righteousness by a man whom he has appointed, and of this he has given assurance to all men by raising him from the dead."[11]

The story of this speech closes with these words:

> Now when they heard of the resurrection of the dead, some mocked; but others said, "We will hear you again about this."
>
> So Paul went out from among them.
> But some men joined him and believed. . . .[12]

This account of a missionary's speech carefully designed to win a hearing within Greek culture poses most of the harder questions speakers must solve in talking to audiences that don't agree from the beginning. Would Paul's personal, religious convictions have been better honored had he *not* suppressed, for this speech, his strong distaste for the Greek religion? This

---

11. (New York: Thomas Nelson, 1959), Acts, XVII, pp. 19–31. Copyright by the Division of Christian Education of the National Council of the Churches of Christ in the United States of America. Reprinted by permission.
12. *Ibid.*, 32–34.

was his first opportunity to talk to some of the most important religious and philosophical thinkers in Athens. He deplored their religion, but to get a hearing he chose not to say so directly (as he had apparently been doing in the streets). He actually used a facet of his listeners' paganism as a means of getting to his own central idea. His choices were rhetorically wise; had he not moderated his criticism of paganism and had he not used the entire situation delicately to assure that he would be heard out, he would have undermined his whole reason for going to the hilltop to talk. If he wanted to convince any leading thinkers in Athens, he had to treat them as we have said in Chapter 3 doubters must always be treated. They must be moved from their strongly held positions and commitments by slow degrees. Generally, though not at every point, that was how Paul approached his task. The account says some listeners rejected the message because Paul still went too far for them when he talked of resurrection. But we are told others were moved far enough to be willing to hear more. Later, it appears, some who heard more came to believe Paul.

There are few records of persuasion that illustrate so clearly the delicacy of judgment you and all speakers have to exercise in order to get even *some* acceptance from those who doubt your "truths." No matter how convinced *you* are, a doubter simply will not see the merits of your ideas if you only "proclaim" them. Doubts and counter opinions are truths, too. Real communication occurs only when speakers' "truths" and listeners' "truths" are accommodated to one another—in the best way rhetorical art allows.

Talk As the Medium

For reasons we shall state shortly, *talk* was an entirely suitable medium for St. Paul's religious message. But talk is not the ideal medium for every kind of material. This means that as a speaker you have further need to adapt your views. You need to present them in the ways that communicate them best. Our courts recognize that some content is better communicated in print than in speech, so an attorney normally prepares a written brief as well as an oral plea. The judge studies the brief at his leisure. If an engineer or any other speaker must deal with highly technical details, he is likely to reinforce what he says with visual or other more efficient communication. An architect prepares floor plans, sketches, sectional drawings, and models, recognizing that building plans are never adequately communicated by speech or writing. Likewise, each speaker must discriminate between what can be told through speech and what is better conveyed in some other way.

The balance of effectiveness is not always against speech as a communicative medium. A person's attitude toward a proposition or toward another person is exceedingly difficult to picture and more difficult to convey through writing than through speech. Feeling or emphasis is better conveyed in person than in print. Speech best communicates the relationships between ideas and human experience. Aspects of an idea or event that have strong human significance are "naturals" for oral communication, and ideas that lack human significance must either be deliberately associated with other matters of human concern or be consigned to another medium. Given the relationship between religious belief and human feeling, Paul suffered no disadvantage because talk was his only available medium of communication with the philosophers.

As a speaker you have both auditory and visual resources. (Never forget that *you* are your most versatile visual resource.) You will need to choose and emphasize content which lends itself to communication through your media and subordinate or exclude from your speech whatever materials cannot be effectively communicated through speech and action.

When using the medium of speech, you may discover that your ideas have to be given shapes and shadings different from those they had when you first thought them or found them. That you will *speak* may demand accommodation of ideas just as much as the prior beliefs of listeners demand accommodation.

We have been focusing in the last few paragraphs on external forces that "hem you in" as you plan and compose speech. There are positive forces, too. You can draw on them to compensate for restrictive pressures.

Handling Ideas

There is seldom only one way of handling an idea. For example, if you find it impossible to demonstrate the existence of life on another planet, you have other options. You can discuss whether conditions on the planet are *potentially* capable of supporting life. Again, many distinctive qualities of a great piece of music are scarcely communicable through words, but this need not prevent you from speaking about the musical work. Though you cannot say all, you can verbally draw attention to some aspects of its structure or *form*. This is precisely the method Leonard Bernstein, Laureate Conductor of the New York Philharmonic Orchestra, used to make meaningful the verbal portions of his justly famous televised lectures on musical comedy, jazz, rhythm, conducting, etc. If one attribute or relationship of a subject does not lend itself to oral communication in a given setting, there is probably some other theme or line of thought, almost equal in importance, that *is* orally communicable.

Speakers confronted with ideas that are difficult to communicate or with purposes difficult to accomplish are like scientists confronted by the fact that absolute certainty and rigorously demonstrable answers are not always possible for them:

There is in the first place the temptation to sloppy thinking—if one knows that rigor can never be attained one is tempted to do less than one's best and let a piece of analysis go that one sees could be improved if one took more time and pains with it. There are situations where a defeatist attitude is too easily adopted instead of pressing the attack to one's utmost.[13]

Very seldom is there no usable analogy, no example, no familiar principle, no easily imagined experience that will create at least an approximate impression of what you want to speak about. St. Paul turned to the methods of philosophical deduction when he wanted to show the superiority of his "Unknown God" to philosophers who were used to this kind of discourse. Thomas Huxley once explained the principles of scientific investigation to an audience of English working men by showing how this kind of investigation resembled investigations of crimes. Huxley's speech is still used as a model of exposition; but it would certainly not be, had he decided to disregard the limitations of his auditors and proceed by rigorously defining induction, evidence, and generalization.

Some years ago Professor Laura Crowell made a careful study of the complicated changes President Franklin Roosevelt and his team of speech writers made in developing an address to the Congress, delivered on January 6, 1941. The speech went through seven different drafts before it was given, beginning with five pages which Roosevelt composed to show his assistants what he wanted. (It is testimony to his art as a composer that 60 percent of this material was appropriate for the final, seventh version of the address.) What Professor Crowell found was that Roosevelt and his staff at first *added* ideas to the initial draft. Then they went through a stage of shifting ideas around in the speech to get the right ones into the important first and last positions. In this process they also began to drop out details and to reduce paragraphs to pithy statements. In the last drafts they seem to have concentrated on sharpening the language—inserting alliteration, parallelism, reconstructing statements to get just the right emphasis, and rearranging statements to achieve climaxes. It was not until the fifth of the seven versions that the final, overall shape of the address began to appear clearly.

As Professor Crowell says, "Often these alterations are not matters of finding appropriate expression for ideas so much as of finding the appropriate ideas for expression." Often only a few words had to be found in order to add major new dimensions to ideas, as in these instances:

> . . . immediacy of the crisis is not the only time relation developed in the preparation of the manuscript. The claim that before 1914 no foreign war "constituted a real threat against *us* or against *any other American nation*" is changed to read "constituted a real threat against *our future* or against *the future of any other American nation*." . . . The time shadow is lengthened differently in regard to the danger of enforced isolation for future generations: "thinking of our children" is amended to read "thinking of our children *and their children*."[14]

---

13. P. W. Bridgman, *The Way Things Are* (Cambridge, Mass.: Harvard University Press, 1959), p. 9.
14. Laura Crowell, "The Building of the 'Four Freedoms' Speech," *Speech Monographs*, XXII (Nov. 1955), 266–283.

Crowell sums up her tracings by indicating that the process was actually one of fitting Roosevelt's "truths" to "truths" of and about American listeners:

> The cumulative effect of these sentences—built to express Roosevelt's concepts of governmental function and relationship, shifted to place the climactic idea in the climactic position, altered and trimmed to add force and effect by the very words chosen—is powerful indeed. Considering that the first wording of the ideas was done by writers with long training on scores of earlier addresses and thus the first sentences embodied much of the style desired, considering that each sentence, each word, underwent severe scrutiny not only in itself but in the light of changes made elsewhere in the address, one begins to understand the power of the final draft.[15]

If experts plan and revise in this kind of detail to "get it right," the rest of us should expect to expend considerable planning, adaptation, accommodation, and revision just to be "adequate" in communication.

Student speakers can do exceedingly well at finding resources by which to solve their communicative problems, as this true narrative indicates.

Bob Barth was one of a class of fifteen students, all but four of whom were college freshmen. Nine were women and six were men. In conference with his instructor Barth revealed that he would like to explain the operation of jet aircraft engines in his next speech to the class but, he said, this probably would be unwise since it was clear that only two of the fourteen students who would be his audience had even an elementary knowledge of mechanical and physical principles. Barth's judgment on his audience was exactly right; most knew nothing and seemed to care nothing for the world of physics and mechanics. Nonetheless, Barth's instructor contended that this was a golden opportunity for an experiment with what careful selection of ideas and methods could accomplish with a difficult audience. Barth reluctantly agreed to do what he could and set doggedly to work designing a speech that assumed little interest and no mechanical knowledge on the part of his hearers.

On the day of his speech Barth began by saying:

> I am going to talk to you today about jet engines. I suspect you think you aren't interested. Probably what's in your minds now is something like this.

Here Barth uncovered a rough but clear drawing of a jet engine "pod" covered with such words as "dangerous machine," "complicated," "for mechanics only," "expensive." He continued:

> The fact is that in principle at least jets aren't complicated. They're rather simple. If you've ever blown up a toy balloon and then let it out of your hands to watch it shoot through the air as the wind escaped, you not only know something about jet propulsion, you've used it. Let's begin right there—with the air escaping out of the balloon.

---

15. *Ibid.,* p. 282.

In this vein, Barth covered simply but accurately the elemental facts about the construction and operation of ramjet and turbojet engines. There was nothing unusual about his delivery, except that it was not as direct and forceful as it ought to have been. The language of the speech was simple and the examples were always from everyday life, but there were few other marks of artistry. Even the charts and sketches that communicated things hard to put into words were freehand crayon drawings on cardboard sheets of different sizes. Yet when Bob Barth ended his talk there was a ripple of applause—the first applause heard in that public speaking classroom. At the end of the hour two young women who had been in the audience exchanged these observations as they walked from the room. "I learned more today than I do in most class periods," said one. Her companion replied, "Yes. And imagine! I even thought I understood that engine!"

What happened? A speaker accepted his audience as he found it, adjusted to its limitations and its needs, and gave it as much information as its little knowledge, his inventiveness and art, and the time would allow. Without fanfare Barth offered his listeners two always alluring reasons for attending: I can help you understand what's been mysterious to you, and you'll find the whole experience much easier than you expect. Scarcely any subject is unusable in speaking if speaker and audience approach it in this spirit.

ORIGINALITY

For the most part this chapter has dealt with how to work your mind efficiently, realistically, and originally in the basic, creative processes good speaking calls for. It is fitting to close with some observations on originality, for much of which we are indebted to one of our former colleagues, an expert teacher, Herbert A. Wichelns.

You may draw information and ideas from printed or oral sources. You may acquire materials from personal knowledge, magazine articles, essays, editorials, or books. You may glean ideas from lectures, plays, movies, television and radio programs, or conversations with fellow students and experts. But once your information is gathered, you must reflect upon it and stamp it with your own personality. Then you must present it in your own words. *To be original you must be able to discover and convey fresh meaning in known matters.* Rarely does even the greatest speaker discuss what was totally unknown before his speech. To realize a truth clearly because you have experienced it in your own mind produces a degree of originality gained in no other way, even though the base for such originality is to be found in readily accepted axioms.

As *you* do when listening, your listeners will be demanding as the price of attention that you have actively thought for yourself, have reached your own point of view, and have reacted as an individual to information you have digested. To be heard with attention and confidence you must exercise judgment in sifting the materials to which you have exposed yourself, and you must test your own reasoning. You must say what you have to say in your *own* way, choosing your *own* words. Since individualized choices in both matter and structure are involved, you should be extremely wary of constructing speeches based on a single source. If you rely heavily on outlines found in debate manuals or study files or upon ideas expressed in a *single* book or magazine account, you cannot hope for originality even though you actually speak the words conveying the final message. If talk is not a fresh accommodation of yourself and your thoughts to *these* listeners in *their* situation, your human relationship with them will surely be tarnished.

Systematic preparation with full consciousness of your listeners' natures and needs is the key to originality in speaking. You must become intimately acquainted with the facts of your subject, and their humanized meanings. You must judge your material with keen awareness of the speech situation into which you will bring it.

Sifting the important from the unimportant takes time and reflection, and for this reason the likelihood of discovering fresh significance in a subject will increase if you begin work early. Ideally, a period of several days should elapse between the period of research and final organization and rehearsal of any important speaking—whether delivered in formal or casual settings. During this "gestation" or "cooling-off" period you should explore—perhaps using such a topical system as we have provided—the meanings and possibilities of what you know. Ideas about your subject should be forced to grow within you; only so can they flower into some final form that is "right" for you, for the speech situation, and for your particular listeners.

It takes imaginative thinking to bring freshness to a subject. You must strive to find the distinct shapes and the potential uses of the materials you use. You must try to see what is unique in your relation to these materials and in their relation to the lives of your hearers. The function of imagination here is not to create the unreal or imaginary but to bring to particular listeners a personalized understanding of your version of reality. Imagination ought to reinforce and animate fact and probability by revealing what happens *in life* if these facts and probabilities are accepted or rejected.

What are some tests of originality? You should be able to defend what you say. You will know more than you have had time—or thought wise—to tell in an initial statement. You will be able and eager to trace ideas to their sources, crediting and evaluating these sources as you talk and afterward. Though you may have borrowed—with acknowledgment—you will always be stating your own ideas, for selection and evaluation of the ideas are *yours*.

If you are original in speaking, you will not rely on others to the extent of repressing your own individuality. You will avoid the hackneyed and be free of clichés because you will say nothing that does not uniquely "fit" the speech situation. Like any other work of artistic merit, your work—your talk—will be the product of personal experience, personal insights, and intense awareness of the natures of those with whom you seek to communicate.

EXERCISES

Written

1. Assume you are to speak to a classmate, or to your entire class, in favor of majoring in the academic subject that interests you most. Identify three lines of thought (topics) that it would be useful to discuss with the audience you have decided on. Identify three other lines of thought that are relevant to your subject but which you would *not* choose to discuss with the listeners you have in mind. Explain the grounds on which you include and exclude each line of thought you cite.
2. Assume you are to give a classroom speech on: "It is important (or is not important) that college-aged voters vote regularly in local and national elections." Which of the sixteen lines of thought listed in this chapter suggest the most promising lines of research for this speech? Explain why the remaining "cues" are not potentially useful as guides to promising information for this speech.
3. Identify the lines of thought (topics) used in some brief, familiar speech such as Lincoln's "Gettysburg Address," Shakespeare's version of Mark Antony's speech over the body of Caesar in *Julius Caesar,* Dr. Martin Luther King's "I Have a Dream" address, or some other. Defend or criticize the speaker's choice of these lines of thought. Were there other topics he might as wisely have chosen? If so, illustrate how one of them might have been incorporated into the speech.

Oral

1. Give a short speech in which you explain two different ways a proverb or a maxim might be interpreted. Or choose a specific process and present two different ways that process might be effectively explained to an audience.
2. Give a brief report on a speech or editorial you have heard or read and in which you believe the creator made exceptionally inventive use of the lines of thought available to him—or failed to take advantage of lines of thought open to him.
3. Form a committee with three or four of your colleagues. Compose an outline or sketch of a speech, editorial, or other practical message intended to accomplish a specific purpose with an audience your committee imagines and describes. When the committee has settled on purpose and audience, use the cuing terms in this chapter to construct a committee's list of *all* the things it might make sense to include in the message. Then cut this list to the topics that *ought* to be covered, and prepare the committee's sketch or outline of the whole message.
4. To intensify your awareness of the many ways most subjects can be treated in speech, divide your class into groups of three; assign a *noun* to each group (trees, girl, car, Eskimo, etc.); have each group member choose a "cue" from page 79 and then prepare and give a 2-minute talk on the assigned subject, using chiefly lines of thought suggested by the chosen cue word. You should discover that there are more interesting things to be said about simple subjects than you supposed.

CHAPTER
5

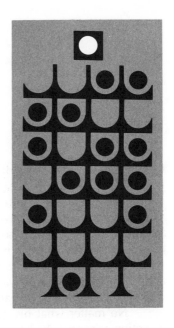

Invention:
General Tactics

In Chapters 3 and 4 we discussed attitudes, feelings, and expectations of listeners and considered ways you can adapt what you say by using general information about the natures of human beings and about types of rhetorical situations. But what we have said does not identify the tactics you will need to use to turn wisely chosen material into "compositions" that will serve *particular* listeners' concerns according to your rhetorical purposes. We shall consider these specific steps for adapting speech material in this chapter and in Chapter 6 look at ways in which the specific goal of a particular talk will further modify your creative activity.

No matter what his goal, any speaker faces two tactical problems of invention as soon as he has collected information to be used in a communication. He has to build *rhetorical proof,* and he has to find ways of *clarifying* his ideas so listeners will grasp them as he intends. These are the two major topics of this chapter.

BUILDING PROOF

A simple way of describing effective talk is to say it is talk which *makes a point and justifies that point.* We shall now consider how these two functions are accomplished. For that purpose let us assume that you have completed the basic inventional processes of choosing a subject and collecting a good deal of information that is pertinent for the speech situation you expect to enter. Now you face the questions: "What is my message going to 'add up to'? Exactly what is it that I am trying to accomplish?" This is a kind of uncertainty experienced speakers know only too well. For all of us the sense of what we want to do in speaking seems plainer *before* preparation starts than after we have acquired all the information it takes to speak sensibly. After general preparation has taken place, most speakers discover they need to take stock *again* — to reset their goals more realistically and express them more precisely. If this happens to you in speech preparation, you are "normal." Now *is* the time to reconsider your communicative purpose intensely.

Purposiveness

It will be important to you and to your listeners that whatever you finally say be unmistakably focused. Whether you openly tell your purpose to your listeners or not, an *exact* goal needs to be plain to you as you give final shape to what you will say. At least *you* must know what specific meaning your communication is supposed to have for those who hear you. They will expect that. To "get the point" of communications is gratifying to them, and if they are to be gratified, you must be able to express two things: (1) the kind of experience you intend the listeners to have, and (2) exactly what kind of content you will put into what you say in order to produce that experience. These two things can be expressed in a single, concise sentence, the standards for which we discussed on pages 25–26 and will consider in further detail in Chapter 6. Just now we want to deal with *why* it is important to think carefully about purpose statements as you begin to "pull together" speech material.

Let's begin with what hard thought about *purpose* can do for *you*. Any subject can be treated in more than one way. In order to speak cogently, you must have decided which of these ways you will use in approaching your particular audience in its unique situation. You dare not be vague, even to yourself. "I want to tell about psychology" does not say which of the hundreds of possible speeches on psychology you are going to frame just now. By contrast "I want to help my listeners to understand what requirements a psychology major must meet" identifies a *specific* speech about majoring in psychology. "I shall explain three milestones in the development of psychology as a science" identifies another, still more sharply focused speech. You could make a coherent, influential speech focused on either of the two last statements—as you could never do by using a vague conception like "I want to talk about psychology." So, your first general tactic in framing a cogent communication on a matter you understand is to formulate a precise statement covering (1) your aim and (2) the range of subject matter to be included in what you will say. Even if you never tell your listeners your specific purpose, this tactical step is necessary in order to direct your own thinking efficiently. You need now to move a step beyond the general conception of purpose that allowed you to make judgments about your speech situation and somewhat sharper goal that guided your search for new and useful information. Now, you need to express your communicative goal exactly so you will have a clear target at which to aim as you sort and shape the material you have collected.

We do not mean that the sharpened statement of purpose should never be changed as you shape your material. You should always feel free to redirect your aim as you learn more about your subject and think more about your audience and your relation to it. Your vision of what you can and ought to achieve should change as your bases for judgment grow. What is important is that in every moment of preparing a speech your purpose should be as incisively clear as your understanding permits. If it is not, you will ramble in preparation, and when you speak your listeners will probably lose their way. It is also true that, for safety's sake, you ought not change purposes for any but clear-headed reasons.

It is important to listeners that what they hear has "unity"—the thrust of precise purposiveness. Listening is not a very efficient way of acquiring information, and listeners need what help they can get to extract the "right" ideas from talk. It is significant that all experiments testing what happens when speakers assert their points and purposes in so many words have demonstrated that this practice helped listeners to understand and retain what they learned.[1] This argues for telling your listeners exactly what your purpose is, if doing so does not introduce disadvantages.

There are times when more will be lost than gained by openly asserting your purpose, or by asserting it early in a communication. This is especially the case when auditors are doubtful or hostile. But it does not follow that you ought to seem to be without purpose at any point. To tell a group of scientists, "I shall show you how science is undermining morals" may arouse so much defensiveness that the scientists cannot listen attentively any more. It may be better to seem to be trying for a lesser purpose, at least at first. Experienced speakers withhold statements of their purposes if listeners are apt to be doubters. They try to secure full attention to their "proofs" by not disturbing the listeners with conclusions until the way to those conclusions has been carefully and inoffensively prepared. But they *have* purpose throughout.

As always in speaking, one must make a judgment about what is a tactically sound way of revealing purpose in speaking. There is no formal rule to follow. The advice we want you to carry away from the last few pages is the following. Careful attention to framing statements of purpose is important in invention, not because we say so, but because speakers need clear purposes as guides to their own planning and because listeners will expend energies inefficiently unless their thoughts are guided toward some, at least apparent, purpose. It is more important that communication *have* purpose than that purpose be formally announced, though announcing and perhaps repeating the purpose of speech can itself have helpful effects on listeners' attention to what is being said.

The forms in which you will want to express your speech purposes (for yourself and for listeners) will vary according to the kinds of specific response you expect. Those variations will be discussed in detail in Chapter 6.

---

1. Among experimental studies supporting this proposition are Donald L. Thistlethwaite, Henry deHaan, and Joseph Kamenetzky, "The Effect of 'Directive' and 'Non-Directive' Communication Procedures on Attitudes," *Journal of Abnormal and Social Psychology*, LI (July 1955), 107–118; Donald K. Darnell, "The Relation between Sentence Order and Comprehension," *Speech Monographs*, XXX (June 1963), 97–100; Ernest Thompson, "Some Effects of Message Structure on Listeners' Comprehension," *ibid.*, XXXIV (March 1967), 51–57.

Proof

The purpose that governs a well-conceived speech guides but does not accomplish the work it forecasts. Ideas, language, and behavior are deployed to do this work. The somewhat military connotations of the words *deploy* and *tactics* are worth taking seriously, for it is, indeed, the "mix" and the placement of "forces" with which you deal in putting together any particular speech.

Your task is always to get someone else to experience something as you would like. You must get people to accept information and use it in special ways if you are to inform them; they must experience heightened desire to investigate if you are to provoke inquiry; they must *re*value their prior knowledge if you are to reinforce their beliefs and attitudes; they must accept *your* interpretations of data and their own interests if you are to persuade them; they must suspend a good many serious concerns if you are to entertain them. Whatever you attempt as a speaker, you ask your listeners to shift their outlooks in some degree. So it is important to think about *why* and *how* people shift their views.

People change views because they think they have found sufficient "reasons" or "proofs" to indicate that to shift would be a "good" thing. Of course, what people think of as "reasons" may or may not involve extensive reasoning. And what seem to them "sufficient" proofs and what seem "goods" may have been identified with much logic or scarcely any at all.

Here are the proofs that listeners demand of a communication before allowing it to change their views.

1. They demand that either the communication or their own experience reveal a connection between what the communication asks of them and their own personal interests. (See Chapter 3, pages 39–43.)
2. They demand that either the communication or their own experience provide "rational" justifications for believing what is said to them.
3. They demand that the source of the communication (the speaker and his sources and sponsors) seem worthy of confidence — at least on the subject of the communication.

A speech, or any part of it, must in some way satisfy these general demands if there is to be change in the attitudes and beliefs of those who listen. You have often made these demands of speakers, though you expressed them within your mind as questions.

Suppose someone is talking to you about an engineering curriculum. Certain questions constantly pop into your mind: Why should *I* care about the engineering curriculum? Why bring this up *now*? Why should I believe the curriculum *is as you say it is*? Why is what you urge on me *better* or *truer* than an alternative? Why should I listen to *you* on this matter?

Whoever talks about engineering curricula can expect these questions to arise again and again in any listener's mind.   And if we substitute another subject, we shall find listeners raising precisely the same questions.   They are commonplace, recurring questions asked by listeners of any speech on any subject.

Notice that some of these questions ask whether the listener's personal interests are going to be satisfied (Why should *I* care?   Why bring this up *now?*); some ask for rational justifications (Why should I believe things *are as you say they are?*   Why is what you urge on me *better* or *truer* than an alternative?); and another asks about the speaker's qualifications (Why should I listen to *you* on this matter?).   If you see to it that these five questions are satisfactorily answered either by what you say and do or by something your listeners are already aware of, your speech will have the personal-interest, rational, and source justifications that audiences demand as the price of shifting their attitudes and beliefs.

To deal with how one builds up personal-interest, rational, and source justifications, we shall have to talk about these kinds of justifications separately, but you should bear in mind that these influences never *operate* separately from one another.   You can demonstrate this by examining your own behavior.   When a speaker shows you that something is in your own interest, do you not think better of him for that same reason?   Do you not almost always find your friends more reasonable than people you dislike?   Have you never said, "I see no flaw in your reasoning, but I don't accept your conclusions anyway"?   We are dealing with proofs that are almost always intricately interrelated, but to talk about them clearly we must treat them separately.

Developing Personal-Interest Justifications.   "Why should *I* care?" and "Why bring this up *now?*" are primitive questions.   They spring from man's basic attributes.   We saw in Chapter 3 that listeners are anxious about things that seem likely to affect their private purposes and interests, that people tend to shut out what has no apparent bearing on their immediate affairs, and that all of us behave in this way by virtue of being human.   You, as a speaker, must give your listeners some satisfying answers to why they should care now.

To see *how* listeners may be shown that their own interests justify what you say, it is necessary to review some elemental psychological concepts. Modern social psychologists generally argue that we behave as we do in consequence of internal forces, sometimes referred to as needs, drives, tensions, or by other terms.   There is general agreement, however, that it is *internal* stimuli that induce us to act as we do.   These internal stimuli direct our activity toward simple or complex goals.   The goals are conditions likely to satisfy our needs or desires, the ultimate sources of the internal stimuli.   The goals may be satisfactions of physiological needs (for food, drink, etc.); some goals reward social as well as physiological needs (the basic need for physical safety and the learned need for social approval may cause us to strive toward the goal of gregarious experience).   Experience teaches us that behaviors of certain kinds tend to bring satisfactions of certain needs, relieving our tensions; thus, we soon acquire predictable patterns of activity to which we regularly resort when we experience the tensions of specific drives. For example, we learn that to drink a cup of coffee at mid-afternoon "picks us up." So, under tension we go through a thirst-satisfying activity. We do not feel any the less gratified because the forces that induced us to act in this way had less relation to thirst than to a need for relaxation.

Similarly we all develop predispositions toward a host of intellectual activities. These are the learnings of special importance to speakers. We learn that experienced people are often better advisers than the inexperienced; so, we become predisposed to accept what, say, a world traveller tells us. Or we learn that Midwesterners are more friendly than New Englanders. We are thereby predisposed to react approvingly if we hear that we shall find it more pleasant to live in Winona, Minnesota, than in Pittsfield, Massachusetts, although we may know nothing of either place. From experience everyone has acquired thousands of such ready propositions—infrequently verbalized and often contradictory to one another. They constitute his fund of attitudes. These predispositions and their intensity—the degree to which we feel it is important to *retain* them—become our guidelines when we judge what ideas and actions are or aren't acceptable to us. With some of our attitudes each of us feels deeply involved, with others less so, and toward some we are all but indifferent.[2]

The paragraphs above contain some statements on which there is difference of opinion among scholars. But a communicator must adopt *some* overall conception of how men and women feel, think, and respond in order to carry out his practical tasks of rhetorical invention. The summary we have offered will serve you as a safe view pending the time when psychologists reach fuller agreement about the mechanisms of changing beliefs and attitudes. It emphasizes a viewpoint especially important to speakers and generally agreed upon by psychologists: We do not address human needs *directly* with our words. Our words and acts awaken or intensify need-produced attitudes which stand in consciousness as self-committing "approvals" and "disapprovals." To weave a tapestry of need-justified experience within listeners, a speaker must "pattern" their attitudinal responses in ways that are accepting of what he offers. He does not "insert" beliefs into other minds; he enables and encourages other minds to evolve their own beliefs and feelings. And if he pays too little attention to the attitudinal patterns his hearers possess, he may miss important opportunities to influence or, worse, allow patterns of judgments to evolve in ways that will operate against him rather than for him.

---

2. For a concise outline of a general theory of attitude change see Irving L. Janis, Carl I. Hovland, *et al., Personality and Persuasibility* (New Haven: Yale University Press, 1959), pp. 1–16. Parts of the summary we have presented derive from C. W. Sherif, M. Sherif, and R. E. Nebergall, *Attitude and Attitude Change* (Philadelphia: W. B. Saunders, 1965).

Below are a few lines from a speech by Dr. Daniel J. Boorstin, historian and Director of the National Museum of History and Technology in Washington, D.C. Dr. Boorstin was addressing the Associated Press Managing Editors' Association on "Dissent, Dissension and the News." It was important for him to distinguish early in the speech between "debate" and "dissent." He apparently wanted to bring his listeners quickly to approve "debate" and to disapprove of "dissent." Notice in the passage below how he attempted to put attitudes into a pattern consistent with his goal. The quotation is broken into thought units, and opposite each unit we have put the kind of response we suppose Dr. Boorstin was working for.

Statements	**Possible Responses**
A debate is an orderly exploration . . .	*Order* and *exploring* are "good." *Debate* has these qualities.
of a common problem that presupposes the debaters are worried by the same question.	*Common interests* and *agreement* make for *order* — debaters have "good" goals.
It brings to life new facts . . .	*Facts* and *newness* are also "good"; *debate* has that "goodness" too.
and new arguments which make possible a better solution.	*Newness* and *better solutions* are "good," so *debate* has further merit.
But dissension means discord.	*Discord* is "bad"; *dissension* has this quality.
As the dictionary tells us, dissension is marked by a break in friendly relations.	*Breaking friendship* is a mark of *discord*; *dissension* has this "bad" quality too.
It is an expression not of common concern . . .	*Dissension* denies the "good" of *common interest*, further rendering it "bad."
but of hostile feelings.	*Hostility* is the opposite of *agreement*, one of the "goods" *debate* develops; another way *dissension* is "bad."
And this distinction is crucial.[3]	[No particular attitude is aroused here. Dr. Boorstin missed an opportunity to fix the pattern firmly with something like: "Debate is productive; dissension is discordant, unfriendly, and unproductive."]

---

3. The complete text of this speech appears in Wil A. Linkugel, R. R. Allen, and Richard L. Johannesen, *Contemporary American Speeches*, 2nd ed. (Belmont, Calif.: Wadsworth Publishing Company, Inc., 1969), pp. 203–211. The excerpt quoted appears on p. 205, as "paragraph" nine.

Notice that Dr. Boorstin offers no formal reasoning, though he does cite the authority of "the dictionary." He makes no verbal attempt to show himself uniquely qualified to say what he does (his reputation may already have done this). The thought he wanted accepted was that debate is valuable but dissent is not. He justified this thought almost entirely by trying to activate a series of favorable and unfavorable attitudes that were already at least latent within his listeners. Boorstin undertook to evoke those attitudes systematically: the favorable ones first and the negative ones afterward. By setting up statements in this way, he arranged matters so that every negative response toward dissension could also remind listeners of the contrasting *merits* of debate—to which they had already committed themselves. If the scheme worked within the speech situation, the listeners experienced an increasing intensity of approval of "debate" as their estimation of "dissension" was pushed lower and lower by Boorstin's remarks. We think Boorstin missed an opportunity to fix his positive-negative pattern by not adding a final, clinching, summative statement at the end. Nonetheless, the passage illustrates how ideas-borne-on-language can be managed for the purpose of regulating a mixture of evaluative attitudes favorable to a speaker's purpose. If Dr. Boorstin succeeded in any degree at all, he supported his own position *through* his listeners' predispositions and self-interests. With preliminary analysis of your listeners' attitudinal patterns you can invent similar, systematic "proofs" for and against ideas you treat.

You will speak on many matters for which the best "proofs" will be already within your hearers, needing only to be awakened and patterned to support what you say. It would be silly to "prove" with statistics, quotations, and formal arguments that students learn better under skillful than under unskillful teachers—especially if the listeners were students! The students' experiences and attitudes would supply proofs more potent than any that could be assembled from outside their skins. They would have learned such attitudes as: disorganized lectures and assignments make it hard for me to learn; teachers who don't allow class discussion are inferior; a showman isn't necessarily a good teacher; good teachers are interested in individuals; and so on. Such attitudinal propositions would only need to be brought to consciousness to become powerful proofs for the proposition that students learn best from skillful teachers.

To identify all the significant attitudes of even a single audience would require research by a corps of social scientists. Some political figures and others have the benefit of this kind of research data, but most of us must try to communicate effectively without those scientific advantages. Even so, we are not without resources. We can use such generalizations about people as were discussed in Chapter 3 to estimate what self-interest justifications reside in our listeners, and we can learn specific facts about specific audiences and situations by general investigation.

You will not need the Gallup polling organization to tell you that the young people in your audience will be more disposed than their parents to endorse idealistic and unqualified propositions. Nor do you need to be a social scientist to predict that people who live in communes are less likely than those who live in fraternities and sororities to have strongly favorable attitudes toward "organization." You also know that more men than women are apt to admire mechanical ingenuity for itself, and that people having difficulty supporting themselves are likely to be more intensely concerned with personal economics than those who have no economic worries. To compose effective speech you need chiefly to ask what your prospective listeners identify as "good for me and mine" and what they think of as "not so good for me and mine." To ask and answer this is to make a kind of survey of attitudes. Common sense will then reveal that a good many of those attitudes can be called up to sustain attention and to justify your ideas. Your common sense will also tell which of those attitudes you will need to skirt lest they leap into a hearer's consciousness as "proofs" against you.

The fundamental point to remember about listeners' attitudes is that your listener may call them up himself, spontaneously, or you may call them up by reminding him of things about which he possesses strong attitudes. Whichever way they arise in his consciousness, it is his attitudes that teach him *why* he should or shouldn't (does or doesn't) care *now*. Your task is to direct his caring toward the conclusions you have in view and not let the caring subside or become associated with things other than those which support you. The biology major whose classroom speech on hunting female deer was described in Chapter 3 and Bob Barth, whose speech on jet propulsion was cited in Chapter 4, illustrated how effective ordinary, but thoughtful, analysis of attitudes "out there" can make speaking. So did Dr. Boorstin's address to the editors. Notice, too, that in these three cases the speakers did not use existing attitudes merely to cause listeners to reaffirm what the listeners already believed; they taught *new* beliefs by interconnecting old attitudes and new information and thus they caused their hearers to generate thoughts that had not previously existed in their minds.

Developing Rational Justifications. Sometimes "Why should *I* care?" or "Why bring that up *now?*" cannot be sufficiently answered by triggering and patterning attitudes. When listeners do not see people, things, and events just as you do—when they are doubters—their prime questions are: "Why should I believe things *are as you say they are?*" and "Why is what you offer *better* or *truer* than some alternative?" Doubt and uncertainty exist when people find nothing or little in their experience that confirms the view being offered them. Your listeners will sometimes possess no supportive knowledge and attitudes; they will sometimes possess beliefs and attitudes that *conflict* with ideas you have and attitudes you need to evoke. Or, perhaps potentially confirming attitudes you need to make use of will be insufficiently prominent in your listeners' consciousnesses to generate the assent you want. In any of these circumstances you must give your audience new ways of seeing—ways that allow the troublesome ideas you offer to "make sense," to seem "rationally justified." What will almost never work with a doubtful or uncertain listener is to *assault* his existing beliefs and attitudes directly.

Though we often talk as though it were, it is not easy to say what a "rational" ground for accepting belief is. Yet doubters and uncertain people are the ones that are really in search of "good reasons," "sound logic," "rational alternatives." A trouble is that what "makes sense" about the things we usually discuss is almost never universally agreed upon. If there is doubt, that is evidence that people who think themselves reasonable can disagree about the doubted point. There is an important point for all speakers here: Whatever *you* may think, anyone who doubts you is just as confident as you are that *his* interpretation of "the facts" is fully rational. For the time being he finds something unsatisfactory about *your* rational processes. Doubtful, uncertain listeners don't feel that *they* have "problems"; for them it is the speaker who is having trouble "being reasonable." Your task is not to prove your doubters "wrong"; it is to prove yourself "right" according to what your listeners are willing to accept as "sound reasons." About the things we discuss most there is almost never only *one* "rational" view.

How different views can be about "What is reasonable?" was illustrated in 1971 when the Supreme Court of the United States heard and decided a case in which the federal government sought to prevent the *New York Times* and the *Washington Post* from publishing excerpts from allegedly stolen secret documents that came to be known as "The Pentagon Papers." The Court rejected the government's case by a 6–3 vote. The vote was decisive, but *not one Justice agreed totally with any other Justice on the proper reasons* for voting on one side or the other. Every Justice felt compelled to write and file his own distinct reasons for voting as he did; so six different "rational justifications" were issued for voting as the majority of the Court did and three different sets of "reasons" were issued for voting with the minority. Why? Because the Justices, like all of us, used different evaluative standards in determining what was most "reasonable." Different perceptions of what was "fact," different interpretations of what the law said, different estimates of what could or would happen in the future, different personal preferences entered into each Justice's "reasoning." These kinds of differences are always in play when any of us makes judgments. Consequently speakers and all other makers of rhetorical communication need to remember very clearly that almost nothing they ever say will seem certain to everyone who hears them. On most matters what is a "reasonable" or "rational" proof depends on who is doing the estimating. The result is that to give another person "rational justifications" is always to satisfy *his* standards of rationality and sufficiency of evidence. It is to align *his* standards of reasonableness and his preferences so they can "accept" what you offer. It is to fill "gaps" in his knowledge until his sense of sufficiency is satisfied.

Then what does "rational justification" sound like in real life? Let us look at an example of intensely "rational" talk created by a college student. Among the classroom speeches we have heard in recent years, one that was especially credited with being well and closely "reasoned" was on the subject, "What Can We Prove about God?" The speaker's central idea was that it is impossible either to prove or disprove in a scientific way that God exists. The subject and purpose, of course, dictated that "rational proof" must be the chief kind of justification used. The excerpt below is from a tape recording of the speech. It illustrates both the potentialities and the limitations of rational justification in spoken communication. The speaker was refuting a familiar type of argument that God *must* exist. He said:

> People who use this type of reasoning about God generally choose some complex kind of natural mechanism and prove—or at least they assume they prove—that the mechanism must have been planned. Thereby, they infer the existence of a Planner. . . . I'll deal [in refuting the argument] primarily with the solar system because we know that better. The followers of this train of thought, of which Sir Isaac Newton was one, say that because the earth and the sun and all the other planets have specific masses and specific velocities, they follow specific courses. They also argue that these courses could not possibly have been selected through the forces of chance. They say these particular orbits were predesigned by some super-being which they call God.
>
> Let me illustrate. Suppose, for example, that this line

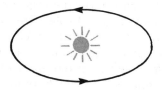

> represents the orbit of the earth around the sun. These people argue that for the earth to take this course by chance is infinitely improbable. Basically, they argue this because in the vastness of what we call space, there's so much room that this earth could as easily have spiraled into the sun, gone straight out into nowhere, or followed a parabolic or hyperbolic curve. But this orbit is the path it chose. Since the path is infinitely improbable, it must have been predesigned. That's the argument.
>
> Now, suppose the earth, rather than following its orbital path, had instead followed this one:

What are the chances that the second path might have been taken? They are equally infinitely improbable. Therefore, the arguers are actually not proving anything, since they are saying, in fact, that all possible courses are infinitely improbable. They aren't proving anything by saying just one of them was chosen. The probabilities for any one path are equal.

. . . no matter what happens in nature, it is infinitely improbable. This is to say, if we try to figure out the probabilities for the fact that it's now snowing here at this moment, it can be proved that it's infinitely improbable that it would snow here today. It is necessary for a whole complex chain of events to occur before it can snow in State College. If the earth weren't rotating at its particular speed, we wouldn't be here with the snow. If the earth were not revolving around the sun as it is, perhaps the climate would be warmer and it would be impossible for it to snow here. If the masses of air had any other set of molecules than they have at this instant, it would be impossible for it to snow. This kind of argument can be applied to anything in nature. Take the existence of a flower in a particular spot. There are an infinite number of places where that flower could grow. So, for a flower that you don't plant but which just happens to grow, it is infinitely improbable that that flower should grow where it does.[4]

The talk continued, pointing out the fallacy of the criticized argument. Said Mr. Zellner, "You cannot explain, just by the complexity of a situation, that the complex had to be planned by some all-knowing mind," but neither can you ever demonstrate the unquestionable absence of such a "planner." Mr. Zellner's listeners found his talk impressively "logical"; so have others who have read it.[5] This kind of response was a credit to Mr. Zellner's ability to justify his views, but the credit did not come because he "scientifically" or irrefutably "proved" anything. The university students who heard him, and some readers, simply found Zellner's reasoning more *probable* than any other reasonings they happened to know about.

We are going to analyze a segment of Zellner's remarks in hopes of showing you the real nature of rational justification in rhetorical communication: that such justification is seldom *final* and that in popular discussions we can seldom prove anything conclusively. All we can do is allay or counter "logical" doubts other people have.

The English logician, Stephen E. Toulmin, devised a way of "laying out" arguments which we shall use to display various features of Mr. Zellner's rational justifications.[6] Professor Toulmin contends that in most arguments, we present some — possibly all — of six different kinds of material. Among them will be: DATA, WARRANT, BACKING FOR WARRANTS, CLAIM. Sometimes, also, we offer QUALIFICATIONS of our CLAIMS in order to forestall or take account of real or anticipated CONDITIONS OF REBUTTAL that, if not guarded against, might make our CLAIMS seem too sweeping or otherwise un-

---

4. Excerpted from a talk delivered by Leon R. Zellner to a class in "Effective Speech," The Pennsylvania State University, March 7, 1965. The talk was in response to the assignment: address the class on "your personal view" on any issue, set of facts, or other matter of concern to you. Printed by permission of Leon R. Zellner.
5. The speech was published in an anthology of speeches: C. C. Arnold, D. Ehninger, and J. C. Gerber, *The Speaker's Resource Book* (Chicago: Scott, Foresman and Co., 1966), 2nd ed., pp. 187–190.
6. Stephen E. Toulmin, *The Uses of Argument* (Cambridge, England: Cambridge University Press, 1958). See especially Chapter 3, "The Layout of Arguments."

acceptable.   Identifying and exemplifying these ideas as we go, we want to show you the nature of Mr. Zellner's reasoning in part of the excerpt above.

Let us look first at the argument Zellner explains so he may later refute it.   One way to diagram the line of reasoning is this:

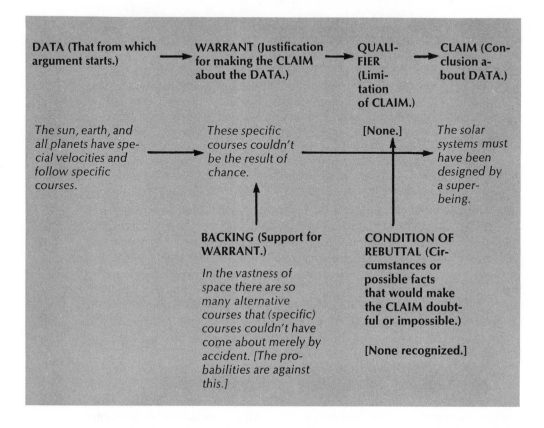

DATA (That from which argument starts.)

The sun, earth, and all planets have special velocities and follow specific courses.

WARRANT (Justification for making the CLAIM about the DATA.)

These specific courses couldn't be the result of chance.

QUALI-FIER (Limi-tation of CLAIM.)

[None.]

CLAIM (Con-clusion a-bout DATA.)

The solar systems must have been designed by a super-being.

BACKING (Support for WARRANT.)

In the vastness of space there are so many alternative courses that (specific) courses couldn't have come about merely by accident. [The pro-babilities are against this.]

CONDITION OF REBUTTAL (Cir-cumstances or possible facts that would make the CLAIM doubt-ful or impossible.)

[None recognized.]

Other people might see this argument as working differently, but for the time being let us suppose that this is a fair description of the argument Zellner is going to oppose.   Let us see how it really works—how "good" it is.

Look first at the DATA.   Will anyone doubt it?   Probably not.   As far as most of us know, it is "scientific fact" and not open to dispute.   Look next at the WARRANT and its BACKING.   This is the part of the argument that sup-posedly explains *why and how* we can legitimately move from the DATA to the CLAIM.   With some BACKING, it is asserted that the specific courses of the solar system "couldn't be the result of chance."   Do you accept it?   If you don't, you can go no further—the CLAIM is not justified and this is not "rational" proof to you.   If it seems reasonable to you, you can go on to see whether the CLAIM seems a "logical" consequence of the DATA and WAR-RANT.   Men have haggled for centuries over whether this CLAIM follows "logically"; you have wise men on your side whether you say it does or doesn't "follow." And that is our point about logical or rational justifications of this sort: Most conclusions we can reach in matters like this are debatable—they are not certain. Sir Isaac Newton and countless others have said this is a "sound" argument, but for as long a time other people have insisted it is no rational justification at all. There are two points at which the argument has been repeatedly attacked (and defended): (1) it can be argued that the WARRANT is "untrue"—that the specific courses of the solar system *could* be the results of chance; and (2) it can be contended "rationally" that even if we agree that the courses of the planets *probably* couldn't be the results of chance, it still would not follow that there *must* have been a super-being who designed those courses. This is Zellner's attack. Our point, once again, is that in arguments like this, all one can do is try to provide enough support and reinforcement for the position he believes in so that his listener will find the contention "sufficiently" rational to accept *as if* it were fully proved.

Mr. Zellner did not find the argument we've just looked at "sufficiently" rational to accept, so he attacked it in hopes of convincing his classmates that he was more "rational" than those who propounded the argument. What did he do? Where did he attack? Though different people may see almost any argument differently from others, it seems to us that what Zellner did was to say that the WARRANT and its BACKING were mistaken—having overlooked something. Mr. Zellner said, in effect, "I will accept the DATA, but I say the WARRANT is mistaken and that without a proper WARRANT you can draw *no* CLAIM at all." Zellner's rebuttal might be diagrammed thus:

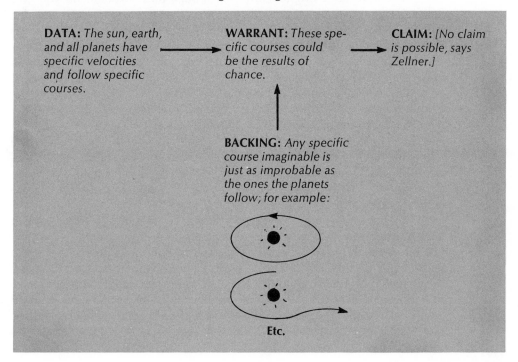

DATA: *The sun, earth, and all planets have specific velocities and follow specific courses.*

WARRANT: *These specific courses could be the results of chance.*

CLAIM: *[No claim is possible, says Zellner.]*

BACKING: *Any specific course imaginable is just as improbable as the ones the planets follow; for example:*

Etc.

If what we have given is a fair explanation of an argument and its refutation, what are we to say about the "strength" of reasoning in rhetorical communication, especially speeches? It seems to us that we must say: The strength of any reasoning is whatever strength the receiver of the communication assigns to it. "Proof," "good reasoning," "sufficient evidence," "strength of argument" and the like are determined in most speaking by what the listeners are willing to think is "reasonable" and sufficient. "Rationality" is judged psychologically as well as logically by those who respond. Go back to the argument Mr. Zellner undertook to refute. Suppose instead of "These specific courses couldn't be the results of chance" the argument had contained as WARRANT the following line from the Koran: "All that is in the heavens and the earth glorifieth Allah." Now, criticize the argument:

| **DATA:** The sun, earth, and all planets have specific velocities and follow specific courses. | **WARRANT:** All that is in the heavens and the earth glorifieth Allah. | **CLAIM:** The solar systems must have been designed by a super being. |

Is the justification for the CLAIM now more rational or less so?

What we are trying to show you through these experiments with Mr. Zellner's classroom talk are these things. (1) Whenever you try to give an idea rational justification, you do it by contending, as best you can, that some DATA *justify* a particular conclusion. Your listener will compare (a) what you say with (b) what his experience says. If there is no conflict, he may go on to make some estimate of what it would "be fair" to infer from *all* of the DATA. (In a sense he creates a set of possible WARRANTS.) Then he estimates the "worth" of the WARRANTS you have offered; if he finds yours "worthy," he may move toward accepting your CLAIM. All this happens in a flash, of course, and the listener needn't know Mr. Toulmin to do it. In any case, the reasoning that makes your justifications stand or fall is the reasoning that goes on inside your *listener's* head. That's the "rational justification" that really counts; *yours* is simply what you offer to direct and otherwise affect that listener's "reasoning."

We are also trying to show you (2) that in the things men and women usually discuss it is largely useless to imagine you can "prove" anything *finally*. A speaker who understands the reality of this limitation will set out to invent patterns of thought that will be accepted as "more reasonable than anything else" in his listeners' views. This is the way "rational justifications" have to be invented even when reasoning begins with such uncontested, physical "facts" as that the sun, earth, and all planets have specific velocities and follow specific courses. Your job, then, is to learn how to handle *probabilities* in ways that are credible *to other people* in specific situations.   This leads to the third thing we have been trying to illustrate.

(3) Rational justifications, like all other justifications in rhetorical speech, succeed or fail depending on how well you adapt them to particular sets of listeners.   Your listeners' knowledge, their standards of "evidence," and their conceptions of what is "reasonable" *in the present situation* are the standards against which you have to work — no matter what *you* think is sufficient and reasonable in the particular case.

A mistake speakers make is to give only their own validations for ideas. Those who do this sometimes discover their listeners are unimpressed.   The real audience may apply more exacting standards of justification than the speaker did.   On the other hand, sometimes speakers bore listeners by trying to meet higher standards of rational justification than the listeners care for. To avoid such mistakes we suggest you make *two* kinds of judgments whenever what you say depends on its being accepted as rational.   Ask yourself: (1) Is my proof "sound" enough so that *I* believe in it, for myself?   (2) How much *more* or *less* will the point require as support in order to satisfy my listeners in the situation where I shall meet them?   If what you say to an audience can be *made* sound enough to satisfy you when you make yourself the "judge" of it, you will meet your responsibilities as a conscientious speaker.   If you adjust what you say to your listeners' demands, you will meet your responsibilities and aspirations as a practical communicator.

There is considerable variety in the patterns of our reasoning and in the forms in which evidence occurs.   Some of the variations will be examined under "Clarifying and Reinforcing Ideas" later in this chapter; others will be treated in Chapter 7, which deals with organizing speech materials.   For detailed treatments of technical reliability and scientific or statistical validity in reasoning you should consult authoritative works on logic, argument, and statistical and experimental procedures.   These matters are not treated here because we believe with the classical writers on rhetoric and speaking that the applicable tests of rationality in speaking are psychological and situational, not formally rule-bound or mathematical.   It seems to us that the formal rules of scientific reasoning are far too abstract to be fruitfully applied in speaker-listener relationships where private rather than universal standards of validity and adequacy normally operate.   Centuries of experience and numerous experimental studies indicate that in the logic of popular communication "One man's meat is another's poison."   What constitutes sufficient rational proof of any idea depends on who is the audience and what the situation is.   The degree to which every speaker is, himself, a powerful proof or disproof of his ideas further indicates that the role of formal logic in popular communication is limited indeed.

The Speaker as a Justification of Ideas.   Why should I listen to *you* on this matter? is asked often. Aristotle pointedly stated the reasons for the question:

The character of the speaker is a cause of persuasion when the speech is so uttered as to make him worthy of belief; for as a rule we trust men of probity more, and more quickly, about things in general, while on points outside the realm of exact knowledge, where opinion is divided, we trust them absolutely. This trust, however, should be created by the speech itself, and not left to depend upon an antecedent impression that the speaker is this or that kind of man. It is not true, as some writers on the art maintain, that the probity of the speaker contributes nothing to his persuasiveness; on the contrary, we might almost affirm that his character is the most potent of all the means of persuasion.[7]

It may seem strange to call upon so ancient an authority to explain the influence of speakers-as-their-own-justifications. The fact is that though no topic has been more diligently studied by experimenters interested in rhetoric, there is still no more succinct and defensible statement on the practical role of a speaker's *ethos* than Aristotle's. He wrote:

As for the speakers themselves, the sources of our trust in them are three, for apart from the arguments [in a speech] there are three things that gain our belief, namely, intelligence, character, and good will. Speakers are untrustworthy in what they say or advise from one or more of the following causes. Either through want of intelligence they form the wrong conclusions; or, while they form correct opinions, their rascality leads them to say what they do not think; or, while intelligent and honest enough, they are not well-disposed [to the hearer, audience], and so perchance will fail to advise the best course, though they see it. That is a complete list of the possibilities. It necessarily follows that the speaker who is thought to have all these qualities [intelligence, character, and good will] has the confidence of his hearers.[8]

Modern scientists have devoted a good deal of effort to exploring the dimensions of *ethos* or what we are calling "the speaker as justification for ideas." On the whole their findings argue that what listeners look for and weigh in speakers are a pair of attributes which Aristotle called "intelligence" and "character" and which investigators of the past twenty years have variously called "competence-trustworthiness," "expertness-trustworthiness," "authoritativeness-character." Something like what Aristotle thought of as "goodwill" turns up in studies that indicate audiences are more readily influenced by speakers with whom they can readily "identify" and in other studies suggesting that we look for and respond to something called "dynamism" in speakers.[9] It is a limitation of virtually all studies of how speakers justify through themselves that the effects of *reputations* have been mainly explored. Yet what is most important to you as a speaker is how what you do

---

7. From *The Rhetoric of Aristotle,* translated and edited by Lane Cooper, pp. 8–9, bk. I, chap. 2. Copyright 1932, renewed 1960 by Lane Cooper. Reprinted by permission of Appleton-Century-Crofts, Educational Division, Meredith Corporation.

8. *Ibid.,* pp. 91–92, bk. II, chap. 1.

9. A good summary of contemporary research on the *ethos* of speakers and the credibility of sources in general appears in Gary Cronkhite, *Persuasion: Speech and Behavioral Change,* pp. 172–178.

when speaking will affect listeners' judgments of your intelligence, trust-worthiness, and your intentions.

We all know that our judgments of speakers' credibility change as we listen to them. We may not notice how radical those changes sometimes are, or why they occur. That striking changes do occur has recently been demon-strated in a series of experiments in which college students listened to bits of tape recorded speeches by the late civil rights leaders Malcolm X and Dr. Martin Luther King, by former president of the International Teamsters' Union James Hoffa, by Governor of Alabama George Wallace, by Reverend Billy Graham, and by Richard M. Nixon speaking as President of the United States. In all tests listeners who were favorable to a speaker before he began to talk became *less* favorable to him after hearing a few moments of his talk, and listeners who felt unfavorably toward the speaker before hearing him became *more* favorable to him after hearing him for a few moments! Very tentatively, Professor Brooks, who conducted most of these studies, proposes this gen-eralization: "Audiences whose initial evaluations of speakers are clearly favorable or clearly unfavorable tend to shift in the opposite direction after a brief exposure to the source's recorded speech."[10] It is too early to generalize that if you are liked before you speak, you will lose ground as soon as you talk or that if you are initially disliked, anything you say will gain a bit of credibility for you. So far, experiments have used tape recorded, introductory passages from speeches by controversial public figures about whom most listeners probably had stereotyped expectations. Nonetheless, the experiments do suggest that the first minutes of talk are exceptionally important to any speak-er's credibility. Perhaps the old adage, "First impressions are lasting," has more significance for speakers than had been supposed.

Certainly modern experiments give added importance to Aristotle's proposition that listeners' trust needs to "be created by the speech itself, and not left to depend upon an antecedent impression that the speaker is this or that kind of man." All that is revealed by the speech—knowledge, analytical power, organizational ability, verbal skill, delivery—can play a part in main-taining, strengthening, or weakening listeners' confidence in what you say and in what you are. It is clear that as speakers we do, indeed, "shape" our credibility even as we go through the stages of composing speech. Every choice we make can, potentially, generate proof or disproof of a spoken message.

To see that claims to intelligence, trustworthiness, and good intentions toward listeners can be built into speech, it will be useful to look at examples of how actual speakers have done this. Consider first a man widely known as a scientist and, at the time he spoke, President of Harvard University. He had just completed a section of an address in which he seemed to have op-

---

10. Robert D. Brooks, "The Generality of Early Reversals of Attitudes toward Communication Sources," *Speech Monographs* XXXVII (June 1970), 154. This report (pp. 152–155) is based upon an earlier one. Robert D. Brooks and Thomas M. Scheidel, "Speech as Process: A Case Study," *ibid.*, XXXV (March 1968), 1–7.

posed to one another a view of the world based on a literal reading of the Book of Job and the "scientific" view offered by Marxism.   Anyone who sets up an opposition of this sort invites a number of questions from listeners: "So, where do *you* stand?" "Are you telling me *I* must choose between these extremes?" "What *are* you trying to do to *me?*" As though recognizing that his reputation as a scientist made it necessary for him to answer such questions, Conant looked back to evaluate what he had just said:

> I have purposely placed before you a false dichotomy — the Book of Job taken literally or dialectical materialism. I have already suggested, I hope, my own predilection; I would not repudiate the nineteenth-century optimism about the continued improvement, with the aid of science, of all the practical arts (including the art of human relations). I would not, however, subscribe to any "in principle" argument about what science can accomplish. I would be certain that for the next century, under the best conditions, the areas of uncertainty and empiricism would remain enormous. As to the Book of Job, I would subscribe to the answer that the universe is essentially inexplicable and I would interpret Job's vision symbolically, using this as one entrance to the whole area of inquiry that can be designated as the universe of spiritual values.[11]

By candidly warning his listeners that he has overdrawn the conflict between spirituality and the scientific spirit, Dr. Conant encourages a favorable impression of his own integrity and, therefore, his trustworthiness as an interpreter and judge. And his caution also enhances his trustworthiness. That Conant, a scientist, will "subscribe to the answer that the universe is essentially inexplicable" is surprising, perhaps. If so, the statement may render his viewpoint all the more acceptable because a listener might say to himself, "A scientist would hardly say a thing like that unless he had very good reason. His training should make him give the opposite answer." Perhaps the most important thing Conant accomplished in these moments was to assure his listeners that he had no intention of misguiding them through "mere" strategies. Though he "placed before you a false dichotomy" in order to emphasize a point, he promised by words and acts that he could be depended upon to give candid, unexaggerated appraisals of any points before leaving them. He appeared to be consciously trying to make himself more trustworthy than he would have seemed had he not explicitly displayed that he was alert to misinterpretations listeners might make of the ways he expressed things.

Establishing that one is *not* extreme or irresponsible is another way speakers can lay claim to listeners' trust. Perhaps no public figure in modern American history has been more obviously concerned to maintain that his positions were not extreme than Theodore Roosevelt. An astute critic writes that Roosevelt deliberately adopted "the rhetoric of concede-and-lead: concede the priority of the audience's self-interest and then on the basis of the

---

11. James B. Conant, "Science and Spiritual Values," a lecture delivered at Columbia University in 1952. In his *Modern Science and Modern Man* (New York: Columbia University Press, 1952), p. 92.

good faith established by the concession lead them to commitments beyond self-interest." What this kind of strategy achieves, the same critic says, is this: "The demagogue reduces rhetoric to the first step alone; the idealist, to the second. Roosevelt's formula was designed to correct the reductionism of each." [12]

On April 5, 1906, Roosevelt pleaded for moderation and regard for balance in the journalism of the "muckrakers," some of whom had been carried far from fact by their zeal to expose corruption. His concede-and-lead habit in persuasion is evident in this excerpt from his famous speech, "The Man with the Muck-Rake":

> It is because I feel that there should be no rest in the endless war against the forces of evil that I ask that the war be conducted with sanity as well as with resolution.
>
> The men with the muck-rakes are often indispensable to the well-being of society; but only if they know when to stop raking muck, and to look upward to the celestial crown above them, to the crown of worthy endeavor. There are beautiful things above and round about them; and if they gradually grow to feel that the whole world is nothing but muck, their power of usefulness is gone.[13]

Like Dr. Conant, Theodore Roosevelt conveys an impression of trustworthiness through the care he takes in defining his position between sensationalism and complacency, while keeping himself on the side of reform. He not only implies this is a sane and sensible position, he declares its opposite is not very sane. He further asserts that he has adopted his position because he is against evil. His tactics in claiming credit for intelligence and trustworthiness are more direct than Conant's, but he is subtle also. His metaphorical imagery, borrowed from John Bunyan's *The Pilgrim's Progress*, could evoke religious or spiritual attitudes of approval in some listeners. Finally, we should note that by casting doubt upon the intelligence and trustworthiness of those he is criticizing, Roosevelt goes a step beyond Conant. He seeks deliberately to detract from the trustworthiness of his opponents.

These are representative ways by which speakers seek to enhance their own images. It is worth noting, too, that in the short excerpt from Dr. Boorstin's address to newspaper editors (page 108) he presumably drew some personal credit for goodwill and good character by associating himself so strongly with the virtues of *debate* (which editors would probably concede) and dissociating himself from *dissension* and *discord* (which editors were likely to disapprove).

There are other more obvious but nonetheless important steps a speaker can take to justify his message through justifying himself as its source. The late Ralph Zimmerman, when an undergraduate at Wisconsin State College,

---

12. Harold Zyskind, "A Case Study in Philosophic Rhetoric: Theodore Roosevelt," *Philosophy and Rhetoric*, 1 (Fall 1968), 245.
13. In *American Public Addresses, 1740–1952*, ed. by A. Craig Baird (New York: McGraw-Hill, 1956), p. 214.

Eau Claire, Wisconsin, did this impressively in a speech entitled "Mingled Blood." His opening words were:

> I am a hemophiliac. To many of you, that word signifies little or nothing. A few may pause a moment and then remember that it has something to do with bleeding. Probably none of you can appreciate the gigantic impact of what those words mean to me.

At a later point Zimmerman tellingly used his own disabilities as proofs in explaining the disease:

> If internal bleeding into a muscle or joint goes unchecked repeatedly, muscle contraction and bone deformity inevitably result. My crooked left arm, the built-up heel on my right shoe, and the full-length brace on my left leg offer mute but undeniable testimony to that fact. Vocal evidence you hear; weak tongue muscles are likely to produce defective L and R sounds.[14]

Mr. Zimmerman's subject matter is exceptional but his method is not. He offers the familiar proof: "Believe me because I have experienced what I speak of."

You have not the initial *ethos* of a Conant or a Theodore Roosevelt nor, we hope, the dramatic physical disabilities of a Zimmerman, but the methods illustrated by these speakers are as open to you as to them. Your speaking ought always to acknowledge, as Conant did, the nature of your rhetorical strategies, the reliability of the ways you analyze and present your subject matter; these things gain for you and your methods strength and respect. It is as open to you as to Theodore Roosevelt to concede what deserves to be conceded, to make clear your avoidance of extremes that your listeners reject, to contrast the good sense of your chosen positions with the lesser wisdom of other views—all the while making clear that you are, for all your care, "going somewhere" in thought. Allusions that associate you and your ideas with that which is intelligent, candid, and in your listeners' interests are also as available to you as to Roosevelt. And "I have seen it" or "I have been there" or even "I have read it carefully" is a claim to respectful hearing which you can use as efficiently as Ralph Zimmerman. All these opportunities are as available to students as to anyone else.

Daniel R. Crary employed all the methods of source justification when he was a senior at the University of Kansas. A college senior is not normally an acknowledged authority on population, but you will have to agree that Mr. Crary gave his listeners ample reason to have confidence in him. At an early point in his speech Crary said:

> But the best conservative information, which is now available from United Nations demographers, says flatly that this increase in population, which has taken us nearly 2,000 years, is going to be *repeated*, not in 2,000 years, but in forty.

---

14. Copyright by the Interstate Oratorical Association. For a full text of this speech see Wil A. Linkugel, R. R. Allen, and Richard Johannesen, *Contemporary American Speeches*, 2nd ed. (Belmont, Calif.: Wadsworth Publishing Company, Inc., 1969), pp. 199–203.

The 1958 publication *Future Growth of World Population* from the U.N. states that the population of the world by A.D. 2,000 will be seven billion. I suppose we've all heard population-explosion statistics which are designed to scare us into subscribing to some socially beneficent endeavor or another, but the United Nations is not passing the hat or trying to scare anyone when it says this (and I quote): "With the present rate of increase it can be calculated that in 600 years the number of human beings on earth will be such that there will be only one square meter for each to live on." Now this puts into question one of the rather old and often-used jokes, which goes: "If all the people of the world were laid end-to-end around the equator, they'd be more comfortable." But if the United Nations' facts are correct, in a few hundred years it may be decidedly more comfortable to stand, thank you. That is purely speculative, but the expectation that world population is going to double in the next 35 or 40 years is not just a speculative game played with almanac and slide-rule. Rather this incredible prospect is the logical implication of what we know to be the facts. And the results are already becoming clear.[15]

Mr. Crary draws to his own support the impartiality of the United Nations' scholars; he is cautious in interpreting information; he rejects hat-passing and "scare"; he lets it be known that he is familiar with more information than he chooses to use at this time. And, happily, he reveals his own humanity by touches of mild, relevant humor.

But Crary's was a formal, very carefully prepared speech. What of the talking that goes on in your classroom and elsewhere? Here is an excerpt from a classroom talk, given in the Spring of 1971 by Robert Dike, to a class in persuasion at the University of Delaware:

As a resident of this state I'm not against normal industrial and population growth, but I am against this dam as a means to supply water for this anticipated growth. There are two basic reasons behind my opposition. The first is conservation; the second, for want of a better title, I've called "governmental injustice."

Believe it or not, the White Lake Creek is the last clean stream in this small state of Delaware. If you ever go up into the area of the Creek, what you'll find is a quiet, scenic, very beautiful forest. I was there recently and, believe me, it is, indeed, beautiful. There are over 30 varieties of wildlife present — ranging from deer and foxes to the rare flying squirrel. And some 143 species of birds and 20 different types of reptiles and amphibians. Plant life is just as richly abundant — more than 250 species — 43 kinds of trees and well over 200 varieties of wildflowers.

No one can doubt that this region is one of Nature's unique havens, but what will happen to this untouched beauty if the dam is built?[16]

Mr. Dike had earlier given his listeners the plans for a new dam. Having now announced his opposition and previewed his reasons, he was moving into a "conservation argument": water impounded by the dam would destroy the

---

15. "A Plague of People," in Wil A. Linkugel, R. R. Allen, and Richard L. Johannesen, *Contemporary American Speeches*, 2nd ed., pp. 220–224. Used by permission of the publisher.
16. This excerpt is from a recording of Mr. Dike's speech provided by Dr. Patricia Schmidt, formerly Instructor in Speech, University of Delaware, Newark, Delaware. Published by permission of Robert Dike.

White Lake Creek area. We believe he established himself as especially credible on this point by making clear his personal acquaintance with the area and by the care of his research suggested by the precision of his statistics and the extent to which he covered types of natural phenomena. We think that in these moments of his speech his "intelligence" and "competency" must have risen in the minds of the other students listening to him. And we think these opportunities for enhancing one's self as a justifying source are open to you daily.

Other methods of providing source justification can be illustrated briefly. Franklin Roosevelt's famous salutation, "My friends—" or his "you and I know" or any speaker's use of the pronouns "we," "us," "our" instead of "I," "me," "my" exemplify small expressions of goodwill and friendly identification with an audience. They are open to anyone's use. Simply to use a cogent argument or to cite the best rather than a second-best authority hints that you have intelligence and knowledge. A dispassionate recital of arguments for or against the position you are taking can suggest: "He's keeping his feelings under control and so is more to be relied on." Demeanor, too, leads to source justification. Listeners prize conversational directness, general pleasantness, and unselfconscious action, voice, and diction because they interpret these behaviors as signs that no ulterior intentions are diverting the speaker's attention from his business with us, his hearers.

In Aristotle's shrewd observations lies what every speaker must remember if he is to give his message personal credibility: not reputation alone, but everything the speaker does in his speech influences the trust his hearers will have in him and in his ideas. Whatever your qualifications to speak, your speech must show (1) that you know enough to deserve a hearing, (2) that you are dealing honestly with your material and with your listeners, and (3) that you have your listeners' interests at heart.

In closing this section on the kinds of justifications listeners demand as the price of acceptance and belief, it is worth repeating that personal-interest justifications, rational justifications, and source justifications never disengage from one another in reality. Each reinforces or weakens the others. To extend a metaphor we have already used, to compose and deliver ideal speech is to weave a fabric of thoughts—some having the color of reason, some the color of personal interest, and some the color of *ethos* magnification. The weaver creates the shadings of coloration that will satisfy those who must purchase the cloth—his particular audience.

CLARIFYING AND REINFORCING IDEAS

Most ideas have to be justified in some degree before listeners will accept them. Sometimes this requires that reasons and evidence (DATA and BACKING) be furnished, sometimes that the source of the idea be rendered more credible. Any cluster of statements put into a speech for such justifying purposes will clarify as well as justify. But an attitude-awakening statement or a bit of rational justification may not, by itself, convey enough knowledge or allow time for a listener to apprehend fully what he is supposed to accept. Additional content, inserted primarily to clarify, to detail or reinforce other ideas, is what writers on the art of public speaking have long termed *amplification*. We must therefore consider not just the "proving" that speaking does but the tactics speakers use to clarify, magnify, or otherwise intensify the likelihood that listeners will catch messages as the speakers meant them to. We shall call these *amplifying* procedures or tactics, but we shall try to show how they can yield justifications along with clarification and vivification.

Speakers clarify and amplify their ideas by at least nine common methods which are briefly discussed below. Notice that we are considering *methods* more than materials here; a single piece of material can serve more than a single amplifying or clarifying function.

Introducing Anecdotes

An anecdote is usually a brief narrative illustrating another idea with which it is connected. To clarify or emphasize the damage a storm can produce, you might tell of a family's experience in a tornado. Fables, parables, imagined episodes, or real incidents all provide anecdotal amplification and often, because of their narrative form, dramatization. The chief considerations in using anecdotes are that one needs to keep them short and sharply relevant to the points they are intended to clarify.

An anecdote, like any other example, offers some rational justification of what it illustrates and clarifies. Moreover, like a narrative, an anecdote sets events before hearers in a dynamic, vivid way; this makes it easier to enlist listeners' personal interests and attitudes for or against what is being clarified. Anecdotes contribute more proof by eliciting strong attitudes than by furnishing grounds for rational justification.

Saying "thank you" is often awkward when an occasion is formal. Consider how William Howard Armstrong used an anecdote to "prove" that he genuinely appreciated the Newbery Medal awarded him at the American Library Association's convention at Detroit, on June 30, 1970, for his story *Sounder*. "The boy" in *Sounder* has no other name. Armstrong used both his former phrase, "the boy," and an anecdote from his own life to amplify how and why receiving the equivalent of the Pulitzer Prize (but for children's literature) was a true source of gratitude. Said Mr. Armstrong:

> And now I find myself in the precarious position of having won a prize for a book called *Sounder,* written for anyone who might like to read it.
> Until I received a telephone call from Mary Elizabeth Ledlie some time

in February, the word Newbery had *not* meant to me a man in England who stocked his bookshop with stories for children. [The award is named for such a man.] But Newberry had been a word to stir the deathless joy and remembrance of a small boy's Christmas. Because if that boy were especially good from somewhere around October 27th or November 12th until Christmas, his father would take him to Newberry's five-and-dime store in town. And after he had looked at all the bows and arrows and red wagons, he could ask the jolly, red-coated Santa Claus — enthroned amid the incense of chocolate and peppermint — to leave them under the Christmas tree for him.

But Newberry's Santa Claus never brought the bow and arrows or the red wagon. So out in the back pasture the boy would cut a maple sapling with his two-bladed barlow pocketknife that he had won for selling Cloverine Salve — guaranteed to cure shoulder-gall for horse and chapped lips for man. Then with sapling and binder twine from the hayloft, the boy would make his own bow.

But tonight it is real. The boy will not have to go home and hammer the Newbery Award out of the top of a Campbell soup can or out of a washer off the axle of his father's hay wagon.[17]

Many people have said "thank you," but few have said it with more grace coupled with intense speaker-audience involvement than Mr. Armstrong — through the powers of anecdote.

Comparing and Contrasting

Comparisons and contrasts also clarify and vivify. One may offer metaphors, similes, or antitheses, or compare and contrast anecdotes, examples, whole arguments, or descriptions. Since we acquire many of our new concepts by comparing or contrasting the new with the old, these methods are especially valuable because they use familiar learning processes. And since conflict and similarity are fundamentally interesting to man, all contrasting and comparing vivifies.

An important distinction is that a comparison or contrast, used primarily to prove, needs to be developed with much more attention to the *literal* likenesses and dissimilarities than do comparisons and contrasts used merely to intensify or clarify. When former Vice President Spiro T. Agnew spoke in 1969 of the "privileged *sanctuary*" of a network studio while criticizing network news reporting, he was attaching an *intensifying* image to his view of broadcasters, but not a "proving" one. But even then, the response to his speech showed that many listeners found in this and other purely "intensifying" metaphors (*plus* their own opinions) bits of "rational support." We cannot say that any comparison or contrast is totally without "rational proof" if listeners accept its legitimacy; on the other hand, any comparison that seems "not quite right" or that seems "far-fetched" to listeners can do no more than add color to speech. It will not, then, "prove."

---

17. William H. Armstrong, "Newbery Acceptance Speech." Delivered June 30, 1970, and published in *The Horn Book Magazine*, XLVI (Aug. 1970), 352–355. Printed by permission of the publisher.

Defining

Defining may be accomplished in several ways. Ideas are commonly defined (1) by classifying them; (2) by differentiating them from other ideas that belong to the same class; (3) by exemplifying them; (4) by inferring their natures from the contexts in which they normally occur; (5) by referring to the etymological derivations of their names; (6) by explaining what they are not; (7) by describing or explaining them from some special vantage point (such as specifying what a musical note is if we view it as a complex of sound waves); (8) by specifying functions, as when a child defines an automobile as a thing to ride in.

The most formal kinds of definition are overused in speaking. This is particularly true of "dictionary definitions" that classify terms and define them etymologically. Definitions that compare, contrast, or exemplify are far more interesting and easier to understand. Classifications and derivations usually demand that the listener think abstractly; therefore it is a good rule to offer these definitions only *after* other modes of amplification have been provided. The formal definitions can then function to sum up other, easier-to-understand definitions, as in the first example below.

> To understand what a barge is, think of a railway coal car. [Example.] Take the wheels off the coal car and imagine the ends of the car are well sloped back toward the bottom. [Further detail by example.] Now imagine the wheel-less car floating in the water—a river, a canal, or possibly the sea. You have what is basically a barge: a floating cargo hauler, unpowered, low, and bulky. [Functional definition with characteristics that classify the barge.] A barge, then, is typically an unpowered cargo vessel used for hauling heavy freight. [Most abstract, classifying definition.]

The following amplification through definition is less easy to take in at a single hearing, so less suited to speech:

> A barge is a large, flat-bottomed boat used for transporting goods. While there are powered barges, most are towed. Modern barges are usually bulky vessels used for hauling heavy freight.

The two explanations are the same in content, but the first proceeds from specific examples and comparisons to the abstract. The second proceeds in the opposite order, first confronting the listener with the most difficult form of amplification and only afterward providing specific, concrete information.

Only occasionally do etymological definitions interest and genuinely clarify. It does not help very much to know that the English word *define* comes from the Latin *definire*, meaning "to limit." It is better to say that *define* means to "explain or set forth the limits of something." On the other hand, if you are trying to explain what *habeas corpus* means in law, the shortest, quickest, and most vivid way to do it is probably to tell your listener that the literal Latin meaning of *habeas corpus* is "You may have the body."   In short, etymological definitions are always available to you, but they ought to be used or rejected according to the *practical* help they will give your particular audience.   Discussion of derivations is not inevitably clarifying or interesting.

Describing

When Aristotle noted that all men like communications that set pictures before their eyes, he pinpointed the chief standard by which to judge the value of a description.   Describing is a process of amplification.

Telling anecdotes, comparing and contrasting, and defining emphasize the special details of whatever is being talked about, but describing usually sets the *whole* of something before a listener.   Unless intended to be humorous or ironic, description ought to focus attention on significant rather than trivial aspects of what is being described.   It should also clarify interrelationships or patterns that give the subject its special character, and it should be as pictorial as the content will allow.

Description can contribute rational justification to discourse as well as clarity and liveliness.   Since any describer fits together the elements that go into his description, he always implies that this is the best way of understanding what he is talking about.   And if we accept his description we accept his version of what is "true" of the thing described.

Observe the functions of vivifying and justifying in this description spoken some years ago by a University of Minnesota student who had for a time owned a restaurant in Minneapolis, Minnesota, in its "skid row" district.

> First let's see where they live.   A typical example is the Anchor Hotel on lower Nicollet Avenue in Minneapolis.   This "hotel" has over 100 dingy, airless, and gloomy rooms on one floor, rooms which are separated only by thin plywood. The walls extend six or eight feet toward the ceiling of the large room.   Each cubicle is covered across the top by chicken wire, and contains a bunk-like bed, a battered dresser, and perhaps a crate or box for a chair.   That's all.   Fourteen windows provide ventilation for these one hundred rooms.   The stench which exists, particularly in the summer time, is nauseating and repugnant.   It doesn't sound very pleasant, does it?[18]

Obviously Peter Karos was pictorializing the surroundings of the "alcoholic bums" he was discussing, but there can be no doubt that he created the description of the Anchor Hotel as a *support* for his statement made a few moments earlier: "If I'm able to change your attitude to one of sympathy and understanding—then we have taken the first step towards eliminating these ghettos. . . ."

---

18. Peter A. Karos, "The Haven of the Defeated," *Winning Orations of the Northern Oratorical League, 1945–1950* (Minneapolis: The Northwestern Press, 1951), p. 188.   A full text also appears in C. C. Arnold, D. Ehninger, and J. C. Gerber, *Speaker's Resource Book*, 2nd ed., pp. 148–151.

Exemplifying

Exemplification is probably the most readily available and most useful of all modes of amplification and clarification. Whether factual or hypothetical, examples can focus listeners' attention on just those features of a subject that the speaker most wants understood. All of us have said perplexedly, "Can you give me an example?" We seem to understand specific cases more easily than generalizations, and most of us gain more satisfaction from specific data than from abstractions. Exemplifying, whether as a part of defining or in the form of anecdote or as an element in description, is the speaker's ultimate weapon where clarification and vivification are his principal concerns.

When examples are used primarily to justify rather than simply to illustrate, they need to be checked carefully, for you must be sure they really support what they are intended to support. Furthermore, examples can become so interesting in themselves that even the points they are supposed to support or illustrate are lost. One of our students not long ago tried to illustrate what "spot reporting" is in radio journalism. His example was a tape recording of a network news reporter's on-the-scene, almost hysterical account of the unexpected murder of Lee Harvey Oswald (assassin of President John F. Kennedy) as Oswald was being transferred from his jail cell in Dallas, Texas. As the student might have foreseen, no listener remembered that this was supposed to be an instance of "on the spot reporting." Predictably all questions at the end of the student's talk had to do with details of President Kennedy's assassination and of Oswald's murder. Examples have great fascination for listeners; they need to be chosen to do exactly what you require of them—no more and no less.

Quoting

Quoting other sources can lend justification to what is said. This is especially true and important if your listeners do not consider you a person of authority on the matter you are discussing. Here's a clear example. We are not complete authorities on how this kind of evidence works in speech, but Professor James C. McCroskey has conducted a number of studies on the matter. So, we shall cite his statement:

> . . . we found that a communicator with moderate-to-low ethos could increase his ethos by including factual material and opinions attributed to qualified sources. This effect, however, was not found in connection with all topics. Whether the audience is familiar with the evidence the communicator uses, or with similar evidence, appears to determine whether the communicator may build his ethos by including evidence in his message. If the evidence is unfamiliar to the audience, it has a favorable impact. Otherwise it has no effect. It is

important to observe, however, that the inclusion of evidence has never been found by experimental researchers to lower a communicator's ethos, even if the evidence has been internally inconsistent.[19]

If on reading our quotation and noticing our footnote you tend to think we probably are giving you "solid" information on the uses of quotation, our point is made. By citing an expert, we have "proved" what we had to say about using quoted materials for rational justification of ideas.

But sometimes you will find it useful to quote others because they have simply said things better than you could. It may be that Oliver Wendell Holmes, Jr., spoke more crisply than anyone else when he said, "The reward of the general is not a bigger tent, but command." If you think so, the line may be useful to you as *amplifying* material, but its "proof" function will not be as strong as our quotation from McCroskey. If Holmes had said, "A general of the army is more interested in the size of his command than the size of his office or tent," you could easily have made the point as well as he—in your own words. To quote would then be pointless. We suggest that it is *never* better to speak someone else's words unless the other's words *carry more weight* or *give more clarity and wit* than yours.

Repeating and Restating

Repeating and restating are important amplifying tactics. Listening is not a very efficient way to collect ideas; consequently, speakers have to give their hearers second and third chances to perceive and understand. Research on the usefulness of repetition suggests that with each of your first three repetitions of a given thought you further increase the likelihood that your listeners will actually grasp the idea. It appears that after the third repetition the gains achieved by each succeeding repetition diminish. There is also evidence that repetitions work more effectively when distributed. Apparently, however, this is not always true with restatement—phrasing a given idea in several different ways. Note the clarification and the emphatic force the British historian, essayist, statesman, Thomas Babington Macaulay gave his idea that the British Parliament might get no second chance to reform the representative system of the early nineteenth century:

> Now, therefore, while everything at home and abroad forebodes ruin to those who persist in a hopeless struggle against the spirit of the age; now, while the crash of the proudest throne on the Continent is still resounding in our ears;

---

19. James C. McCroskey, *An Introduction to Rhetorical Communication,* 2nd ed. (Englewood Cliffs, N.J.: Prentice-Hall, Inc., 1972), pp. 72–73. Most of the findings referred to here come from McCroskey's "Experimental Studies of the Effects of Ethos and Evidence in Persuasive Communication," D. Ed. dissertation (The Pennsylvania State University, 1966). See also James C. McCroskey, "A Summary of Experimental Research on the Effects of Evidence in Persuasive Communication," *Quarterly Journal of Speech,* LV (April 1969), 169–176.

now, while the roof of a British palace affords an ignominious shelter to the exiled heir of forty kings; now, while we see on every side ancient institutions subverted and great societies dissolved; now, while the heart of England is still sound; now, while old feelings and old associations retain a power and a charm which may too soon pass away; now, in this your accepted time; now, in this your day of salvation, take counsel, not of prejudice, not of party spirit, not of the ignominious pride of a fatal consistency, but of history, of reason, of the ages which are past, of the signs of this most portentous time.[20]

Here the tightly packed, paralleled restatements of the time-is-running-out theme make Macaulay's meaning unmistakable and the idea impressive. A safe general rule for amplifying through repetition and restatement is to *distribute* repetitions of an idea but to use restatements both sequentially and distributively.

Any repetition—whether in the same or in different terms—increases the probability that the repeated idea will be perceived by a listener. Even unvaried repetitions tend to make listeners accept what they hear as true. In both repeating and restating, the method that clarifies tends also to justify. And if one variously rephrases content so as to awaken strong attitudes—as Macaulay did—a great deal of personal-interest justification can be built into speech even though repetition and restatement are essentially amplifying procedures.

Quantifying

Statistics clarify and often support or prove because they express quantity in the language of numbers. Therein lie the strengths and weaknesses of statistics as amplifying materials.

The danger of highway travel can be variously expressed. One can dramatize it through anecdote or example; one can compare it to the danger of air travel; one can describe congestion and consequent dangers. One can also express this danger statistically; but now one shifts from word symbols to numerical symbols. By this shift we gain much in precision, but we lose much in imagery. We may say there were 500 traffic fatalities in Powhatan County which has a population of 1,500,000 people. This is a precise expression of traffic deaths in that county. But to get this precision, the conditions under which 500 people died, all the consequences of their deaths, and much other information have to be dropped out of the story. We have chosen to represent people and things by numbers. Moreover, the language of numerical expression has specialized rules—a kind of special grammar. What is it the numbers represent? Considering what they represent, and how the counting was done, what may or may not be inferred? What kinds of statistical manipulation are

---

20. "On Parliamentary Reform," an address to the English House of Commons, March 2, 1831. In *Speeches* (New York: Hurst and Co., n.d.), p. 91.

allowable, given these numerical representations of reality? Such are the normal questions any use of numbers raises. Unless you tell your listeners— in so many words—how your statistics may and may not be interpreted, there is a strong possibility your statistical amplifications will confuse or even mislead. This means statistics *alone* are not very useful to listeners; they require numbers *plus* analysis of their meanings. It doesn't mean much to say that in 1960 Kennedy defeated Nixon for President by 118,550 popular votes. It means more to say that this was the voting margin and that there are more people than that in Topeka, Kansas, or Paterson, New Jersey, and that it's only a few thousand more than the population of Pasadena, California. Such distributed comparisons would emphasize the *narrowness* of the margin—which would be the real point of citing the figure.

Even with their limitations, statistics are invaluable amplifying materials wherever quantitative attributes and relationships have to be clarified. Because they are so valuable for these purposes, it is all the more important for you to remember (1) that you must often compensate for the dryness of statistics, and (2) that it is usually not enough merely to supply statistics—you also need to explain their alternative interpretations.

To compensate for the abstractness of statistics and to focus attention, it is well to round off figures (let 1611 become "slightly over sixteen hundred"). It is also useful to present any series of statistics visually as well as orally. Note that concentrated clusters of statistics become confusing. Distribute them within your speech if you would hold attention. Finally, because statistics can only express quantitative attributes and relationships, it is well to amplify them further by using imagistic materials.

Using Audiovisual Aids

Rightly introduced and used, audiovisual aids become valuable amplifying materials which can give you clarity, vividness, and personal-interest or rational justification. The proper reasons for introducing aids are to save or reinforce words, to bring ideas closer to reality, to render the abstract concrete, and to enhance attention through introducing change or movement. Too often speakers associate only charts and graphs with visual aids. The raw materials for audiovisual reinforcements are much more numerous. They include photographs, maps, charts or graphs, models, mock-ups, blackboard drawings, assistants who help with demonstrations, sound movies, slides, video tapes, musical instruments, disc and tape recordings, and still more. But the most versatile and convenient audiovisual aid any speaker has at his disposal is himself. This is a fact you ought never forget. If you do, you may end by neglecting your best and easiest-to-manage resource and involve yourself unnecessarily with gadgets that are less effective than the human body.

One basic principle should be observed in deciding whether to amplify ideas with audiovisual aids: Unless the aid is less complicated than the idea being clarified it will confuse or distract. Specific considerations are important too. Any aid you use must be relevant and well timed. Your listener demands as the price of attention that whatever aids you use be: see-able or hearable or both, understandable, and interesting. The speaking situation will determine what is tasteful and appropriate, and what physical properties the aid must have to be seen, heard, and understood. You (or someone available to help you) must be able to manage and control your aids without disturbing the intimate relationship you need always to maintain with your audience. There is nothing intrinsically wrong with an hour-long documentary film or a twenty-minute segment of an opera, but *speech* cannot *contain* either because the speaker cannot maintain a continuing association with his hearers.

There seems almost no end to the ways in which audiovisual aids can be misused in speaking situations; almost all misuses grow out of disregard for the fact that audiovisual aids potentially endanger the speaker's own mastery of purpose, audience, and occasion. "Who is in charge?" is always a pertinent question when audiovisual aids are brought in. The following true story presents a set of extreme circumstances, but it illustrates how and why unsophisticated use of audiovisual amplification can turn a speech into something very different.

The student's chosen subject was "The Treatment of Snakebite." Having introduced his subject, he startled his audience by releasing a white rat from a cardboard canister. The speaker announced that the rat's name was Maudie, and whipped out a hypodermic needle. Plunging the needle into Maudie, he explained that he was giving the animal an injection of snake venom. Maudie would expire within a few seconds. Meanwhile, he would explain what steps a human being should take if bitten by a poisonous snake. To clarify these steps the speaker now drew grease-pencilled lines and circles on his forearm to indicate where incisions should be made in cases of snakebite. But Maudie was dragging herself about, gasping her last in full view of everyone. Naturally, her troubles drew even the speaker's attention away from his explanations. He interrupted himself to comment: "Oh, yes. Bleeding at the mouth—quite natural at this stage." The speech, of course, was a failure, as any thoughtful person could have foretold from the moment this speaker decided to introduce poor Maudie as an "aid."

Quite apart from the charges of cruelty and bad taste with which listener-spectators had every right to counter this speaker's claims to good sense and good character, the poisoning of a rat was foreseeably irrelevant to his purpose. It would set in motion forces he could not control, and it was predestined to direct attention away from his message. Movement, attitudes of revulsion, surprise, the life-death contest, grim realism, suspense would be at work to grip listeners' attention. No comparable forces would be working for the speaker's message—however good his grease-pencil drawings or his exposition of them. Any speaker who introduces charts that are too detailed or passes items through the audience while he talks or involves himself with overly complicated mechanisms makes the same fundamental mistake as Maudie's executioner: he abdicates his proper position of command.

What we want you to see is that audiovisual materials used for their own sakes can overwhelm speaker and speech. "A picture is worth a thousand words," it is said.   But if pictures or other nonspeech content can convey one's entire message, the speaker ought to send the pictures and omit the speech.

Without doubt, audiovisual resources can be exceptionally effective means of clarifying, vivifying, and proving.   The variety of these resources multiplies as graphic and acoustic technologies advance, and we cannot possibly illustrate and discuss their full potentialities.   However, to stimulate your consideration of what may effectively aid your speech, we offer a partial list of audiovisual materials which speakers have successfully (and unsuccessfully) used:

The object itself
Models: complete, cut-away, mock-ups
Motion picture film clips
Photographic slides
Photographic enlargements
Maps
Blackboard or other sketches, diagrams, outlines
Graphs: bar graphs, pie graphs, pictorial graphs
Schematic representations: organizational charts, genealogical charts, etc.
Sound tapes and disc recordings
Video tapes
Other people: as demonstration assistants, examples, etc.
Staged scenes

The list could be extended.   The point to understand is that any device whatever which will present an idea to the five senses — sight, hearing, touch, taste, and smell — can clarify, vivify, and prove what you want to tell through speech.

A few *do's* concerning the effective use of audiovisual resources deserve to be remembered as important guidelines:

1. Introduce visual and other external resources where you think your best verbal-personal presentation is likely to fall short of complete clarity.
2. Always *verbalize* what it is your listeners are *supposed* to see, hear, and understand from any audiovisual resources you introduce.
3. Where more than a few seconds are to be devoted to an aid, let your hearers know what they are to learn from it *before* introducing it; then, restate what should have been learned *after* using the aid.
4. Design or edit all aids to eliminate or hide objects and material that are irrelevant to your immediate purpose.   Eliminate whatever might send listeners' thoughts in directions you do not wish them to go.
5. Use your aid where you need it, then get it out of sight and hearing so your audience cannot dwell on it when you want them to attend to something else.

6. If possible, pretest sight lines and sound levels from all positions in which listeners will be during your speech. And pretest the workings of your aid if it has to operate in any way.
7. Give *your* attention to the audience when using audiovisual aids, not to the devices. You are still the *chief* messenger, and your listeners need your attention even though they are receiving part of your message through another source.
8. Always prefer the *simplest* form of audiovisual stimuli capable of doing what you need done. For the same reasons, keep machinery to the minimum for getting your task done.

The most important advice for all speakers who take advantage of audiovisual resources is: *Keep yourself in charge* and *maintain the closest possible personal relation with your hearers.* You are still the chief messenger!

We do not believe any authors, teachers, or other advisers can plausibly say to you: "This is precisely the way to compose a speech." In the last several chapters we have been trying to say: "When you compose *any* speech for *any* situation, you have at your disposal this large array of resources and tactics for fitting your message and yourself to the rhetorical situation you will enter." To this we can only add that you will be especially well advised to review your choices of speech materials a final time, once you have selected them. At that point hold in your mind the general proposition that *variety* is also a quality that contributes to holding listeners' interest and encouraging their belief in what you say. Ask yourself whether your speech materials not only serve your purposes but serve by giving your listeners a variety of *kinds* of information. Look back to Chapter 3 at the table of "Special Resources in Ideas and Language" (pages 62–64) and ask whether your materials and the ways you plan to use them will take the fullest possible advantage of these opportunities to make your talk interesting. Sometimes a few substitutions of materials here and there can give speech variety in method and so enhance its impact.

In this chapter we have set out the importance of making clear, at least to yourself, the purpose of your communication. We have considered the possibilities and importance of combining personal-interest, rational, and source justifications so your listeners will find "good reasons" for listening to you and for believing you. We pointed out nine other ways available to you for clarifying, vivifying, and indirectly supporting what you believe. Exactly how you will blend these types of material will depend partly on your subject and partly on your relation to your subject and to the needs of your listeners and the social groups and systems to which they belong. What blend of content is right, only your judgment can determine. We hope to have offered sound suggestions for *ways* of thinking about such matters. If you *always* keep your listeners' needs, values, attitudes, and goals in mind when discovering and choosing speech materials, you will be taking the most important step toward sound inventional decisions.

What you want to accomplish with your audience puts some special constraints on rhetorical invention, of course. We shall therefore conclude our study of invention by considering in the next chapter what special tactics are yours depending on whether you plan to inform, inquire, reinforce views, persuade, or entertain.

EXERCISES

Written

1. Before beginning other preparation for your next speech write out a "Choice of Subject" paper containing the following information: (a) an exact statement of your proposed speech subject; (b) an exact statement of your specific purpose; (c) a brief essay explaining why your subject and purpose are timely, significant for you and your audience, amenable to oral presentation, and manageable in the time available. Present this to your instructor for evaluation or have two or three classmates read it over and tell you whether they understand exactly what it is you plan and whether it seems a wise plan for the audience you will meet.

2. Evaluate each of the following statements. Indicate how well each meets the criteria for good expression of a specific purpose. Properly rephrase any statement you find unsatisfactory in wording.

    a. Don't adopt the sales tax.

    b. This is a speech to clarify the processes by which committee chairmen are chosen in the United States Senate.

    c. I want to explain that women ought to receive the same pay as men when they perform the same jobs and that in general their equality with men should be universally recognized.

    d. Economic and social effects of the growth in the United States' tourist industries since 1960.

    e. It takes study to appreciate the art of motion pictures.

3. As you prepare your next talk, label in the margins of your outline what *kind* of supporting or amplifying material you are planning to use at each point. Then write a short paragraph contending that you have achieved the best degree of *variety* in supporting material that is open to you. Discuss your defense with your instructor or one or two of your classmates.

4. Identify and evaluate (a) the kinds of justification and (b) the forms of amplification used in the following excerpt from Leonard Bernstein's lecture, "The World of Jazz":

> But I find I have to defend jazz to those who say it is low-class. As a matter of fact, all music has low-class origins, since it comes from folk music, which is necessarily earthy. After all, Haydn minuets are only a refinement of simple, rustic German dances, and so are Beethoven scherzos. An aria from a Verdi opera can often be traced back to the simplest Neapolitan fisherman. Besides, there has always been a certain shadow of indignity around music, particularly around the players of music.
>
> I suppose it is due to the fact that historically *players* of music seem to lack the dignity of *composers* of music. But this is especially true of jazz, which is almost completely a player's art, depending as it does on improvisation rather than on

composition. But this also means that the player of jazz is himself the real composer, which gives him a creative, and therefore *more* dignified status.[21]

Oral

1. With a group of four or five classmates choose a subject to talk about. Almost any subject will do. Assign to each member of the group *one* of the nine ways of clarifying and reinforcing ideas discussed on pages 124–135. Have each member of the group prepare a 1-minute statement about the agreed-upon subject, using primarily the single method of clarifying and reinforcing ideas that was assigned to him. After each group member speaks, discuss the advantages and disadvantages *any* speaker will face when he chooses to amplify ideas by that method.

2. Working in groups as suggested in Exercise 1 above, assign each group member the task of using *one* of the three ways of building "proof" discussed on pages 106–124 in a 1-minute talk about some aspect of the topic the group has chosen. Following each presentation discuss how the 1-minute talk could have been made stronger (a) by using additional kinds of justification for what was said and (b) by better use of the particular kind of justification assigned to the speaker.

3. Using a group like that suggested in Exercises 1 and 2 above, choose a subject for an imaginary speech to be given in a situation you have imaginatively worked out. In group discussion phrase the ideal central idea for the imaginary speech, agree on what main points ought to be made about it, and make a list of what tactics of invention would be especially important in developing each point.

4. Prepare and deliver a one-point informative speech in which you use at least four different forms of amplification.

5. Prepare and present a short speech on some aspect of a subject you know your classmates disagree about. Try to build enough rational justification into your speech to satisfy a skeptical listener. After the speech, invite a listener who agrees with you and one who still disagrees with you to evaluate how well you proved your point. Conduct a class discussion of their evaluations of your proof.

6. Present an oral report on an advertisement or advertising campaign. Discuss the ways in which personal-interest, rational, and source justifications are used in this advertising.

21. From Leonard Bernstein's televised lecture "The World of Jazz," in *The Joy of Music* (New York: Simon and Schuster, 1959), p. 97. Used by permission of the author.

CHAPTER
6

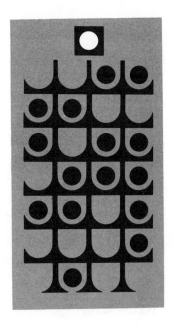

Invention
in Relation
to Purposes

This chapter concludes our consideration of the discovery and selection of what to say in a speech. In Chapters 3, 4, and 5 we tried to generalize about all speeches and all speakers. But your specific purpose affects your choice and management of what to say. Here, then, we shall examine how each of the normal objectives in speaking (to inform, to induce inquiry, to reinforce, to persuade, to entertain) influences your choices.

SPEAKING TO INFORM

There are times when speakers are fully satisfied if their hearers understand what is said. Then we tend to think of their talk as informative. We could as easily call it explanatory or expository. A teacher's lecture and a physician's explanation of how a disease must be treated are examples of this kind of speech. Whether understanding is a speaker's overall objective or the objective of only a part of his talk, the aim to inform requires him to find particular kinds of material and use them in special ways that meet the distinctive standards listeners impose when asked to accept knowledge understandingly.

What kinds of content are especially appropriate when you set out to inform? Any material clarifying such attributes and relationships of a subject as are listed on page 79, excepting the attribute of desirability. Also, whatever clarifies any of the five relationships listed on page 79 will be potentially informative. Material that concerns the *desirability* of anything is never purely informative. It implicitly or explicitly raises questions about debatable matters: "goods," "bads," "betters," "poorers." Material that affirms or denies desirability forces speaker and listener into the realm of persuasion. However informative, talk about desirabilities must always be persuasive as well. The result is that a speaker who raises questions of desirability must meet the standards of persuasive speaking as a purely informative speaker need not.

The standards peculiar to informative speaking are: (1) *accuracy,* being true to fact in both detail and proportion; (2) *completeness,* being comprehensive enough to cover the subject promised by the specific purpose; and (3) *unity,* providing knowledge that will be intelligible as a whole. Like many other propositions about oral communication, these standards of good informative speaking are simply the expectations of audiences. When a speaker indicates he wants us to understand, we begin watching whether what he says seems "true," whether there is enough detail to allow us a "full" understanding, and whether what we are being told "adds up" to anything that seems to "fit together."

Mistakes in Explaining

A speaker who undertakes to explain how a tape recorder works will err if he seems to say that all tape recorders use cassettes (many use reels); he will err in a different way if he says nothing about the different playback systems recorders have; and he will err in another fashion if he does not recognize that the whole idea of having a tape recorder is to preserve sound and to reproduce it conveniently. If a speaker makes all three errors, he will have violated all the basic demands listeners place on people who try to inform them. He may not be rejected for an error of fact or an omission of some details or for not saying why what he is talking of exists, but unless these mistakes and omissions are corrected in the listeners' own minds they will understand less than the speaker's full explanation.

Another mistake common in giving information is failing to "pull the details together." A way to protect yourself against this is to write out your specific purpose and then examine it carefully to see that your statement expresses all, but no more than, you want your listeners to understand. A very good practice is the following. Write the words: "When I finish I want my listeners to understand *that. . . .*" Insert after "that," a single clause completing the sentence and expressing what you want to accomplish. "When I finish I want them to understand *that* the Battle of Gettysburg was a battle of maneuver rather than firepower," is a precise subject sentence. "When I finish I want my listeners to understand the Battle of Gettysburg" is useless as a subject sentence because it gives you no focus and promises the listener no clear prevision of what it is he is supposed to learn.

Even if audiences didn't need so much help in discovering what you do and don't intend to cover, your own self-interest argues for taking great care in phrasing subject sentences whenever you plan to talk informatively. Without expressing your purpose to yourself in exact terms you are likely to try to cover too much, to gather material you cannot use, and to have trouble organizing your ideas.

Maintaining Interest

Maintaining interest is also often difficult in talking to inform. Some material does not have inherent qualities that draw attention. Then you will need to choose special materials that associate these qualities with what you explain. Through special attention to style and delivery you may also be able to intensify the attention value of what you say. Specific examples, comparisons and contrasts, brief narratives, real and figurative analogies are especially useful. So are all facts that are close to the experience of your listeners—even facts that appear threatening.

The anatomy of the housefly does not seem a subject on which to build an engrossing speech, but a student speaker did just that by finding concrete and threatening amplifying materials. The housefly is hairy. This unexciting fact assumed significance when the speaker amplified it by saying that the fly's body hairs are easily befouled as he moves around filth, and the same hairs easily pollute human food when the fly later alights on it. The fly's digestive system is not universally arousing, but the speaker centered her exposition on the fact that the insect's digestive system is not capable of handling dry matter, thus it is necessary for him to salivate or regurgitate on dry food in order that he may wet it and make it edible. In explaining the mouth, legs, and wings of the fly the speaker used visual aids and other attention-compelling methods. That exposition of the housefly's anatomy did not lack for attention or understanding. Our discussion of Bob Barth's speech on jet engines (see Chapter 4, pages 96–97) illustrates comparable ingenuity in locating the kinds of information that compensate for remoteness, technicality, or dullness of subject matters which must be lucidly explained.

Speakers often neglect another opportunity when explaining difficult subjects. It is the opportunity to treat the subject matter *as if* it were other than it literally is.

No one has ever seen a sound wave. Sound waves do not behave precisely like the water waves we call ripples. Nonetheless, it is customary to explain part of the behavior of sound waves *as if* the waves acted as ripples spreading outward when a stone is dropped into water. There are many aspects of sound that cannot be explained properly by this *as-if* treatment; nevertheless, the treatment will serve as long as we confine our attention to specific aspects of how sound waves spread out from their source. The whole point of hunting for *as-if* treatments is that people build new knowledge upon the knowledge they already have—through comparison and contrast. Some aspects of a steel rolling mill can be made both clear and interesting if we think of the steel *as if* it were dough and the mill *as if* it were equipped with kitchen rolling pins. One must be careful that listeners understand that an *as-if* treatment is not a discussion of actuality; yet, informative speakers should search for such potentially useful ways of explaining.

Other Valuable Materials

Several other kinds of materials are especially valuable in informative speaking. Types of material that clarify were discussed in Chapter 5 (pages 124–135). Of special use are comparisons and contrasts, definitions that exemplify and specify functions, descriptions, examples, restatements, and presenting information through visual aids as well as speech.

We have been discussing informative speaking *as if* information-giving really existed completely apart from inquiry, reinforcement, persuasion, or entertainment. It seldom does, but we can talk clearly of only one thing at a time. Clear explanations persuade us to believe; they encourage us to seek more knowledge; they reinforce our feelings; and they are often entertaining in the sense that new learning is pleasing. Good informative speaking frequently persuades. When President Nixon announced his then unexpected "price-wage freeze" in 1971, he "explained" the policy and also sought to persuade people to accept. Or consider a different situation: If a speaker tries to explain methods of contraception, he will almost surely be interpreted as endorsing their use. On controversial matters "pure" explanation is almost impossible just because speakers are naturally thought to "stand with" whatever they present, however dispassionately. It is also often the case that the strongest persuasion is the clearest exposition of how and why things *are* as you say.

To summarize, your main goal may be to inform people. When it is, the important thing is to be careful to specify to yourself (and usually to your auditors) exactly what you want understood. Information about any characteristic of what you explain *may* be useful, except that statements about its desirability will always involve you in persuading listeners to believe your *endorsement* of the subject as well as your explanation of it. When your main business is to clarify and amplify, comparisons, contrasts, references to what is familiar, examples, narratives, and analogies are likely to be especially useful to you because these materials tend to provide "built-in" elements that draw and hold attention. And you ought not forget that those who inform accurately, fully, and pointedly often turn out to be the most persuasive of communicators!

SPEAKING TO INDUCE INQUIRY

Do speakers ever address others without having the "answers"? Unquestionably, though when this happens the audience is likely to be small and select. An executive or chairman meeting his staff or committee often has to set out the nature of a problem before asking for discussion through which it is to be solved. To take a more formal case, a city manager may have to describe to a mass meeting the nature of his city's water-supply crisis, and present alternatives from which the citizens must choose a solution.

Creating a Spirit for Inquiry

If group problem solving is a part of the work of your class, you will notice that creating a spirit of inquiry is the primary goal expert chairmen seek to attain in their opening remarks.   And a formal speech to induce inquiry is simply a longer presentation of the ideas that under different circumstances would have formed the agenda of an inquiring discussion group.

If you look about you, you will see more speech aimed at inducing inquiry than you may have expected.   One apartment mate may notice a sink drain is slow.   What shall we do?   Consult the landlord or superintendent?   Let it go?   Try to fix it ourselves?   Call and pay a plumber ourselves?   The person noticing the problem may bring it up with his or her partners, describing and estimating the problem, expressing what "ought to be," and reviewing the possible actions.   Or in another case any of us might introduce into conversation the question of what policy our government should have toward conscientious objectors.   If we wanted serious discussion of that issue, we might speak for a few moments, not merely informing in the usual sense but not persuading either except to the extent of trying to make the others see that the subject deserves serious reflection, now.   In such speech situations speakers usually want to set out the conditions within which a solution needs to be found and to stimulate listeners to look for, evaluate, and choose a desirable solution.   They may even be trying to encourage discussion in open forums that they expect to follow their remarks.[1]

Questions and Answers

The subject sentence of any continuous remarks to induce inquiry ought to express a precise question to be answered.   Such a sentence might be put thus: "When I finish I want the audience to be prepared and motivated to answer the question, '..?'"   The words, "be prepared and motivated," represent key aspects of the inquiring speaker's assignment.   Whether he puts these words in a formal statement of purpose or not, his function is always to pave the way for a serious search for real answers. To do this he must explain the problem and, insofar as he can foresee, suggest directions in which a viable solution might be looked for.   These parts of his task are primarily informative, but unless he can also answer his hearers' ever-present question, "Why should *I* care?" little will result from his speech. Whoever undertakes to induce inquiry must accept the dual responsibilities of preparing and motivating his audience to try to solve a problem.

The fact that people who speak to induce inquiry do not "know the answers" frequently keeps them from even identifying the proper *questions!* People can be sensitive to difficulties and have standards or goals by which to

1. Exposition of this kind of speaking may also be found in J. H. McBurney and Ernest J. Wrage, *The Art of Good Speech* (New York: Prentice-Hall, 1953), chap. 13, "The Methods of Inquiry."   Recognition that formal speaking of this kind does occur can be found in the writings of Cicero and Quintilian and even in the works of lesser but earlier authors.   Our discussion of this topic draws upon many of these sources and, at several points, goes somewhat beyond what has heretofore been said.

measure solutions and yet possess no clear idea of what question needs solving. An English writer, Arthur Young, noticed this state of mind among the revolutionists in France in 1792:

> I have been in much company all day, and cannot but remark, that there seem to be no settled ideas of the best means of forming a new constitution. . . . In these most interesting discussions, I find a general ignorance of the principles of government; a strange and unaccountable appeal, on one side, to ideal and visionary rights of nature; and, on the other, no settled plan that shall give security to the people for being in future in a much better situation than hitherto; . . .[2]

Young identified a great source of difficulty in France at the time of the Revolution. Most leaders simply lacked the wisdom or experience to distinguish among: questions inviting inquiry, questions that must be debated in order to choose or not choose a solution already known, and philosophical questions ("rights of nature") to which no *final* answer could ever be found. They framed and debated philosophical questions, not questions of practical action. Some of the excesses of the period occurred because they debated their philosophical questions as though they were issues of absolute and practical right and wrong.

A campus speaker who says he wants to raise the question, "What is student government good for?" or "What are the inalienable rights of women?" or "Is racism eradicable in America?" is in the same difficulty as the French leaders. The speaker senses that problems exist but frames questions having no clear, final answers. The questions invite interminable debate about definitions and values; they postpone the possibility of practical, improving action. The poser of such questions does not recognize, as most philosophers do, that for every philosophical proposition about a definition or value there is, somewhere, an alternative proposition; this is the reason definitions and values are matters of debate from generation to generation. Meanwhile people have to *choose* from among *available* definitions and *choose* among conflicting values to get their daily business done. The student speaker we are imagining really wants to alter events, but he poses questions as though matters concerning "good," "inalienable rights," and the *future* of "racism" could be *settled* by discussion and debate. If change must wait for agreement on such questions, there will be little change at all.

Differences in Questions

Anyone wanting to induce inquiry for other than purely learning purposes needs to recognize that questions of fact (especially *future* fact) and philosophical definition can only be *judged*; they do not in themselves generate thinking

2. *Travels in France.* Quoted in *The Debate on the French Revolution, 1789–1800,* ed. Alfred Cobban (London: Nicholas Kaye, 1950), pp. 51–52.

about practical alternatives. Questions of policy and of action serve best to generate inquiry because people can agree — temporarily at least — on *practical* definitions and move from these to weigh the *apparent* wisdom of alternatives. Our campus speaker must decide whether to try to invoke inquiry about practical alternatives or seek philosophical reflection, without limits, on the uses of government in general. This speaker needs to decide whether listeners are to think about student government *as a concept* or search for answers to specific problems existing *in* student government on a specific campus. It is equally necessary to decide whether listeners are to study how to produce some kind of "Bill of Rights for Women" or try to locate *actions* that could enhance the day-to-day rights of women. On racism the issue is whether to invite a search for some prophetic pronouncement about the future or a search for courses of action that might minimize or eliminate racially discriminatory behavior.

Our point is that if you want to open practical inquiry instead of lengthy philosophical discussion or extended debate, you need to be very careful about what your questions *seem* to ask your listeners to do. If you phrase questions so you seem to ask for decrees, definitions, and decisions about ultimate values, you may not be replaced by Napoleon as the French revolutionaries were, but you will tend to invoke exchanges that produce only opinions but not actions. It is therefore especially important that your subject sentences in speaking to invoke inquiry be precisely phrased to invite exactly the *kind* of inquiry you want.

Phrasing your subject sentence is important also because the sentence must not only define the kind of inquiry wanted but pose a problem that can be dealt with in the time at your listeners' disposal and one that can be solved through the listeners' available knowledge and other resources. Problems need not be *completely* answerable to be worthy of inquiring consideration, but at least your listeners ought to be able to make satisfying progress toward a final answer. If they have too little time or too few resources to allow any decisions at all, your invitation to inquire can only frustrate them.

Distinctive Aspects

With a single exception, the kinds of ideas that can be pertinent to inquiry are like those appropriate to informing. The exception is that *desirability* is a topic that *must* be treated if the problem to be explored involves *policies*. For example, whether campus conduct should be regulated by student government finally becomes a question of whether such regulation would be desirable. It is the same with virtually all questions about courses of action or about how values ought to be applied. The desirability of such actions or applications must at some point be explored, either by you or by those who pick up the inquiry after you have stimulated it.

The distinctive pattern of organization into which main ideas fall in a speech of inquiry is discussed in Chapter 7 (pages 183–185). The divisions of an inquiry are useful guides to the materials needed in developing speech of this kind.

Inquiring speech normally begins with discussion of a problem and proceeds toward solutions deserving consideration by reasonable people. This kind of thought movement is not inherently interesting. The speaker, and therefore the listener, moves from point to point with judgment suspended. Even at his close, the inquirer may or may not have revealed a preferred solution. There are, thus, few natural climaxes. There is no inherent sense of energetic progress or satisfying release from the tensions. In return for asking his listeners to defer judgment and to sustain the tensions of inquiry, the speaker ought to repay them by using the most interesting clarifying and vivifying materials available to him. He ought to use those amplifying tactics that do most to aid his auditors to grasp his message (see Chapter 5, pages 124–135).

An inquiring speaker assumes a special leadership role. He presides over a collaborative search for a "best choice." In this role he must be careful to demonstrate his own knowledge of the subject, his impartiality concerning the decisions he is asking his listeners to make, and his candor in dealing with both content and listeners. Few tactics are more resented than attempts to maneuver audiences toward a preselected conclusion under the pretense of inviting them to inquire freely.

Questions, not propositions, stimulate inquiry; so, the subject sentences of speeches to induce inquiry ought to contain clear expressions of potentially answerable questions. Where the issue for inquiry concerns a matter of policy, *desirability* and all the other attributes and relationships we commonly talk about can suggest discussable aspects of the problem and of solutions. Because of their inductive character, speeches of inquiry usually need to be specially enlivened by the most interesting amplifying tactics that are available and relevant. Those who induce inquiry assume the roles of informant and leader; therefore all they do and say must show their personal qualifications for these roles.

SPEAKING TO REINFORCE BELIEFS AND FEELINGS

From time to time we speak simply to reinforce existing beliefs and feelings. We speak of the values of education on a commencement day; we assure a friend that he is right in claiming that it takes more brains to play football than to play baseball. The aim of such talk is to make the listener feel or believe something more than ever or, possibly, to make him prefer some of his beliefs over others.

Speech that reinforces beliefs and feelings is a kind of persuasion. We are considering this kind of speech apart from what we shall shortly call "persuasion" for two reasons. The materials you need for reinforcement are unique, and when you develop points and themes in this kind of speaking you will amplify more than you will justify.

Limitation in Ideas

When you set out to reinforce beliefs or feelings, your search for discussable ideas becomes limited to ideas your listeners already have some knowledge about. Whether you talk about education, physical fitness, or scientific method you will locate your most useful ideas for reinforcement *in the knowledge and attitudes your listeners already possess.* When you have found these, your task is to develop those themes in ways that connect these ideas *with important values the listeners already have.* The essential process of reinforcing beliefs and feelings is connecting familiar ideas and attitudes with *high* (or low) values. To this extent, speaking to reinforce allows you, as speaker, the least intellectual freedom of any customary type of speaking. You work within the framework of your listeners' *existing* beliefs, feelings, and value systems. This is why speaking to reinforce can be heard in all societies, no matter how totalitarian or censorious. Even where freedom of speech is closely restricted, there will always be some approved ideas and some "proper" values which can be extolled. And there will be certain "improper" ideas which can be connected with "improper" values for purposes of denunciation. Hence, speaking to reinforce (positively and negatively) occurs in all known cultures and social systems.

Uses of This Type of Speaking

Despite its limitations, speaking to reinforce beliefs and feelings has important uses. Through it, religious congregations are sustained and social and political virtues such as pride and mutual respect are maintained as active forces. Indeed, the shared values that bind us into social groups form the subjects of most of the important reinforcing communication that occurs. Without reinforcement through speech and other media, social bonds would begin to atrophy and any society would begin to drift toward anarchism.

The audience determines on what subjects a speech of reinforcement may be made. Whatever the audience already believes or disbelieves and whatever values they hold in high esteem or plainly reject can become subject matter. (One can reinforce disbelief or rejection as readily as belief or acceptance.) But not every existing belief or disbelief is appropriate for discussion at any time. People who attend meetings of ethnic groups indicate by attending that their beliefs about nationality or race are, just then, of high importance. Whoever addresses such a meeting must recognize that it is beliefs about nationality or race that are to be reinforced and not, say, beliefs about commerce or education. But many persons who attend such meetings will also be members of business, educational, and political groups; nonetheless, during an ethnic gathering these people will be only secondarily conscious of their other associations. They will be unready to hear commercial, educational, or partisan talk unless ethnic values are stressed. The same people may on another day gather as businessmen or as political partisans. Then, there will be occasion for reinforcing beliefs about business and politics. The same general situation applies in religious convocations, educational commencements, lodge meetings, voters' groups, and so on. Wherever there is *an* identification among all or most listeners, there is occasion and often need for reinforcement of beliefs and feelings through connecting familiar ideas with the familiar values that bind the hearers together.

What we have just said implies that rhetorical situations inviting speech that reinforces are often ceremonial, but not invariably so. Anniversaries, religious and other observances, rituals of various sorts, "kick off" meetings, locker-room half-time sessions, rallies of all sorts are among the situations that invite speech that reinforces beliefs and feelings. But so, also, do dating and lovemaking!

Procedure

Assuming a moderately formal circumstance for reinforcing speech, how does one proceed after having taken inventory of the listeners' known ideas, attitudes, and values? You ask what the exigences are—the special needs—of the situation and select themes or a specific subject that fits those needs. Now it will be time to formulate a subject sentence that can guide you in searching for further materials and composing an appropriate message. You will help yourself and your listeners if you adopt the following formula for framing the subject sentences you use in this type of speaking. Write the words, "When I finish I want my listeners to (believe, feel) (more, less) strongly *that* ....
..............." Compose a clause to follow the word "that." Decide whether it is predominantly "belief" or "feeling" you wish to intensify or diminish, and eliminate either "more" or "less" according to your intention. A finished subject sentence might read: "When I finish I want my listeners to *believe more* strongly *that* personal acts of pollution control are worth doing."

The unique feature of a subject sentence for reinforcing is that it ought to express the *degree* of intensification or diminution for which you are going to strive. And it is useful to express, too, whether it will be ideas or emotions on which you will concentrate. Our formula will remind you of both needs.

Except for the limitations we have discussed, the reinforcing speaker's search for ideas differs little from the searching we discussed in Chapter 4. Any of the attributes we commonly assign to things and people and any of the relationships we commonly assert or argue (see page 79) can suggest potentially discussable themes for justifying greater or less belief or feeling. There are, however, two special bits of advice that can help you when you aim to reinforce.

We borrow our first piece of advice from Aristotle, who observed that in his day speeches of reinforcement consistently made beliefs or feelings impressive (or unimpressive) by connecting them with recognized "goods" or their opposites. He saw speakers linking ideas with justice, courage, temperance, grandeur, liberality, gentleness, prudence, wisdom, etc. He contended that ideas seem more, or less, impressive depending on how much they contribute to or are consistent with these qualities and others the listeners admire. If you will listen to reinforcing speech in our own day, you will find it working in just this way. So, in amplifying your themes or "points" you will be well advised to show that the beliefs or feelings you are magnifying or diminishing enhance or diminish the major "goods" your listeners prize generally and prize specially because of the rhetorical situation they are part of.

The other item of special advice is: It is better to develop a train of thought that is simple and clear than to try to render an idea impressive in several different ways. Enlargement of an idea is preferable to multiplying its features. An ancient Greek speech is still an ideal model in this respect. In his famous funeral oration commemorating the bravery of Athenians who had died in the first year of the Peloponnesian Wars, Pericles expressed the pith of his whole discourse thus:

> Taking everything together then, I declare that our city is an education to Greece, and I declare that in my opinion each single one of our citizens, in all the manifold aspects of life, is able to show himself the rightful lord and owner of his own person, and do this, moreover, with exceptional grace and exceptional versatility.[3]

His whole address, as Thucydides reports it, merely amplifies these tightly related thoughts concerning the city for which the dead had fought. A lesser speaker might have insisted on discussing the way the heroes died, the justice of the war, the qualities of victories and defeats, and the gratitude of living Athenians—all in a misguided effort to multiply listeners' feelings of gratitude to the dead. Pericles wisely chose a single theme and amplified it: Athens' worth ennobles its fallen soldiers. His speech had focus.

Distinctive Aspects

What makes speech to reinforce successful? You need to amplify hitherto unnoticed connections between "goods" your listeners already value and the

---

3. Thucydides, *The Peloponnesian War*, trans. Rex Warner (Baltimore: Penguin Books, 1954), p. 119.

idea or attitude you want to reinforce. Some examples will illustrate ways of doing this, and you can work out other variations on the basic method.

In 1967, a Purdue University freshman named Charles Jarrow gave an unusual speech which he called "The Case for the Non-Voter." He wanted to *diminish* belief in the desirability of having a high turnout of voters in elections and *magnify* confidence in present American practices in voting. To do these things he first noted that although enlarging the percentage of regular voters is an almost sacred ambition of many Americans, the highest turnouts of voters actually occur in *totalitarian* countries where elections "are actually meaningless." Having given "high turnout" this negative association with totalitarianism, Jarrow compared voting in the United States with voting in other *democratically* governed countries. This showed that "their voting percentages match ours quite closely." Thus present practice was positively associated with democracy. Finally, Jarrow showed that those who do not vote regularly in the United States are actually the *least informed* among the eligible voters; thus, said he, "we have what might be termed a kind of 'natural selection' among voters," and we should be thankful for it.[4] By the end of the speech Jarrow had affirmatively associated admiration for democracy and informed voting with the *status quo,* and distrust of totalitarianism and uninformed voting with high turnouts at the polls. We may suppose he at least unsettled some values by these strategies of reinforcement.

Winston Churchill used the same general methods of associating values, making vital and important the rather platitudinous notion that the British and the Americans should "never cease to proclaim . . . the greater principles of freedom and the rights of man which are the joint inheritance of the English-speaking world." To reinforce this idea he said:

> . . . this means that the people of any country have the right . . . to choose or change the character or form of government under which they dwell; that freedom of thought should reign; that courts of justice, independent of the executive, . . . should administer laws which have received the broad assent of large majorities or are consecrated by time and custom. Here are the title deeds of freedom which should lie in every cottage home. Here is the message of the British and American peoples to mankind.[5]

Undoubtedly Churchill's careful choice of value-laden words helped to make the virtues of self-government, freedom of speech and thought, and independent courts of popular law dignify the importance of "proclaiming."

Abraham Lincoln used the same general methods at Gettysburg; however, he found the virtues he would speak of by studying the *setting* for his

---

4. Charles Jarrow, "The Case for the Non-Voter," in *On Speech and Speakers,* H. Bruce Kendall and Charles J. Stewart, eds. (New York: Holt, Rinehart and Winston, Inc., 1968), pp. 229–231.
5. "The Sinews of Peace," delivered at Westminster College, Fulton, Missouri, March 5, 1946. The text of this speech (also called "The Iron Curtain Speech") is available in many sources. Quoted here from *The Sinews of Peace: Post-War Speeches by Winston S. Churchill,* Randolph S. Churchill, ed. (Boston: Houghton Mifflin Company, 1949), p. 97.

speech. He found them in the familiar dedicatory scene. Simply to "dedicate this cemetery" would not sufficiently dignify the occasion, he seems to
have thought. To the ordinary act, he attached the value-laden concept,
"dedicate ourselves." And this idea was in turn associated with still higher
national goals. Thus, he reinforced the notion that the military cemetery was
important as both a personal and a national symbol.

Though undertaking to magnify or diminish ideas and values people
already believe in is frequently a ceremonial function, purposiveness and
clarity are no less important than elsewhere. But perhaps because they work
so much with familiar ideas, speakers who undertake these tasks are often less
exact than they should be in framing their purposes. Focus, as we have tried
to show, is a special virtue in such speaking. Once clear, purposive focus has
been found, your tasks become (1) to amplify familiar ideas and values in
ways that serve your purpose by means of (2) pointing up hitherto unthought-of
attributes and relationships.

SPEAKING TO PERSUADE

We now turn from this special form of persuasion to the typical problems of
persuasive speaking.

The only realistic standard of excellence in persuasive speaking is:
Did the speaker engender as much change as the circumstances, including his
own sense of responsibility, permitted? Speakers often wish for changes they
cannot completely achieve. They must then settle for less than their desires.
Norman Thomas was a constant spokesman and political candidate for the
Socialist Party in America for nearly three decades. Though he was never
elected to office and won but a tiny proportion of his hearers to his party, he
has been repeatedly credited with popularizing political and social reforms
later adopted as their own by Democrats and Republicans. It would be absurd to say that such a persuader's achievements were negligible or his public
persuasion unsuccessful because he won no office. The only fair question to
ask about Mr. Thomas' powers as a persuader is: Did he engender as much
change as the unfavorable views of his audiences and his own sense of responsibility permitted? The general answer must be that his persuasion was
at least creditable, despite his failures at the polls. It is not the *absolute effect*
of persuasion that testifies to its excellence, but *the comparison between the
effect and what was reasonably possible considering all the circumstances.*

Special Demands

What special demands does persuasion place upon you, in addition to the
demands characteristic of all speaking?

Justifying, as well as amplifying, is essential. Both must have motivational importance for the audience. This ought to be true of all content in all speeches, but it is crucial in persuasion. Hearers' own interests must supply justifications for change. This point was forcefully expressed by the Scottish rhetorician, George Campbell. His language and psychological theory now seem quaint, but his general point concerning persuasion is unmistakably sound:

> . . . when persuasion is the end, passion also must be engaged. If it is fancy which bestows brilliancy on our ideas, if it is memory which gives them stability, passion doth more, it animates them. Hence they derive spirit and energy. To say that it is possible to persuade without speaking to the passions, is but at best a kind of specious nonsense. The coolest reasoner always in persuading addresseth himself to the passions some way or other. This he cannot avoid doing, if he speak to the purpose. To make me believe it is enough to show me that things are so; to make me act, it is necessary to show that the action will answer some end. That can never be an end to me which gratifies no passion or affection in my nature. You assure me, "It is for my honour." Now you solicit my pride, without which I had never been able to understand the word. You say, "It is for my interest." Now you bespeak my self-love. "It is for the public good." Now you rouse my patriotism. "It will relieve the miserable." Now you touch my pity. So far . . . [is it] from being an unfair method of persuasion to move the passions, that there is no persuasion without moving them.[6]

A twentieth-century psychologist might reject Campbell's technical distinctions among fancy, memory, and "passion," but he would agree that there is no changing the attitudes or feelings of mankind without engaging the desires that Campbell called "passions." The modern psychologist would agree with Campbell that "the coolest reasoner" must certainly fail to change views unless aided by feelings. This necessity of enlisting active desires is one of the special demands the persuader's aim imposes on you.

In order that active drives toward belief and action may operate within hearers, it is sometimes necessary to refrain from expressing all that you believe. You may even avoid asking for all the opinion change you would really like to attain. The reason is that what men cannot yet understand, what they are not intellectually or emotionally ready to receive, is more likely to trouble them than persuade them. St. Paul's sermon on Mars Hill (pages 91–93) illustrates how audiences' limitations affect what persuasive speakers dare say. Paul deliberately claimed less than he might have if his audience of Athenian philosophers had been intellectually and emotionally ready to examine his teachings without bewilderment. Most persuaders find themselves in comparable situations and dare not claim all they would like to claim for fear of destroying their opportunity to change *some* beliefs. The situation is not unlike that of a teacher. He must teach what his students are now ready and able to learn; if he goes farther, he will perplex and perhaps frustrate, not teach.

---

6. *Philosophy of Rhetoric*, ed. Lloyd Bitzer (Carbondale, Ill.: Southern Illinois University Press, 1963), bk. I, chap. 7, p. 77. Originally published in 1776.

The persuader's situation is often still more critical; if he goes too far he may generate rejection of his entire position.

Consulting All Sides

The general controversiality of the things we persuade about can create special problems in persuaders' preparation. There are sources of information so strongly committed to the various sides of controversies that they cannot give us a whole view of the issues and evidence. One does not expect to receive the whole story about a labor dispute at either the labor union headquarters or from officials of the disputing corporation. Nor is one likely to get all the facts from hearing the witnesses for only one side in a court case. Less obvious but equally biased sources of information abound on almost all controversial issues.

You need to consult all sides in your research: read *The Nation* and *The National Review*, *The New York Times* and *United States News and World Report*, if your subject involves a liberal-conservative controversy in politics. See that you get the positions of union and management, if your subject concerns a labor dispute. Getting both sides will not necessarily give you the whole story. You are likely to come away from this kind of investigation with a good deal of extraneous information. But you will know where opponents differ and where they agree. Where they agree, you may probably accept; where they disagree, you must search for more facts by firsthand investigation and by consulting the most impartial sources available. Using both modes of research you will ultimately acquire a reliable body of material for the construction of arguments.

What we have just said may sound idealistic, but it is practical too. Of all speakers, the inquirer and the persuader must be most jealous of their reputations for integrity. Persuaders, like inquirers, presume to lead and advise. Thereby they place their own reliability at issue. You do not readily accept the advice of people who know less about the matter than you do. So it is with all persuadees. What they especially want from their advisers is consistent evidence that the adviser fully understands and reasons well about the matter at issue, and that he counsels in their own best interests.

An important way a persuader can show that he is both informed and fair is to recognize the existence of other views as he talks. Experimentation has almost uniformly shown that recognizing opposing views in persuasion has more durable influence than giving one-sided presentations. Only when an audience already agrees or when it will never be exposed to "other sides" does it seem safe to be one-sided. But "two-sidedness" raises the further question: Shall we present our own views before or after conflicting views? A great deal of research has been carried out on this and related questions, especially on whether what is discussed first (primacy) or what is discussed later (recency) has greater impact on persuadees. The findings are not definitive, but the following seems a fair statement of what experimental research suggests at this point to practical persuaders.

It is plausible to think that when a listener hears the "other side" of an argument and hears it refuted or otherwise "taken care of," he is conditioned or "inoculated" against that side. It will thereafter require more persuasion to get him to accept that "other side" than it would had he never heard that side discussed.[7] On this principle, then, you ought to make your own position as attractive as possible *before* you handle counter views. You will thus take advantage of the fact that ideas seem to gain adherence over competing ideas when they are attractively presented *first* in a series. Once your own position has been established you ought to recognize conflicting views and show that they are less credible than your own. In this way you may "inoculate" your listeners against competing conclusions and, at the very least, give your own stand the best positioning advantages you can. To all of this we add two thoughts: (1) a persuader who recognizes and reasonably disposes of "other views" is showing that he both knows his subject and can reason about it; and (2) if listeners think the "opposition" was *justly* handled, his *ethos* is apt to rise.

Constructive and Refutational Discourse

What we have just said about the importance of recognizing opposing views implies that effective persuasion normally involves both constructive and refutational discourse. Constructive argument builds up the persuader's side of his subject; refutational argument challenges or otherwise exposes weaknesses in contrary views. The technicalities of developing these two sorts of arguments are best studied in courses devoted specifically to persuasion and argumentation. As a beginning student of speaking, you can carry out your work if you follow these guidelines in developing constructive and refutational arguments:

1. No matter what motivational justifications you offer for your position, you must satisfy your listeners that you have not taken your position irresponsibly. You must give some kind of evidence that you have taken it for sensible and essentially rational reasons. (Concerning the development of rational supports see Chapter 5, pages 110–117.)
2. You need to show your listeners why the position you have adopted is more sensible

---

7. The classic studies of one-sided *vs.* two-sided persuasion were done during World War II and were reported by Carl I. Hovland, Arthur A. Lumsdaine, and Fred D. Sheffield in *Studies in Social Psychology in World War II*, vol. 3: *Experiments on Mass Communication* (Princeton: Princeton University Press, 1949), see especially pp. 201–227. There has been little direct research on how refutation of the "opposing view" affects persuasion, but nothing so far established casts doubt on the supposition that "opposing views" ought to be "taken care of" somehow if they are introduced to listeners. For concise discussions of experimental evidence on these matters (to 1967) see Ralph L. Rosnow and Edward J. Robinson, *Experiments in Persuasion* (New York: Academic Press, 1967), pp. 69–70 and 99–104.

and responsible than other positions they may have heard of (or may hear of in the future).   This usually means you must give your audience both rational and self-interest justifications for rejecting alternatives to the position you endorse.

3. The ultimate justification for any position will be, for your audience at least, your constructive proof that your position is better for them.   Hence, the bulk of persuasion is constructive.[8]

What chiefly distinguishes the persuasive speaker from the informant, inquirer, or entertainer is that his *primary* test in choosing available materials for proof or amplification is always, "Has this material enough promise or threat for my listeners so I may expect their outlooks to shift a bit because I have used it?"   He must be unusually sensitive to George Campbell's previously quoted reminder: "That can never be an end for me which gratifies no passion or affection in my nature."   A persuader dares not stop the search until he finds materials that will make a psychological contribution toward altering human experience.

SPEAKING TO ENTERTAIN

When a speaker decides to entertain, he commits himself to hold attention agreeably by diverting listeners' thoughts from matters of high seriousness. Often, though not invariably, the task is to provide amusement.   Another way of defining entertaining speech is to say it so completely interests listeners that they have almost no sense of working to acquire the full significance of what is said.

Notice that entertainment *may* be amusing but is not invariably so.   A first-rate travelogue can be entertaining but not basically amusing.   Many narratives and descriptions entertain us with varying degrees of humor.   So, a speaker planning to entertain listeners should recognize that being humorous is not the only option open.

Treatment of Subject Distinguishes This Type

Any subject—any theme that will hold attention agreeably in a diverting rather than highly serious way is a potential subject for entertaining talk.   The *treatment* of the subject is the distinguishing mark.   Treat any subject lightly, divertingly, and you can make it entertaining.

Typical occasions for entertaining talk allow extraordinary latitude for choosing subjects.   These occasions tend to be convivial gatherings or situations where no stronger motivation than curiosity has brought people together.

---

8. For an excellent, detailed treatment of these responsibilities in argumentation see Douglas Ehninger and Wayne Brockriede, *Decision by Debate* (New York: Dodd, Mead, 1963), especially pp. 81–95 and 252–266.

Wherever listeners are willing to be diverted from the usual and the serious there is a rhetorical situation for entertaining speech.

Where casual curiosity has created the speech situation there is occasion for entertaining speech that is not predominantly humorous. Light, straightforward treatment of whatever subject is the speaker's "specialty" is usually expected. Consider two of many possible settings. A Rotary Club invites the public to a post-luncheon period during which Mr. So-and-So will talk about his recent visit to India. A sorority invites Miss Blank who won a gold medal in Olympic competition to a coffee hour. Obviously Mr. So-and-So's trip and Miss Blank's Olympic achievement prescribe each speaker's subject. Few listeners in either place will be deeply informed or consumingly interested in either India or Olympic competition. Most will be there chiefly to "see" the traveler or the champion. The traveler has to say things in a fairly formal way because of the structure of his situation. Miss Blank will doubtless be asked to "tell us" at some point or points during the coffee hour. But in both places the speaker's task will be to give special information in popular terms that will satisfy the listeners' casual curiosity. This dictates that each should be prepared to give special prominence to whatever is most colorful, most human, most tantalizing about the prescribed subject. Whatever discourse has these characteristics is almost certain to be entertaining. It need not be as objective or as comprehensive as less entertaining speech on India or Olympic competition prepared with a purpose of informing.

Distinctive Aspects

From what we have said, one may draw several important inferences. *Speech that entertains differs from other speech primarily in the way subject matter is treated.* The more agreeable and diverting the amplification and delivery of ideas, the more entertaining speech will be. The difference between informing, inquiring, and persuading on the one hand and entertaining on the other is chiefly a difference of manner, not of matter. A second inference is that *to be entertaining a speaker must regard the pleasure of his audience more highly than the logic of his subject.* This does not mean that to be entertaining one must be inaccurate; on the contrary, accuracy at least in some details is essential. What arrests us is usually some disproportion of attention to specific details: detailed attention to the colorful garb of Indian women without much attention to, say, the social significance of their dress, or ludicrously detailed attention to the rigors of training for Olympic competition without much attention to the results of it. The entertaining speaker must remember that the interesting *parts* of his subject are often more important than the *whole*. It is in this sense that he sacrifices the logic of his subject to the pleasure of his audience. A third inference to be drawn about speaking to entertain is that *while good humor is always entertaining, entertainment does not necessarily*

157

hinge upon the presence of humor. This inference has been amplified by our earlier examples.

Since it is the *treatment* of material that makes speech entertaining, you will want to give special attention to stylistic resources in developing speech to entertain. (See Chapter 9, pages 211–245.) . However, to create entertaining language, you first find ideas that lend themselves to entertaining treatment. Once again, a review of the attributes things and people possess and the relationships that may exist among these attributes (page 79) can suggest potentially entertaining thoughts. Any attribute of anything has potentially humorous possibilities if examined in enough detail or distorted in some fashion. Charlie Brown and Lucy and Linus in the comic strip "Peanuts" constantly create humor by treating the *existence, nonexistence, forms,* and *possibilities* of things absurdly. George Bernard Shaw played trenchantly but amusingly with the attribute of *degree* and with *causality* when addressing students at the University of Hong Kong:

> That war [World War I] was made by people with university education. There are really two dangerous classes in the world. There are the half-educated, who have destroyed one-half of civilization, and there are the wholly educated, who have nearly completely destroyed the world.[9]

The Reverend Richard Whately, Anglican Bishop of Dublin and also an able rhetorician, developed an entertaining refutation to arguments denying that Jesus lived by applying the tests of *possibility, causality,* and *existence* too strictly to the life of Napoleon. He thereby "proved" that Napoleon could not have lived.[10] "The Conspiracy Against Lefty" was the title of one of several, delightful, informal talks we have heard left-handed students make by exaggerating (while preserving some realism) what it is like to be left-handed in a right-handed world. The young woman who alleged "conspiracy" deftly jumbled *causes* and *possibilities* together when she "established" that the entire horse breeding, training, and equipping industry is managed by "right-wing plotters" who "brainwash" every newborn foal to resent all left-handed persons who try to approach in "a natural and convenient manner." Any subject—idea, person, object, experience—has or can be given amusing relationships to other ideas, persons, objects, or experiences. It is amusingly *conceivable* attributes and relations for which entertaining speakers hunt when their special goal is to amuse.

Interrelated Points Concerning Entertaining

Three other, interrelated points need to be made concerning the content of speech that entertains. They can be stated briefly, but their importance is considerable.

---

9. "Universities and Education," delivered February 12, 1933. Reported in *The New York Times,* March 26, 1933. Note Shaw's exaggeration—one of the most common techniques for creating humor.
10. *Historic Doubts Relative to Napoleon Bonaparte* (1819).

1. *Only in entertainment is it sometimes advantageous to make no sense.* Sometimes the nonsensical bears just enough similarity to the sensible to amuse us. Here lies much of the fun of Lewis Carroll's *Alice in Wonderland* and comedian Danny Kaye's outrageous double-talk.
2. *What entertains in speaking is that which is quickly and easily understood.* Private jokes or asides and private experience are not entertaining. In entertaining speech all meaning is public—familiar and easily grasped. Even nonsense must contain a semblance to sense, or the response is not amusement, only bafflement. It is true that working puzzles can be entertaining, but puzzling speech is not. The reason is that speech moves swiftly through time, leaving listeners no opportunity to work puzzles as they appear.
3. *An entertaining speaker may properly disregard or even do violence to the natural logic of his subject, but he will please his hearers best if his speech has some kind of thematic logic.* This will give the audience the satisfaction of having been pleased by *something,* not just some *things.* Even the nightclub gag man recognizes this audience demand for structure in entertainment. If artful, he will separate his mother-in-law jokes from his insurance-company jokes, giving each group the status of a thought unit within his patter. As though further adapting to the preferences of modern audiences, more and more comedians now develop entire monologues around single themes treated humorously. In so doing, they emulate the practice of the best among entertaining speechmakers.

Entertainment can be used without being the dominant objective of a speech. Comprehensive speech of serious intent certainly can contain subordinate units of entertainment, provided they do not becloud the serious content.

In closing our three-chapter survey of how content for speeches is discovered and selected we have examined the special opportunities and difficulties that arise when you set out to inform, induce inquiry, reinforce beliefs or feelings, persuade, or entertain. We have seen that some of these special purposes limit the range of ideas from which you may draw content, and that each kind of purpose imposes its special manner of treating ideas after they are found. If any generalization is to be drawn from our survey in this chapter, it must be that you cannot be wholly successful until you have determined your specific purpose in speaking. Without understanding your specific task you cannot know what materials are useful to you nor can you know precisely how to treat them.

It would be an error to infer from what we have said that mixed purposes never occur in good speech. Informing, persuading, and entertaining, for example, can all be found in almost all first-rate speech. But if speech is first-rate, one purpose will dominate, nor will there be any confusion about which purpose dominates any *part* of the speech. If your primary intention is to persuade, your informing sections will have the features of informative speaking but will plainly serve your dominant persuasive intention by providing a base for it. Entertaining subsections will provide momentary diversion without distorting your information-giving processes or demeaning the importance of your persuasive content.

EXERCISES

Written

1. Write a brief essay on differences between speech materials that "prove" propositions and those that "amplify" ideas.
2. Choose a general topic such as "The Cost of Living" or "Clothing" and outline three different kinds of speeches that could be given on some aspect of the topic. For example, outline a persuasive, an informative, and an entertaining speech on "The Cost of Food Is Rising."
3. Read a speech of your own choosing and write a critique in which you:
   a. Identify what seems to have been the speaker's dominant purpose in speaking.
   b. Identify any subsections of the speech in which the purpose of communication seems to have shifted temporarily (e.g., from a dominant purpose of informing to a subordinate purpose of entertaining or persuading).
   c. Evaluate the speaker's success in making shifts from primary to secondary aims and back to his primary aim. (Did he indicate to his listeners that he was shifting purpose? Did he indicate why he was doing this? How successful was he in keeping his dominant purpose clear despite temporary shifts? Was the total impact of his speech strengthened or weakened by temporary changes in purpose? If weakened, how might this effect have been avoided?)

Oral

1. With two other members of your class choose a simple topic such as earth, tools, books, or some other. Let each member of the group prepare and give to the class a 2-minute talk that makes three points about the chosen topic, one talk giving information, another persuading, and the third entertaining. Afterward compare and contrast the different kinds of materials each speaker used and the different ways he or she had to use them.
2. Prepare and give to your class a short speech of inquiry on the question, "What is the best way we could conduct our class in order to get helpful feedback from the audience in our next formal speeches?" When you have opened up the problem and suggested directions in which a solution might be sought, preside over a class discussion seeking to devise a plan for handling feedback and criticism during a forthcoming set of classroom speeches.
3. Among the more difficult topics on which to inform are those in which abstract or aesthetic concepts have to be made clear. For practice with this kind of speaking prepare and give a 2-minute talk on how people should go about "understanding" or "appreciating" some specific artistic object (a statue, piece of jewelry, architectural form, bit of poetry, or other).

4. Prepare and present an oral report on the kinds of content used in some speech to entertain which you have read or heard. Indicate also what special treatment was given this content. (Speeches by Mark Twain or Will Rogers, or recordings by such entertainers as Mort Sahl or Stan Freberg might be chosen for discussion in this exercise.)

5. Prepare and present a brief talk on why it is unwise for those who speak to inform or to induce inquiry to color their speech content with personal value judgments.

6. Prepare and present an informative talk in which you assess why some allegedly good speaker failed in a major attempt at persuasion. (Certain campaign speeches by William Jennings Bryan, Richard Nixon, or George McGovern might be examined. Or you might consider a television editorial you have recorded and can present to the class and then discuss. Or a poor lecture by a usually good teacher could be considered.)

CHAPTER
7

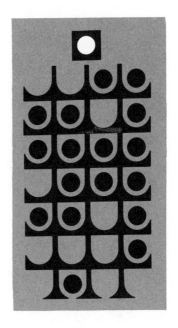

Disposition:
Organizing Materials

> . . . form is the creation of an appetite in the mind of the auditor, and
> the adequate satisfying of that appetite.
>
> <u>Kenneth Burke, "Psychology and Form"</u>[1]

In his book *The Image,* Kenneth E. Boulding points out that a modern view of
physical processes postulates that there is an omnipresent tendency "for things
to run down." He continues, "The end of the universe, according to this
picture, will be a thin, uniform soup without form. It is toward this comfort-
less end that all physical processes are moving." By contrast, Boulding insists, the record of history exhibits another tendency, "the tendency for the
rise of organization":

> It is the capacity for organizing information into large and complex images which
> is the chief glory of our species. . . . Our image of time . . . goes far beyond that
> of the most intelligent of lower animals, mainly because of our capacity for lan-
> guage and for record. . . . Closely associated with the time structure of his
> [man's] image is the image of the structure of relationships. Because we are
> aware of time, we are also aware of cause and effect, of contiguity and succes-
> sion of cycles and repetition.[2]

The organization of an oral message is the application of this distinctive
human capacity and appetite for organizing our environment into ideas we
want to give to other people. This is more easily said than done.

The thought of a swimming pool, in your mind, may be encrusted with
what are *for you* memories of friendships made while relaxing beside the
pool; pleasing sensations of cool water on hot days; cookouts and so on. But
you can never implant this entire cluster of remembrances in anyone else's
mind. The elements of the cluster must be detached from one another. They

---

1. From Kenneth Burke, *Counter-Statement,* originally published in *The Dial,* LXXIX (July 1925), 34–36,
Quoted from Morton D. Zabel, ed., *Literary Opinion In America* (New York: Harper & Row, Publishers, 1962),
II, p. 668.
2. Ann Arbor: University of Michigan Press, 1956), p. 25. See Chapter 2, "The Image in the Theory of Organization." Used by permission.

must be verbalized in some sequence that enables the other person to create out of his own experiences another cluster of images and sensations comparable to yours. You must show him the *connections* that join the different ideas into the *whole* memory you have. The more special or private the relationships are, the more difficult it will be to convey them in familiar public terms. Some thoughts and sensations are so highly personal that we almost never succeed in communicating them. Because we cannot always, through language, line up the aspects of these sensations in any way that exhibits all of them with their precise interconnections, we have trouble reproducing the experience. Try, for example, to express in words what it feels like to swallow a mouthful of ice-cold water on a day when it is 100° in the shade and you haven't had a drink for three hours. This is a problem for poets, not artisans in public speaking.

DEMANDS FOR ORGANIZATION

Happily, most matters about which we speak publicly can be verbalized in structured forms that meaningfully convey their internal natures. The fact that we share conceptions of the relationships we call time, cause, effect, contiguity, cyclical succession, and repetition makes it possible to communicate at least the basic experiences and thoughts we acquire. Even listeners with poor perceptions can see relationships if we organize our thoughts with careful regard for the patterns all men are accustomed to perceiving. A speaker must invariably remember, however, that (1) listeners do not take in as much detail as readers, so he must show relationships very plainly — sometimes obviously; (2) the object of all effort to organize ideas for public speech is to transform the shape of the speaker's thought into shapes that a particular audience will be able to recognize; (3) it is foolish to try to organize the ideas of a speech before most of the ideas have been located and the specific purpose of the speech has been identified.

Audiences insist that they be helped to understand what a speaker says. Their insistence is partial expression of their natural wish to see the interrelationships among ideas; to see which ideas are primary and which are subsidiary; to detect the rationale behind the overall pattern of a speech. When you depart from an order of thought anticipated by your listener, or from an apparently logical order of thoughts, you had better explain why; otherwise your hearer will find the flow of thought chaotic. He may suspect you of deliberately trying to mislead.

Listeners lose interest when discourse does not seem to be advancing toward a psychologically meaningful goal. Because they are human beings with a need to organize, listeners demand progression and a sense of constructive variety. They want cumulative, psychologically satisfying effects. A

165

speech, then, must build, point by point. Somewhere a climax must be reached. This high point is usually near the end of the discourse, but it may and sometimes does occur earlier. In either case it will be psychologically satisfying if points along the way are given time, detailed development, and intensity proportionate to their relative weights within the total structure. Listeners anticipate that somewhere in your speech all the necessary information will be in, all arguments developed to the point of acceptability. They expect, in short, that all roads will lead to Rome. In this they are simply displaying the chief glory of their species.

Not all decisions about organization of oral communication derive from the natures of audiences. Some ought to depend on your own responses to the structure of your ideas. If you find your plan too complicated to use easily, you have probably created a poor organizational structure. Uncertainty about organization is often a main cause for lack of confidence in yourself and your materials. It is only when you are satisfied that *you* understand how each piece of supporting material is related to each other that you will be able to proceed with assurance.

Content can impose patterns of organization, too. Once material is discovered and gathered, you will begin to sort it. Sorting may show that such materials as anecdotes, questions, examples, and statistics tend to group under a particular set of topics or arguments. Thus, materials about topography or scenery will lend themselves to spatial organization, producing description. Historical materials may virtually demand to be handled in narrative, chronological form.

How materials ought to be "weighted" in relation to one another may also be determined by your research. As you move through the inventional processes we have discussed in Chapters 4, 5, and 6, you may evolve an image of your speech which will have to be changed when you undertake to structure all you know. You may be startled by how little there is to say about a pet idea, for example. Then you have the choice of discarding a seemingly weak contention or of backtracking to search for new information.

More often, you will find that you have too much material for the available speaking time. Upon sifting and sorting data you may discover that you have support for twelve or thirteen significant ideas. You may then discard those ideas which are least fruitful, those least likely to gain audience acceptance, or those least necessary for your purpose. On the other hand, you may decide to regroup and reorganize your material. Very often when material seems to yield too many main points the problem is that secondary ideas are being mistaken for broader ones and ought to be used as support or amplification for the larger concepts.

The processes of elimination or reorganization may seem painful. You may have to cut your speech repeatedly. Should you discover that your speaking time has been encroached upon by unforeseeable circumstances, you must sacrifice still more material and do it without destroying form. It happens even to the famous. Franklin Roosevelt found it necessary to cut his 1932 speech accepting the presidential nomination. The plane in which he flew from Albany to Chicago was hours late, which meant that he would appear before an audience wearied by waiting to hear him. He wisely decided that his speech would have to be shorter than he had planned. Samuel Rosenman, who assisted him with the speech, writes:

> With each radio report, we were falling further and further behind schedule; and more and more paragraphs came out of the acceptance speech. This lopping off of material on which we had worked so long and so hopefully was a painful process. I know that there were some jewels dropped on the airplane floor that day. It is likely, though, that the cutting process hurt us more than it did the speech.[3]

Such may be your feeling, yet rejection and red-pencilling will often result in conciseness and sharper focus. The tightening that comes from excision usually enhances the organic unity of a speech.

Should you choose to regroup speech materials, you will find, each time, that you need to discover a new rationale, a new set of topics. Often this regrouping is less difficult than it at first seems. Many good speakers insist that the fewer the points in a speech, the better. If you are giving a short speech, you ordinarily ought to assume that you have time to develop three or four main points at most.

By slicing your material in a new way those twelve or thirteen points will fit under three or four main heads. One or two of the thirteen may now appear expendable and others will probably prove to have been sub-points all along. You will keep the audience in mind if you proceed wisely, realizing that two or three points acceptably substantiated are more valuable for most purposes than a half-dozen points lightly touched and dropped.

Arrangement of main points according to strength deserves serious consideration. When you have decided upon the points to be amplified or supported, questions arise about their placement. Knowing that audiences are likely to pay closer attention and to be least tired during the early part of a speech argues for putting your strongest point first. But knowing that listeners are also likely to remember the ideas they have heard most recently argues for placing your strongest point last. As we indicated in Chapter 3, despite numerous experiments, there are no "rules" by which you should choose between these alternatives.[4] All you can be sure of is that the first and last positions in any series are more impressive than the other positions. Therefore, it is sensible to place ideas of less importance in the intermediate positions. Experienced speakers employing three points favor placing them in 1–3–2 or 2–3–1 orders of strength. In dealing with four points they favor 1–3–4–2;

---

3. Samuel I. Rosenman, *Working with Roosevelt* (New York: Harper & Brothers, 1952), p. 75.
4. Ernest Thompson, "Some Effects of Message Structure on Listeners' Comprehension," *Speech Monographs,* XXXIV (March 1967), 51–57.

1–4–3–2; 2–3–4–1; or 2–4–3–1 orders of strength.   Your final decision has to be one of *judgment*.   It ought to rest on whether special features of content or situation lead you to "bet" that primacy or recency will here be the position of greatest emphasis for your particular audience.

While we usually think of organization or disposition of entire speeches, the principles of clear organization also operate for the various points within a discourse.   If you use narrative, chronological order is almost inescapable.   Interrupting narrative for expressions of personal opinion almost always diverts attention from the main movement of thought.   Yet, there may be circumstances where spontaneous insertion of definitions or other clarifying detail is necessary if you are to adapt to your audience.   The questions to be asked about any break in an established order of ideas are: "Is this departure relevant?   Will this deviation from the thought pattern *help* to achieve my purpose?"

Occasions and settings influence organization of ideas less often than do audience, speaker, and material.   The occasion may require initial acknowledgments or personal greetings, but these are minor audience adaptations.   A setting may also more severely narrow your choice.   For example, a Washington's birthday celebration may call for a eulogy of George Washington.   Speakers have found that eulogies are successful when the praise of the man is structured by recounting incidents in his life or describing his traits of character.   When speakers depart from a pattern because the occasion itself is unexpectedly changed by some distraction such as the rattle of jackhammers outside the window, a sudden power failure, or the unexpected appearance of an important personage, modification of the message is as much a matter of audience adaptation as of adaptation to the occasion.

Plainly the disposition of ideas, their orderly arrangement, is not random.   Nor can it be done by rule.   Organizational choices are wisely made only after careful consideration of the audience's expectations; the speaker's capabilities; the nature of the data used to achieve the speaker's purpose; and, incidentally, the circumstances prevailing at the time of delivery.

MAIN COMPONENTS OF A SPEECH

The number of "parts" of a speech has been an issue of debate for centuries. Today's convention is that a speech should have Introduction, Body, and Conclusion *unless* there are strong reasons for building it otherwise.   The proportions of these parts depend upon the subject matter, the occasion, and the speaker himself, but most often they depend upon the audience's expectations and motivations.   There will also need to be clear connections which link the three main portions.   These linking parts are major transitions.   Normally, then, as in other works of art such as plays, poems, and musical compositions, a speech has a beginning, a middle, an end, and internal transitional elements. We shall consider these separately.

The introduction to your speech should fulfill demands made by all of the elements in a speech situation. Since it is a beginning, it must (1) attract the initial, favorable attention of the audience; (2) provide necessary background for the audience so they may comprehend what follows; (3) be suitable to the occasion; and (4) contribute to your own ease during a crucial period of adjustment. In addition, the introduction ought to be coordinated with and must relate to the body of the speech. It is not a preamble nor a prelude without relation to what follows.

At the outset, you must gain attention in such a way that your listeners will want to go on listening. Any of the methods for achieving attention may be employed, but the most useful ways are to refer to something familiar or something novel. You may start with a reference to the occasion, to its purpose, or to other things about which the audience already knows. You may begin with greetings, an anecdote, or analogy. Tradition may dictate what you will say at the beginning. Or you may need to awaken the audience by sharpening the focus of their attention. Where this is so, unusual facts or stories, shocking or startling assertions, unfamiliar statistics, telegraphic headline fragments, or other striking materials may enable you to create curiosity or suspense. Reference to your own interests and needs, especially if they are similar to those of your audience, may create common ground and cause your audience to want to listen. A modest statement of your qualifications for speaking on the subject you have chosen can make your listeners want to hear more.

Most audiences want to be given reasons for listening. They are always ready to ask, "Why should *I* listen? What's in this for *me?*" And, often, they want directions about what to listen for. The ways in which you can touch off an audience's powers of concentration are limitless, yet none is truly useful unless it will at once seize attention and favorably dispose your audience to what follows.

It is often essential for you to provide background knowledge your hearers must have from the outset. It may be necessary to provide preliminary information about new materials, details you will use in amplification, or the relationships between main points and your central proposition. Such basic information may be provided by way of a preview which will furnish a context for what you are going to say.

It may be necessary to define unfamiliar terms to be used later in your discussion or to define familiar terms so the audience will understand special meanings you plan to assign to them. A short, historical review may help.

Especially where argument from precedent is involved or where your subject is one that listeners have not thought a great deal about, it is useful to employ a history of the question.

Definitions and histories are sometimes supplemented or replaced by statements of those matters you will or will not deal with in the body of your speech. Items so singled out because you intend to pass them over or because they seem irrelevant are often called "waived materials." You simply state that you will not consider them and give your listeners your reasons. Giving main points to be developed later by amplification or support is what the Romans called "division"; today it is sometimes called "initial partition." The tactic is useful when your audience needs to know the path you intend to take. Of course, you would not offer such statements if you wished to preserve suspense or feared that revealing your entire plan so early might make some listeners defensive. Initial partitioning is not a useful introductory tactic in speeches developed inductively or in those designed for unfriendly audiences. There, even the subject sentence is often withheld until the end.

In speeches constructed on a deductive pattern you ought to include the subject sentence of your speech as a final item of your introduction, or as an initial item in the body of the speech. As we have already said, the subject sentence is delayed in most indirect sequences. Wherever it appears, it ought to be carefully expressed in a single, economical, unambiguous sentence as was pointed out in Chapters 2 and 5.

Not all the items we have mentioned will be included in any one introduction. What your listeners *need* to know before you proceed should dictate how much and what kinds of orientation materials you offer. An example of a student's introduction for a speech appears in the Exercise Section of this chapter on pages 188–189. It is selective yet suggestive. You will find in it some of the principles discussed in this section.

The introduction is a part of the speech which, given the right circumstances, may be omitted altogether. It is not necessary if an audience is already attentive and interested in your subject, if they expect you to speak, if they already possess the background information, if they are highly motivated, or if the occasion exerts no special pressures. College professors can often dispense with introductions after the first few lectures. If their audiences are oriented and motivated, introductory remarks become superfluous. You, however, should be cautioned about omitting introductions. Rarely can an introduction be omitted when you speak to an audience for the first time; never, when your audience is not entirely ready to pay attention from the outset.

Body of the Speech

The body of a speech comprises (1) the main points, (2) the material which supports or amplifies these points, and (3) transitional phrases or sentences.

Earlier we discussed sorting and sifting materials in order to arrive at main points and determine their psychological weighting and placement.[5] When these stages of preliminary analysis have been completed and you know your main points, you next word the main ideas.

Where possible, main points ought to be worded in parallel phrasings to provide balance, thus making them easier to remember. They should also be worded to elicit the responses you seek from your audience. Main points for informative speeches should be simple, clear assertions. In speeches of inquiry the main points are often worded as questions which are then explored or answered with information. Main points for persuasive speeches should be assertions, slanted in wording to express your point of view and to support the main proposition embodied in your subject sentence. These main points should be "contentions" or "reasons" closely linked to the subject sentence so that they become the foundation stones upon which the core idea rests. Main points for speeches of reinforcement are framed in essentially the same ways as those for speeches of persuasion. For speeches designed to entertain, main points again take the form of assertions.

In all cases the final form of your main points should respond to the interrelated demands of the material, the audience, your habitual mode of expression. The ways of arranging these main points into patterns will be discussed later in this chapter. Under the discussions of the various patterns you will also find some examples of wordings for the different purposes.

Transitions[6]

Listeners cannot easily review what you have said after it has been spoken, as they might turn back and reread the pages in a book. Therefore, you will need to provide careful transitions if your speech is to be clear at all points. Transitions are words, phrases, sentences, or groups of sentences which join ideas together. If clear and smoothly worded, they contribute to the organic unity and the clarity of your speech.

Transitions are like signposts. They tell your audience where you have been, where you are, or where you intend to go. They are most frequently needed at the completion of a main idea, before you move on to the next one; but you may also need them as connections between subsidiary points or phrases leading to the ideas in single sentences.

Since we have already considered that . . . , we should adopt. . . .

In addition to . . . there is another outstanding reason (element, factor, consideration, fact). . . .

---

5. See pp. 167–168.
6. This section is based in part upon an explanation of transitions originally written by Harry P. Kerr, University of Maine, Farmington, Maine. Used by permission.

We have seen . . . , yet it remains for us to observe. . . .

But . . . is only one important viewpoint.   Equally important is. . . .

Since . . . is so, what can be said of . . . ?   (Questions can often be useful as transitions.)

Where the thought connection to be emphasized is between sub-points, or where the thought relationships are easy to comprehend, a phrase or even a single word such as "so" or "yet" may be adequate to tie ideas together.   Some examples of such phrasings are:

More important than all this is the fact that. . . .

In contrast to. . . .

Looked at from a different angle the problem seems to be. . . .

This last point raises a question: . . . ?

What was the result?   Just this. . . .

On the other hand. . . .

When this has been done. . . .

And so you can see that. . . .

Seek variety in transitions.   Avoid using only stock phrases or repeating the same few phrases over and over.   While you should not be afraid to be obvious in your transitions, you should avoid being too brief.   A mark of an unpolished speaker is his tendency to use only "and," "also," or "like" as transitions.   He gives the impression of having tacked his ideas together, of having joined them to one another carelessly.   Yet he is in a better position than the speaker who melts from point to point or vaguely gropes his way from topic to topic.   Good transitions (1) show that the speaker is moving from one idea to another, (2) demarcate completed ideas, (3) indicate the relationships between the ideas involved, and (4) remind the speaker of his sequence of thought.

Conclusions

The final segment of your speech, its conclusion, performs functions demanded by the audience, the material, the occasion, and yourself.   In this segment the audience normally expects at least (1) a restatement of your core idea or (2) a summing up of main points which clarify or prove your thesis.   Both restatement and summary may be needed.   Almost any body of material needs a final rounding out that fuses subject matter with intent. To emphasize a detail or simply to fade into silence obscures meaning. The audience should not feel at the end of a speech that they have been left hanging, that the speech ended too abruptly, or that the subject is still up in the air. *The final moments of a speech ought to be used to drive the core idea home.* The audience should know that you have finished, and you should feel satisfied that you have accomplished your purpose and produced an intended final impact. This does not mean that your final sentence ought always to be a restatement or summary. True, recapitulation is the main function of most conclusions, but one's last sentences are often strongest if devised to challenge the audience to further thought or action, or to operate as a coda to one's central theme. Final sentences may echo the beginning sentences or constitute a return to a text or refrain, thus providing a frame for all you have said. A "thank you" at the end of a speech may detract from the central idea and an otherwise strong final impression. Indeed, any remarks of appreciation used as last sentences ought to be carefully considered since they may destroy the focus of an otherwise effective conclusion.

As we have said elsewhere, it is conceivable that you will speak in a few situations where you need not utter "concluding words." These circumstances will be rare. The most common ones are those in which someone else will conclude what you have said very briefly, as when one person explains that the treasury is empty, knowing that a colleague will immediately make an appeal for money.

Introduction, subject sentence, body, transitions, and conclusion will, with rare exceptions, be parts of every speech you will deliver, though they may be cast in different designs from speech to speech. It remains for us to consider the most common structures or designs employed in arranging materials.

USABLE PATTERNS OF ORGANIZATION[7]

Four conditions will usually determine the most appropriate pattern for a given speaking situation: (1) the particular type and degree of response you seek from the audience; (2) whether the audience is favorably, unfavorably, or apathetically disposed toward your subject, your central idea, and you as a speaker; (3) how much knowledge your listeners possess about your subject;

---

7. The descriptions of the cause-effect, problem-solution, withheld proposal, and open proposal patterns in this section are based upon explanations originally written by James A. Wood of the University of Texas, El Paso. Donald E. Williams, University of Florida, prepared the original explanation of the reflective sequence. Used by permission.

(4) how you can best relate your specific purpose to the pertinent interests and desires of your audience.

The standard patterns commonly used in structuring ideas in practical speaking include: (1) chronological, (2) spatial, (3) topical, (4) ascending and descending orders, (5) causal, (6) problem-solution or disease-remedy, (7) withheld proposal or indirect sequence, (8) open proposal or direct sequence, (9) reflective sequence or pattern of inquiry, (10) Monroe's motivated sequence, and (11) elimination order. Each is explained in some detail below.

Patterns may be thought of as primarily logical or primarily psychological. The chronological, spatial, topical, causal, and problem-solution are structures which are primarily logical. Ascending and descending orders, withheld- and open-proposal sequences, and elimination order are methods which may be considered primarily psychological. The reflective sequence and Monroe's sequence are at once logical and psychological in that they adapt material to audiences psychologically by offering it in a problem-solution structure.

We make these distinctions to show you that psychological patterns of audience adaptation may be superimposed upon logical patterns. For example, ascending or descending orders may come into play as you arrange ideas topically or spatially. In like manner, elimination order may be employed in treating causes, effects, or possible solutions. In some instances two psychological orders can be used in handling a particular logical arrangement. For example, ascending and withheld-proposal orders may be used as you develop a topical pattern.

Patterning ideas is not an either-or affair; it is a matter of clarifying psychological and logical relationships by adding the meanings of various structural systems to the basic meanings of speech content.

You should bear in mind that a pattern need not be followed rigidly or in its entirety to be useful as a general scheme for organizing materials. It may be used for the organization of a whole speech, for only a particular segment, or for a relatively brief statement you might make in a discussion. For example, in a speech you might have a chronologically arranged section within the introduction and a problem-solution arrangement in the body; or you might have a cause-effect pattern for the problem section of a problem-solution speech. Generally speaking, introductions ought to be organized independently of the bodies of speeches, and the conclusions usually reflect the patterns of organization used in the bodies of speech materials they conclude.

Chronological Pattern

The chronological pattern is a time order, enumerating occurrences in the sequence in which they happened or giving directions in the order to be followed in carrying them out. Material will often dictate this kind of ordering. Chronology, an order most useful in recounting events, is almost mandatory in narration. Chronological patterns may be used in all kinds of speech units. They are used commonly in connection with informative purposes. A time sequence usually allows climactic development, arousing curiosity and creating suspense. Segments of speeches chronologically developed can be found in the narrations of circumstances leading to crime in Clarence Darrow's famous summation at the trial of Loeb and Leopold, or in Daniel Webster's classic speech for the prosecution in the Knapp-White murder case. Examples of entire speeches developed chronologically include many eulogies, speeches of nomination, historical lectures, demonstrations, and instructional discourses.

One weakness of chronological patterning is that such important considerations as cause, effect, desirability, form cannot easily be emphasized without interrupting the movement-in-time that gives chronology its chief interest value.

Spatial Pattern

The spatial pattern, as the name implies, is a structure based on the relationships or parts of a whole as they exist in space. In building such a pattern you proceed systematically, describing how something looks or functions. Normally you will describe from left to right, top to bottom, bottom to top, or front to back. Sometimes you will describe by moving from that portion at the center to those on the periphery. For instance, you might describe the control panel in an airplane by pointing first to those centered instruments most often used before moving out toward the surrounding instruments which are less frequently used. You would then be using a pattern of descending importance which happens here to become identical with the pattern of spatial description. In all spatial arrangements you will need to mention each part or aspect *according to plan;* haphazard coverage makes spatial relationships hard to understand.

Spatial structure is especially useful in giving information. A fire extinguisher might be described from top to bottom, a painting from right to left, the floor plan of a house from front to back or story to story. The order in which to proceed when describing spatially will ordinarily be up to you. Your decision on which space portion to take up first ought to hinge on your estimation of how you can be clearest for your audience while highlighting the important relationships among parts. If these standards leave you more than one good way of describing spatially, choose the one that is easiest for *you* to present.

Topical Pattern

The topical pattern is really one in which there is no easily labeled speech structure. The label "topical" is assigned to organizational schemes which we cannot otherwise account for. Some call them "classification orders" to denote that some kind of orderly categorization accounts for the patterning. Some would say topical patterns are those which arise from the subject matter, that these are patterns evolving out of the "natural parts" of the subject, its aspects, types, or qualities. The word "topical" gives us a clue. A communicator trying to order his ideas asks himself where the places are to which we go for argument or clarification and comes up with such an answer as: "We often look at social, political, or economic aspects of arguments." Thus he *invents* a *special* classification of materials. It may be only one of several schemes of organizing data. Another might have been: public interests versus private interests. In this way we think of the topics we might use, select from them; and they, as we choose to arrange them, become the bases for organizing the ideas in a speech. A topical pattern is an arbitrary grouping of themes pertinent to a particular subject and speech purpose. It is adaptable to any purpose but inquiry. The only demand upon such a pattern is that the audience accept the divisions as reasonable and suitably comprehensive.

In an impromptu speech in Philadelphia, February 22, 1861, Abraham Lincoln adopted a simple but easily understandable topical arrangement treating (1) the principle of unity reflected in the Declaration of Independence and (2) his determination to sustain the Union at all costs. He might as easily have chosen to discuss the (1) economic, (2) social, and (3) political benefits of maintaining the Union. Or he might have discussed the (1) legal and (2) historical justifications for the Union. All of these arrangements might be identified as topical.

Ascending and Descending Orders

Should you choose to use ascending and descending orders you place patterns, aspects, types, or qualities in sequence according to their increasing or decreasing importance or familiarity. That is to say, you move from the most to the least important or from the most to the least familiar points or vice versa. You start with the strongest argument and move to the weakest or start with the weakest and move to the strongest. You may start on common ground and move into unfamiliar territory, or you may begin with an unusual aspect or argument and lead the audience to what they already know or to what is already uppermost in their minds. In the case of descending order, for example, you would explain how pulp is processed for the manufacture of paper by taking up the most commonly used process, the ground-wood process, and move through your speech to the soda, sulfite, and alkaline processes, which are used less frequently and are less familiar to most people. Similarly, in a speech on population control, the familiar argument that natural resources of the earth will soon be used up would precede less striking arguments about political and cultural consequences of an exploding population. If you simply reverse the sequence so less known or weaker arguments come first, you achieve ascending order.

Ascending-descending orders are suitable in speaking to inform, to persuade, or to reinforce. The pattern might also be adapted for use in a speech to entertain. The choice and construction of ascending and descending orders hinge on your judgments of the relative importance of your materials; on your estimate of what will help your listeners to remember and give them a sense of climax; and, sometimes, on whether you have time to develop enough points to make ascent or descent psychologically meaningful.

Causal Sequences

Causal patterns are used in situations where one set of conditions is given as the cause for another set. In such cases, you may begin with a given set of conditions as the cause and allege that these will produce certain results or effects; or you may take a given set of conditions as the effect and allege that these resulted from certain causes.

In most uses of this pattern the specific purpose is to urge elimination of those conditions which function as causes. To achieve this specific purpose, however, you may need to persuade your audience of one or more of these: (1) that the effects are really undesirable to them; (2) that the alleged causes are truly responsible for these effects; and (3) that elimination of these causes will not result in other, undesirable consequences. The first two concerns must either be evident to the audience or must be proved. The third may sometimes be safely disregarded.

The most common use of this pattern is one in which a speaker points out that certain undesirable conditions *(effects)* now exist and then explains that these are caused by certain other conditions *(causes)*. The speaker *may* carry his reasoning through a chain of two or more effect-cause relationships in order to get from the present undesirable effects to the cause which he asks his audience to eliminate. This kind of development might run thus:

I. The nations of the world now spend billions of dollars on armaments. (Present undesirable effect.)
II. This money is spent because the people of the world live in perpetual fear of war and aggression. (Establishing first effect-to-cause relationship.)
III. People live in such fear because there is no international authority strong enough to prevent war. (Second effect-to-cause relationship establishes the real cause of the present undesirable conditions.)

IV. Billions of dollars and much warfare will be saved by establishing stronger authority in the United Nations. (Audience urged to adopt proposal eliminating prime cause and thereby eliminating effect.)

Frequently, a speaker will point out that certain existing conditions will cause undesirable effects in the future and so should be eliminated. The normal sequence is to begin with the present causes and then describe the anticipated future effects. Sometimes a more artistic sequence can be achieved by visualizing the future effects for the audience first, then linking these effects to the present undesirable causes. One might structure a unit of speech thus:

I. The nations of the world are drifting toward a third world war. (Future, undesirable effects.)
II. This drift is being caused by rampant nationalism. (Present conditions cause future effect.)
III. Therefore, all nations should be made to submit all international disputes to the United Nations' settlement. (Appeal to audience to eliminate present causes in order to avoid future effect.)

Sometimes a speaker draws an analogy between a cause-effect relationship and another similar cause-effect relationship which is already accepted by his audience:

I. At the present time, the nations of the world are permitting country X to ignore international authority. (Establishing present conditions as cause.)
II. Because the League of Nations did not force Hitler and Mussolini to keep international peace, a world war was necessary to stop aggression. (Referring to past and accepted cause-effect relationship.)
III. Present disregard of X's actions toward her neighbors could eventuate in war. (Drawing parallel undesirable effects from parallel causes.)
IV. Therefore, the United Nations should force X's obedience to international authority. (Appeal to audience to eliminate present causes in order to avoid future effects.)

Although causal patterns are generally used to advocate the removal of some condition, they can be used to advocate that certain conditions be encouraged. In this use you would show how something desirable to your audience (effect) results from other things (causes); therefore, they should set these causes in operation in order to secure the effect. Such a pattern might run:

I. We want permanent peace in the world. (Establishing condition, effect, as desirable to audience.)
II. Permanent peace results from democratic nations' armed superiority over potential aggressor nations. (Establishing cause for desirable effect.)
III. Therefore, let us enlarge our sea and air power. (Appeal for audience to favor conditions designed to cause desirable effects.)

Causal patterns are also often used in informing to describe the relationships of parts of what is being explained, such as the causes of inflation or the effects of X-rays on human tissue. On occasion, speeches to reinforce and entertain are cast in this pattern.

Often the biggest difficulty in using causal patterns in either persuasive or informational speaking is making clear that a valid cause-effect relationship actually exists between the two sets of conditions. The demand to be met is primarily the listeners' need to see a clear and logical demonstration that genuine and significant (for them) causal relationships do exist. In turn, to use causal patterns requires that a speaker be capable of cogent thinking and that the materials used in the speech lend themselves to causal development.

Problem-Solution Sequence

The problem-solution pattern presents an audience with a problem and proposes a way to solve it. This pattern is also called the "disease-remedy" or the "need-remedy" pattern. Here, you point first to the existence of a problem or evil and then offer a corrective program which will be (1) practicable and (2) desirable. The corrective program must be capable of being put into effect, and it must be capable of eliminating the problem or the evil in question. It must also be one which will not introduce new and worse evils of its own. This is an issue long debated regarding the control of nuclear weapons. Does the control proposed erode national sovereignty in ways more dangerous than nuclear arms?

The specific purpose of speaking in a problem-solution pattern is to urge listeners to adopt the conditions embodied in the solution. This type of organization usually serves well in the following situations.

1. Where the audience is aware that a problem exists and is interested in finding a solution to it, you may advocate one solution as the best of several possible answers. Although you will generally describe the problem briefly, you will be primarily concerned with showing how your particular solution will solve the problem in the best possible way and how any alleged disadvantages of your solution may be avoided. This latter concern, avoiding new difficulties, will frequently involve you in anticipatory refutation, which means you will have to dispel arguments against your proposal even though they have not yet been advanced by anyone.

2. Where the audience is only dimly aware of a problem or need, the problem-solution pattern still serves well. Listeners can be made aware of the problem's exact nature; then, perhaps, the solution will become evident. Here you are primarily concerned with focusing your hearers' vaguely felt needs upon the specific problem you have isolated. You want the audience to see that their interests are vitally affected by the problem. Although you should at least indicate the evident solution, your chief concern is to show that

a specific, serious problem does exist. Where your audience is not initially aware of their difficulty, it is unlikely that in a single speech you can do more than establish a precise sense of need; but not even in these circumstances can you disregard the solution section of your sequence altogether. If you do, you will leave the hearers up in the air. You must at least indicate that there *are* ways of solving the problem.

3. There are situations where the major concerns of both the preceding settings are combined. Sometimes you can carry your audience from awareness of a problem through to a readiness to act on a particular solution.

Now your task is (1) to sharpen awareness of the problem and (2) to show why your solution is the most suitable. Such speech might be structured thus:

I. A serious problem of juvenile delinquency now exists in the United States. (Referring to felt need.)
   A. This problem not only poses a threat to our personal welfare and property but costs us millions of dollars in taxes for police protection. (Establishing importance of problem to audience.)
   B. Youthful offenders are now too commonly released with neither punishment nor correction. (Focusing felt need on specific problem.)
II. This problem can be solved by imposing stiffer fines and jail sentences on juvenile criminals. (Statement of solution to specific problem.)
   A. By making youths responsible for the consequences of their actions we will deter them from criminal activities. (Showing *how* proposal will solve the problem.)
   B. The use of special jails will keep juveniles apart from older, hardened criminals. (Meeting objections to proposal.)

Variations on the problem-solution pattern are sometimes used. One variation is that of alternating or staggering portions of a problem with portions of the solution. For example, the cost of a project may be seen as one aspect of a problem, the workability of the project as another. Finding time for the project may be a third. Taking each up in turn and providing the solutions for cost, workability, and time as you present these aspects of the problem may psychologically satisfy your audience better than if you had discussed all of the problem and then its total solution. A second variation occurs in informing, as when you *show how* people were faced by a problem and how they solved it. One might report how halfway houses came to be established to meet the problems faced by people seeking to overcome drug addiction. The pattern may be used to inform even if the solution is not yet in effect, provided the answer has been decided and is no longer a question for debate. Problem-solution arrangements may also be adapted to reinforce belief and feeling or, more rarely, to entertain.

From what we have said it can be seen that problem-solution patterns are direct responses to audiences' needs. An audience must feel or be made to feel that a problem exists or that an evil is present before it will accede to a solution. Often the felt need will originate in you so that you have the initial need for this pattern. Where this is true, you must make the audience feel that the needed action is justified in terms of their interests. Speech materials also affect your choice of this organizational pattern. They must be capable of being divided into clear-cut problems and solutions. The occasion will determine to some extent those items which you select to depict a problem and to explain a solution. Thus, all forces in the communicative setting are at work in the final determination of how and whether a problem-solution pattern can be evolved.

Withheld-Proposal or Indirect Sequence

The withheld-proposal or indirect sequence presents individual cases or instances as the bases for a conclusion about additional members of the same class.

The most important characteristic of the indirect sequence is that when using this pattern you give your audience examples, or some basic assumptions and facts, before you present any generalized inferences or conclusions of your own.

This pattern is especially useful when you speak to a hostile audience. Sometimes it is the only pattern that will enable you to persuade, because it permits you to begin an argument with material your audience knows to be true or with assumptions they accept. A common ground of agreement is established with the audience; when inferences are logically drawn from these accepted materials, the audience must either attack the logic involved or admit that you may be right. This pattern is also effective because it reflects man's normal thinking processes — reasoning from examples and assumptions in order to reach decisions.

Indirectly structured speeches generally operate in one of two basic patterns. In the first a number of examples is given, and a generalization is inferred. The plan might be:

I. Our city was charged with polluting the lake by improper sewerage control during last year.
II. Regulation 73 on smoke abatement was enforced against only three companies in the city during the first six months of this year, though fourteen complaints were filed.
III. Days on which air pollution alerts were officially announced to city residents increased by 35 percent over last year during the last six months.
IV. Three of five retirees from the pollution abatement office of the city were not replaced last year.
V. This city administration is not living up to its pledge to improve the quality of our physical environment.

In using this pattern it is essential that your induction meet your own and your listeners' logical tests for acceptable generalizations.

In a second type of indirect pattern you first give basic assumptions or premises which are acceptable to your audience; then you give the facts of the specific case about which you are speaking; finally you apply your basic premises to the specific case.

I. The property tax is our primary source of public support for education.
II. Property taxes more than doubled between 1960 and the early 1970's.
III. The property tax particularly oppresses the elderly.
IV. The property tax oppresses low-income workers who own their own homes.
V. We have no choice but to redesign our tax structure.

Several specialized, indirect patterns usefully support central ideas. One of these is the applied-criteria pattern in which propositions of fact or value are argued by first setting up criteria or standards and then showing that the alleged fact or value matches them. Another specialized use of indirect presentation develops when what at first appears to be a pattern of inquiry (described below) concludes by showing or strongly implying that only one solution solves the problem. The so-called implicative pattern resembles an incomplete, indirect pattern in that description, narration, and exposition are used for persuasive purposes. Word pictures, stories, and explanations hint at conclusions. Arguments presented may or may not be stated in formal fashion. In any case, the method is implicative because the audience is left to draw its own final conclusion or application.

As we have noted, indirect sequences are useful in dealing with hostile audiences and where materials can be divided into acceptable and known, unacceptable and unknown. Concerns of speakers also invite use of this pattern. If you are more adept at presenting materials indirectly, in the soft-sell manner, than at approaching audiences directly, you may favor this pattern. The mood of the occasion may also prompt its use. So, once again all elements of speaking situations can enjoin adoption of a withheld-proposal sequence. Furthermore, indirect presentation is feasible regardless of the speaker's purpose.

Open-Proposal or Direct Sequence

The open-proposal or direct-sequence pattern of organization is in one sense a deductive order and stands in contrast to the indirect sequence. In using this pattern you urge the audience to accept a proposition on the grounds that its validity, morality, or practicality necessarily follows from accepted axioms or principles.

The direct sequence is simple to use. Essentially, it consists of telling your audience what you intend to prove or explain and then giving the arguments or clarifications that support your thesis. On many occasions you will use several different arguments or divisions of clarification supporting your subject sentence, and these can be grouped into categories. A person advocating certain legislation might develop arguments showing that it is morally right, legal under the constitution, of economic benefit, and practicable. A speaker explaining road building might cover route planning, grading, and surfacing. These divisions could form the main heads of the body of a speech. They could be arranged in a sequence that gave additional climactic or logical force to the development (the proposal is *desirable;* it is *also practical;* moreover it will have *no significant disadvantages*). Your major concern in applying the open-proposal sequence should be that the sub-propositions be arranged in the clearest, most natural, and most logical order.

The direct or open-proposal sequence includes, among its variations, the topical arrangements which are so common in giving information. It also includes the list-of-advantages pattern for persuasion. In this scheme the case for a proposition of policy is structured to present a list of benefits arising out of the proposed policy. This variation is closely related to problem-solution organization in that each alleged advantage implies or demonstrates a problem and solution.

In general, an open-proposal sequence is most suitable where listeners are fairly familiar with your subject and where they have favorable or openminded attitudes toward your position. The significant advantage of this system of organization is that you can give a number of arguments or kinds of clarification efficiently while keeping your audience always aware of what you are trying to prove or clarify and how you are going about it.

As in the case of the indirect sequence, whether you adopt or avoid the direct-sequence presentation depends on the outlook of your audience, the way subject matter may be reasonably divided, your skill with direct versus indirect presentation, and the tone or spirit of the occasion.

Reflective Sequence or Pattern of Inquiry

The reflective sequence or pattern of inquiry is a pattern of organization based upon five steps in reflective thinking outlined by the philosopher John Dewey — (1) locating and defining a problem, (2) describing and limiting the problem, (3) suggesting possible solutions, (4) evaluating and testing the solutions, and (5) selecting the preferred solution.

To use this pattern requires that you and your listeners be willing to suspend judgment about a problem. This willingness comes from experience and reflection; life teaches us that snap judgments are often wrong, and that sound opinions are usually based on careful consideration of numerous factors. An inquiry and its reflective pattern of organization are appropriate when you are willing to assemble information and ponder various solutions with your audience before reaching a decision.

In a state of mind touched by doubt you invite your audience to join you in a quest for the best solution or the best answer to a question. You develop your speech so that your listeners feel the problem is their problem, not yours alone. And you do all you can do to give the audience and yourself a better basis for coming to a sound decision. This is the function of a speech of inquiry.

Such speaking is obviously both informative and persuasive. It persuasively asks hearers to ponder, to weigh and consider, to explore; but it does not ask audiences to adopt all of your opinions.

An inquirer both resembles and differs from an informative speaker. The man who gives us information is conversant with his subject; his aim is to impart his understanding. An inquirer, on the other hand, does not enjoy the same degree of certainty. He is experiencing a degree of discomfort about his subject, discomfort caused by his inability to settle on a really satisfactory choice among competing solutions or answers. He is certain of some things, for he has studied and thought about the problem that vexes him. (1) He can formulate and clarify the question. (2) He has analyzed the nature of the difficulty and has penetrated beneath its symptoms to its causes, to basic facts. (3) He understands the criteria for a good solution. (4) He knows what solutions are available. His doubt concerns the relative worth of the solutions or the relative validity of the answers. His aim is to impart his information to the audience and to enlist their help in the final determination.

To orient his listeners to his subject, an inquirer first provides them with an understanding of the problem they share. He informs them of its troublesome symptoms and of its underlying causes, carefully distinguishing between symptom and cause. He may also review the problem's historical development, or he may give the details of a controversy that needs to be settled.

He doesn't stop there, however. He next considers the criteria which an acceptable answer must meet. This is an important and often missed step. He must satisfy himself that he has formulated the right criteria, since the acceptability of any solution will depend on what standards are chosen. Though he must consider criteria in every case, inquirers do not always find it necessary to present and justify them in the speech. Some are obvious and readily taken for granted: safety on the highways, democracy, speed in settling legal cases. Such standards hardly need formal presentation and if they do, they require no justification. Sometimes criteria need to be presented but are too complex for explanation apart from discussion of solutions. This might be the case with the aims of a foreign policy, or with the nature of the good life. In such cases criteria will be presented piecemeal as various solutions are discussed. But consideration of criteria is integral to inquiry, so formal presentation of criteria is usually advisable.

Having clarified a problem and said what is necessary concerning standards, an inquirer using the reflective sequence turns to the alternative solutions or answers. This is generally the most important element in his speech; hence, he should allow sufficient time for it, restricting preliminary sections to what is absolutely essential. For each solution he explains and assesses. He explains the solutions or answers. He assesses or evaluates each thoroughly and fairly in light of the pertinent criteria.

In concluding his speech an inquiring speaker should try to make his audience continue to inquire. Their reflection on the subject should not stop when the speaker stops. In fact, inquiry on a large scale—group inquiry— often begins after a speech of inquiry has been delivered. The speaker may well conclude by presenting the salient questions which his listeners should consider as they continue their search for the best solution. Or he may point out the *direction* in which he thinks the best answer will be found.

A speaker who would really inquire may suggest, but he will not urge, acceptance of a specific solution. He may omit Dewey's fifth step altogether. All five steps need not be included in every inquiry. Indeed, some inquiries go no farther than steps two or three. Others omit step one. The pattern, in short, is subject to considerable variation according to the requirements of speaker, audience, and occasion.

The speaker's own state of mind comes first in justifying this pattern of organization. The readiness of the audience to accept a pattern which does not provide for the conclusive settlement of a problem may also be a consideration. Speech materials have less influence on the selection or rejection of this pattern since the same materials at once lend themselves to informing, persuading, or questioning. The occasion is a determinant in that the situation must be one in which men can deliberate. An atmosphere of puzzlement, of careful consideration, will most often suggest to you that a pattern of inquiry is your best scheme of organization.

Monroe's Motivated Sequence

Professor Alan H. Monroe of Purdue University developed this pattern of organization which bears his name. Based on the normal process of human thinking, it is thought to be especially effective in motivating listeners' responses to speakers' purposes. The sequence consists of five steps: Attention, Need, Satisfaction, Visualization, and Action.

In persuasive speeches, which Monroe sees also as speeches to actuate and to reinforce, all five steps are used. The speaker (1) gains attention; (2) establishes a need for change of some sort; (3) shows how the change needed can be brought about or "satisfied"; (4) visualizes what will happen if the need is or is not met—that is, he pictures the good or bad results of following the course he suggests; and (5) appeals directly for action, either mental or physical.

In the speech to inform, Monroe's fourth type, only the first three steps are used, and the "Need" step becomes the "need to know" rather than the "need to believe" or the "need to act." In the speech to entertain, his fifth and last kind, either only the "Attention" step is used, or others are used as the entertainment becomes a parody of informative or persuasive speaking.

This sequence, more than any other, is psychologically planned to lead your audience's thinking naturally and easily from a vague interest in your subject to a definite acceptance of the attitude or action you are advocating. Each step in the sequence is built on the preceding steps. The motivated sequence can be used in a variety of speeches, but it is chiefly useful when you face an audience that has little interest in your subject or when you want to arouse a strong and specific response in your listeners. Here is how the pattern might be developed if you were selling a vacation tour:

I. Your next vacation ought to be better than those dull visits you've paid to crowded, metropolitan beaches in past summers. [**Attention.**]
II. What you really want this summer is privacy plus comfort plus informality. [**Need.**]
III. Maurice Island promises long, quiet beaches, luxury living at moderate prices, and come-as-you-are attitudes. [**Satisfaction.**]
IV. Each of the four beach hotels that occupy the island's twelve miles of tropical, sandy beach reproduces a different nation's night life. [**Visualization.**]
V. The plane is chartered and the fare is reasonable; Miss Krider will give you literature, take your reservation, or better still accept your checks if you will talk with her at the door before you leave. [**Action.**]

You will notice that you have been exposed to and perhaps have used this pattern of ideas before! But do not miss the fact that the structure is psychologically sound for promoting international cooperation, rousing lethargic voters, showing people how to study better, or even giving a speech to entertain.

Because it is both logically and psychologically based, Monroe's motivated sequence is in whole or in part usable with most kinds of material, in a wide variety of situations, and by any speaker willing to work his ideas into the most psychologically inviting form to which they are amenable.

Elimination Order

Elimination order is a pattern of organization wherein several or all possible interpretations of a subject or solution to a problem are considered and all but one are eliminated as undesirable, impractical, or incorrect. This strategy is sometimes called the method of residues because whatever remains at the end is the matter to be accepted by the audience.

The method of elimination is often used as the fourth step of what is otherwise a reflective sequence. This adaptation is especially advantageous when you wish to present an investigation for the purpose of persuading rather than inquiring. At the point of considering solutions you may eliminate all known solutions except the one you advocate. The same patterning may be applied during the second half of a problem-solution or need-remedy speech where more than one solution or remedy must be considered. Thus, this pattern may be thought of as a variation which can be incorporated within either reflective or problem-solution systems or it may be treated as a scheme of organization applicable to a whole speech.

Factors affecting your choice of this organizational system arise from the audience and from your own concerns. Both you and your audience must be willing to investigate more than one kind of "answer." The speech materials must allow discussion of more than one course of action or possibility. The occasion also affects your choice: time must be available for full explanation and for testing the possibilities, and the atmosphere must favor a several-sided consideration of the subject. Thus, once again, all four elements in the speech situation are involved in determining whether elimination order is a wise choice for disposing your speech materials.

We began this chapter by considering man's special need to find relationships and any speaker's consequent need to clarify and show the movement of his thought. Disposition of the content of a speech is essentially further adaptation. It is adaptation to the human propensity to search for structure and unity in all things. Our examination of the normal parts of speeches (introduction, body, and conclusion) and of patterns of organization has been a survey of various ways by which speakers have learned to answer the universal demand for organization.

Most of the time a reasonable adaptation to the necessities of audience, subject, speaker, and occasion will make it necessary that speech begin by orienting the listener to speaker and subject (introduction). Properly adapted speech will continue with a systematic message that makes listening easier and surer by conforming to a structural pattern familiar to both listener and speaker. It will conclude with some reinforcement of the total experience of hearing the speech.

We have discussed the standard patterns of organization, first, because public speech is an art form through which relationships are exhibited in familiar, public terms. The standard patterns of organization are simply the most familiar—the most public—systems our society uses in verbal communication. Second, while not all speech can be effectively structured according to one of the standard patterns we have discussed, all speech will have at least a segment that can be best conveyed according to one of the familiar patterns. These patterns, then, are optional systems among which you will constantly choose. We hope that by understanding what they can accomplish and what they cannot, you will be able to choose wisely. Third, most speech and most situations in which you speak will permit you to select from the standard patterns.   You can adapt to man's need to order his perceptions if you develop what you say in accordance with one of these patterns; if you do not do so, you may achieve effective presentation but you are more likely to achieve obscurity.   Fourth and finally, we have discussed patterns of organization in detail because we wished to demonstrate once more that the art of speaking is an art of social adaptation in which the interrelated requirements arising from content, speaker, audience, and occasion must always be weighed.

EXERCISES

Written

1. a. Choose a subject area, such as air pollution, current methods in secondary education, or the Democratic party in America today.

b. Carefully write out three subject sentences for the subject chosen.   One sentence should be devised for a speech of *information,* another for a speech of *persuasion,* and the third for a speech of *inquiry.*

c. Write out the main heads for each of the three subject sentences you have composed.

2. Write an essay in which you evaluate the following introduction according to the requirements for a good introduction found on pages 169–170.

Drunken Drivers

From the wreckage of the crash, two persons extricate themselves.   The first seems to be an elderly, well-dressed businessman, who, after surveying the wreckage, pulls out a young man and helps him to his feet.   The young man obviously needs help; his gait is unsteady, his eyes are bloodshot and bleary, and his speech is almost unintelligible.   The onlookers are convinced by these signs that he is drunk, which is confirmed by the strong smell of alcohol which is obvious a few feet away.

As the police cars pull up, the crowd is assured that the young man will get what is coming to him.   He can get out that his name is William Schultz, and he is a taxi driver, but he is unable to give the police his address, does not know where he is by a few miles, yet insists that he had nothing to drink.   The officers dutifully administer a test commonly known as the "Balloon Test" to him.   After the balloon is blown up, the contents are passed through a tube containing a purple liquid on what looks to be a wad of cotton.   The purple color disappears if the air passing through it is filled with alcohol, the policeman explains, and the faster the color disappears, the drunker you are.   At the end of the test, however, the purple color is still there, causing some bewilderment among the spectators and the policemen.   Some more tests will be taken down at the station.

It is now the older man's turn for examination.   As expected, he gives a good account of himself.   He is Milton P. Jones, an executive, on his way home from a business conference. He admits to having had a few drinks two hours earlier with his lunch, but the policemen are unable to smell alcohol on his breath. He is also asked to take the balloon test, and, within a fraction of a minute, all color disappears in the glass tube. Befuddled, the policemen take them both down to the station for further examination.

From the evidence placed before you, every person in this room must have some thoughts as to who the guilty party is. Young Mr. Schultz appears to have all the physical attributes of a drunk, while Mr. Jones is surely the victim of this terrible crime. We'll come back to these men and their particular case in a few minutes.[8]

3. Assume that the following sets of main heads have been taken from the "bodies" of outlines for speeches. Evaluate each set for (a) the wording of the main points, and (b) the overall pattern of organization. Give detailed reasons for your judgments.

   a.   I. Every speech should have an introduction, body, and conclusion.
       II. Should the introduction get attention and make the speaker's purpose clear?
      III. A conclusion should summarize and put the entire speech into focus.

   b.   I. The social, political, and economic instability of underdeveloped countries is a potential breeding ground for Communism.
       II. We must increase our financial aid and technical assistance to these countries to head off the threat.

   c.   I. Economical and efficient means of smoke prevention have been devised.
       II. Heavy smoke darkens the sunlight.
      III. Smoke is harmful to public health.
       IV. Smoking is a bad habit.
        V. The annoyance, filth, and unhealthful effects of smoke have caused an agitation for smoke prevention in large cities.
       VI. Gas and electricity may replace coal for many domestic uses.
      VII. Imports of residual oil cause much unemployment in coal fields.
     VIII. Since smoke is injurious and preventable, immediate steps should be taken toward its elimination.
       IX. Efficient smokeless furnaces have proved a success.
        X. Smoke hinders good ventilation.
       XI. Smoke prevention in large cities should be compulsory.
      XII. Electric locomotives may be used in place of steam.
     XIII. Many fires are caused by faulty furnaces.
      XIV. Coal smoke damages the lungs.
       XV. One important step is to sign the Anti-Smoke League petition.

4. Locate the text of a speech in an anthology of speeches, an issue of *Vital Speeches,* or a volume of the Reference Shelf series (H. W. Wilson Co.) devoted to speeches. Read the speech carefully. Identify the overall structure of the speech. Support your labeling of the pattern in a paragraph or two in which you cite specific portions of the speech which led you to choose the label you did.

---

8. This introduction was composed by Renee Ehrlich for an introductory course in public speaking. Used by permission.

Oral

1. a. In class discussion choose several subject sentences for impromptu speeches. Such sentences as: "The automobile is primarily a vehicle for human transportation"; "Donation of blood to the Red Cross is worthwhile"; "Grades in college should be abolished" will serve.

b. Assign each of the subject sentences chosen to three different members of the class, and also assign to each of them *one* of the usable patterns of organization discussed in Chapter 7, e.g., chronological, spatial, problem-solution, causal.

c. Allow time for each of the three students to prepare 2- to 3-minute impromptu speeches using the pattern assigned.

d. After hearing the speeches, discuss the suitability of each pattern to the subject sentence assigned. Also evaluate the speaker's ability to produce a recognizable pattern of organization on short notice.

2. Make a 2-minute speech about a classroom you are familiar with. Treat at *least* these main headings:

> Blackboard areas
> Lighting
> Seating arrangements
> Virtues and flaws as a classroom

Determine and be ready to defend the sequence in which you order your points and your choice of a central idea. Be sure to append appropriate introductory and concluding remarks.

3. Here is a problem in isolating a usable central idea and in arranging main points and amplifying material. The miscellaneous facts below have (or can be given) relationship to one another. Using them as your basic material, give a 2-minute talk in which you have at least two major points amplifying whatever central idea you choose. Be sure to show by clear transitions how the main points relate to the central idea (and to each other if that is important). Here is your basic material:

> In dealing a hand of 13 cards from 52 in bridge, the probability of drawing a perfect hand (13 spades) is 1 in 635,013,559,600. In a four-handed poker game, the chances of getting the highest possible hand (royal flush) are 1 in 649,739. If you are a white, female American, aged 19, insurance companies estimate that you have 57 more years to live. If you are a white, male American, aged 19, the estimate is that you will live 51 more years. If you are a girl and 19, there is 1 chance in 8 that you will marry within a year, but if you are a male and 19 there is but 1 chance in 25 you'll marry within a year.

CHAPTER
8

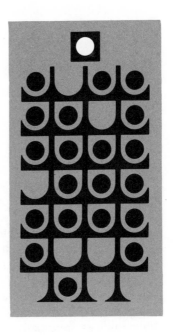

Disposition: Outlining

Outlining the speech on paper is essential for careful disposition (ordering) of materials and adequate preparation for extemporaneous and manuscript speaking. Constructing an outline insures that your ideas will be arranged and fully enough supported or amplified. It further insures that you will have considered the logical relationships among ideas and the weights and emphases you wish to accord them.

From an outline you can perceive shape and definiteness because your conscious attention will be drawn to the existence and proportioning of the parts of the speech. Contours of both the overall and internal structuring will emerge to reveal internal development and climaxes or the lack of them. While outlines are usually skeletal maps of a speech, sometimes they are such complete plans that they are almost manuscripts.

FUNCTIONS OF OUTLINES

You, as speaker, must decide what kind of outline is best for you, how far to go in preparing your thoughts for oral delivery. In some classroom situations you may be required to construct *content* or *technical* outlines in order to reveal to a teacher your planned content or strategies. You may be required to submit *full-sentence, phrase,* or *key-word* outlines, depending upon the degree of preciseness and refinement the teacher demands as evidence of preliminary planning. In any case, you will outline or prepare some sort of speaker's notes to keep thoughts clear and sharp.

If you are a beginner, you will find sentence outlines most helpful. Since full sentences express the complete thoughts to be presented at each point, their use insures that you will frame each thought fully and understand its juxtaposition and relationship to other complete thoughts. While thoughts may be symbolized on paper by mere words, indeed by symbols even simpler than words (a cross or a circle), most beginners find themselves handicapped when using shorthand outlines resembling grocery lists. The more experienced you are, the more likely you are to be successful in using abbreviated methods in outlining.

For maximum effectiveness, your method must be suited to your individual needs. Outlining will serve *you;* audiences seldom see outlines. Utility is the mark of a good outline; no rigid set of rules for structuring a speech on paper is possible.

Speakers resort to various devices to jog their memories. Indeed, the whole matter of *memoria,* which the ancients saw as command of the entire speech and which we discuss at some length in "Rhetorical Theory: A Heritage" in the Appendix, is greatly aided by structuring and placement. One speaker may underline main heads in his outline; another may place asterisks at various points. Still another will draw pictures. Yet another will include notations of the kinds of material he is including: example, story, statistics; he may even mark the vocal variations he wants to produce: loud, soft. No one can say that any of these practices is wrong; for an outline is an instrument, a tool for the speaker. The single exception occurs in the learning situation.

You are asked to submit an outline to your teacher in order to receive helpful, constructive criticism. Your outline, then, is no longer a private paper. It is, instead, a record of preparation to be shared with another interested person who is to make suggestions. This shared paper must be understood by your teacher as well as by you. Since this is so, you must take special care to make ideas and their relationships clear both visually and verbally. You and your critic must agree upon a system of outlining. You may be asked to employ full sentences, at least to begin with, because your reader can understand them better than phrases or words. A single word offered in support of another single word may not be comprehensible to your teacher, and it will not indicate whether you have thought through your ideas. For instance, you may know what you will say when you have written the word "Economic" and listed "Cost" and "Profit" as supporting ideas, but your teacher may not see clear-cut connections between these sketchy symbols. He may be led to conclude that at this particular stage of speech preparation your ideas have not been fully enough refined, that they are still in vague or fuzzy condition. And, in fact, you may really have slipped in your own thinking. For your reader's sake and for your own you must take special care in preparing your papers so that ideas and their relationships are kept clear.

As a teaching device your instructor may prescribe that you not only construct a "content" outline showing the ideas in your speech but that you add technical labels. He may ask you to indicate your kinds of proof and amplification, sources of attention, or the pattern of structure exemplified. When these labels are added to an outline, you have in reality two outlines. One maps ideas to be uttered; the other maps strategy and tactics. It is common for the inexperienced to mix these two types of mapping. In making outlines you will not give symbols to Introduction, Body, Conclusion, because these are not parts of the idea structure of the speech. It is useless in constructing a "content" outline to write simply "story" or "statistics" beside a sub-point number without indicating what you intend to say.   To identify your tactics or methods enables you to straighten out in your own mind just what it is you are doing as you order ideas and just what kinds of ideas you are ordering.   Sometimes your teacher may ask you to use these technical labels in order to test you.   But such labels alone will not enable you to tell others what you will say.   Alone, they produce an unsatisfactory paper for you to refer to should you decide to deliver a second version of your speech before a second audience.   An outline reading as follows would be of little help were you to try to determine what the speaker who made it intended to say.

Introduction

I. Story. — Using novelty, stereotypes, familiarity.   Chronological order.
II. Subject sentence.
III. Definitions.
    a. By function.
    b. By classification.

Body

I. Argument. — Open proposal pattern.
    a. Quotation — familiar.
    b. Statistics — visual aids.
II. Argument. — Developed inductively.
    a. Report of Experiment.
    b. Report of Second Experiment.

Conclusion

I. A Summary.

This record would be of little value either to a teacher aiming to evaluate supports or proofs, subject sentences, or attention values, or to a speaker trying to recapture from his personal files what he said six months ago.

COMMON PRACTICES

No hard and fast rules govern outlining speech, but customary practices have been found trustworthy.   These practices satisfy the requirement of speakers, materials, audiences, and occasions.   They promote the clarity, the organic unity, and the adaptation so necessary for successful speaking.   They produce a visual image of a speech which can help you and, indirectly, your audience.
    What, then, should you do in constructing an outline?   What should you look for as you check over your outline?   Provided you are following commonly accepted practices, you should look for the following:

A Clear Indication of the Basic Divisions of the Speech: Introduction, Body (sometimes labeled Discussion or Proof), and Conclusion.   Since these labels are not parts of the idea structure of the speech but are technical notations, they will not normally be given symbols.   Numerical and alphabetical symbols ought to be reserved as indicators of relationships.   Usually the names of the basic divisions of your speech are centered on the page and go unsymbolized.   This placement insures that you have an introduction and a conclusion and that you are aware of what constitutes these portions of your speech.   In those infrequent instances when no introduction is used, its absence is readily apparent if one forms the practice of identifying each division actually to be included.

A Consistent System of (a) Symbolization and (b) Indentation.   This aids in clarifying relationships and in helping you to remember those relationships. The system of symbols you use is up to you; consistency in their use is essential.   It matters little whether Roman numerals, capital letters, or Arabic numerals are used to indicate main heads and subheads.   What matters is that each time a type of symbol occurs it signifies that the ideas thus identified are of approximately the same importance or weight.   Uniformity in symbolization will indicate clearly the value you assign to your material, and the different symbols assigned will show which ideas are subsidiary to which.   Since you will be working out a structure idea by idea, you should place only one symbol before any one idea.   This serves as a caution against composing compound sentences containing more than one thought.   If you follow the rule: one symbol for *each* idea, you will be reminded to break compound statements in two.   You will need to check very carefully in making a phrase outline to see that each symbol stands beside an idea rather than beside a fragment of one or a phrase that represents — for you — several ideas.

Indentation, the physical arrangement of ideas, further reveals values assigned and stirs the memory.   If each new idea has a clear indentation, that fact announces to you when it is time to embark on a new phase of your thought structure.   Ideas subsidiary to other ideas should be indented under the subsuming thought.   In this way it will be easy to see that supports and amplifications are subordinate points.   Your visual image of your speech will then be of a network of ideas with the least important ones indented farthest from the left-hand margin of the page.   Though none of the ideas you set down on the page is, ideally, expendable, it will be less of a calamity should an idea given minor weight (one farthest indented) be forgotten.

In outlining inductive patterns, a common practice is to symbolize and indent points and sub-points in the same way you do for deductive patterns, then to place supporting or amplifying sub-points in parentheses.   Such practice indicates that the examples, statistics, and definitions subsumed by a point are to be presented *before* the point being amplified or supported.

An outline is not always constructed to indicate the order in which ideas will actually be introduced when the speech is delivered.   However, it is imperative to follow the outlined orders when utilizing chronological or ascending or descending order patterns. When using inductive patterns, such as the withheld proposal, speakers will more often depart from idea structures as they appear on paper.

Absence of Single Sub-points.   Wherever one idea is subordinated to another, it indicates a splitting of the subsuming idea for purposes of amplification or support. Usually more than one piece of information is needed to develop a point adequately. Yet, one definition, one example, or one opinion sometimes may suffice to clarify or prove to an acceptable degree. Audience needs may occasionally be met with only one item of amplification. More often, a single subordinate item would be better reinforced if there were other, parallel items. If not, it may very well be combined with the idea to which it appears to be subordinate. In any case, an outline containing a multitude of single sub-points should be viewed suspiciously. It is likely that the ideas contained in it have not been developed to the point of audience acceptance and that necessary information and proof have been overlooked. Only when you are absolutely sure that one and only one piece of proof is necessary should a sub-point be allowed to stand alone.

Discreteness of Ideas.   In outlines, ideas should not be lumped together nor should they overlap. An outline is a structure intended to display relationships clearly. This fact dictates that each idea stand separately within the structure. The need to reveal the relationship of each idea to other ideas is an additional argument for full-sentence outlining. Sentences, if correctly constructed, are expressions of complete thoughts. Be wary of the compound sentence in outlining; it contains more than one idea, making it impossible to follow the principle of one symbol, one idea. Therefore, "ands" and "ors" should rarely appear in the sentences of an outline; they bear special checking when they do appear.

Appropriate Symbolization and Placement of Subject Sentences.   Since the core idea (subject sentence, main proposition, central idea, or specific purpose) is the most important idea in the speech, it deserves the highest rank in symbolization. This main proposition or assertion should be unmistakable in your outline. Some teachers and students prefer to label this proposition or assertion "central idea," "main proposition," "subject sentence," or "specific purpose" rather than affixing number or letter symbols, because it is of highest rank in the hierarchy of ideas symbolized in the outline.

In the sample outlines at the end of this chapter and in the diagram on page 197 we have both symbolized and labeled the central idea, indicating that either method is acceptable and that both are common in outlining. No matter which of these practices is followed, the central idea should never appear as a sub-point nor should it be indented beneath any other point. In deductive patterns this central sentence will usually appear near the end of the Introduction or near the beginning of the Body of the speech. Wherever it appears, the central idea should be designated by a symbol or label indicating that it is of most weight or value. Graphically, it should at least be accorded the same rank by indentation as the other most important items in the section. The same is true in symbolizing or labeling and in indenting the central idea when outlining inductive patterns, such as the withheld-proposal sequence. The main idea should be given the symbol and/or label and indentation that reveals it is a statement not outranked in importance by any other ideas in that section of the speech. Whether the central idea appears in the Introduction, Body, or Conclusion, it is the most important idea in that division of your outline.

Clear Transitions. Transitions should be uniformly indicated and set off from the rest of the structure. Points of linkage and internal summaries should be clearly indicated. If they are symbolized and indented in the same manner as other parts of the outline, they should be given technical labels such as "Transition" or "Internal Summary." A common practice is to treat these portions of the speech differently from main points or sub-points, omitting symbols but marking them off by enclosing them in brackets or parentheses. This practice shows that you have given careful attention to how you will move from one point or sub-point to another and to the necessity for repetition and review.

If the above practices are observed, a diagram of an outline will look like that printed below. For a short speech you may not need to outline in as full detail as this diagram indicates, but we illustrate in detail for your future reference.

Title

Introduction

I. ....
   A. ....
   B. ....
II. (Central Idea) ....
     (Transition: ....)

Body

I. ....
   A. ....
   B. ....
     1. ....
       a. ....
       b. ....

2. ....
   a. ....
   b. ....
C. ....
  1. ....
  2. ....
   a. ....
   b. ....
     (1) ....
     (2) ....
  (Transition: ....)
II. ....
A. ....
  1. ....
   a. ....
   b. ....
   c. ....
  2. ....
  (Transition: ....)
B. ....
  1. ....
   a. ....
   b. ....
     (1) ....
     (2) ....
     (3) ....
       (a) ....
       (b) ....
   c. ....
   d ....
     (1) ....
     (2) ....
  2. ....
   a. ....
   b. ....
  (Internal Summary: ....
  ....)
III. ....
A. ....
  1. ....
   a. ....
   b. ....
  2. ....
B. ....
  (Transition and/or Internal Summary ....
  ....)

Conclusion

I. ....
  A. ....
  B. ....
  C. ....
II. ....

Bibliography
(or Statement of Sources)

....
....
....
....
....
....

     Two items appearing in this diagram remain to be considered: title and bibliography or statement of sources.

TITLES

The final act in the composition of your speech is ordinarily the selection of a title. Informal situations make titles less necessary than those in which you will be introduced, but a title provides a label for use by those reporting your speech, recording it, or referring to the event of which your speech was a part. Titles are normally composed last since that is when you can best cast your eye back over the total composition and decide upon a phrase characterizing it. But sometimes a title will evolve from the very first pieces of data you encounter in the process of invention.

     Good titles attract attention by being (1) brief, (2) relevant, and (3) provocative. They arouse interest and reveal to some degree what the speech is about by emphasizing its theme.

     A title must be brief for practical reasons. An audience stops listening before the end of a title such as: "The History and Significance of the Indian Tribes in the Western New York Area from the Years 1770 to 1790 with Special Emphasis upon the Youth between the Ages of 12–18 and Their Role in War Making." A better title would be "The Warring Indian Braves of Western New York during the Late Eighteenth Century." A long title is also impractical for publicity purposes; a title should be short enough to fit on a poster or into a one- or two-column newspaper head. When a speech has no title or a long and unarresting one, newspapermen often invent one. Reporters did just that when they retitled Franklin D. Roosevelt's "Speech to the Teamsters'

Union, September 23, 1944," the "Fala Speech."   They also shortened the title of his "Speech at the Dedication of the Outerlink Bridge, Chicago, Illinois, October 5, 1937," to "The Quarantine Speech."   The second of these "tag titles" identifies the essential theme of the speech, but the first does not.

Your titles ought to arouse curiosity.   Images can help since they serve as shorthand symbols which stir up mental pictures.   William Jennings Bryan's "Cross of Gold" is a classic example, yet we can think of other lesser-known titles such as "Skeletons All?" "Little Fences and Barriers," and "The Big Fraud."   Such images in titles arouse initial attention and are remembered after the speech has been delivered.

These four titles seize attention but are still not ideal.   They do not tell us precisely what the speeches are about.   To a degree they are riddles. Bryan's speech might have been titled "The Economic Cross of Gold."   The "skeleton" of "Skeletons All?" represented a nonvoter, and a good title might have been "Present but Not Voting?"   "Little Fences and Barriers" might better have been "Fences and Barriers that Separate Us," and "The Big Fraud" would have been clearer as "Social Security or Insecurity?"

BIBLIOGRAPHIES

The educated man knows the sources of his knowledge and his opinions.   He is able to acknowledge how and where he acquired his ideas and facts, and he does so voluntarily.   In preparing outlines and manuscripts he annotates ideas and quotations not his own and does so as a natural recognition of other people's contributions.

You may be asked to include a bibliography or "Statement of Sources" with your outline.   Occasionally acknowledgments of sources may appear in the outline proper.   They should certainly appear there when the sources are mentioned in the speech itself.   More often such acknowledgments will be appended at the end of the outline as a communication to the instructor or other reader.   Your teacher, as a critic, wants to know what you actually found useful, and you, yourself, at some future date may wish to relocate the sources.

There are many forms for bibliographical entries.   The important objectives are to be complete and consistent.   The following forms may be used when you are asked to cite your sources.   Comments on the scope and value of printed sources are enclosed in square brackets.   The notes on other materials are given in informal description.

Observation:

During the week of August 12–19, 1973, I took part in NROTC naval maneuvers and saw the things I describe under Point I of the Introduction.

Interview:

On May 12, 1973, I talked with President J. B. Smith of X Company for about an hour and got the ideas on management's problems which appear in Section III of this outline.

I have drawn at many points on the courses I have taken in business, economics, and oral and written communication.

Book:

Lash, Joseph P., *Eleanor and Franklin Roosevelt: The Story of Their Relationship Based on Eleanor Roosevelt's Private Papers* (New York: W. W. Norton, 1971).
[The early chapters of this volume provided me with information on Mrs. Roosevelt's childhood which I did not find anywhere else and which stood me in good stead in developing Point I in the Body of my speech.]

Articles:

A. *From Periodicals:*

Asimov, Isaac, "I Can't Believe I Saw the Whole Thing!" *Saturday Review,* LV, No. 36 (September 2, 1972), 25–32.
[The definition of "holography" used in the Introduction of my speech and the historical materials used under the first main point of the Body of my speech come from this source.]

B. *From Books:*

Kauffmann, Stanley, "The Film Generation," in Allen Kirschner and Linda Kirschner, eds., *Film: Readings in the Mass Media* (New York: Odyssey Press, 1971), pp. 151–163.
[Some of the material I used concerning the role of sex in current films (see Point II) are taken from this essay.]

C. *From General Reference Books:*

"John Donne," *Encyclopaedia Britannica,* 9th ed. (New York, 1878).[1]
[Most of the biographical material in my speech came from here.]

Newspapers:

A. *From Signed Articles, Editorials, and News Accounts:*

Povich, Shirley, "Germany Loves Olympians," *The Washington Post* (August 23, 1972), sec. D, p. 1.
[Information concerning Germany's preparations for the 1972 summer Olympic games and evidence indicating the friendliness of the natives of Munich were drawn from this article.]

B. *From Unsigned Articles, Editorials, and News Accounts:*

"Ping, Pong, Plunk," *The New York Times* (August 26, 1972), p 24.

---

1. In citing any *Britannica* since 1932 it is advisable to use the date of printing: "John Donne," *Encyclopaedia Britannica* (1971).

[This editorial criticizing Peking's veto blocking the admission of Bangladesh to the United Nations furnished support (backing) for the argument comprising Point III.]

Pamphlets (where the author or editor is not credited):

The Crime of Genocide, United Nations Office of Public Information (New York, 1959). [The text of the convention (international agreement) passed by the General Assembly in December of 1946, quoted in my speech, was contained in this source.]

SAMPLE OUTLINES AND SPEAKER'S NOTES

The two outlines which follow will serve to illustrate good outlining procedures and preparatory methods. The first is an outline for a speech of information six minutes in length. It contains good examples of structure and of outlining mechanics. These outlines are as detailed as any you will probably ever make. Your own needs and your instructor's expectations may require you to prepare less comprehensive outlines than these, but the principles of outlining and of documenting outlines are fully illustrated in these samples because at some time you may need to prepare in this much detail.

The Artificial Kidney Machine[2]

Introduction

I. Although we haven't made any giant steps in controlling air or water pollution, we have found a way to eliminate body pollution.
  A. What is body pollution?
   1. Body pollution is the loss of function in both kidneys.
   2. This results in the inability of the person to filter out the wastes from the blood.
     a. Uric acid begins to pollute the body.
     b. Excess water is also built up within, due to the lack of efficient urinary output.
  B. How has body pollution been eliminated?
   1. Through the use of the artificial kidney machine, the blood is purified.
   2. Hemodialysis or simply dialysis is the term given to this process of cleaning the blood.
(Central Idea)
II. Living without kidney function is not only possible, it is safe, painless, and relatively simple, if one has access to an artificial kidney machine.

---

2. Adapted from an outline prepared for an informative speech in a beginning course in public speaking at Herbert H. Lehman College, City University of New York. The author of the outline was Miss Randy Cohn. Used by permission.

Body

I. What is the basic structure of the artificial kidney?
   A. I will limit my discussion to the Drake-Willock Kiil combination dialyzer, since it is the one used most frequently in the United States.
   B. The artificial kidney consists of two main parts.
      1. The upper part is made up of three boards and a frame.
      2. The electrical portion composed of the heater, delivery system, and trouble detecting devices make up the bottom half of the unit.
      3. (Visual Aid Number 1 — Picture showing the main parts of the artificial kidney machine.)
      (Transition: After seeing the artificial kidney, one cannot help but wonder how it operates.)
II. How does the dialyzer work?
   A. The dialyzer works on the principle of osmosis.
      1. Osmosis is the tendency of a fluid to pass through a semipermeable membrane in order to equalize concentrations on both sides of the membrane.
   B. The upper portion of the kidney is set up in such a way that it can be compared to a double-decker sandwich.
      1. The boards would be the bread.
      2. The dialysate or cleaning liquid would be the butter.
      3. The membranes would be the lettuce.
      4. The blood ports, through which the blood flows, are in the position of the meat.
   C. By realizing this positioning, it is easy to see that the membranes serve as the semipermeable membrane through which the blood passes its unwanted wastes and excess water into the dialysate.
   (Transition: In order for the machine to be effective, the person must come in contact with it.)
III. The blood of the person being dialyzed can be sent to the machine in one of two ways.
   A. The shunt is a piece of flexible silastic tubing which is embedded into an artery and a vein of the arm or leg.
      1. It has a portion which is visible.
      2. The visible piece of tubing is separated at a connecting piece; much like two drinking straws attached by a smaller piece of straw.
   B. The other method is by the use of a fistula.
      1. A fistula is an internal operation.
      2. It requires the use of needles to be inserted into enlarged veins of the arm.
      (Transition: In conclusion, I would like to remind you that people who have lost complete kidney function may lead a normal life.)

Conclusion

I. Dialysis can be carried on at night.
   A. Depending on the machine used, dialysis takes either 6 or 10 hours.
   B. The person may sleep without fear, due to a complex alarm system sensitized to the slightest problem.
   C. There is no pain involved.

II. We should value our health and protect it.
  A. There are signs we can all look for in order to determine possible kidney trouble.
    1. Puffy eyes and swelling ankles are significant.
    2. Intense thirst and low back pain are also present.
  B. To protect your kidneys you can do a couple of very easy things.
    1. Make sure you drink a few glasses of water a day.
    2. Strep throat is the number one cause of kidney infection; therefore, take care of all sore throats.

Bibliography

Observation:

Since March 1969, I have been involved with the hemodialysis program at Grasslands County Hospital, Valhalla, New York. The majority of my knowledge comes from this experience.

Interview:

I have had the opportunity to speak with Dr. S. Weseley and Mr. Roger Smith, both prominent members of the staff at Grasslands, along with other people and patients involved in the program.

Books:

Longmore, Donald, *Spare-Part Surgery*, Doubleday and Company, Inc., New York, 1968, pp. 53–59.

Pamphlets:

A Chance to Live, U.S. Department of Health, Education, and Welfare (Washington, D.C., 1968).

Instruction Booklet #2, Drake-Willock Mobile Dialysis Machine operation and maintenance.

The Modified Kiil Dialyzer, Cobe Laboratories, Inc.

The second outline illustrates suitable procedures for a persuasive speech. It was prepared by a student for an eight-minute presentation.

The Big Fraud[3]

Introduction

(Central Idea)
  I. Beware of Social Security: a poor investment.
    A. Students preparing to enter the work force will be most affected and have the least to gain from Social Security Insurance.
      1. They will contribute for 46 years at the highest rates in history.

---

3. This outline was submitted by Mary M. Collins. Used by permission.

    2. Their contributions will far exceed what they could ever hope to achieve in benefits.

  B. They must be alerted to the inequities of this system.

(Transition: Before telling you more about this fraud, I'd like to mention a few of the facts.)

II. Social Security Insurance was born at the height of the depression when 22 million were unemployed.

  A. It was a crash program to free citizens from economic fear, care, and want.

    1. It provided money with dignity to those in need.

    2. The requests for welfare were reduced.

  B. The present system is not fulfilling the promise made back in 1935 with regard to financial security.

Body

III. In the beginning Social Security Insurance was a good deal.

  A. Until 1939, whatever money the worker contributed was returned to either the retired worker or his estate.

    1. This "money-back guarantee" was cancelled in 1939.

  B. Ida Fuller was the first person to receive benefits and is still receiving them— $12,000 later.

    1. She paid in less than $70 to the plan.

    2. She participated in the plan for only two years.

(Transition: For *Ida* it was a good deal; for *you*, it's *not!*)

IV. Under present law Social Security Insurance is not a good deal.

  A. A person now 18 will contribute approximately $19,270 by the time he reaches 65 and will not receive interest on his money.

    1. If deposited in a bank, the contributions could earn presently $5\frac{1}{2}\%$ interest.

    2. Money doubles every 14 years in a bank.

  B. The maximum benefits one could receive assuming one lived till 79 years of age would be $80,888.

    1. Internal Revenue actuarial tables show life expectancy at 71.9 years.

  C. There are many inequities in this system.

    1. Participation is compulsory.

    2. This "insurance" does not have the restrictions and regulations imposed on private insurance plans.

    3. The plan used is "pay as you go"—no reserves.

    4. Funds can be used for any purpose the government decides upon.

    5. This "gift" can be revoked, increased, or decreased by Congress.

    6. There are gimmicks attached which prohibit receiving checks under certain circumstances.

V. The solution is to get the government out of the insurance business.

  A. Encourage growth of private investment plans rather than hamper them.

  B. Manage your own money in your own way rather than entrusting it to Uncle Sam.

Conclusion

VI. After three decades the promise of financial security is still unfulfilled.

  A. Constant clamoring for more indicates that Social Security is not enough.

B. Let's do all we can to abolish Social Security Insurance.

C. The fraud is being perpetrated on *you*. Beware!

Statement of Sources

1. Anonymous, *Social Security—Medicare Simplified* (Washington, D.C.: *U.S. News and World Report,* 1969).

    [This book was easy to understand and provided basic material. Pages 219–223 were especially useful.]

2. Douglas, Paul Howard, *Social Security in the United States* (New York: Arno Press, 1971).

    [This volume contained historical material which I found useful, in part.]

3. Ellis, Abraham, *The Social Security Fraud* (New Rochelle, New York: Arlington House, 1971).

    [Ellis suggested leading arguments and some of the wording of main points. My title was also suggested by this source.]

4. McKinley, Charles, and Robert W. Frase, *Launching Social Security: A Capture-and-Record Account, 1935–1937* (Madison, Wisconsin: University of Wisconsin Press, 1970).

    [I found most of this book much too technical, but it was an aid on the historical aspects of my topic.]

5. Scheibla, Shirley, "Memo to Young Workers," *Barron's National Business and Financial Weekly,* LI, No. 27 (July 5, 1971), 5 ff.

    [Figures under IV. A. and B. came from this source.]

6. *Social Security Benefits for Students, 18–22,* United States Department of Health, Education and Welfare, Social Security Administration Pamphlet No. SS 1–48 (Washington, D.C.: U.S. Government Printing Office, October, 1969).

    [Some of this material aided me in adapting to my specific audience.]

7. *Social Security Benefits—How You Earn—How to Estimate,* United States Department of Health, Education and Welfare, Social Security Administration Pamphlet No. SS 1–47 (Washington, D.C.: U.S. Government Printing Office, January, 1970).

    [This pamphlet was an easy to understand, valuable, authoritative source.]

Speaker's Notes

The speaker's notes for the speech outlined above might have looked like this:

The Big Fraud

Intro: Beware of Social Security = poor investment
Students entering work force—you—most affected
Contribute 46 yrs at highest rates
Contributions exceed benefits
Program born at height of Depression, crash program

Body: In beginning, good deal!
           Money-back guarantee—cancelled
           Ida Fuller, example—how worked well
      At present, *not* good
           18 yr old, by 65 = \$19,270: *vs.* money in bank
              (doubles every 14 yrs)—no interest on yours
           S.S. maximum at 79 = \$80,888
      Six inequities of system:
           1) Compulsory
           2) No regs. (as there are for private ins. co's)
           3) Pay as you go—*no reserves*
           4) Funds can be used for any purpose
           5) Congress can revoke—increase or decrease
           6) Gimmicks
      Solution: *Get Gov't out of business!*

Concl: Promise—still unfulfilled
      Don't let it happen *to you.* Beware!

Note that the brevity of these notes would make it possible for the speaker to fit them on two or three 3″ × 5″ cards which might be used unobtrusively on the platform.

An outline is the basic tool by which an extemporaneous speaker fixes the design of his speech as a composition, tests the reasonableness of that design, represents to himself and others the relationships among his thoughts, and fixes his speech plan in his own mind. A completed outline is a visual representation of how speech materials are going to be disposed or handled in the speech to come. Both making an outline and reviewing it are invaluable aids to what ancient writers on rhetoric had in mind when they used the Latin term *memoria*—the speaker's ultimate command of his material, his plan, and his own thinking processes in the moments of delivery. These being the justifications for making outlines, the only legitimate justification for any formal procedure in outlining must be that it is practically helpful. It is on just such a practical basis that we have tried to weigh the merits of outlining procedures in Chapter 9.

The mechanics of outlining are good or bad in proportion to how well they serve your needs and the needs of any constructive critic. Six common practices in outlining are invariably helpful:

1. Clear identification of the basic divisions of the speech: Introduction, Body, and Conclusion.
2. Use of consistent systems of symbolization and indentation to signal the relative importance of the relationships among ideas.
3. Recognition that the appearance of single sub-points in an outline is likely to indicate that a relationship has not been clearly thought out.

4. Firm adherence to the rule of discreteness in outlining; one thought per symbol; one symbol per thought.
5. Clear and unmistakable identification of the central idea or subject sentence.
6. Clear and unmistakable identification, in uniform fashion, of important transitions and internal summaries.

The sample outlines we have provided for your study and analysis conform to these practices in most details. They illustrate the general principles of disposition we have discussed in Chapter 8.

EXERCISES

Written

1. Arrange the eleven statements below as an outline for a main point in a speech. There is no title, introduction, or conclusion. Select the sentence containing the main point and give it proper place and status in your outline.

Political bribery may be increased considerably due to heart transplants.
Some feel the poor man deserves it.
The families of the poor cannot afford prolonged private care without surgery.
Saturday Review of February 3rd reports an incident in which a prominent New York politican used his influence to have a half-hour conference with Dr. Christiaan Barnard when he was in Washington, D.C., in order to discuss the possibilities of his securing a heart transplant.
Heart transplants are ethically questionable.
Some feel the rich man who can afford surgery should receive it.
The poor are the only means of support for their families.
The January 6th *Science News* states, "A million dollars could buy a patient almost anything . . . including a new heart."
There are inequalities shown in deciding whose lives are to be saved through the miracle of heart transplants.
How many other unreported incidents of this sort will be revealed in the near future?
Some feel it should be the man or woman with special talent.

2. Make a list of suggestions for improvement of the outline entitled "The Big Fraud" (see pages 204–206).
3. In a sentence or two evaluate each of the following speech titles:
   a. "What You Must Do"
   b. "Acres of Diamonds"
   c. "Billy the Kid—Juvenile Delinquent?"
   d. "A Case for Euthanasia in the United States Today with Special Emphasis upon the Role of the General Practitioner in the Rural Areas"
   e. "Goya"
   f. "From Trees to Paper"
   g. "Drug Addicts: The Living Dead"

h. "Some Evidences of the Pedagogical Philosophy and Techniques of Quintilian as They Are Found in Modern Speech Education"

i. "The Sleeping Dragon"

j. "The Eternal Verities"

Oral

1. Outline a speech by one of your classmates as you listen to him deliver it. Arrange for a conference during which you compare the outline you composed with the outline he used. Look for similarities and differences between the outlines and discuss why these occurred as they did.

2. Compose an outline for a 6-minute speech of information or persuasion. Observe the suggestions made in this chapter and in Chapter 7.

3. Here, in proper order, are the items of a "blank outline." Choose a suitable subject, organize the items of the outline with proper symbols and indentations, and fill the blanks with ideas appropriate to the subject you have chosen. Be prepared to give this short speech extemporaneously at your next class meeting.

I wonder whether you have thought enough about _____(subject)_____.

I would define _____(subject)_____ like this: _____.

You can see what I mean by thinking of these examples:

My first example is: _____.

Another example is: _____.

What causes [or results from] _____ is this: _____.

An example of how this happens is _____.

Another example is _____.

We usually think of _____ as something remote from our everyday lives, but there are cases where it makes a lot of difference to people like you and me.

One everyday influence it has [had] is [was] _____.

Another influence is [was] _____.

My conclusion is that the next time we hear people talk about _____ or think of it ourselves, we ought to remember it is no vague thing but something that can touch our lives as closely as in _____(refer to examples used)_____.

CHAPTER
9

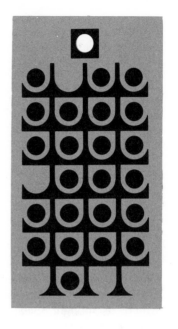

Style

> Among all other lessons this should first be learned, that wee never affect any straunge inkehorne termes, but to speake as is commonly received: neither seeking to be over fine, nor yet living over-carelesse, using our speeche as most men doe, and ordering our wittes as the fewest have done.
>
> Thomas Wilson, "Arte of Rhetorique"[1]

Man's expression of inner self probably emerges more clearly in his style than in any other aspect of his communication. The verbal ways in which a speaker symbolizes thought reveal his capacities to discriminate among meanings, to conceive ideas clearly, to represent them precisely. Styles reflect men's adjustments to their times. The relatively unguarded expression found in speaking mirrors habits of thinking with special sharpness. Thus examination of style provides information for conclusions both about accommodations to society and about society itself.

Speech consists of ideas converted into words. *Acoustic* words are the basic symbols of all oral communication and expression. When we speak these acoustic symbols stimulate the listeners, and they stand for our ideas. We encode our thoughts and express our emotions in sound, hoping that the listeners have the necessary aural repertoire of meanings to decode the message accurately or nearly so. The fundamental problem of oral style, then, is to find and use language that is at once true to our actual meanings and within the capacities of particular listeners to interpret with a high degree of accuracy. Hence, Thomas Wilson's advice to Englishmen learning to use English for formal purposes is still applicable: not the strange but the "commonly received," not the "fine" and not the "careless" but the precise and telling—for listeners—become the goals in developing a style for speaking. The work of speaking is not finished until ideas and feelings are *couched in the language of speech*, voiced, and given further meaning through bodily action.

The words we choose as symbols of our ideas, their capacities to stir

---

1. Thomas Wilson, *Arte of Rhetorique* (London, 1585), p. 162.

meanings in listeners' minds, and the influence of their combinations *are* our ideas insofar as they are verbally communicated. One may say, "The posterior portion of the mansion embraced a rude pergola under which a saucy damosel attired in a bathing costume reclined." Or, "The rear of the house supported a rickety arbor beneath which sat a beautiful girl in a bathing suit." Or, "The back of the club propped a saggy shade below which a hot bikinied babe laid." The ideas are basically similar, but the images communicated surely are not. The reason lies in the individual words and in the ways they have been combined. Since the primary concern in oral communication is to arouse exact meaning, success depends very much upon the speaker's ability to choose and combine verbal symbols for aural reception. If we are to be practical we must be concerned with the art of creating efficient, telling "style."

THE NATURE OF STYLE

Oral style is that part of rhetorical art which emerges from choices and combinations in language. The force of style derives from the meanings of words, their grammatical construction, and their collective psychological impact. We define style, as applied to the rhetoric of oral discourse, as *the personal manner of utterance or expression giving ideas impact and movement.* Style in this sense is the result of the most complex and personal of all the adjustments involved in human communication. You will be creating and controlling the processes of style as soon as you have selected an idea or have begun to arrange ideas in logical and psychological sequences. Some language decisions are made during stages of invention and disposition; but whole speeches almost never exist, even in the mind, until after the problems of language have been faced directly.

You will not always speak extemporaneously, even though that mode of speaking finds most favor with most people. There are many formal situations in life which call for carefully symbolized speech. People do not ordinarily "speak off the tops of their heads" or even from "just a few notes" at inaugurals, commencements, dedications, or funerals, or in making technical reports. These occasions hold great significance; they are often once-in-a-lifetime events for those involved. Whether everyday situations or special ones, they call for particular care in choosing word symbols and often they dictate writing down one's verbal choices ahead of time. The more formal or technical the situation is, the more vital care becomes. Our purpose in this chapter is to discuss resources you have when you need to make careful choices in solving the problems of style. We shall also consider the general role style plays in oral communication of all serious sorts.

We shall use the term "style" in a limited sense. Style may be thought of as a quality pervading all of a communication, including the way it is uttered.   Gestures and facial expressions operate as symbols to stir up thought, so style in delivery is worthy of consideration.   However, in this chapter we shall consider style only as it relates to verbal composition, the conversion of ideas into words.   The selection of words and their combination into thought units are our special topics in the pages that follow.

We want to emphasize at the outset that we do not conceive of style as either decoration or the exhibition of mere facility with language.   Many think that style is, as Lord Chesterfield said, "the dress of thoughts."   They think of verbal style as clothing or covering, as something you *put on* ideas or *do to* them.   Ideas are looked upon as windows to be trimmed, or as Christmas trees; composition then becomes work from which you step back to see if the baubles and tinsel you have applied give interesting effects.   This view we reject.

This concept of style as exornation, as superimposed beautification, is often associated with an equally erroneous conception that the object of working on problems of style is to produce something to be exhibited.   When speakers try to dazzle their audiences with clever wordings or to impress them with long or archaic words or with quaint expressions, we think they misconceive the function of oral language.   They miss its necessary relationship to idea, audience, and occasion.

We believe that when language is truly effective it arises *from* and is *at one with* thought.   Rather than worry about what to do with an idea or how to exhibit it, we believe one should try to think clearly in the first place so that he searches for words that say accurately and clearly what he is thinking.   We agree with George Henry Lewes:

> We see at once the mistake directly we understand that a genuine style is the living body of thought, not a costume that can be put on and off; it is the expression of the writer's mind; it is not less the incarnation of his thoughts in verbal symbols than a picture is the painter's incarnation of his thoughts in symbols of form and colour.   A man may, if it please him, dress his thoughts in the tawdry splendour of a masquerade.   But this is no more Literature than the masquerade is Life.[2]

What Lewes says of writing and literature applies even more forcibly to public address.

In our definition of style we emphasized personal manner, impact, and movement.   In the remainder of this chapter we shall try to help you to see ways of achieving impact and movement as you develop a style of your own.   Topics we shall treat are the constituents of effective style, considerations imposed by orality, and special communicative resources offered by conventional forms in language.

---

2. George Henry Lewes, "The Principle of Beauty," in *Representative Essays on the Theory of Style,* ed. William T. Brewster (New York: Macmillan, 1921), p. 217.

CONSTITUENTS OF EFFECTIVE STYLE

A useful way of looking at style is to consider the general qualities or traits of language that contribute to effectiveness. These are qualities that combine to constitute a speaker's personal, distinctive way of speaking and the variations within it. They are attributes or constituents of style *as listeners view style.* Whether they understand the uses of language well or not, your listeners are always asking themselves whether what you say is *accurate* in relation to what you probably mean. They also ask whether what you are saying is *clear, appropriate,* and *economical* in relation to the task you have undertaken. Listeners respond specially to *forceful, striking,* and *lively* language that keeps interest up and gives ideas the "right" emphases. From listeners' points of view your speech, however individualistic, must seem "good" in at least these six ways.

Accuracy

Whatever is said has some quality of accuracy; any thought expressed has some amount of precision or fuzziness, as a listener sees it. Your accuracy, then, depends on your ability to choose words which will represent as exactly as possible to listeners what you want them to understand. The precision and range of your vocabulary will partly determine the degree of verbal accuracy you can attain. If you use "infer" for "imply" or vice versa, no listener can get your meaning precisely. Would it be better to say, "I *telephoned* my father" than to say, "I *contacted* my father"? The first is more specific, more accurate, and, therefore, clearer. You will solve problems of accuracy best by concerning yourself with the concreteness and exact meanings of words. After all, a large vocabulary is a source of *in*accuracy if one does not attend to precise, conventional meanings.

Grammatical accuracy—observing the conventions your listeners respect most—ought to govern your choices in fashioning your symbols into meaningful clusters. It has been said since classical times, and modern experiments and surveys have repeatedly confirmed it, that whatever listeners take as "slips" in grammar will negatively affect your image as a speaker. Conventional grammar is expected by audiences unless unique features of a situation authorize the unconventional. With educated audiences your standards ought to be the same as Cicero's:

> . . . nobody ever admired an orator for correct grammar, they only laugh at him if his grammar is bad, and not only think him no orator but not even a human being; no one ever sang the praises of a speaker whose style succeeded in mak-

ing his meaning intelligible to his audience, but only despised one deficient in capacity to do so.[3]

The literature of experimental research done with college students as subjects confirms each of Cicero's points, though it appears that college-educated listeners do not so much "laugh at" as "regret" grammatical inaccuracies in speaking.

A third concern in achieving accuracy ought to be for what is "correct" for one's specific occasion. Matters of accuracy, correctness, and appropriateness come into blended consideration here. If you need to produce a particular tone or feeling, you may need to choose between several levels of language, any of which might be accurate to your basic meaning. For example, the formality of an occasion may force a special choice. In a parliamentary situation, for example, "I agree with George's idea" may accurately reflect your attitude, but it is both inaccurate and inappropriate to the ways of doing parliamentary business. "I support the motion presented by George Green" would have both accuracy and propriety for this situation. Your level of abstraction and the technicality of your language can be *both* accurate and appropriate only if your immediate audience understands what you say and the occasion justifies the way it is said. The most convivial gathering of astronauts would allow levels of technicality and precision that would be bafflingly imprecise and inappropriate for a high school class in general science. And the same could be said of the "in language" of motorcycle buffs.

What is accurate enough to be efficient in speech is always modified by who speaks, to whom, on what idea, and under what circumstances. The "right" language must meet all these tests at once.

Clarity

One cannot, of course, be clear if he is inaccurate. But what listeners demand as clarity involves more than the kind of precision discussed above. At the beginning of his discussion of style in *The Rhetoric*, Aristotle said: "We may therefore . . . regard it as settled that a good style is, first of all, clear. The proof is that language which does not convey a clear meaning fails to perform the very function of language."[4] So you must ask yourself, "How clearly have I expressed the idea? How completely will my audience understand me?"

Aristotle went on to say: "Clearness is secured through the use of name-words [nouns and adjectives] and, verbs, that are current terms. . . ."[5]

3. *De Oratore*, trans. H. A. Rackham (Cambridge, Mass.: Harvard University Press, 1948), pp. 41–42, bk. III, chap. 14.
4. From *The Rhetoric of Aristotle*, translated and edited by Lane Cooper, p. 185, bk. III, chap. 2. Copyright 1932, renewed 1960 by Lane Cooper. Reprinted by permission of Appleton-Century-Crofts, Educational Division, Meredith Corporation.
5. *Ibid*.

His judgment is still sound.   Listeners prefer concrete to abstract words. Moreover, good transitions and simple, familiar sentence structures help them, no matter what their levels of sophistication.   So, the more directly you say what you have to say, the more likely you are to be clear.[6]

What your listeners are *ready* to understand ought also to be a major consideration in deciding *how much* you can say and still be clear.   How far you go in amplifying, in detailing your explanations and arguments, ought to be determined by thinking about how much your listeners already know — or how little they know.   One can easily say too much to be clear.   You ought not try to tell listeners who know very little about jazz what "schools" of jazz have developed.   However artful you are, those listeners must first understand the basic musical forms that make jazz jazz instead of something else.   In such a case you would be wise to explain what jazz *is* and leave exposition of the "schools" for another talk.

To put the points another way, you may be entirely accurate about an idea and still be unclear.   This is especially important to remember when you deal with technical materials.   Except with sophisticated listeners, clarity will demand that you interpret precise ideas by filling in definitions of terms, analogies, contrasts, and the like.   But just there, another danger must be watched for and avoided.   *Mis*information can be communicated clearly.   To explain the transmission of sound it is clarifying and accurate, up to a certain point, to ask listeners to think of sound waves as spreading out as ripples do when a stone is dropped into water.   The comparison and the associated language having to do with water can help an uninformed listener greatly.   But if he is allowed to think of sound waves as *looking like* ripples, he will be misinformed.   The "water language" must be quickly abandoned once the image of the spreading movement has been established, for sound waves travel through walls and holes as water waves do not.

As the examples above suggest, clarity is a goal you work for relative to a particular audience, but your idea, itself, is inevitably a controlling factor, too.   And the occasion on which you speak may influence you if it is of a special nature.   But your own preferences should influence you least in making choices of language.   There is the rub!   Your clarity, for yourself, will tempt you to disregard your listeners' clarity, the opportunities your subject offers you, and special aspects of your occasion.   Clarity thus becomes a matter of *self-discipline*.

Propriety

Propriety, or appropriateness, is also characteristic of any good oral style. Speaking, unlike the writing in an essay or a novel, is meant for a particular

---

6. You will find Rudolph Flesch's *The Art of Plain Talk* (New York: Harper & Brothers, 1946) exceedingly helpful and informative on this point and others.   The work deals chiefly with writing, but the principles and methods discussed are valuable to speakers.

audience gathered in a particular place at a particular time. Particularity and close adjustment are the goals of oral style, not universality or adaptation to respondents in all places at all times.

One's style must, of course, be appropriate to the subject matter treated. "The style again," as Aristotle declared, "should not be mean nor above the dignity of the subject, but appropriate. . . ."[7]   To describe a commonplace operation, such as changing a tire, in flowery language would be ridiculous. Such menial subjects are not good ones for stylistic experimentation. To depict a sunset in plain vernacular is to rob the subject of meaning and of its inherent emotional quality. To say "the sky was kind of red, sort of like a tomato or a radish," would be as inappropriate as to say of a tire, "the shiny black vulcanized rubber besmirched by dust and grime, ought to be carefully loosened from the band which girdles the wheel."

As we have said, audiences as well as subjects impose standards of appropriateness. You could hardly use the same vocabularies or formalities in phrasing when talking to a group of college alumni, to a group of boy scouts, and to persons lacking in formal education. The words used for these groups would vary as would the amount of elaboration necessary for clarity and interest. Yet, in adapting to each particular audience, you must still be careful to be always yourself. You must not sell yourself *or* your listeners short. A college graduate who tries to sound at different times like a farmer at a Grange meeting, a juvenile delinquent at a boys' reformatory, and a college professor in the classroom is play-acting. Somewhere he will slip and become ridiculous. So in tailoring your style to an audience, do not forget that you can and must tailor it to yourself—and to your listeners, the occasion, and the subject. *Your style*, as Buffon noted, *is you*, yourself. It is a very personal thing. It forms your manner of expression. Straining too hard or trying too strenuously to adapt to an audience or striving for a special level of style, as some beginning students do, usually results in style which smells of the lamp or sounds like a caricature of someone else. You, as you are, define what *can* be appropriate for you, even after all other controls have been considered.

Style must be appropriate to subject matter, audience, and speaker, and must still be appropriate to the particular occasion. To use the same style in a corporate business meeting or at a professional meeting as you would use for informal remarks at a fraternity gathering would be to court disaster. On certain occasions it is traditional to be formal and to strive for niceties of expression. On other occasions it is more appropriate to be relaxed, informal, and to indulge, with taste, in slang and colloquialisms. Common sense will usually let you solve these problems of adjustment—and still remain yourself—if you think about them.

---

7. *Rhetoric, op. cit.*

Economy

Most of us use too many words when we speak. We clutter thoughts so that even when we are not obscure, we irritate with unnecessary circumlocution. Listeners want efficiency. That is why they want clarity and interestingness.

By economy in language we mean the right choice of words, in right amount, and in best order for instantaneous intelligibility. We mean economy of the listener's attention.

In his essay "The Philosophy of Style," Herbert Spencer emphasized the importance of economizing the "mental energies" and "mental sensibilities" of auditors or readers. "To so present ideas that they may be apprehended with the least possible mental effort, is the desideratum towards which most of the rules . . . point," he said.[8] Spencer claimed that the secret of effect lies in right choice and collocation of words, the best arrangement of clauses to clarify the ranks of principal and subordinate propositions, judicious use of figures of speech, and creation of a rhythmic sequence of syllables. He summarized his "principle of economy" thus:

> A reader or listener has at each moment but a limited amount of mental power available. To recognize and interpret the symbols presented to him, requires a part of his power; to arrange and combine the images suggested requires a further part; and only that part which remains can be used for realizing the thought conveyed. Hence, the more time and attention it takes to receive and understand each sentence, the less time and attention can be given to the contained idea; and the less vividly will that idea be conceived.[9]

Extreme brevity is characteristic of passionate language, but the fewest number of words for effective expression is not always the smallest number possible. Economy of attention is economy only if the idea is fully clear and understandable. At times, economy in style means not brevity or frugality but the necessary amplification. A further fact to consider is that speech needs to be more ample than writing. One reason is that listeners cannot review or reexamine unless speakers provide the necessary words.[10]

No one can tell you exactly how to judge in advance of speaking when you have thought out just enough to say about a point or other unit of speech. But as you speak you have one major way of gauging what is needed. You can watch listeners closely, looking for facial and other evidences that they have or have not understood, have or have not accepted what you are saying. If you have prepared sufficient material and several different ways of stating things, you will find it possible to enlarge your discussions of ideas when you

---

8. *The Philosophy of Style,* p. 11.
9. *Ibid.*
10. This point is discussed on pp. 225–228 in the section on "Oral and Written Style."

see signs of uncertainty and to cut out unneeded bits of amplification and re-statement when you receive signs of acceptance. It is, in fact, a great advantage that in planning and rehearsing for extemporaneous speaking you can and probably will evolve several ways of saying more things. In final presentation, then, you can work from the briefest to the amplest expression of any point if "feedback" from listeners shows that *more* than a minimum of right words in best order is needed for intelligibility.

Force

Listeners like language that has drive, urgency, and action. It compels them to pay attention as it propels ideas forward. Economy, precision, and simple grammatical constructions produce force. Spencer supplies the link when he says, ". . . other things equal, the force of all verbal forms and arrangements is great in proportion as the time and mental effort they demand from the recipient is small."[11] Modern research in linguistics and stylistics bears him out. The simplest, easiest, and so most forthright construction in English is the simple, subject-verb-object or modifier. This form you first experienced when you first read "I see the ball." Interfere with the sense between "I" and "see," and you will complicate understanding and also lose force: "I, to the best of my judgment, see the ball." The complexity of an idea or the character of your situation may make the more complicated kind of construction all but inevitable (e.g., "The measurement, taken at 70 degrees Fahrenheit, is 60 millimeters"), but you should know that force and simplicity are always sacrificed if you interfere with your listener's natural, simplest, thought movement from the subject to the predicate of a sentence or clause.

Some words are more forceful than others. It appears that it is not length or the origin of a word that makes it complex and unforceful. It is the number of "interior" meanings the word contains. Rudolph Flesch explains:

> Language gadgets . . . are of two kinds: Words by themselves, like *against*, and parts of words (affixes), like *dis-*. The more harmful of the two for plain talk are the affixes, since the reader or hearer cannot understand what the gadget does to the sentence before he has disentangled it from the word it is attached to. Each affix burdens his mind with two jobs: first, he has to split up the word into its parts and, second, he has to rebuild the sentence from these parts. To do this does not even take a split second, of course, but it adds up.[12]

You need not avoid all complicating and force-diminishing affixed words, but wherever there is a choice you ought to prefer the simplest word that will be accurate. The student who said, "Your response is a variant of the teleological argument for the existence of God," was unnecessarily complex. He was,

11. *The Philosophy of Style*, p. 33.
12. Flesch, *The Art of Plain Talk*, p. 42.

therefore, less forceful than he could have been. He could have said, "Your answer is like the argument that since the world seems orderly, a God must have organized it." He would have used more words, but they would have been simpler. His grammar would have been a bit more usual, and the "gadgety" word "teleological" would not have been present to steal force and clarity.

There is no clear empirical proof of it, but experience argues that listeners like active terms more than passive ones and pictorial words and phrases more than abstract ones.[13] You can insert words that denote or suggest actions. You can also keep as much of your talk as possible in the active voice. Then, both vocabulary and grammar will work toward successful communication. Any college student can approximate that precision, clarity, appropriateness, economy, and force that Leonard Bernstein attained in a televised broadcast. He was doing the difficult job of speaking about a musical composition:

> Whether you call this kind of weird piece "cool" or "crazy" or "futuristic" or "modernistic" or whatever, the fact is that it is bordering on serious concert music. The arrangement begins to be a *composition*. Take away the beat, and you might not even know it's jazz at all. It would be just a concert piece. And why is it jazz? Because it is played by jazz men, on jazz instruments, and because it has its roots in the soil of jazz and not of Bach.[14]

All the constituents of style we have so far discussed are present in this short passage from the speech of a brilliant expositor. Notice especially, however, that *no* subject is separated from its verb by intervening thought; of 86 words only about 15 (depending on one's method of analyzing) are "gadget terms"; action words and descriptive words are scattered throughout; and the passive voice is never used. The English language offers you the same resources for creating straightforward, forceful style. What is required of you is forethought about simplicity and force, and, of course, clear ideas to begin with.

Striking Quality

The characteristic of good style which we choose to call "striking quality" gives speech heightened effect. Writers have called this characteristic "interestingness," "impressiveness," "ornateness," "vividness," or "beauty."

We reject "beauty" because speaking is usually a utilitarian art. Its primary function is never to be beautiful. A speech admired for the sole reason that it aroused the imagination as a poem might would be suspect as rhetoric.

---

13. See pp. 231–240, "Figures of Speech" for fuller discussion of the second of these points.
14. From "The World of Jazz," a televised lecture first published as part of Bernstein's *The Joy of Music* (New York: Simon and Schuster, Inc., 1959). The text of this lecture is also available in Arnold, Ehninger, and Gerber, *The Speaker's Resource Book*, pp. 67–76. The quoted passage appears on p. 76.

Similarly suspect would be one whose main virtue was that it was euphonious. Some words are beautiful, others seem ugly in sound. Some mental images produced by words are lovely, others seem repulsive. The revolting as well as the attractive can draw our attention and subsequently have an effect. Beauty may be a constituent of striking quality, but it is not the only element in the quality. The unknown writer called "Longinus" said in *On the Sublime:*

> . . . the choice of proper and striking words wonderfully attracts and enthralls the hearer, and that such a choice is the leading ambition of all orators and writers, since it is the direct agency which ensures the presence in writings, as upon the fairest statues, of the perfection of grandeur, beauty, mellowness, dignity, force, power, and any other high qualities there may be, and breathes into dead things a kind of living voice. All this it is, I say, needless to mention, for beautiful words are in very truth the peculiar light of thought.[15]

Longinus also pointed out, ". . . stately language is not to be used everywhere, since to invest petty affairs with great and high-sounding names would seem just like putting a full-sized tragic mask upon an infant boy."[16] Buffon echoed him: "Nothing is more inimical to this warmth [the luminosity of style] than the desire to be everywhere striking."[17]

The quotations from Longinus and from Buffon suggest the delicacy of deciding how to express ideas verbally. From one side aspirations for accuracy, clarity, economy, and simplicity ought to tug at any speaker, but from another side the wish to make at least some ideas impressively striking ought to draw him, too. Even in ordinary conversation, and much more in formal speaking, striking phrases often have their place. It is probably not too much to say that the history of John F. Kennedy's life will continue to be something a little "special" to Americans because he uttered the uniquely formal sentence, "Ask not what your country can do for you — ask what you can do for your country." The "turn of phrase" embedded a familiar idea within history and made it one specially associated with Mr. Kennedy. The college student who said, "The Inner City does this — it crushes and shatters thousands; it is our shame" struck a strong blow for really serious consideration of urban decay. In telling of his summer's work in Harlem he wanted very much to "shake up" his fellow students on the subject. His striking phrasing helped to accomplish that; and you may have similar needs from time to time.

Striking quality in language comes from giving poetic turns to words while keeping them prose, from painting word pictures which stir listeners' emotions, from combining words in unexpected and sometimes alliterative or euphonious ways. It is the *unique* expression that seizes listeners' attention specially. And in most circumstances at least a bit of uniqueness can serve almost any speaker's purposes. Aristotle's advice was, ". . . it is well to give

---

15. Longinus, "On the Sublime," trans. W. Rhys Roberts, in J. H. Smith and E. W. Parks, *The Great Critics*, 3rd ed. (New York: W. W. Norton, 1951), pp. 95–96.
16. Smith and Parks, *The Great Critics*, p. 96.
17. Cooper, *The Art of the Writer*, p. 151.

the ordinary idiom an air of remoteness; the hearers are struck by what is out of the way, and like what strikes them."[18] "Remoteness" presumably leaves the impression we have called "uniqueness" in expression. But as Longinus and Buffon warned, not everything is important enough to bear the honor of unique phrasing. So the subject matter you are handling at any moment of speaking severely controls whether you should apply striking phrases. And, of course, what your listeners are familiar with will define what will prove striking to them. Your own taste can also govern when and where to strive for special phrasings. You may be fond of imagery, pleasing sound combinations, and unusual turns of phrase. As long as this fondness does not produce exhibitionism it is all to the good, and striking quality is likely to become a mark of your oral style. But it does not follow that effective speaking cannot be accomplished without striking quality; the passage just quoted from Bernstein is an illustration of that fact. Or, is Bernstein's very simplicity "striking"?

Particularly important in any decision to try for the striking is the occasion. Ritualized occasions for speech cry out for touches of originality. Awards are presented and accepted constantly, and welcomes and farewells must be said. The usual has been said many times, in usual ways. In such circumstances a speaker's major goal might be to speak the old in a fresh way, to seek striking variations on old, familiar themes.

Liveliness

Force, economy, and striking quality contribute to liveliness in oral communication. If the mission of rhetoric is to endow ideas with movement and if its goal is, as C. S. Baldwin said, "the energizing of knowledge and the humanizing of truth,"[19] then there is no more important stylistic quality oral discourse can have than liveliness. If speech is to reach climaxes of reason and emotion, there must be both energy and the kind of movement that propels ideas forward through influential form.

Aristotle recognized the basic devices that generate liveliness when he said that listeners ". . . like words that set an event before their eyes; for they must see the thing occurring now, not hear of it in the future."[20] The speaker, he said, must "aim at these three points: Metaphor, Antithesis, Actuality."[21] He thereafter advised that speakers make their verbal pictures move — that they make them motion pictures rather than still photographs, as moderns might put

---

18. From *The Rhetoric of Aristotle,* translated and edited by Lane Cooper, p. 185, bk. III, chap. 2. Copyright 1932, renewed 1960 by Lane Cooper. Reprinted by permission of Appleton-Century-Crofts, Educational Division, Meredith Corporation.
19. See his *Ancient Rhetoric and Poetic* (New York: The Macmillan Company, 1924), p. 247.
20. From *The Rhetoric of Aristotle,* translated and edited by Lane Cooper, pp. 207–208, bk. III, chap. 10. Copyright 1932, renewed 1960 by Lane Cooper. Reprinted by permission of Appleton-Century-Crofts, Educational Division, Meredith Corporation.
21. *Ibid.,* p. 208, bk. III, chap. 10.

it. The goal is not still-life images but "objects . . . invested with life," and thereby "an effect of activity."[22]   The successful stylist is one who ". . . makes everything live and move; and movement is activity."[23]

In discussing "actuality" Aristotle says,

> We have said that liveliness is secured by the use of the proportional metaphor, and by putting things directly before the eyes of the audience. But we still have to explain what is meant by setting things "before the eyes," and how this is to be effected. What I mean is, using expressions that show things in a state of activity.[24]

Liveliness comes from injecting animation, conflict, suspense, actuality (or realism), specificity, and proximity into what you say. It comes from using the present tense and the active voice. It comes from economy in wording, from simple rather than complex structuring, from vivid imagery, and from any other resource of language that sets moving images before the minds of listeners.

Relate events in a "you are there" rather than an "I was there" fashion. Take your audience with you as you re-live the suspenseful moment when your boat capsized or your car crashed. Let the audience feel the tape breaking across your chest at the finish line of a race, the touch of your friend's hand at the moment of good-bye, the pull of your muscles as they lift a rock or kick a football. Make your images cumulate and build. Let your appeals to sight, touch, taste, hearing, and smell, to thermal and kinesthetic sensitivity, so combine that images in the mind are experienced. Combining images and constructing a *past* experience in the *present* tense might produce such a passage as: "I smell the pines. The morning air is crisp, and I hear the crunch of snow beneath me as I plod up the path. My tired muscles seem to cry out at every step." In this sequence, four kinds of sensory images combine to bring a whole experience to reality. Experiment with animation, actuality, and imagery and you will find that your speeches can attain realism and movement. What you say can run to its goal rather than limp to its conclusion.

Demands for liveliness come above all from listeners. Hearers want to be moved, to respond empathically, to be excited by ideas. At other times, they prefer to be lulled, at least briefly. Bouncing, vigorous, hard-muscled style fits some occasions and not others. An extremely lively style may be out of place at eight o'clock in the morning. The solemnity of a commencement or a worship service may call for gentle pace rather than for vigorous movement. But whatever the occasion, clear, concrete images are never out of place. Liveliness through metaphor, antithesis, realism, and progressive movement of ideas is possible with or without high excitement. That is fortunate for some speech materials lend themselves better to lively discourse than

22. *Ibid.*, p. 211, bk. III, chap. 11.
23. *Ibid.*, p. 212, bk. III, chap. 11.
24. *Ibid.*, p. 211, bk. III, chap. 11.

others. Narratives are especially susceptible to animated treatments while inquiries often demand your diligent search for the means to liveliness.

To say that liveliness is the most important of all qualities of good oral style is no exaggeration; it is a forthright summary of all we have just said. Accuracy, clarity, propriety, economy, force, and striking quality are constituents of good style, but they are constituents of the ultimate virtue of speech that influences — liveliness.

ORAL AND WRITTEN STYLE

It is worth emphasizing that speaking is not writing. Both deal with words, sentences, and language in general. And written style often has oral elements. Still, to compose for the ear is not to compose for the eye.

James A. Winans once said, "A speech is not an essay on its hind legs." He meant that an essay is not oral even though it may be rhetorical. The chances are that your essays, themes, and term papers, if read aloud, would lack some of the traits your speaking ought to have. Proof of the differences lies mainly in everyday experience.

Little research has been done on the differences between oral and written style.[25] What experimental evidence there is provides us with points of departure rather than decisive generalizations, and the differences between oral and written style seem differences not of kind but of degree.

Drawing upon available research and upon our personal observations, we arrive at the following hypotheses which we invite you to test in your speechmaking. In contrast to written prose style, good oral style uses:

1. More personal pronouns.
2. More variety in kinds of sentences.
3. More variety in sentence lengths.
4. More simple sentences.
5. More sentence fragments.
6. Many more rhetorical questions.
7. More repetition of words, phrases, and sentences.
8. More monosyllabic than polysyllabic words.
9. More contractions.
10. More interjections.
11. More indigenous language.
12. More connotative than denotative words.

25. See for example, Gladys L. Borchers, "An Approach to the Problem of Oral Style," *The Quarterly Journal of Speech,* XXII (1936), 114–117; Gordon Thomas, "Effect of Oral Style on Intelligibility of Speech," *Speech Monographs,* XXIII (1956), 46–54; Joseph A. De Vito, "Comprehension Factors in Oral and Written Discourse of Skilled Communicators," *Speech Monographs,* XXXII (1965), 124–128; James W. Gibson, Charles R. Gruner, Robert J. Kibler, and Francis J. Kelly, "A Quantitative Examination of Differences and Similarities in Written and Spoken Messages," *Speech Monographs,* XXXIII (1966), 444–451. The last study includes a valuable survey of contemporary studies of oral and written style.

13. More euphony.
14. More figurative language.
15. More direct quotation.
16. More familiar words.

Aristotle recognized much the same differences when he said:

> . . . each kind of rhetoric has its own appropriate style. The style of written prose is not that of controversial speaking. . . . A knowledge of both the written and spoken style is required. . . . The written . . . style is more finished; the controversial is far better adapted to dramatic delivery. . . . On comparison, speeches of the literary men sound thin in the actual contests; while those of the orators sound well but look crude when you hold them in your hands — and the reason is that their place is in a contest.[26]

We urge students, when working on speech manuscripts, not to worry about how the speech looks on paper. If one brings only the standards of writing for the eye to bear upon writing intended for the ear, he will be applying irrelevant criteria and he will fail to apply other, important criteria. For example, the principles of paragraphing have limited relevance to composing what will be heard. Outstanding speakers exhibit widely varying practices for marking off major and minor ideas on the manuscript page. Whatever is done, the convenience of the speaker, not the general reader, must be served.

The same is true of sentences. Speaking appropriately uses many more sentence fragments than formal writing. Every novelist who is expert in writing dialogue and every good playwright knows this well. So, to apply formal standards of sentence construction and sentence completeness in evaluating the manuscript form of a speech would be to force the communication to follow rules that need not and do not normally apply. Consider a fragment from Franklin D. Roosevelt's address, "The Philosophy of Social Justice Through Social Action."[27] Using the best available records, L. LeRoy Cowperthwaite's judgment of what Mr. Roosevelt actually said in Detroit is quoted below. Notice how little the language resembles what we ordinarily call polished writing *for the eye*. Notice the broken sentence structures. Doubtless they were rendered smoothly meaningful by pause and vocal inflection. Notice the reinforcement gained by repetition of the words "crippled children" — reinforcement that writing for the eye might achieve in less obvious ways. This is a very carefully established sample of the *oral* style of one of the most successful political speakers in the history of the United States. This is the way he *talked:*

---

26. From *The Rhetoric of Aristotle,* translated and edited by Lane Cooper, p. 217, bk. III, chap. 12. Copyright 1932, renewed 1960 by Lane Cooper. Reprinted by permission of Appleton-Century-Crofts, Educational Division, Meredith Corporation.
27. The text of President Roosevelt's speech excerpted here is based on an official stenographic report, his own manuscript, and a recording. This text appears in full in Arnold, Ehninger, and Gerber, eds., *Speaker's Resource Book,* 2nd ed., pp. 135–139.

Take another form of poverty in the old days. Not so long ago, you and I know, there were families in attics—in every part of the Nation—in country districts and in city districts—hundreds and thousands of crippled children who could get no adequate care, crippled children who were lost to the community and who were a burden on the community. And so we have, in these past twenty or thirty years, gradually provided means for restoring crippled children to useful citizenship; and it has all been a factor in going after and solving one of the causes of poverty and disease.

Our point is not that good communication composed for the ear must look exactly like this on the page. The page of a speech manuscript should, however, display the variety of language forms and the myriad of reinforcing and emphasizing devices that listeners require of thoughts that are being developed *acoustically*.

Impaled on paper, some sentences of a speech will look strange, and many constructions will depart from the standard patterns of good visual communication. Other differences will reflect the sixteen special qualities listed above. Usually, the text of a speech ought to exhibit fewer "howevers," "thuses," and "therefores" than an essay might; it ought to contain such words and phrases as "but," "and so," or "the result of high cost is." These last are simply the connectives of normal conversation.

Speeches ought to contain few indefinite pronouns. "This" and "that" are ambiguous words for a listener. They always require him to remember some noun used earlier. It is often hard to recall that the "this" now heard actually means the "cathedral" heard five or ten seconds previously.

Whether you are writing or speaking, you will convey meaning more forcefully and usually more clearly if you use verbs in the active voice. There is more efficient meaning and more action in "The dog bit the man" than in "The man was bitten by the dog." "It is believed by most observers that a decision will be made by the President on Thursday" is bad writing and stupid speaking. Listening is neither easy nor a highly efficient way of absorbing information. Good oral style compensates for these limitations by its directness; one of the easiest, most obvious compensations is to use active verbs as much as possible, in the present tense where that is appropriate. There are times when the detachment produced by the use of passive voice is desirable, but ordinarily active voice serves best.

Scientific evidence does not justify an unqualified declaration that if you incorporate in your speaking such qualities as the sixteen we have enumerated and if you keep your talk in the active voice as much as possible, you will achieve a successful oral style. The point we want to stress is that oral style needs to be adapted to the special circumstances under which speaking takes place. Crucially important is that speaking is heard, not read. This is what dictates that oral style be conversational, personal, and responsive to the thought processes of listeners. We believe that if you try to inject the qualities we have been discussing into your spoken language, you will begin to increase your conversational quality and rid your speaking of whatever written or essay-like sound disturbs and hampers efficient listening.

THE RESOURCES OF LANGUAGE

Altering one's vocabulary in adapting to the necessities of practical speaking is an adjustment virtually everyone is aware of. But as you become part of a systematic situation and communicate within it when you speak, you and your listeners share a language which is a subsystem of signs and symbols that are adjustable to the requirements of the larger system that is a speech situation. That language is a system of optional *words* is only its most obvious characteristic as a resource. The language system you have available contains a wealth of other procedures and patterns from which you can choose in developing improved oral style. Some of these options we discuss below.

Connotation and Denotation

Words are symbols; they stand for and suggest ideas. No word has exactly the same meaning for any two individuals. Words uttered are combinations of sounds which travel through air. We endow them with meaning. The meaning assigned depends upon the human being who perceives the sounds. His background makes him interpret word symbols in particular and sometimes peculiar ways. Parental authority, environment, and learning experiences all combine to determine exactly what a word will mean to any one of us.

As sounds or print, words always have at least two kinds of meaning: denotative and connotative. Some words denote much and connote relatively little—for most people. Denotative words are thought to be more logical, objective, impersonal, and extensional. They refer explicitly to objects and actions outside the mind which are verifiable through observation. Purely denotative words require few further words of explanation. A fairly denotative statement would be, "President Jones called the meeting to order. Secretary Smith read the minutes of the last meeting."

Connotative words are those which, for most people, have important emotive, subjective, personal, and intensional meanings. Their meanings are turned toward the self, are private, suggestive, and depend upon the individual's emotions. Such words as "mother," "homecoming," "democracy," "black," and "lover" are rich in connotation. They arouse emotional responses, create images in the mind, and evoke the established attitudes of the listener. These words can be explained—rendered precise or "public"—only through the use of other words.

Most words, of course, are both connotative and denotative because their objective meanings touch off personal reactions. The word "house" can in many cases be considered denotative, as in a sentence reading, "There were twenty houses in the three-hundred block of Elm Avenue." This same word in other contexts may call to mind a particular house or a particular experience with a house and thus becomes strongly connotative.

In distinguishing between the two kinds of meaning, Professor S. I. Hayakawa is helpful:

> . . . the extensional meaning is something that cannot be expressed in words, because it is what the words stand for. An easy way to remember this is to put your hand over your mouth and point when asked to give the extensional meaning.
>
> The intensional meaning of a word or expression, on the other hand, is that which is suggested (connoted) inside one's head. Roughly speaking, whenever we express the meaning of words by uttering more words, we are giving intensional meaning, or connotations. To remember this, put your hand over your eyes and let the words spin around in your head.[28]

Word Choice

The fact that words have connotations and denotations shows that our systems of language are imperfect as precise representations of reality. Semantics, the science of word meanings, deals with some of these imperfections. It is enough to say here that confusion in word meanings poses many problems for speakers. It is almost too much for them to hope that they will stir up the exact meanings they intend. Almost any symbol may mean one thing to a speaker and quite another to his listeners. So speaking ought to be making choices and revisions in order to maintain practical control over intended meanings.

A word choice is a mistake, of course, if it implants an unintended message in the mind of a listener. As the illustration at the beginning of this chapter suggests, word choices *can* and *do* change meanings. Mental pictures are altered and modified by changes in wording. To say, "I saw a *red* bicycle" prompts a different image from "I saw a *pink* bicycle" or "I saw a *fuchsia* bicycle" or "I saw a *vermilion* bicycle" or ". . . a *Chinese red* bicycle" or ". . . a *Coca-Cola red* bicycle." The manufacturers of nail polish could extend the lists of reds *ad infinitum*. Similarly, to say, "The child skipped *gaily* down the street" is different from saying the child skipped "merrily" or "joyously" or "boisterously," or even "happily." But a change of adjective or adverb is secondary to a change of noun or verb. Substitute "lad" or "youth" or "teen-ager" or even "girl" or "boy" for *child,* and the meaning changes instantly. Or substitute "shuffled" or "skated" or "strolled" for *skipped* and the mental picture is again modified drastically. To stir up an

---

28. S. I. Hayakawa, *Language in Action* (New York: Harcourt, Brace, 1946), p. 47.

intended meaning, just any word will not do even though it conforms to all grammatical conventions.

At times the wrong choice of word, a malapropism, can make meaning ludicrous or spoil the mood created by a speaker, undoing several minutes' work. We think of the student who said that a speaker's body was "stagnant" when he meant "static," and of the student who spoke of "illiciting" rather than "eliciting" audience responses. We also think of the student speaker who, in describing a thief's actions during a robbery, coined a new word when he declared that the thief "slurked" around the corner. Whether the intended meaning was "slunk around" or "lurked at" or "sneaked around" was found out only by questioning the speaker. When he was questioned something fundamental came out: the idea, the image, was not exactly clear in the speaker's own mind. His coined word was in fact a way of evading clear, denotative meaning. From these examples, we gain two basic guidelines for making meanings serve rather than hinder you: (1) Determine your own exact meaning. (2) Once you know your meaning select from the accepted terms the one or ones that conform most closely to the meaning in your own mind. But select those terms which are also unlikely to connote anything incompatible with your immediate rhetorical purpose within the situation you plan to enter or have entered.

Word Changes

Another resource (and possible source of trouble) in language is that it is a system of meanings in a continual state of flux. Meanings of words can change with locality and with time. Some phrases are indigenous and even peculiar to geographical areas. In one region of the country people buy "hot dogs and pop," in another "frankfurts and soda," and in yet another "wienies and tonic." And verbal expressions come and go as fads change; other sayings have special meanings to particular in-groups at particular times. Depending on your speech situation, you may speak clearly and appropriately of motorcycles as motorbikes, cycles, or bikes. If you are talking about the 1950's, a young person wandering about the country had better be called a "beatnik," but the same kind of person of the 1970's could perhaps be better identified by saying he joined the "street people." A "skin flick" was a "stag film" on campuses some years ago; today the term equates for many people with "X-rated movie." "Black" and "Negro" are specially sensitive terms in the 1970's, and one needs to know an audience well to determine which will carry precisely the denotation and connotation one wants at a given moment. Some words are added, some are replaced. Words and expressions also become tired and worn out. Certain expressions become clichés: "black as pitch," "blue as the sky." It is rare for the vocabulary of any society or person not to shift. It grows, it shrinks, and the word shadings change.

Shifts in man's way of symbolizing meaning present opportunities and problems to speakers. In deference to an audience you may need to speak their particular language, of their particular time, and according to their judgments of what is appropriate to the immediate situation. If you can fit into that "language system" naturally, you will have considerable rhetorical advantage. Happily, if you cannot use their language system and still be yourself, almost any audience will accept with good grace the "standard" usages and meanings of "General American" speech and "standard" English grammar. So, the flucuating character of language systems gives you two options for communicating effectively: (1) Adjust to the language system of your audience wherever it is natural for you, and (2) in all cases of doubt adopt the current patterns of language that are understood and respected across regions, in-groups, and decades.

Figures of Speech

Historically figures of speech have been classified, divided, and described at tiresome lengths. Worse, many have been given names which are obscure. But the fact remains that just as there are "standard patterns of organization" with which Western culture has familiarized us, there are also standard maneuvers with words which prove emphatic, argumentative, and sometimes striking in all Western languages. The Belgian philosophical writers, Chaim Perelman and L. Olbrechts-Tyteca, restored to these turns of language their proper status in the arsenals of speakers and rhetorical writers when they published *The New Rhetoric,* originally in French, in 1958. In the English translation of their work these authors make the following observations which every serious rhetorical speaker ought to take seriously:

> From antiquity, and probably from the moment man first reflected on language, one has noticed certain modes of expression which are different from the ordinary, and they generally have been studied in treatises on rhetoric; hence their name, *rhetorical figures.* . . . Rhetorical figures increasingly came to be regarded as mere ornaments that made the style artificial and ornate. . . . If the argumentative role of figures is disregarded, their study will soon seem to be a useless pastime, a search for strange names for rather farfetched and affected turns of speech. . . .
>
> In order that there may be a figure, the presence of two characteristics would seem essential: a discernible structure, independent of the content, in other words a form (which may, under the divisions recognized by modern logicians, be syntactic, semantic, or pragmatic), and a use that is different from the normal manner of expression and, consequently, attracts attention.[29]

---

29. Chaim Perelman and L. Olbrechts-Tyteca, *The New Rhetoric: A Treatise on Argumentation* (Notre Dame: University of Notre Dame Press, 1969), pp. 167, 168.

Later, these authors repeat a long-lost point about these linguistic manipulations: that they can "argue" or "persuade" as effectively as, and sometimes more effectively than, formally structured arguments or "appeals." Perelman and Olbrechts-Tyteca say further:

> We consider a figure to be *argumentative,* if it brings about a change of perspective, and its use seems normal in relation to this new situation. If, on the other hand, the speech does not bring about the adherence of the hearer to this argumentative form, the figure will be considered an embellishment. . . .[30]

The main point here is that there are certain recurring ways of putting words together that in Western languages from ancient Greek to modern English have special kinds of impact. We think you ought to be aware that these verbal forms exist, that they are in common use, that they sometimes "embellish" what is said and sometimes "argue" as sharply as the "arguments" illustrated in logic and debate books. If you do not know these basic tactics of linguistic practice, you can only stumble about in disciplining your own oral style and you will frequently not know, or will misunderstand, what happens to you when you listen to speech. These are practical reasons for asking you to think about verbal maneuvers that have strange names but very consistent and influential consequences.

Some thirty distinctive "figures" are commonly used in modern written and spoken discourse. It is not as important to know their names as it is to recognize them as resources and influences in talk. Among those most often used in ordinary speech are the following, illustrated with excerpts from speeches.

Simile is a *direct comparison* between things which are essentially dissimilar except in the particular qualities alluded to in the simile. This kind of comparison contains the words "like" or "as." For example, "There are voices hot, like scorching blasts from a furnace . . . and others cold as if they came from frozen hearts" (Peter Marshall, "Letters in the Sand").[31] Or

> Five score years ago, a great American, in whose symbolic shadow we stand today, signed the Emancipation Proclamation. This momentous decree came as a great beacon light of hope to millions of Negro slaves who had been seared in the flames of withering injustice. It came as a joyous daybreak to end the long night of their captivity. (Martin Luther King, Jr., "I Have a Dream").[32]

Metaphor is an *implied* comparison between two essentially dissimilar things. Words such as "like" or "as" are omitted. As you can see, the dictionary's distinction between simile and metaphor is wholly technical and of no practical consequence. We might be wise to go back to Aristotle's unpedantic position that the term "metaphor" is a sufficient word with which to

---

30. *Ibid.,* p. 169.
31. In Catherine Marshall, *A Man Called Peter* (New York: McGraw-Hill, 1951), p. 322.
32. In Wil A. Linkugel, R. R. Allen, and Richard L. Johannesen, eds., *Contemporary American Speeches,* 2nd ed. (Belmont, Calif.: Wadsworth Publishing Company, Inc.), pp. 290–291. Used by permission.

talk about *any* stylistic comparison between essentially different things. Does it matter, in the practical impact, that "like" or "as" is missing from Robert F. Kennedy's remark below? We think not. Said Kennedy: "Yet I suppose that the end of the academic year is one of those watersheds of life where a backward then a forward look becomes almost mandatory" (Robert F. Kennedy, "Speech Delivered at California Institute of Technology, Pasadena, California").[33]

From a practical standpoint the important thing about Marshall's, King's, and Kennedy's verbal tactics is that all three men *made a claim and implied an argument* by means of them. Marshall implied that we should prefer hot voices to those from "frozen hearts"; King implied with "seared in the flames of withering injustice" that the "injustice" had been far worse than "mere" injustice; and Kennedy implied that commencement was a point of change in life where you do something predictable. (But see *irony* below.) Whether these speakers were conscious of it or not, all three made quick arguments through metaphoric comparisons. If Marshall did not wish to denigrate "cold" voices, he used the wrong verbal form. If King did not intend to magnify the injustice he was talking about, he used the wrong verbal form. If Kennedy did not mean to treat commencements lightly, he spoke with the wrong kind of metaphor.

Metaphors (and similes) have serious effects, then. They can enhance, denigrate, or embellish. They are stylistic procedures we all use, and you will be wise to consider their probable impacts, use them often, but in ways that will serve your purposes precisely.[34] You will make metaphoric comparisons. We all do. They enliven speech and affect listeners' attitudes. They therefore need to be chosen purposefully and with a sharp eye to your listeners' tendencies and biases. Then, they will work for you rather than against you.

Rhetorical question is a question designed to produce an effect but not to evoke an overt answer unless, perhaps, an answer verbalized by the speaker. For example, "Now how is this news determined? A small group of men, numbering perhaps no more than a dozen anchormen, commentators, and executive producers, settle upon the 20 minutes or so of film and commentary that's to reach the public" (Spiro T. Agnew, "Television News Coverage").[35] Whether answered in the minds of listeners or answered explicitly by a speaker, this question form *reinforces* its own answer. If the listener answers within himself, he strengthens his own commitment to that answer by producing it in his own terms. If the speaker answers his own rhetorical

33. In Thomas A. Hopkins, ed., *Rights for Americans: The Speeches of Robert F. Kennedy* (Indianapolis: The Bobbs-Merrill Company, Inc., 1964), p. 246.
34. A major empirical investigation of the effects of sustaining comparisons metaphorically is reported in John Waite Bowers and Michael M. Osborn, "Attitudinal Effects of Selected Types of Concluding Metaphors in Persuasive Speeches," *Speech Monographs*, XXXIII (June 1966), 147–155. Experimental evidence reported there indicates that sustaining a single theme metaphorically at the conclusion of a speech affects the attitudes of listeners in ways significantly different from the effects generated by an unmetaphorical conclusion.
35. In *Vital Speeches*, XXVI, No. 4 (Dec. 1, 1969), 99.

question, as Mr. Agnew did above, he makes his answer seem more significant than if he had not used the question form.   His answer now has the added importance of being a response to a live and specific query; the answer cannot seem to a listener a statement without an excuse for being.   There is, of course, a limit to when and how rhetorical questions can argue by emphasizing.   It is unsafe to raise rhetorical questions unless you are entirely sure your listeners *will* produce answers agreeable to your purposes.   Otherwise their internal answers or their uncertainties about how to answer may simply call your point into question.   Similarly, to ask and answer a rhetorical question creates more problems than it solves if listeners are not certain to accept *completely* the answer as you propose it.

Antithesis (an-'tith-ə-səs) is a parallel construction of words, phrases, or sentences which contains opposed or sharply contrasting ideas.   Expressing the antithetical ideas in similar (parallel) language injects an additional "claim" that the matched ideas "really are" opposed or contrasting.   John F. Kennedy said, "Let us never negotiate out of fear.   But let us never fear to negotiate" ("Inaugural Address," 1960).[36]   The paralleled wordings of the two parts of Kennedy's antithesis tend to "argue" that fearful negotiations and negotiating out of fear are genuinely opposed things which we should "never" do.   (And notice that in this construction Kennedy created an opportunity to *repeat* his key injunction, "let us never.")   By emphasizing in this verbal matter the oppositions you want to talk about, you, too, can add touches of strength to your general claims that they are indeed opposed.   By using parallel wordings in expressing things that are *alike* you can similarly emphasize through verbal form that they are indeed alike in the ways you say.   This structure is usually called *balanced* phrasing.

Onomatopoeia (‚än-ə-‚mat-ə-'pē(y)ə) occurs when you choose a word in which sound suggests the meaning of the word.   Notice the suggestive, descriptive function of "clattering" in this example: "The free Irishmen marching everywhere today to the tune of 'O'Donnell Abu' and 'The Wearing of the Green' are a dramatic contrast to the clattering of hobnail boots on darkened streets, the sound that marks the enslaved nations" (Robert F. Kennedy, "Speech Delivered to the Friendly Sons of St. Patrick of Lackawanna County, Scranton, Pennsylvania").[37]   The symbol of enslavement, the "hobnailed boots," is surely made a bit more threatening because Kennedy chose to make them "clatter" rather than just "sound."   He might have achieved a similar but slightly different effect if he had said, "the *thud* of hobnail boots." "Thud," like clatter, is an onomatopoeic word.   So are "ripple," "crunch," "slither," and many other standard English words.   All are available to you as means of adding realism and sometimes threat or promise to points you want to make.

Pun is a word substituted for another having a suggestively different

36. In Linkugel, Allen, and Johannesen, eds., *Contemporary American Speeches,* 2nd ed., p. 300.
37. In Thomas Hopkins, ed., *Rights for Americans: The Speeches of Robert F. Kennedy,* p. 195.

meaning or a suggestively similar sound. For example, "Churchill said aptly, that Jaw, Jaw is better than War, War" (Hubert H. Humphrey, "The Open Door").[38] The effects here are several. The parallelism of sound (Churchill, an Englishman, would have said "waw, waw") reinforces the contrast Churchill and Humphrey want to stress: talking is *much* better than warring. In short the sounds stress the antithetical qualities. But there is also a touch of humor in equating "talking" or "negotiating" with "jawing," thus suggesting that even the crudest talk is better than "waw." In all, Churchill's phrasing plus his dialectal way of saying the word "war" constitute a subtle argument that all negotiation is preferable tò warring.

Less subtle uses of puns may inject humor without much "argument." The problem is, one may seem to try too hard for the humor. Obvious puns like, "She seized the hen; fowl deed!" have caused some to call puns "the lowest form of humor." We suggest that they need not be "low forms" and that truly imaginative puns can be valuable linguistic resources to speakers.

Irony implies something different from, usually the opposite of, what is stated. Sarcasm is a form of irony.

> To guarantee in advance that the President's plea for national unity would be challenged, one network trotted out Averell Harriman for the occasion. Throughout the President's message, he waited in the wings. When the President concluded, Mr. Harriman recited perfectly. He attacked the Thieu Government as unrepresentative; he criticized the President's speech for various deficiencies; he twice issued a call to the Senate Foreign Relations Committee to debate Vietnam once again; he stated his belief that the Vietcong or North Vietnamese did not really want military take-over of South Vietnam; and he told a little anecdote about a "very, very responsible" fellow he had met in the North Vietnamese delegation. (Spiro T. Agnew, "Television News Coverage")[39]

There have been a few attempts to discover empirically what persuasive effects irony (and the related form, satire) has. The findings are by no means definitive, but they suggest that these forms of saying-other-than-what-you-mean do not *change* attitudes very much but may be excellent ways of reinforcing existing attitudes.[40] Agnew, of course, was seriously argumentative in saying that Harriman "recited perfectly," but ironic statements can also be playful. The man who said, "Sin is something to be looked at with gentle, sad hatred" was being more playful than intensely persuasive, but his irony also "argued" subtly concerning the nature of temptation.

Climax is the arrangement of words, phrases, or sentences in series according to increasing value or strength of impact. For example,

---

38. In Linkugel, Allen, and Johannesen, *Contemporary American Speeches*, 2nd ed., p. 244.
39. In *Vital Speeches*, XXVI, No. 4 (Dec. 1, 1969), 98.
40. Two studies by Charles R. Gruner encourage these judgments. See "An Experimental Study of Satire as Persuasion," *Speech Monographs*, XXXII (June 1965), 149–153 and "A Further Experimental Study of Satire as Persuasion," *ibid.*, XXXIII (June 1966), 184–185. We are, of course, inferring that the effects of irony are probably comparable to the effects of its sustained form, satire.

> There is no place in this Republican Party for those who would infiltrate its ranks, distort its aims, and convert it into a cloak of apparent responsibility for a dangerous extremism.
>
> And make no mistake about it—the hidden members of the John Birch Society and others like them are out to do just that!
>
> These people have nothing in common with Republicanism.
>
> These people have nothing in common with Americanism.
>
> The Republican Party must repudiate these people.
>
> I move the adoption of this resolution. (Nelson Rockefeller, "Extremism")[41]

There has been much discussion and experimentation seeking to determine exactly how climactic arrangement persuades. The best conclusion seems to be that structuring language in this fashion *can* add persuasiveness, but that under some circumstances creating an anticlimactic structure in which the strongest thought comes first rather than last can yield at least an equal persuasive force. We cannot advise you beyond saying that to emulate Governor Rockefeller when you feel it would be wise to build up to a telling point cannot possibly take away from the force of your key idea and may significantly strengthen it.

Repetition is the reiteration of the same words or phrases or sentences in order to reinforce ideas. Evidence drawn from experience and experiments indicates that repeating is one of the surest of all means of giving ideas emphasis. That new immigrants are accepted as Americans much more readily than blacks is certainly made unavoidable as a proposition in this excerpt:

> If you and I were Americans, there'd be no problem. Those Hunkies that just got off the boat, they're already Americans; Polacks are already Americans; the Italian refugees are already Americans. Everything that came out of Europe, every blue-eyed thing, is already an American. And as long as you and I have been over here, we aren't Americans yet. (Malcolm X, "The Ballot or the Bullet")[42]

Here Malcolm X combined the power of repetition with the force of antithesis (white versus black experience) to contend that his point was inescapably true.

Alliteration is repetition of sounds in words or in stressed syllables within words. Judiciously used, the repeated sounds can hold listeners' attention to an emerging idea and can sometimes render the idea easier to remember. The first of these functions is surely served in the question, "Shall we sit in complacency, lulled by creature comforts, until we are engulfed in chaos?" (Hubert H. Humphrey, "The Open Door").[43] Sometimes repetition combines repetition of idea plus sounds that further reinforce the idea, as in Lincoln's sentence, "As our case is new, so we must think anew and act anew." The

41. In H. Bruce Kendall and Charles J. Stewart, eds., *On Speech and Speakers* (New York: Holt, Rinehart and Winston, 1968), p. 322.

42. In Irving J. Rein, *The Relevant Rhetoric* (New York: The Free Press, 1969), p. 49.

43. In Linkugel, Allen, and Johannesen, eds., *Contemporary American Speeches*, 2nd ed., p. 243.

sound, therefore the meaning, of "new" is thrice repeated and "newness" is made easier to remember.

Personification is the endowment of objects, animals, or ideas with human attributes. They can by this means be given qualities that seem attractive, unattractive, powerful, weak, and so on. Or motives may be assigned to things that ordinarily would not be seen as motivated. Consider Leonard Bernstein's "For Gilbert and Sullivan, along with those other geniuses, Johann Strauss and Offenbach, had led the American public straight into the arms of operetta" ("American Musical Comedy").[44] Bernstein makes "the American public" fall in love with — not just accept — operetta as a musical form, and by doing so he probably reports more accurately than if he had said the public "accepted" or "became interested in" operettas.

Personification offers an exceedingly valuable way of making persuasive statements about abstract or inanimate things and ideas. Congress may be seen as a giant enmeshed in procedural details. The personifying metaphor clearly argues that Congressional inactivity has a particular kind of cause and that the human capabilities of Congress are more or less painfully constrained. The possibilities of thus activating, humanizing, and arguing on behalf of your ideas should always be thought about as you make final choices in preparing to speak.

Synecdoche (sə-ˈnek-də-( )ke) is the substitution of parts for wholes or of wholes for parts of things. For example, "We tie all countries close together, put each doorstep on a universal ocean, but how are we to direct these accomplishments to improve the basic qualities of life?" (Charles A. Lindbergh, "The Future Character of Man").[45] As Perelman and Olbrechts-Tyteca point out, what happens when a part is made to stand for the whole of something or vice versa is that sometimes attention is focused on a characteristic aspect of a whole (the characteristic dramatized by the part) and sometimes attention is drawn to the class to which a specific thing belongs (by naming the class rather than the thing itself). Thus "sail" for "ship" or Lindbergh's "doorstep" for "geographical boundary" argues that the power-source of the sailboat or the entrance-exit features of a country are the major things one should think about just now. Conversely Lindbergh implies that every individual, international decision belongs to a grand class that is of crucial importance, decisions affecting "the basic qualities of life."[46] In each case the figure of speech focuses attention on specifics or on the general and makes a subtle argument that whatever listeners associate with *those* entities are the factors they should think of just now.

Hyperbole (hī-ˈpər-bə(ˌ)le) is exaggeration or overstatement used for

---

44. In Kendall and Stewart, eds., *On Speech and Speakers*, p. 287.
45. In *Vital Speeches*, XX (March 1, 1954), p. 294.
46. For a more general discussion see *The New Rhetoric* (Notre Dame: University of Notre Dame Press, 1969), pp. 334–337.

purposes of emphasizing without deceiving. This tactic works in the same general way as synecdoche; here the aspects that are exaggerated or over-stated are emphasized as uniquely important at the moment. Malcolm X once emphasized the monetary wealth of a university audience in this way: "And if you realize that for anybody who could collect all of the wages from persons in this audience right here for the next month, why they would be so wealthy they couldn't walk" ("A Debate at Cornell University").[47] Perelman and Olbrechts-Tyteca show that the function of hyperboles is "to provide a refer-ence which draws the mind in a certain direction only to force it later to re-treat a little. . . ."[48] Exaggeration taken seriously in any literal sense that deceives cannot function as dramatization of a "right direction." It cannot overdraw or magnify so that the listener will willingly retreat to what was really meant. Bernstein's phrase, "led the American public straight into the arms of operetta," is truly hyperbolic as well as a personification. The public did not literally have a love affair with operetta; any listener knows that and knows that is not what Bernstein means. Seeing the real truth of the matter, the listener willingly retreats to the "true" position, that the public became exceptionally fond of operettas. And the "truth" of Bernstein's point becomes more credible because the listener has actively participated in locating the degree of enthusiasm that rightly represents historical reality.

There are additional, less well known figures of speech which we shall discuss below because they are used by speakers more often than by writers.

Aposiopesis (ˌap-ə-ˌsī-ə-ˈpē-səs) is the practice of breaking off ut-terance of one thought without finishing it, in order to express another, due presumably to the emotional state of the speaker. The cause of self-interrup-tion might be anger, sorrow, fear, or some other strong feeling. Many sentence fragments will fall in this category. For example,

> Property rights, property rights is what the United States Constitution is based on. You should know that. . . . Property rights. People who didn't own property could not vote when this country was first founded. (Stokely Carmichael, "Speech at Morgan State College")[49]

Carmichael effects a special claim for the importance of "property rights" in two stylistic ways: (1) he interrupts himself to say, "You should know that," and so claims "property rights" is so important a concept that he is almost "carried away" by its importance, and (2) the very breaking up of his own grammatical structure gives him occasion to repeat the phrase three times for further emphasis.

Epanorthosis (ˌepə.nȯ(r)ˈthōsəs) is retracting or cancelling what one has already stated. This form of utterance has some of the same effects as

---

47. In Haig A. Bosmajian and Hamida Bosmajian, eds., *The Rhetoric of the Civil Rights Movement* (New York: Random House, Inc., 1969), p. 80.
48. *The New Rhetoric,* p. 291.
49. In Bosmajian and Bosmajian, eds., *The Rhetoric of the Civil Rights Movement,* p. 120.

aposiopesis. To say, "The town was aflame—I mean of course the center of the town" specially emphasizes that the fire was at the *center* and not everywhere else. If the *correct* location weren't especially important, the speaker would presumably not bother to correct himself. Leonard Bernstein once used this method of retraction to alter the direction of his listeners' thinking and to "argue" the special importance of a "new" perspective on what he had already said: "By this time I've probably given you the impression that jazz is nothing but Blues. Not at all. I've used the Blues to investigate jazz only because it embodies the various elements of jazz in so clear and pure a way" (Leonard Bernstein, "The World of Jazz").[50]

Apophasis (ˌap-ə-ˈfā-səs) is the ostensible omission or concealment, through denial, of what the speaker has really in fact declared. For example: "I am not pleading so much for these boys as I am for the infinite number of others to follow, those who perhaps cannot be as well defended as these have been, those who may be down in the storm, and the tempest, without aid. It is of them I am thinking, and for them I am begging of this court not to turn backward toward the barbarous and cruel past" (Clarence Darrow, "The Plea of Clarence Darrow").[51]

Darrow was in fact pleading for his clients, but by denying the primary importance of the Loeb-Leopold case he could make their case a part of a larger and perhaps more significant set of issues. A particularly unpleasant use of the tactic of apophasis occurs in statements like, "I could of course dwell on my opponent's record of mishandling funds, but I won't." Psychologically such a statement functions much like Darrow's. The idea denied is emphasized because the denial calls attention to it. But Darrow's use of the form is much less transparent than the second statement; moreover, it could have been true to Darrow's real intent.

The catalogue of figures of speech could be continued for there are other ways of bending language to the service of special or emphatic meanings. The figures we have identified are those that are probably already in your day-to-day speech. They are figures that are common in English usage but are too seldom focused on as usages that can drive points home with the strength of complicated arguments. They are not, however, the forms of speech we use all of the time. We seem to save them for special moments of meaningfulness; hence, each startles listeners mildly and so momentarily rivets attention and potentially makes a unique set of claims about ideas and things.

A skilled speaker needs to know these special ways in which he can achieve special emphasis and direct minds persuasively if subtly. A speaker who does not know and understand at least the sixteen special usages we have

---

50. In Arnold, Ehninger, and Gerber, eds., *The Speaker's Resource Book,* 2nd ed., p. 73.
51. In Maureen McKernan, *The Amazing Crime and Trial of Leopold and Loeb* (New York: The New American Library, 1957), p. 192.

discussed simply does not know the affective possibilities his language system offers him.   He is inept, resembling a landscape contractor who knows everything about his business except the conditions under which plants thrive or die.   To refine your access to the resources of language, reflect on why these figures of speech work as they do.   Look for them in speeches you hear and read, examining what they achieve or fail to achieve for those speakers. Learn, too, the distinctions between figures of speech that prove functionally useful and those that stand out ostentatiously and distractingly.   In preparing to speak, review at some stage how figures might help—or hinder—when emphasis, vividness, and subtle argument are needed.   There is nothing unusual about using figures of speech to create effects in listeners; what differentiates expert speakers from casual ones is that the experts choose their figures and understand their workings while casual speakers only follow habits and fads without knowing why.

THE DEVELOPMENT OF A STYLE

We have been implying that perhaps you should alter your style of speaking. But you already have your own particular manner of utterance or expression— good or bad.   Consider the other members of your speech class.   You will notice that some of them stand out from the rest in style.   One may help you see more visual images, let you see and feel the things talked about.   Another may have a rough-hewn style—terser, plainer, or more homespun in wordings. Still others may be abstract, or habitually use colloquialisms, clichés, or slang, or be exceedingly precise in explanations.   Why these styles impress you as distinctive may be difficult for you to determine, but every speaker has habits that favor particular kinds of language or specific sets of stylistic devices. Each consciously or unconsciously endows his speech with particular characteristics of style, the style of each has hallmarks, and yours does, too.

You and your classmates have different oral styles in part because you work differently.   When you revise and reword, you modify and change ideas in order to say what you mean.   Or you just don't think ahead about language. Do you really make full use of your linguistic opportunities?   Even when you speak extemporaneously you need to express yourself as accurately as possible. Even there you may try out wordings as you work from your outline or speaker's notes.   You need not freeze wordings.   You can build a reservoir of alternative, effective phrasings.   At every point in composition you make choices which give your style the qualities that distinguish it as yours.   At all times, it is important that you remember that while readers may flip back through a book to re-read thoughts, listeners can never re-listen to your speech.   It must be clear to them upon first hearing.

As we said, you already have a style of some sort.   You have a vocabulary at some stage of development and special habits of expression peculiar to you. Your background, prior education, and methods of writing have exerted influence on your style. Some of your habits of expression are good ones which need emphasis. Probably others are faults to be eradicated. Improvement comes from developing your strengths and removing your weaknesses. You start by surveying your present speech style and work from there. It takes a long time to change a style; you cannot expect fixed changes to emerge overnight, but you will be surprised at how you can modify your style through conscious attention and experimentation.

Your aim ought to be to nurture variety. An inflexible style will not meet the demands of enough different speech situations. As Herbert Spencer said, "To have a specific style is to be poor in speech."[52] The many adjustments necessary to meet the demands of specific speaking situations preclude the use of any one style in all cases. The style of a chemistry or mathematics lecture would hardly be suitable for a popular lecture on the advancement of science. An inspirational sermon would be poorly couched in the jargon of a salesman. In a sense, then, improvement of your oral style involves developing styles within a general way of talking that is both effective and your own.

Not purpose but situation governs the characteristics of a style that is practically effective. Some people think that informative speaking is distinguished by language of fact and explanation, the diction of definition, example, comparison, and literal vocabulary. We believe that such broad generalizations are unsatisfactory. It seems to us that the situation for informing rather than the purpose determines what is appropriate in a given case. This is why there is no section in this book in which style is matched to speaking purposes. No one characteristic of style is exclusively associated with any one purpose. What you need is personal, distinctive style within which many variations may be made as you adapt to the requirements of ideas, audiences, occasions, and your own needs. What is it that you are to adapt? The resources imbedded in language itself.

What sort of program for long-range improvement should you follow? To manage your speech well, try to:

1. *Become language conscious.* Become sensitive to good and bad uses of words. Discover your faults in grammar and those points of style where you seem to be most limited. Ferret out such weaknesses as want of vividness, poor syntax, malapropism, use of clichés. Listen carefully. Read widely. At times read aloud to test the "orality" of your prose.

2. *Increase your speaking vocabulary.* Try consciously to extend the number of words and phrasings at your command. Do not go out of your way to master unusual words and unique phrases; learn the meanings of language you normally encounter but do not understand. You are after the most accurate and most appropriate words. Keep a dictionary handy and refer to it whenever you see or hear unfamiliar words. *Roget's Thesaurus* will also help,

---

52. Herbert Spencer, *The Philosophy of Style*, p. 27.

but look up its synonyms in the dictionary to fix precise meanings in your mind.

3. *Write.*   By expressing yourself on paper you will learn to make conscious word choices.   Writing will improve your vocabulary and the accuracy with which you use words.   Aim for the best written expression when writing for the eye and the best oral expression when writing for the ear.

4. *Rewrite.*   Once you've written a speech or a part of one, put it aside; but come back to it, and rewrite it.   The best speech makers who work from manuscript often put their speeches through several drafts.   Franklin Roosevelt, master of the craft that he was, put some of his speeches through as many as twelve drafts before he was satisfied.   Benjamin Disraeli wrote, re-hearsed alone and before friendly critics, and rewrote again — in order to speak extemporaneously!   In rewriting, smooth out wordings, correct unclear con-structions, tinker with phrasings, rearrange language and ideas.   By polishing your utterance on paper you will make it more precise and vivid, whether you are to speak from manuscript or extemporaneously.

5. *Study published and live speeches.*   Note what makes for success and failure in style.   Take cues from the good models.   Avoid the faults of bad ones.   Imitate the style of others, but for practice and exercise only.   Do not study the style of great speakers to copy them; study them to incorporate their best attributes in a distinctive style suited particularly to you.

6. *Speak in public.*   Take advantage of opportunities to refine your expression of ideas in both conversation and public address.   Speak as often as possible.   The more you speak, especially in the extemporaneous and im-promptu modes, the better you will become at finding ways to finish phrases and statements effectively no matter how you started them.   The more ex-perience you have with thinking on your feet and symbolizing your ideas as they develop in your mind, the more fluent and attractive your style will be-come.

Style is that part of the art of speaking which emerges from choices and combinations of language.   Its grammatical aspects and its psychological im-pact have been the subjects of investigation in the preceding pages.   A "per-sonal manner of utterance which gives movement and impact to ideas" is not decoration to be exhibited but a facet of speechmaking derived from reason-able and imaginative management of words.

Wording and thinking are inseparable processes wherever communica-tion deserves its name; hence, style in speaking must always be viewed as one more means to winning a particular set of responses under particular circum-stances that comprise the rhetorical situation or system which you enter as speaker.

The origins of the word *style* and the meanings assigned to it through history remind us that what we call oral style cannot be separated from the whole act of speaking, except for purposes of analysis and discussion.   Style, good or indifferent or bad, is present in all speech.   Its qualities color listeners' perceptions of what is said and of the entire rhetorical situation. Nonetheless, there is no universally suitable set of stylistic qualities appropriate to all speakers even though their purposes resemble one another's and though they speak in comparable situations. This is why we have contended that each speaker must understand, for himself or herself, the various resources of language. It is with such understandings that each individual can develop through practice and experience the particular patterns of verbal style suited to his or her needs and talents. Happily audiences and rhetorical situations allow for and respond favorably to individuality in speakers, provided that individuality does not disregard the general principles upon which language operates as social force.

Language, as system, is so complicated no one as yet fully understands its workings. There are, however, some basic features of linguistic influence that we can all understand in an elemental way. These are the features speakers need to appreciate. Words have denotative and connotative meanings. To a degree at least these are open to speakers' artistic use and control. Figures of speech offer special resources for achieving clarity, force, and even argument and persuasiveness. Systematic attention to what dictionaries, thesauruses, and good models offer as guides to using linguistic resources enlarges any speaker's capacity to meet the demands of different rhetorical situations. In preparing for and in engaging in speaking only your sensitive judgments of the demands of your subject, your audience, the situation in which you will find them, and your own abilities can guide you toward effective linguistic choices. We can point out your resources; we cannot offer you language for all occasions. There is none. We can stress that all listeners in all situations ask their speakers for accuracy, clarity, propriety, economy, force, striking quality, and—above all—liveliness in verbal expression. But your listeners, not we or you, will define these stylistic virtues. Nonetheless, college students, statesmen, ministers, lawyers, teachers, and thousands of others have consistently demonstrated that, given some understanding of language, thoughtful readiness to adapt, plan, and practice can yield appropriate style as we have defined it: *The personal manner of utterance which gives movement and impact to ideas.*

EXERCISES

Written

1. Below are the first, second, and final versions of a statement from Lincoln's "Gettysburg Address." In a paragraph or two discuss what language problems Lincoln tried to eliminate as he worked on the speech and which of the successive changes he made seem to you to have yielded gains (or losses) in effective communication of the ideas of the statement. Be sure to say *why* each change was an improvement or a regression in stylistic effectiveness.

First draft: We have come to dedicate a portion of it as a final resting place for those who died here, that the nation might live.

Second draft: We have come to dedicate a portion of it as a final resting place for those who here gave their lives that that nation might live.

Third draft: We have come to dedicate a portion of that field, as a final resting place for those who here gave their lives that that nation might live.

2. Choose a speech from *Vital Speeches* or from an anthology of public addresses. Study it carefully. Write an essay in which you (a) identify the major stylistic devices the speaker used to support his ideas; (b) point out particular word choices that give special clarity, propriety, and economy to the language; and (c) identify instances in which figures of speech function argumentatively or otherwise persuasively.

3. Rewrite the following sentences for oral delivery:

a. Therefore, it is evident that before you can provide an elucidation of the operational functions of the system for the propagation and dissemination of information you would be required to make a thorough investigation of the public relations branch of the corporation.

b. If one had one's preference, one would be likely to hold a preference for one's own photographic equipment with which to photograph one's own favorite subjects.

c. Easily seen is the fact that the playing field is surrounded by a large metal fence over which the ball often passes when a home run is made.

d. Even although I had been selected to represent my college, had planned my itinerary to the meeting, which incidentally was held sixty miles from the college itself, had packed my clothing for the journey, which I did the night before, had reserved my seat in the airplane, which was a jet and was flight 107, and had persuaded my close friend, whose name was Mark Smith, to convey me to the airport, I was still in fear that the weather would prevent my going to the convention at all.

e. "Like I said," she said, "Jane's cheeks looked as red as roses, however, I discovered that the effect was all due to the application by her of cosmetic in large quantity."

4. Rewrite the following paragraph in such a way as to give it the motion-picture quality discussed in the section of this chapter devoted to liveliness.

My most embarrassing experience was when I was a boy. It was the result of my getting into a place I had no business being. I had crawled under our old back porch and had found some paint cans. I pried off the tops with a stick. Then I had put my hands into one can after another. First I put them into a can of green paint. Then I put them into a can of red paint, and then into a can of yellow. The color which resulted was an ugly brown. When I finally finished, my clean clothes had paint dribbled all over them. I was a mess. What was embarrassing though was that I couldn't get the paint off. After a licking by my mother, a bottle of turpentine was given to me, and I tried to get the paint off with that. I rubbed and rubbed with a cloth, but there was so much paint it just wouldn't come off. I was embarrassed for a whole week because it was summertime, and I looked as if I were wearing a pair of brown gloves. I guess I felt most foolish when my piano teacher came to give me my lesson, and I had to explain why my hands were as they were. I also felt very foolish on Sunday. I was sure that everybody was looking at my hands when I was up there singing in the choir.

5. a. Identify the kinds of imagery used in the following passage taken from a speech
   by a college student.

> The quiet rural atmosphere had been effectively shattered. Chickens and feathers
> flew fast and furiously from both sides of the road. Cattle, only a moment before
> peacefully pastured, ran in aimless directions. Farmers' horses became frightened
> and reared into the air. A low-slung sports car, flashing and brilliant yellow in the
> afternoon sunlight, thundered through the rural village, a beautiful blonde movie
> queen at the wheel. An aroused policeman hauled the straw-haired beauty over to
> the side of the road, arrested her, and brought her before a justice of the peace who
> fined her five dollars. The indignant beauty thrust a 10 dollar bill into his hand and
> stalked out of the courtroom. "Just a minute," shouted the judge, "your change."
> "Keep it," she hurled back as she hopped into the auto, "I'm going out of here a hell
> of a lot faster than I came in."[53]

   b. Identify the figures of speech used in the above passage.
   c. List the kinds of imagery *not* used.
   d. Write a paragraph commenting upon the strengths and weaknesses for speech in
      the rhetorical style of the passage.

Oral

1. Compose and deliver a 2-minute persuasive talk in which you use (a) at least three
   different figures of speech and (b) at least three different kinds of imagery.
2. Using a speech you delivered during a prior session of your class and drawing upon
   what you now know about style, rework the speech or a portion of it and deliver
   it again. Discuss the effects of your deliberate stylistic changes with your listeners.
3. Some subjects are harder to talk about in words than others. For example, it is more
   difficult to find words to describe an abstract painting than it is to find words to
   describe an automobile. As an exercise in expanding your awareness of linguistic
   resources, prepare a short talk on one of the following subjects or a comparable
   subject:
   a. How abstract art tries to communicate.
   b. *Form* as communication.
   c. Red and yellow are "warm" colors.
   d. "Quick hands" are essential in a basketball player.
   e. Charisma is a quality public leaders need.
   f. Here's what to look for in (a statue, a piece of jewelry, tailoring in clothing, a top
   quality first baseman, or other quality-oriented items of a similar sort).
   g. The reason this (car, book, movie, music group) was the best I've seen or heard
   is ....

---

53. From the manuscript of a speech entitled "Seven Years of Silent Excitement," by Nelson T. Joyner, Jr.
Used by permission.

CHAPTER
10

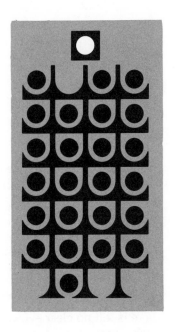

Delivery

After surveying empirical research on delivery as an influence in communicative speaking, an author recently wrote:

> In summary: (1) visible action does not harm communication and perhaps helps; (2) certain deficiencies in the audible code, though listeners consider them unpleasant, do not affect comprehension. The conclusion to draw from the second point is not that speakers should cease striving for excellence, for clearly good delivery does no harm. The meaning rather is that in the whole complex of content, style, arrangement, and delivery no one presentational element, such as fluency or voice quality, is likely to affect the outcome significantly.[1]

There is still no clear evidence that any particular presentational behavior will surely affect your listeners' responses if that behavior is within those listeners' range of previous experiences. Nonetheless, we point out that problems of oral delivery have preoccupied speakers and theorists since the beginnings of Western thought about speech communication (see pages 330–336).

One is tempted to believe that this pervasive concern with aspects of delivery reflects the inner needs and insecurities of speakers more than the pragmatic demands of speech situations. Indeed, the psychology of speaking publicly and the enthusiastic searches for "rules" of delivery in modern times tend to confirm this suspicion. Because we believe the *way* you think about delivery is very important to whether you speak well or ill, we want to preface discussion of *your* delivery with some comment on the chief ways delivery has been thought about in the last hundred years. We think important cautions for all of us are embedded in that record.

Energetic attempts to create rule-bound systems exemplify man's desire to guard against uncertainties in speech. We do take risks of losing face when we speak. Physical and vocal activities furnish cues by which other people judge our worth and self-control. The crucial question for those who practice the art of public speaking is: Can the risks of speaking be minimized by adopt-

---

1. Wayne N. Thompson, *Quantitative Research in Public Address and Communication* (New York: Random House, 1967), p. 92.

ing rules of delivery? This is a question men and women of Western culture have been disputing since the days of Gorgias and probably before.

Four philosophical approaches have been made in attempts to arrive at a mode of superior delivery: the *imitative* (which recommends copying the delivery skills of others); the *mechanical* (which attempts to arrive at rules based upon empirical analysis); the *impulsive* (which throws all cautions to the winds); and *think-the-thought* (which may or may not ignore the action of body and voice as it emphasizes concentrating upon ideas).[2]

During the past decade there has been renewed interest in delivery as it concerns bodily action as communication. Scholars and popular writers have turned their attention to "action communication," "action language," "body language," and "nonverbal communication." Their interest is akin to that of the elocutionists (see pages 332–334) in that they are attempting in scientific ways to chart, annotate, and explain the aspects of human behavior which do not involve words. Exactly what that does and does not mean is difficult to state. Eisenberg and Smith say:

> All communication except that which is coded in words is generally referred to as *nonverbal communication*. This rubric is in one way unsatisfactory. The term "nonverbal" aggregates different kinds of behavior which have in common only the quality of not being structured by a linguistic system. Like the term "nonhuman," which covers an infinity of life forms from protozoa to gorillas, nonverbal denotes that which is not included in the concept verbal, but tells us little about what *is* included.[3]

Some distinctions, helpful to understanding these specific concerns, are made by other investigators. (1) Nonverbal communicative functions are continuous whereas sounds and letters have definite beginnings and ends. Because of starts and stops anyone can choose *not* to talk verbally but no one can choose not to communicate nonverbally. (2) Nonverbal communication is taken in through several senses simultaneously. You can feel, smell, see, and hear a message and its source at one and the same moment. In contrast, verbal cues are taken in by fewer of the sense organs.[4] (3) Nonverbal cues yield less cognitive content than verbal ones, because language can easily indicate objects and relationships. (4) Nonverbal cues are in many instances better suited for projection of emotional states.[5]

The kinds of nonverbal communication investigated by those working

2. These approaches may be investigated by consulting: S. S. Curry, *The Province of Expression* (Boston: The Expression Co., 1927), pp. 301–325; Richard Whately, *Elements of Rhetoric*, Douglas Ehninger, ed. (Carbondale, Ill.: Southern Illinois University Press, 1963), especially pp. 346–353; Frederick W. Haberman, "John Thelwall: His Life, His School, and His Theory of Elocution," *The Quarterly Journal of Speech*, XXXIII (Oct. 1947), 294; Joshua Steele, *Prosodia Rationalis: or An Essay Towards Establishing the Melody and Measure of Speech, to Be Expressed and Perpetuated by Peculiar Symbols* (London, 1779), and Gilbert Austin, *Chironomia or a Treatise on Rhetorical Delivery* (London, 1806).

3. Abne M. Eisenberg and Ralph R. Smith, Jr., *Nonverbal Communication* (Indianapolis: Bobbs-Merrill Company, Inc., 1971), p. 20.

4. Jurgen Ruesch, "Nonverbal Language," in Robert Cathcart and Larry Samovar, eds., *Small Group Communication* (Dubuque: William C. Brown & Co., 1970), pp. 260–263.

5. Eisenberg and Smith, p. 22.

in this field, as classified by Ruesch and Kees, are: (1) "sign language," the use of gestures in place of words, numbers, and punctuation signs; (2) "action language" such as walking, eating, drinking, and making love; and (3) "object language," comprising the intentional or unintentional use of objects such as furniture, clothing, and architectural elements in communicating feelings and ideas.[6]

Others have classified what is included in the study of nonverbal communication differently. Some speak of paralanguage, proxemics, and kinesics. The study of paralanguage is concerned with voice set and nonverbal vocalizations. The influence of vocal properties such as resonance, rhythm, rate, and pitch and the effects of sounds such as "ums" and "ers" and silences between words fall within the purview of this class of nonverbal communication. Proxemics, a second broad category of nonverbal communication, deals with the spatial relationships that exist between a speaker's body and other people or objects in communicative settings. Kinesics or body movement has been viewed as a separate kind of communication by means of facial expression, head action, posture, walking, and gestures made by the arms and hands. Kinesics as defined by its originator, Ray Birdwhistell, is a system for classifying body language much as linguistic systems classify elements of language. Kinesics, however, has come to be used as a term signifying all study of all body movement. Birdwhistell says:

> Kinesics is concerned with the abstraction of those portions of motion activity which contribute to the process of human interaction. . . . Kinesics is not concerned, as such, with the movement potential of the human species, but rather with those portions of the movement spectrum which are selected by the particular culture for patterned performance and perception.[7]

In 1970, Birdwhistell said that the methodology of kinesics was, as yet, extremely crude and that its claim to being a science rested on the canons dominating its operations and the postulates upon which its operation depends. In his view, the body of accumulated knowledge about kinesics did not yet warrant the label, "kinesiology." He saw research done during the five years prior to 1970 as being devoted chiefly to refining methodological procedures and as a fruitful beginning in the development of kinesics as an infant science.

It is obvious that the results of the systematic study of nonverbal communication have implications for both informal and formal speaking. However, almost all research thus far completed deals with nonverbal communication in interpersonal or one-to-one situations. Some of what is said nonetheless applies directly to public communication. Studies in "prekinesics," a subarea of kinesics, define the movements of which the human body is capable. Birdwhistell estimates that the human face is capable of 250,000 different

6. Jurgen Ruesch and Weldon Kees, *Nonverbal Communication: Notes on the Visual Perception of Human Relations* (Berkeley: University of California Press, 1956), p. 189.
7. Ray L. Birdwhistell, *Kinesics and Context* (Philadelphia: University of Pennsylvania Press, 1970), p. 190.

expressions.[8] Mehrabian says that 55 percent of the impact of a face-to-face spoken message results from facial expression.[9] A generalization coming from experimentation with eye movement asserts that greater proximity in human relationships results in less eye contact.[10]

Such findings, of course, help us understand the importance of body and voice as channels of communication. Up to this time, however, only scattered bits of information bear directly upon the problems of speaking in public. The research accruing from the renewed interest in nonverbal behavior has for the most part failed to take *public* communication into consideration. What is chiefly implied for public speech is that recognition and adaptation to nonverbal feedback from audiences may be even more important and subtle than has been supposed. One pair of authors has said:

> The effective group member or public speaker constantly surveys his auditors to judge their reaction to him and his ideas. Even a group or audience that appears to be relatively passive sends many messages about their degree of involvement and acceptance of what is being said. Failure to look at the speaker, small nervous gestures, an overly relaxed posture, can all signal boredom.[11]

We shall deal with such interchange of nonverbal signals repeatedly as we explore the problems of speech delivery in the remainder of this chapter.

DELIVERY AS ADAPTATION

The approach to delivery which we advocate is a modification of Whately's theory reinforced by the teachings of James A. Winans. We hold that to think your thought is not enough, though it is primary. We feel that you ought to achieve both a keen sense of communication and a vivid realization of your idea at the moment of utterance, that you work to control all the channels of action—mental, physical, and vocal—to support and reinforce ideas. There are no hard and fast rules for this. Delivery must be adapted to all the demanding elements in the speech situation: the material, the audience, the occasion, and the speaker himself. None of these elements is ever frozen or absolutely set; all make fluctuating demands. Even so, there are certain principles which may be followed to achieve effective, adaptive delivery.

---

8. Birdwhistell, p. 8.

9. Albert Mehrabian, "Communication Without Words," *Psychology Today*, II (September, 1968), 53.

10. Michael Argyle and Janet Dean, "Eye-Contact, Distance and Affiliation," *Sociometry*, XXVIII (1965), 289–304.

11. Eisenberg and Smith, p. 64.

General Principles

Good delivery helps the listener to concentrate upon what is being said; it does not attract attention to itself. If this is adopted as a governing premise, we can further say that to reach this objective you will need to do the following things:

1. *Remember that you are not speaking to perform or to exhibit yourself.* Delivery should be viewed as a means to an end, not as an end in itself. During speaking your message is the most important thing to be exhibited. Your mission should never be to show off your body, your grace, or your clothing. You must concentrate on meanings.

2. *Think about the meaning of what you say as you speak.* To create or re-create ideas vividly at the moment they are being uttered means that you reactivate a subject and ideas to support it, that you regenerate the enthusiasm that led you to speak in the first place. This enthusiasm must last from the first moments of preparation through the last syllable of your speech. You must be in control of assimilated ideas so that they are at your bidding. You must have become so intimately acquainted with them as you structured, worded, and orally rehearsed them that no matter what happens during the actual presentation of your speech, you will be master of your feelings and of your audience's responses. Professor Winans, who formulated this precept, put your needs well when he said:

> . . . there should be full and sharp realization of content. And this includes more than bare meaning; the implications and emotional content must also be realized. The reference here is not merely to those striking emotions commonly recognized as such, but also to those attitudes and significances constantly present in lively discourse: the greater or less importance of this or that statement, the fact that this is an assertion and this a concession (with an implied "granted" or "to be sure"), this is a matter of course while this has an element of surprise, and so on through all possible changes.[12]

The ideas you work with must be in your grasp so that you can support them through your own behavior, vigorously and forcefully. The ideas you have painstakingly worked over must come alive. They must flow. You must be running over with them. You must be able to lose yourself in your speech and still maintain control of your experience.

No matter how well you know your materials, you ought to give the impression of meeting the ideas for the first time. You ought not be serving up limp remnants from creative experience. What was alive as you prepared and as you rehearsed orally must come to life again in the actual speech situation. Overrehearsal, loss of enthusiasm, repetition to the point of being "sick of the

---

12. From *Speechmaking* by James A. Winans. Copyright, 1938, D. Appleton-Century Company, Inc., p. 25. Reprinted by permission of Appleton-Century-Crofts.

whole thing'' will promote mechanical, boring, dull delivery. The process of speaking, you should remember, is one of creation, then re-creation for the sake of listeners.

3. *Cultivate a keen sense of communication.* This third step, which we also borrow from Professor Winans, is closely allied to the second. Thinking of public speaking as dialogue rather than as soliloquy will help achieve this keen sense. Talk *with* the audience, not *at* them. Dwell on ideas until you are sure of the response for which you work. Try to feel on the platform what you experience during verbal exchanges with your friends over the dinner table, on the athletic field, or in bull sessions. We experience this sense of sharing minds daily; trying to recapture the same sense in public speaking makes for lively delivery. By assuming a false, tense, artificial mood we rob public speaking of the urgency and eagerness it ought to have. As Professor Winans said:

> We should make sure in our efforts to bring this communicative tone into our delivery that it springs from mental attitudes; for it, . . . should [not] be assumed as a trick of delivery. The attempt to assume it is likely to result in an over familiar confidential or wheedling tone which is most objectionable.[13]

4. *Be direct.* People are seldom evasive when they are in earnest. Look the audience in the eye. If you look elsewhere, so will your audience. If you look at your audience, they will look back at you. Looking at a spot on the back wall will not produce directness. You will give the impression that you are in a trance. A dead-fish stare while you call up ideas and wordings will not do. Neither will darting your eyes from person to person or addressing one side of the audience to the exclusion of the other. In the first instance eye contact will be so fleeting that it will be no contact at all. In the second, a whole segment of the audience will think that you have ignored them.

Your eyes are decidedly expressive parts of your face. Haven't they been called "the windows of the soul"? Eyes and mouth more than other parts of your body, reveal your emotions. And it is your *feeling* for content that delivery needs to convey. So you should face front and direct your eyes to your listeners. Try looking at a segment of the audience or at one or two people in a particular area of the room as you develop an idea. When you have finished with that idea, and as you start the next one, direct your gaze to another part of the audience. As you move to subsequent ideas, refocus each time. Then you will talk with your audience, not at them or past them.

Directness is fundamentally a matter of direct eye contact. Attain this much and the probabilities are that you will also be tolerably direct mentally, vocally, and physically.

5. *Punctuate and support your ideas with your body and your voice.* Channel your physical resources to reinforce your message. Let your bodily

13. *Ibid.*, p. 28.

actions and your vocal intonations operate as warm, emphatic communication. In speechmaking, facial expressions, gestures, pitch changes, variations in vocal rate and volume, pauses, shifts in posture, and walking take the place of the commas, italics, exclamation points, and question marks in written communication.   Intelligibility and clarification often depend greatly upon support and emphasis from your physique.   Learn to use *yourself* often and with control.   Some special considerations in this connection are discussed below under the heading "Bodily Action" (pages 255–258).

6. *All aspects of your delivery should promote conversational quality.* If the ways you say things have the qualities we have referred to in discussing the five principles above, your speech will tend to be much like your best conversation: meaningful, reflective of content, clearly intended for listeners, direct, and supported by natural physical and vocal behavior.   But the larger your audience and the more formal your situation, the more your presentation will need to differ mechanically but *not in manner or intention* from everyday conversation.   We noted differences between conversation and public speech in Chapter 1 (pages 3–4).   We observed that public speech contrasts with conversation in that we speak more loudly, are relatively uninterrupted, focus attention more sharply, are more systematically prepared, and have less opportunity to perceive auditor's responses in detail.   But effective formal speaking still retains important characteristics of good conversation: directness, spontaneity, animation, and emphasis.   It is, therefore, conversational in *quality* though not in *style*.   Reproduced conversation does not satisfy.   Public speech needs to sound like conversation enlarged — more dignified, more systematic, and more forceful than conversation under informal circumstances. Yet as far as is possible, a speechmaker has to suggest to his listeners that his *attitudes* toward them remain essentially those of one person conversing with others.

Thus, effective public communication dare not be exhibitionism; it must be sensitive re-creation of ideas by a speaker whose whole being directs, punctuates, stimulates, and focuses meaning — after the manner of a conversationalist aware of enlarged responsibilities and responsively alert to the messages his listeners send back to him.

7. *Focus the attention of the audience on meaning.*   Influence of some sort is any public speaker's goal.   His manner must direct attention to the meaning of the moment, be it an image created with words, a contention of importance, a visual aid, or some other communicative element.   But the task is not to direct attention toward only those stimuli bearing basic meaning; one must also act in ways that exclude irrelevant stimuli which might produce interfering "noise."   Manner of delivery can often displace distractions that come from other sources — a flapping window shade, a smell from a laboratory down the hall, your listeners' fatigue.   With strong stimuli stemming from your own behavior such interference can be overcome.   Bodily movement and vocal variations are always available to you as means of focusing or refocusing listeners' attentions.

8. *Monitor delivery to generate and respond to emotional and physical experiences of listeners.* A recent survey of theoretical and experimental literature relating to audience response or "feedback" in communication emphasizes that an adequate account of how human communication works must recognize that *both* speakers and listeners have *personal goals* which *each* party must (a) recognize and (b) adapt to, if ongoing communication is to succeed.[14] Accordingly your delivery must clearly communicate your goals in relation to your listeners. It must also signal that you are receiving and adapting to signals from your listeners implying their goals—their rising or declining interest, their physical and psychological needs. To a large degree your own signals that you are aware of and are responding to your listeners' goals are the cues listeners "read" to discover whether you mean what you say and whether you are being "direct" toward them.

Your manner generates other responses in listeners. What listeners see and hear causes them to have physical and emotional reactions resembling what they see signs of. If you seem fidgety, your audience is likely to become so. If they detect that you are tense and rigid, your listeners will experience like physical states. If you are confident or indecisive, smiling or depressed, tough or soft in manner, listeners will feel so, too. Your manner thus determines the experiences listeners have and whether they are pleasant or unpleasant. So, a fundamental task once invention, disposition, and language choice have been completed is to conceive of the sort of delivery that will *show* your full meanings to your audience.

Just thinking about and discussing how speakers maintain lively contact with listeners and generate desirable emotional and physical experience can make your behavior more "natural" and conversational. A recent experiment showed that inexperienced speakers who had considered and discussed using feedback from listeners subsequently used dramatically fewer "ahs," "ers," and other vocal signs of unease than similar speakers who had given no special thought to capturing and responding to "feedback cues" from audiences.[15] In short, just knowing there *are* messages for you "out there" and determining to respond to them as you speak are likely to help you monitor your delivery and generate among listeners the kinds of emotional and physical experiences that will reinforce your message.

Bodily Action

We implied earlier that the chief instruments of delivery are physical actions involving the face, limbs, and torso and expressive use of the voice. The

14. Donald A. Clement, "Feedback in Human Communication: An Analytic Review of Conceptual and Empirical Treatments," Unpublished M.A. thesis. The Pennsylvania State University, 1972.
15. See Steven C. Rhodes, "Some Effects of Instruction in Feedback Utilization on the Fluency of College Students' Speech." Unpublished M.A. thesis, The Pennsylvania State University, 1972.

broad principles we have just outlined apply to any aspect of delivery, but bodily communication deserves some special consideration.

Any speaker must understand that his actions are of two kinds: overt and covert. Overt action is open to inspection, easily perceived by an audience. Covert action is covered or concealed. An audience may sense even concealed action. For example, the contractions of hidden muscles of the throat or leg are actions audiences may sense without being able to locate the muscular activity itself.

Strong feeling often turns covert action into overt action. A spectator at a football game may so strongly wish his team to score that he actually crouches, reproducing the thrust he wants a ball carrier to prepare for. The spectator will not go all the way in his response; he will perform the action only partially. For fear of audience censure, he is likely to inhibit his actions, allowing only muscular contractions partly hidden beneath his skin and clothing. Less dramatic but similar behaviors occur constantly during public speech. It is not unusual to see speakers, moved by indignation or determination, bring a clenched fist into sight from behind the lectern or rap hidden knuckles as they utter strong words.

Whether evident or concealed, all action associated with speaking expresses something. The practical question is whether the actions express relevant meaning and whether they do it conventionally. In order to talk clearly about what kinds of actions serve practical ends it is useful to have a few common terms by which to refer to specific kinds of bodily action.

Descriptions of Action.   "Eye contact" is the phrase used to denote the focusing of the eyes upon the audience. "Posture" or "stance" usually refers to the position of the whole body. "Movement" is the label ordinarily used to indicate walking or other movement of the entire body. "Gesture" is the word used to indicate movement of the hands and arms. "Facial expression" is self-explanatory, as are "head action" and "shoulder action."

Gestures are labeled in three ways. One set of terms indicates their functions: emphatic, descriptive, and suggestive. Other terms indicate the position of the hand at the time of the gesture: palm up, palm down, clenched first, and index finger. Still another set is based upon inherent qualities of gesture: habitualized, natural, and nervous.

Good Gestures.   To communicate well, gestures need vitality, proper coordination, good timing, integration with other bodily movements, habitualization, and appropriateness. Also, good gestures must reveal that some energy is still held in reserve. Good gestures employ broad strokes in large situations and subtle movements in small ones, and usually they just precede the ideas they reinforce.

Principles of Good Bodily Action. The questions students ask are: "How shall I walk?" "How shall I stand?" "How shall I move?" "What shall I do with my hands?" "How can I register feeling in my face?" We answer with no prescriptions. Mechanical planning and execution, which prescription implies, do violence to the individualized nature of effective public speech. However, some general guidelines can be offered.

1. Action should be in key with audience temperament and should prompt the reactions sought.
2. Action should suit the occasion.
3. Action should reinforce, enhance, and emphasize meanings.
4. Action should never belie what the speaker is saying.
5. Action should refine the focus of attention.
6. Action should contribute to the speaker's comfort by being easy and unlabored.
7. Action should reveal the speaker's total concentration upon expression and communication of his message.

The Demands for Action. Any audience demands stimuli to direct attention and increase understanding. Listeners like animation. They drowse if the speaker's body is asleep, if movement and gesture are vague, unchanging, or monotonous. In short, listeners want to see meaning as well as hear it.

Special audience requirements for action derive from the ages of listeners. A group of small children listening to a talk on Africa may wish the speaker to be the elephant he describes. The five-year-old demands much action, for his attention span is short and his comprehension level, comparatively speaking, is low. His imaginative level is high, so he responds with delight when a speaker is literal and offers representational action in amplifying ideas. At the other extreme, if you were to address a gathering at a home for the aged, you would disturb your audience if you used a great deal of action or action that was especially fast. Unless you aimed at humorous effects, you would not assume your hearers had never seen an elephant. The postures and gestures that gave joy to the child by seeming to represent the trunk of the animal are absurd in the sight of the mature. In general, the younger the audience, the more plentiful and suggestive action may be. The older the audience, the more likely it will be that reserved and subtle action is meaningful and fitting.

Each message, too, exerts special demands for bodily action. Since the listener's eye reads only the speaker's body and its surroundings, it receives whatever signals the speaker gives to clarify his message. As we have noted, action is part of the punctuation of a speech. A sensitive listener knows that an index finger shaken in the right way or brought down forcibly upon a table is in reality an exclamation point, just as a spread palm in horizontal position may serve to underline. Some material requires special bodily action for proper emphasis. Often, too, material calls for clarification through total bodily movement. A step or two in a new direction during a transition breaks and refocuses listeners' attention as a speaker moves from point to point. Other material calls for literal, physical description. For example, the easiest way to suggest spherical or square shapes is by gestures. During demonstrations of techniques necessary in military, gymnastic, or dance instruction, action is not just inherent in the material, action *is* the material, a part of the message to be conveyed.

Occasions may also govern action, as in religious ritual. Quick, jerky movement in a softly lit, sedate, ceremonial setting would normally be as inappropriate as would lazy, languid movement at a political rally. Even the time of day influences what is appropriate in action. When it is late and an audience is tired, speakers do well to increase the flow and variety of their movements.

Mental and bodily activity are coordinated if natural. Coordinated action expresses a speaker's concerns as it conveys his meanings to listener-viewers. It is also fortunate that speakers who experience tensions and lack of confidence can disperse those strains by moving meaningfully. Unhappily, however, purely nervous movement can belie the practical meanings of words spoken. The remedy found practical over centuries is to direct action toward *reinforcing ideas*. Action is then most likely to be appropriate to what is said, to the audience, to the occasion, and to the speaker's need for nervous relief.

Voice

Those who define speech broadly argue that nonverbal elements, a shrug of the shoulders or a crook of the finger, constitute "speech," but it is impossible to conceive of speech consisting of gestures alone. All public speech requires vocal ability.

Management of your voice, then, ought to be of serious concern to you. You must be able to use your voice flexibly. Yet, a sound course in public speaking cannot be a course in voice training. Voice improvement is most wisely achieved by individual work on poor habits or by a separate course of study. Poor vocal habits ought to be remedied by private exercise and practice. Public, group exercises consume valuable time which ought to be devoted to speechmaking.

Minimum skill in vocal communication means that you must (1) be heard, (2) be understood clearly, and (3) be free from annoying vocal habits and distortions. Most of us can fulfill these minimal requirements. Some fail to meet the requirements simply because they have acquired poor habits in the formation of particular sounds—a "p" sounds like a "b," a "th" like a "d," or an "l" like a "w." Others' voices rasp or squeak, so that the quality distracts from what is being said. But most of us are endowed with adequate physical equipment for acceptable voice production. We make sounds which are usually heard and understood. We may be sloppy and inaccurate, yet every day we convert ideas into sounds which convey meaning. But it is still universally true that anyone, no matter how pleasant his voice and clear his diction, can do better. Even the Laurence Oliviers and Paul Newmans, after years of experience, continue to exercise their vocal mechanisms to improve intelligibility and quality.

Ideally, good voice does not attract attention because of peculiarities identifying it with a particular class of persons or a particular locality. But it is not our intention here to provide a manual for those who wish to eliminate regional dialects, upgrade substandard speech, improve voice and diction through drill and exercise, or correct defects. Therapy to remove defects or to improve manipulative skill is a highly individual matter to be undertaken in addition to, and many times before, work in speech composition. Here, we intend to explain how normal vocal behavior relates to speaking.

Voice, like action, must be under the speaker's control. You must think what you are saying. You should not be affected or "speak with your mind on your larynx," but you ought to pay attention to understandability and vocal flexibility. To attain clearness and variety a good speaker needs to be generally acquainted with the process of producing meaningful sounds and with the variables of vocal expression: articulation, volume, rate, pitch, and quality. He can then refine his habitual control over these natural resources.

Voice Production. Speech is an "overlaid function" of the speech organs because each of them has some other primary purpose such as breathing or swallowing. Inspiration takes place as air is taken into the lungs through the nose and/or mouth, passed through the pharynx (throat), the larynx (voice box, vocal folds, or Adam's apple), the trachea (windpipe), the bronchi, and bronchial tubes. (See Figure 10–1.) As air fills the lungs, they expand; the chest walls within which they are contained move outward and upward to create the partial vacuum that causes this lung expansion. The muscles which control the actions of the ribs come into play in this raising of the ribs and consequent expansion of the rib cage. During this action, the front wall of the abdomen also expands as the diaphragm—the muscular floor of the chest and the roof of the abdomen—moves downward compressing the visceral organs. When the rib muscles and the diaphragm relax, the latter moving upward in a recoiling action, the size of the chest cavity is again reduced and the air forced out of the lungs and through the trachea. As this exhalation takes place, the air passes through the larynx, between the vocal folds which vibrate to produce sound as the air passes through the glottis (the opening between the vocal folds). The length and thickness of the vocal folds and their state of tension are responsible for the pitch of the voice produced.

The voiced and unvoiced sounds produced during exhalation are given character and quality as they are resonated from the surfaces of the pharynx, mouth, and nasal cavities. The sounds are reflected from these surfaces and reinforced by them. Finally, certain sounds are turned into consonants by the

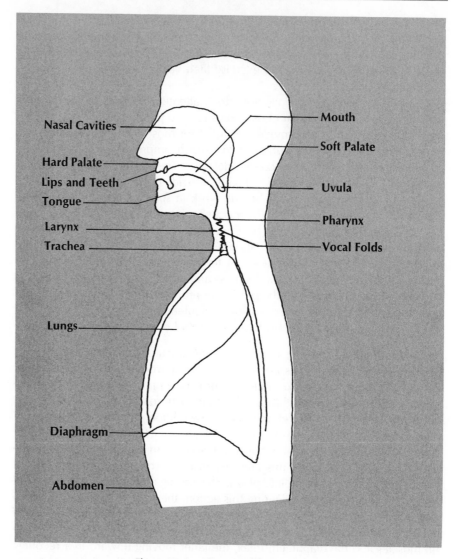

Figure 10–1.   *Diagram of the vocal tract.*

articulators: the tongue, the teeth, the lips, and the soft palate, which controls the passage of air between the mouth and nose. These sounds combine to form words, and the cycle is complete. (See Figure 10–2.)

From this simplified description we see that the production of voice is a motor process involving breathing; a phonation process involving the vibration of the vocal folds; a resonation process involving the reinforcing surfaces of the mouth, throat, and nose; and an articulation process involving the formation and codification of specific sound symbols.

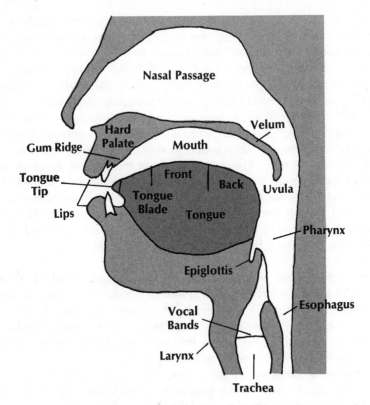

Figure 10–2. *Diagram of speech mechanism.*

The cycle we have described repeats itself over and over again as we speak, and what happens at the various stages in the cycle is responsible for the distinctive attributes of the voice. The physical adjustments and modifications which take place during speech and the general physical condition of the speaker are responsible for the individuality of each human voice. It has been argued that our voices are as distinctive as our fingerprints. Certainly we know we can readily identify one another by voice alone, that by the sound of the voice we know who is at the bottom of the stairs or around the corner.

Articulation. The most effective speakers attain a high degree of clear, distinct, sound formation. They are not content to slur over words, to drop off word endings, to run together sounds which ought to be kept separate, even though such slovenly practices do not always lead to misunderstanding. They aim for distinctness. Where the elision of sounds is called for, they naturally blend the sounds skillfully. They guard against mistakes in articulation which result from addition, omission, or substitution of sounds. That is to say, they do not add sounds as in "athalete" for "athlete," "exscaped" for "escaped," "acrost" for "across."   Nor do they in most settings omit sounds by saying "reglar" for "regular," or " 'nuff" for "enough."   Nor do they substitute one sound for another by saying "hypmotism" for "hypnotism," "cartoon" for "carton," "ya" for "you," or "fella" for "fellow."   They pronounce words *in accordance with the conventions acceptable to their particular audiences.* Generally speaking, their authorities are dictionaries, community leaders, and experts in the field in which a given word is commonly used.   They are attentive to "-ing," "-tion," and "-nd" word endings unless there are strong reasons for sounding otherwise.   They aspire to neat, businesslike utterance that is relaxed and unlabored.   They aspire to meet the highest demands of their audiences for clear, controlled, understandable utterance.   Meanwhile, they seek to create personality images which please their audiences and themselves.   And lest all this seem idealistic, let it be said that no speaker loses influence by conforming to the best standards of his audience and occasion. He does lose standing if he falls short of these demands.

Volume.   Appropriate volume is the degree of loudness which meets the needs of the audience and the physical setting.   Without straining, an audience ought to hear every word a speaker says, no matter what the size of the place in which he speaks.   Where loud, strong utterance is required, a speaker ought to be able to produce it, but where the situation calls for soft or soothing utterance, a speaker must be equal to that necessity.

Beginning speakers are often unskilled in assessing the demands of audience for vocal force.   Some beginners speak in tiny, whispery, subdued voices which cannot be heard beyond the fifth row because they are unable to judge how forcefully sounds must be produced in order to reach the rear of the room.   Just as often, a beginning speaker speaks with too much volume. He unnerves his audience with too much force because he erroneously thinks that all speeches ought to be delivered loudly.   He is like those people who think they must shout into the telephone in order to be heard at the other end of the wire.   Often this speaker thinks that to be intense he must increase volume.   Much intensity is, of course, of a very quiet sort and achieves its influence by its very want of volume.

To make proper adjustments to situational demands for volume requires experience and practice.   Where a student speaker repeatedly misjudges, a hearing test is in order.   It may be that he does not hear himself accurately and as a result is using more or less force than needed.

Rate.   Optimum effectiveness in speaking requires a rate of speaking suited to the abilities of the audience to comprehend and to the emotional coloring or mood to be conveyed.   Beginners tend to race through formal speeches, stumbling over words, slurring them and blurring articulation.   The audience cannot then keep up.   Ultimately, listeners may come to feel they are running a losing race and so give up. The remedy is disciplined self-control on the speaker's part. If he paces utterance to *meaning,* his listeners will have no cause to complain.

Where ideas are not under control, are not at the speaker's beck and call, rate may become inappropriately slow, lagging behind the listeners' abilities to comprehend. Again, the result is irritation. The audience wishes the speaker would "get on with it."

The cause of slowness may be poor preparation. Perhaps the speaker is finding his ideas for the first time in slow, disjointed wordings while his audience waits impatiently. The cause of undue rapidity may be want of the keen sense of communication we have already discussed. Meaningfulness, self-discipline, and consideration for the audience are the only serviceable roads to improvement.

Ineffectual pausing and phrasing are characteristic of poorly managed rate. The too-rapid speaker does not take time to group words into meaningful thought units; nor does he stop frequently enough for the audience to catch up with him and absorb his ideas. The too-slow speaker breaks ideas within thought groups so that meaning is distorted or lost; his pauses are simply stops during which he collects his thoughts. He hesitates, often filling the resulting silence with "uhs" and "ers." His disfluency destroys meaning and effectiveness, and is often taken as a sign of lack of self-control.

A skilled speaker controls rate as he observes cues which signal that listeners are or are not absorbing his message. If he sees frowns or puzzled looks, he may slow down, at the same time modifying content by repeating what he has already said or by adding new ideas to make his point clearer and more acceptable. If he sees his listeners staring vacantly or assuming lolling, indifferent bodily postures, he may speed up or slow down in order to produce variety and thus recapture attention. If he sees knowing smiles or heads nodding in agreement and understanding, he may speed up since he has been given a "go" signal which says that what he is saying is readily understood and he need not belabor it. Speed ought to match the rate of comprehension. In all these ways he can respond adaptively to feedback.

The content of speech often demands variations in rate and certain quantities (meaning elongation of particular sounds, usually vowels). A blow-by-blow description of a boxing match would sound ludicrous if delivered at largo pace and with elongated vowel sounds. Similarly, to describe a quiet, calm, romantic canoe ride in rapid rate, sounds of short duration, and abrupt, staccato rhythms would neither reinforce meanings nor create appropriate mood. Just as rate ought to match comprehension, it ought to suit the material's emotional tone.

If rate is correlated with meaning, mood, and feedback, it will be varied. To speak at the same rate throughout is monotonous and invites listeners to turn their attention elsewhere if it does not lull them to sleep.

Pitch.   Flexibility in pitch is a further attribute of skilled speakers; lack of variety in pitch is as hampering as lack of variety in volume or rate. Monotone in pitch, volume, and rate can destroy the meaning of even the best ideas and the attentiveness of the most willing listeners.

Each of us has a pitch level which is natural and normal. Hanley and Thurman say, "Research findings for superior young adult male and female speakers are that their average (habitual) pitch levels are C_3 and $G\#_3$ respectively . . . or one octave and two musical notes, respectively, below middle C."[16] These authors and other authorities recommend that no one institute a program for relocating his habitual pitch without prior medical consultation. They further add:

> Pitch (frequency) is a function of balances among length, tension and mass in the vibration of a taut string, which your vocal cords resemble to a considerable degree. In your vocal mechanism these balances or adjustments have been arrived at over a span of many years. Your average level changed from infancy to childhood to young adulthood, where you now stand. In the absence of better information, we believe, it should be assumed that your physiological maturation has been as normal in the larynx as it has been in your upper arm, or ankle, or any other anatomical locus. If this is true, if you have normal cords that vibrate under normal tension, then the frequency at which they vibrate most often is the best, most effective, most efficient frequency, the optimum pitch level, the one at which you can produce sounds longest, with least effort. Temporary movements away from that frequency are good, for obvious reasons. But an ill-considered shift of any magnitude away from that habitual level can result in vocal strain and other more serious effects. . . .[17]

Some speakers unintentionally adopt pitches too high or too low. This is especially true at the beginnings of speeches and at points where tenseness and nervousness impair ability to vary pitch levels. From any such artificial pitch it is difficult to inflect upward or downward for emphasis or meaning. Thus a speaker who does not take such steps to reduce tension as were discussed in Chapter 2 will find himself adopting pitch levels that do not allow reasonable expression of meaning.

Changes in pitch are effected by raising or lowering the key of the voice either gradually or abruptly between or within words. Gradual changes in pitch are referred to as "slides," since we actually slide from one key to another. Abrupt changes are called "steps." The ways in which we modify pitch often determine what we mean and the degree of emphasis we place upon an idea. Through inflection it is possible to convey meaning opposed to the meanings of one's words. "Oh, no" inflected upward by means of a step may convey disbelief. "Oh, no" inflected downward by means of a slide

---

16. Theodore D. Hanley and Wayne L. Thurman, *Developing Vocal Skills,* 2nd ed. (New York: Holt, Rinehart and Winston, 1970), p. 184. By permission of Holt, Rinehart and Winston, Inc.
17. *Ibid.,* p. 185.

may indicate indecision. "Oh no" inflected downward by means of a slide may indicate dismay or may mean "yes."

Demands for pitch changes come most often from the material of speech. If public speech is to have conversational quality, inflection and stress must resemble the inflections and stresses of lively conversation. In ordinary conversation we do not think much about pitch inflections, stresses, or changes of key; we automatically make changes consonant with meanings. Public speakers need to respond to their materials as they would under normal circumstances, then their pitch patterns are unlikely to belie their words. But if your habitual pitch and stress patterns do not serve you well in impromptu and extemporaneous speaking, we suggest that you seek the help of a speech specialist who can competently analyze your speech patterns and devise a program of retraining. The public setting is not a suitable place to think about pitch and stress patterns; there, the task is to *use* the conventional patterns you have elsewhere learned to command.

In addition to variety in pitch, an audience demands the comfortable empathic responses which result from appropriateness in inflection. If an audience perceives from inflections that you are not thinking what you are saying or that you lack enthusiasm or are falsely enthusiastic, if they see that you are uncomfortable and therefore unable to move freely within a pitch range, you cannot expect them to respond appreciatively or comfortably to your message.

Your own need for flexibility in pitch arises from your need to avoid feelings of strain. Also, you listen to your own voice as you speak and are stimulated or bored by what you hear.

Occasion and setting, too, must be considered in establishing pitch controls. Pitch helps to establish mood. High pitch can create impressions of tension and excitement; low tones can help to convey solemnity or calmness. Pitch and the power to project adequate sound are related. To fill a large hall or to speak above competing noises you must adopt your most comfortable and efficient pitch range so that all resources of a relatively relaxed vocal mechanism are at your disposal in overcoming the difficulties imposed by the setting.

Quality. Quality is produced by changes in the shapes and sizes of the resonators: pharynx, mouth, nasal passages. It is common practice to say that a speaker's voice is breathy, nasal, denasal, pectoral, oral, guttural, metallic, strident, or orotund. These terms are really attempts to say something about what is happening along the path of the breath stream which produces sound. To say a voice is *nasal* means that an unusual amount of the breath stream emanates from the nose strongly reinforced by resonance in the nasal passages. To speak of a voice as *denasal* means that there is little nasal resonance on the "m," "n," and "ng" sounds due to some closure of the nasal passages. What we have called nasal is sometimes spoken of as positive nasality; denasal quality is sometimes called negative nasality.

To say a voice is *pectoral* is to imply that the sound seems to be reinforced in the chest or pectoral regions. It is doubtful that chest resonance really occurs, but some voices sound that way. To refer to a voice as *oral* is to indicate that vocal placement seems forward in the mouth so that sound seems reflected off the teeth and gum ridges. *Guttural* voices are those that seem especially reinforced low in the back of the throat. *Metallic* or *strident* voices sound as though they are heavily supported by strained and tense surfaces, presumably those within the mouth including the hard palate (roof of mouth). *Orotund* voices are those thought pleasant because they seem reinforced by a suitable balance of relaxed surfaces, which suggests that the cavities involved must be rounded. The truth is that none of these descriptive terms accurately describes acoustic phenonema in any precise way, but the terms do describe our psychological reactions to what we hear. They enable us to talk meaningfully about these perceptions, and they remind us how ready listeners are to make judgments on the basis of vocal quality.

Breathy and *aspirate* describe voices produced by inadequate control over the breath stream. When more breath is released than is needed to vibrate the vocal folds efficiently, the result is a whispery sound, usually of inadequate volume. Often the reason for this phenomenon is that the vocal folds are not firmly approximated; the air passing between them causes *some* vibration but also some sheer escape noise comparable to the sound of whispering.

The ways a speaker tenses the muscles involved in voice production and resonation and his general physical condition determine his vocal quality to a large extent. Tensed muscles are likely to produce *metallic* quality; too much relaxation is likely to produce unconventionally *nasal* sounds. A person in excellent physical and nervous condition is likely to manipulate his resonators so as to produce satisfactory vocal quality. A person in full control of all his muscles is likely to produce full, resonated tones. An invalid or aged person who lacks control over his general musculature has poor control of his speech.

Qualities suitable for public speech cannot be assumed at will, but elimination of what Hanley and Thurman call "negative tonal characteristics" is possible through special training and through self-analysis and discipline. The effort sometimes needed to achieve agreeable vocal quality has its rewards. The conditions that quality depends upon contribute to your general well-being. The empathic effects of good vocal quality support effective communication. Strained voices produce comparable strains in listeners and, of course, no "negative tonal characteristic" can produce affirmative aesthetic experience.

Knowing how voices are produced, how vocal sound is articulated, and what effects flow from various attributes of voice and utterance is a necessary basis for exercising that self-control all effective speaking requires. However, one ought not to try to perform vocal or articulatory experiments during communication; that is the time to reveal the precision of muscle and quality control that comes from private experimentation and reflection. You ought to experiment with your vocal resources, as with your bodily resources, but do so in practice in order to establish the habits and acquire the versatility essential to understanding and favorable, empathic responses on the part of listeners.

Empathy

As we have said, bodily action and vocal quality during speech are visual and acoustic stimuli that can affect listeners empathically. A major part of the impact of delivery comes about because as human beings we have, as Berlo says, "the ability to project ourselves into other people's personalities." This is his definition of *empathy*,[18] the topic we must now consider.

The German word for empathy, einfühlung, provides a clue to distinctions we ought to make between sympathy and empathy. Sympathy is ordinarily thought of as a feeling *toward* another person or being, a feeling *for* him or it. Empathy—einfühlung—is a "feeling in with." Our natural ability to take the role of another vicariously is the source of our empathic behaviors. Shaffer, Gillmer, and Schoen have said these ". . . empathic actions, postures or expressions are not deliberate mimicry and the persons displaying them are usually unaware of what they are doing. As non-voluntary acts, therefore, they are explained in the same manner as suggestion."[19]

It is plain that people who listen to others *do* involuntarily "feel in with" those who talk with them. The implications of this fact for you as a speaker are quickly apparent. As far as is possible you need to act and sound in such ways that the audience receives sensations (or suggestions) that support your meaning. They must perceive your behavior as invitations to participate in experiencing your message.

As we said when discussing nonverbal communication, there is no such thing as *not* emanating communicative cues when one faces an audience. The issue is simply whether the bodily and vocal cues you send out invite participation in your message or invite participation in some experience irrelevant to it. We have all heard speakers whose rates of utterance and bodily actions were so slow we wanted to "push" them along. And we have all heard speakers so gravel-voiced that we participated more in their throat conditions than in the messages offered by their words. Undesirable responses are occurring whenever listeners squirm, close their eyes, look out the window, or yawn. They are participating in experience extraneous to the speech. But when a listener nods his head in agreement, smiles at you, laughs with you,

18. David K. Berlo, *The Process of Communication* (New York: Holt, Rinehart and Winston, 1960), p. 119.
19. Laurence F. Shaffer, B. Von Haller Gillmer and Max Schoen, *Psychology* (New York: Harper & Brothers, 1940), p. 195.

leans forward when you lean toward him, you may be sure that he is "feeling in with" you and your meanings. To communicate fully you need to work for these visible signs of audience participation. This is what adaptive delivery is—being sensitive to listeners' reactions, identifying them, reacting to them, and guiding them. The most effective speakers plan very little of their delivery. They reach out and invite naturally; they watch for cues that listeners are joining in; and they try by voice and action to illustrate full participation in the meanings of what they are saying.

You will be able to generate empathic support for your ideas if you develop conventional vocal and bodily behavior and add to that full realization of your own meanings at the moment of utterance. Coordination of matter, manner, and listeners' perceptions is less the product of inspired moments than of moments of communication prepared for by careful inventional and stylistic choices "fixed" within your natural control by rehearsal.[20] Empathic response is harder to achieve when speeches or parts of them are read from manuscripts or notes, but reading is sometimes necessary. We turn next, therefore, to the topic of reading speech materials in public situations.

READING IN PUBLIC SITUATIONS

The Speaker Becomes Reader

Almost anyone who functions in a community or other public role has sooner or later to read while trying to place ideas before listeners. The material may be your minutes of a meeting, your report for a committee, a special passage supporting the ideas of your otherwise extemporaneous speech, or an entire speech prepared in manuscript form because of some special demands of the occasion. At such times you become a public reader as well as a public speaker. Assuming such a role means that you take on the responsibilities of an interpreter—one who stands between an author and an audience. When he presents his work from memory, a speaker similarly stands between the author he was and the speaker he is. Since the position of a reader is intermediate, the primary demands upon him come from the material. Elements in the occasion and the conventions of the audience force only minor modifications in his behavior. His personal skill affects his communication, but the material to be read chiefly determines what ought to be done.

If we put aside private reasons such as personal convenience or uncertainty, there remain but two good reasons for reading to an audience: (1) to bring something new and unusual to the fore or (2) to give listeners meanings

---

20. For extended discussion of extemporaneous speaking and rehearsal for this kind of speaking, look back to Chapter 2, pp. 29–30; 33–34.

which they would not get from reading the material by themselves either silently or orally.

Reading a speech or a portion of it involves stirring up meanings in those who listen. By uttering the sounds signified by black marks on a white page, you take responsibility for translating the marks into meaning. You must endow the printed words with the meanings their composer, or you, if you happen to be the author, intended them to have. Where you were the composer, you presumably know what the words mean; the problem is to revitalize your own ideas. If someone else composed what you choose to read, you must understand what that author meant before you can give the meaning to others. Whether you undertake to revitalize your own ideas, or to bring to life what another author meant, you have analytical work to do before you read.

Most people read badly because they are not aware of what is involved in getting and giving meaning. This is sufficient reason for discouraging beginners from reading their speeches. We cannot treat oral interpretation fully, but we can offer basic suggestions to public communicators who must sometimes read. Since a public speaker's reading is primarily for utilitarian rather than aesthetic purposes, the observations that follow focus on reading to convey practical meaning, leaving out of consideration the equally legitimate object of giving pleasure.

General Principles

The following suggestions are arranged in the approximate order in which you are likely to confront the problems discussed.

Discover Author's Purpose and Method. To determine an author's purpose and method, sift the material for clues. Is the communication essentially utilitarian? Aesthetic? Or does the author's intent fall somewhere between? At the utilitarian end of this imaginary continuum might stand a technical report or the minutes of a business meeting. At the aesthetic end you would expect to find love lyrics. Any author's purpose will lie somewhere along the line between these types. Consider the different communicative purposes that distinguish a news report, an editorial, a personal essay, a fictional narrative, a scene from a play, a ballad, a sonnet.

When an author's purpose is practical, as the news reporter's and editorialist's purposes usually are, he may explain how a thing can be done, why it should be done, or how to get people to do it. He may simply describe. Or he may explain through abstract proof. Most authors have the same purposes you have: to inform, persuade, reinforce, inquire, or entertain. This tells you what tone or mood to adopt in your general delivery. It also gives you a framework for further analysis of the material.

Discover the Complete Meaning.   One of the chief causes of poor reading is failure to obtain complete meaning from the material. To discover the purpose is not enough. You should learn what the material says and what the author's attitude is. In so doing you may have to turn to other materials and read about the author or read critical essays written about the material.

Getting the full meaning entails knowing the meanings of all the words. You must know their dictionary meanings and their denotative and connotative meanings. You will also have to study the contexts of these words before you can interpret them precisely as *this* author meant them. Associations and the responses words touch off are important. Make sure, then, that you are aware of the referents intended by your author. Examining language carefully, a task you may find glorious or laborious, will be essential if you are to grasp the material to reconstruct suggested meanings, and to respond empathically to the ideas.

To achieve complete meaning you will sometimes have to study the setting for the material. The historical period depicted or to which the piece belongs may be as much a matter for concern as its objective meaning. You may have to answer for yourself such questions as: "Who is saying this?" "Why is he saying it?" "Who is the intended listener?" Whether the words were spoken on the steps of the nation's Capitol during an inauguration or in the give-and-take of a Lincoln-Douglas debate will affect the manner in which you read them.

Knowing the author's mood—his expression of attitude—is a related requirement. You, as the middleman, must reflect feelings in harmony with the author's and for that reason, unless you are an experienced and accomplished reader, sight reading can be dangerous. The establishment of mood is especially important to effective presentation of materials with aesthetic purposes. You cannot quote poems and stories effectively unless you understand and are able to transmit mood. Even your reading of utilitarian material is enhanced if you can adopt the manner that reflects your author's feeling toward the subject about which he wrote.

Sometimes paraphrasing a passage or writing a précis will aid you in assimilating its full meaning. You must undertake whatever research, peripheral reading, or repetition is needed to discover complete meaning. Only if you understand the whole can you understand how to read a work or any of its parts.

Discover the Structure and Unity of the Selection.   Every well written composition—even a passage—has perceivable structure and unity. Some planned development of ideas dominates the work. If you can see what lines of thought or feeling contribute most to the structural pattern and the unity of the material, you have important hints about what to emphasize in reading. If you quote at length, you have need to examine the form the author has chosen as his medium of expression. News story, prose narrative, ballad, sonnet, and dramatic scene have distinctive structural patterns. For example, the most important facts or meanings are usually found near the start of a news story, but near the end of a dramatic scene. What is worth quoting, what is representative of the author's meaning, and what must be emphasized are all revealed by attention to the structure and unity of the work and of its parts.

Discovering structure also means examining grammatical constructions so you can see minor relationships. Paying close attention to transitions can also help. Whether you are concerned with minor or major structural features, your purpose is basically to discover what relational patterns you must express by your manner of utterance.

Cultivate a Sensitivity to Rhythm. Some of the subtlest shadings of meaning achieved through language are conveyed by changes in rhythm, changes in the beat or measure of sounds. This is especially true of poetry but it is also important in some prose. If you choose to quote Daniel Webster, Winston Churchill, John F. Kennedy, or Martin Luther King, you will seldom convey the full meaning of a passage if you do not express the rhythmic patterns so characteristic of these speakers' prose. Only by preserving rhythm, or by breaking it, can the meanings of some authors be conveyed. It is seldom necessary to do so with poetry. If you quote poetry you should be careful not to let meter dominate your utterance to such a degree that you destroy meaning. The extreme example of this fault is the small child's sing-song recitation of poetry. Your capacity to "hear" rhythmic meanings and reproduce them will often determine what you should and should not try to quote.

Cultivate Imaginative Capacities. A further requisite for good reading is imagination, the power to see what others cannot in a combination of words. Watch for authors' unique achievements, their use of special patterns of expression, new relationships between ideas, and new word pictures. The more aesthetic the author's purpose, the more valuable imagination is in interpreting his material.

Imagination comes from experience and from temporarily divorcing yourself from reality. It comes, in part, from a capacity to dream. Let your mind range as you work over material to be read. Visualize the possibilities. Create several versions of possible meaning in your mind, then choose the best one for your final interpretation. All of this is useful even if you are quoting yourself.

Cultivate Ability to Group and Pause. Grouping or phrasing is the art of breaking a text up into ideas or speech units. A word is a grammatical unit; the idea is the speech unit. According to W. M. Parrish:

> When we are creating thought as we go along, as in conversation, we generally make the grouping clear to our hearers, that is, make our ideas distinct. In reading from the printed page, our eyes must be trained to run quickly along the suc-

cession of words and organize them into proper groups before the voice attempts to utter them. If the voice fails to communicate this grouping to one's hearers, it fails to communicate meaning, for meaning lies in the grouping. And if we make a false grouping, we falsify or destroy meaning.[21]

In reading poetry the inexperienced tend to group mechanically at the end of each line, a practice to be avoided. You must learn to group by thought. Realistic grouping is no less necessary in quoting prose, though the problems are less complex.

You should be aware that there are two types of punctuation, oral and written. Oral punctuation makes meanings clear to an auditor by noticeable changes in voice or action, as written punctuation makes similar meanings clear to a reader. The two kinds of punctuation do not always coincide. There are many times when you will want to ignore the written punctuation altogether. Pausing at every comma, semicolon, or period does not always enhance meaning. It may confuse. One who reads aloud must determine in advance which written punctuation will assist him in grouping audible thought and which will not. Punctuation in oral reading, as in speaking, is achieved by changes in volume, rate, or pitch, and by gestures and other bodily movements which make groups of words stand out clearly and so convey units of meaning incisively.

A pause is a psychophysiological event. Proper pausing does more than any other one thing to make reading natural and realistic. "There is never any need to pause for breath alone, as the pauses for thought are so many that the lungs may always be full, a necessary condition for good voice support. . . . We must learn to fill the think tank and the lung tank, automatically and simultaneously."[22] A pause is not mere silence. It is not a dead stop. In a true pause silence is pregnant with meaning. When the voice stops for a true pause, thought continues. The reader sees ahead and gains command of the next idea; the listener digests what has been said and becomes curious about what is to come. Pauses help both reader and listener to apprehend the relationships among the words and phrases.

Professor Parrish explains why young readers do not pause. He says:

First, they lack confidence. The excitement of reading before others causes a nervous acceleration of what is normally too rapid a rate of utterance. Under such circumstances, the cessation of vocal activity for a fraction of a second seems an ominous silence full of dreadful possibilities. The reader feels that his audience will begin to wonder whether he has not broken down. . . .

A second reason why young readers seldom pause is just that they do not *deliberate*. They skim. Their minds do not *dwell* upon the ideas to be com-

21. Wayland Maxfield Parrish, *Reading Aloud*, 4th ed. (New York: The Ronald Press Co., 1966), p. 21. Copyright © 1966 The Ronald Press Company. Used by permission of the publisher.
22. S. H. Clark and M. M. Babcock, *Interpretation of the Printed Page* (Englewood Cliffs, N.J.: Prentice-Hall, 1940), p. 5.

municated. As surely as the mind begins to dwell upon the ideas being expressed, there will be a focusing on separate word-groups (how else *can* one think?), and these word-groups will generally be separated from each other by pauses.[23]

We add, parenthetically, that Parrish's observations are true of speakers as well as of readers.

Cultivate Ability to Subordinate Ideas. You must realize in reading, as in speaking, that ideas are not all of the same value. Some ideas are subordinate to others. They support and amplify. In your analysis of material to be quoted you must look for these relationships. Then you must try to *convey* these relationships of degree by voice, gesture, and movement. Emphasize the most important ideas and de-emphasize the less important ones. If you read every word in the same way with the same rate, pitch, and volume, you will be boring. The variety of enlarged conversation clarifies the meaning inherent in printed material. Thinking the thought, feeling the meaning, and releasing voice and body to reinforce these experiences are your best means of expressing discovered relationships.

Cultivate Ability to Maintain Visual Directness. Preserving visual directness is an even greater problem when reading to an audience than when speaking to them. Speakers who bury their noses in books or who gaze at papers on the lectern destroy the liveliness which ought to prevail during public speech or reading. As Henneke says,

> The reader has a special eye problem. He must look at his manuscript and still maintain eye contact with his audience. His best answer is a compromise. His eyes should follow the manuscript until he is certain of what he is going to say. Then he may look at his audience until he has completed saying that phrase or group of phrases.[24]

In this way readers may read without wholly destroying the intimate speaker-audience relationship that gives speech its special social meaning.

Preserving visual contact with an audience during reading is a skill attained only through practice. To take in a group of words, then to lift your eyes and focus upon the audience as these words are uttered requires that you remember what the eye first took in long enough to deliver it meaningfully and without interruption. The process demands a high degree of physical coordination with memory. Some beginning students who find it difficult to achieve this resort to memorizing quotations. The better way is to familiarize yourself thoroughly with all quotations or excerpts before speaking. If you proceed wisely in this task you will find you are following precisely the steps

23. Parrish, *Reading Aloud*, p. 36. Copyright © 1966 The Ronald Press Company. Used by permission of the publisher.
24. Ben Graf Henneke, *Reading Aloud Effectively* (New York: Rinehart, 1954), p. 143.

of analysis and practice we are recommending on this and the immediately preceding pages.

In short, visual directness—or its absence—usually reveals whether the reader has thoroughly or haphazardly prepared to read.

Cultivate the "Illusion of the First Time."   Flexibility and variety are essential for all good speaking or reading.   In extemporaneous speaking one responds afresh to ideas sifted though never fixed by preparation, but in reading from memory or the printed page it is fixed content and form that must be recaptured.   The speaker's stimulus is never quite static, unless he overprepared; the oral reader's stimulus is inevitably static.   The material is precisely that thing to which he responded again and again during preparation.   Thus, the illusion of fresh experience with content is much harder to convey when reading than when speaking.

It is not limitations of vocal and bodily equipment that constrain most oral readers; it is inability to recapture whole meanings and to respond with full powers of intellect and imagination while under the stresses of public communication.   There is no easy remedy.   As is true with other arts, so it is here: given understanding of how to study material and of the resources of delivery, practice, evaluation, and more practice produces the controlled but lively responses to static stimuli that superior reading requires.   Here a reader resembles a musician.   The "illusion of the first time" to which audiences enthusiastically respond is largely the result of experience and painstaking practice.   For the speaker who reads only brief passages in the midst of extemporaneous speaking there is this encouraging fact: careful analysis, modest experiments with the resources of delivery, plus less than formidable amounts of practice can produce meaningful readings of utilitarian prose and uncomplicated kinds of poetry.

DELIVERY AND SETTINGS

Whether you speak extemporaneously, read, or both, the space in which you move determines to a considerable degree how you will need to regulate your posture, gestures, and movement.   The amount and the character of the action you use to reinforce and punctuate your message will be affected by the physical spaces and objects to which you must relate.   If your setting is open and spacious, you will ordinarily move considerably more and use broader gestures; you would be more restrained if your setting were a confining one.   If you speak or read from a platform in a stadium or field house, you will have to make large, wide gestures, move in somewhat exaggerated ways, and speak in a loud voice just to make the physical aspects of your communicative behavior have meaning for your listeners.

Proxemics, as we have said, is the study of distances between interacting human beings and treats also the communicative significance of a speaker's distance from such inanimate objects as lecterns, chairs, curtains, and other furnishings of his environment. The findings of scholars in proxemics have significant bearing upon notions about speakers' control of space and immediate, physical settings.

In almost all manners of speaking, space and communicators' relations to space contribute significant parts of the total message communicated. Your relation to space is *not* a matter of taste or haphazard choice. Yet you, yourself, may have passed up opportunities to look, before speaking, at what spaces and furnishings were available for your use in a room where you were to speak. Very many speakers fail to test, before speaking, what kind of vocal modulations a room allows or demands. Salesmen, lecturers, and even office personnel often study systematically what positions, postures, and furnishings give them advantages and disadvantages in relation to their clients or audiences.

One cannot give "rules" for regulating and adjusting to physical features of a setting. All we can do is urge you to look carefully in advance at what space and furnishings will *do to you* as a communicator and how *you* can manage them to your advantage. Common sense will usually tell you some adjustments to make. If, for example, there is no lectern or desk about which to center your speaking and thus provide a point of focus for the audience, what shall you do? You can still succeed. How? A way of learning to think about how to use space and furnishings is to test out alternatives.

Figures 10–3, 10–4, 10–5, and 10–6 are diagrams of rooms in which we have both made speeches and taught, and we have watched students like yourself try to make speeches and conduct meetings in these spaces. We invite you to consider: (a) What does the arrangement of the office space pictured in Figure 10–3 "announce" about the two faculty members occupying this space? (b) How would you want to rearrange this office if you and the other desk occupant wished to communicate to others that you were of *equal* importance? (c) Where would you stand or sit to make a report in this room?

Ask further how a sensible speaker ought to direct his movements behind and around the lectern as it is placed in Figure 10–4. What would a speaker have to do with his movements in order to maintain effective communication with the audience indicated in Figure 10–5? Where would you position yourself in Figure 10–6 if you were to preside over a meeting or make a report to ten people gathered in the room with the furniture arranged as indicated? Would you move any of the furniture? If you will make your judgments on these and like matters and discuss them with friends and colleagues, you will have begun to sensitize yourself to the uses (and abuses) speakers can make of the physical settings in which they talk.

Another benefit of considering carefully the physical settings in which you speak is that you will often discover that they have persuasive effects. It is no accident that portraits of the leaders of the party are often displayed

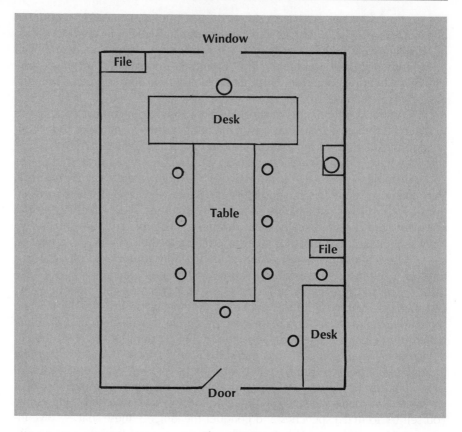

Figure 10–3

in the halls where national political conventions are held or that flags, bunting, emblems of brotherhoods or unions, of parties and patriotism adorn the walls and platforms of meeting rooms.   These create atmospheres and moods that modify the persuasiveness of what is said in such places.   These inanimate symbols have meanings and stir up memories.   They are there because it has long been known that they are important in reinforcing certain kinds of speaking.   It was not by chance that Hitler often spoke in gigantic stadiums at night with flags massed, torches flaming, and drums beating or that there were bugles blaring prior to his entrance into these carefully staged settings.   Nor was it by chance that Mussolini always spoke from balconies, which he had built to order when none was available.   Neither is it strange that speeches before mobs seem to get most effect if delivered from elevated places above the crowds or before symbolic façades.   Words uttered in such settings have different meanings from the same words delivered in the sometimes sterile and cold settings of college lecture halls.

    The place in which you deliver a speech, then, is first a space in which

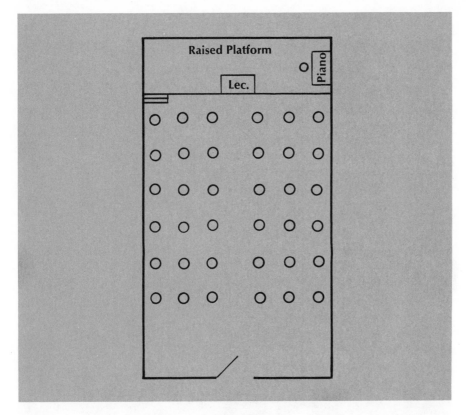

Figure 10–4

to move; second, it creates a part of the occasion, especially if it contains visible symbols which will reinforce what you have to say or detract from it. Your task is to calculate ways to use or counteract the space and the symbols in the midst of which you try to attain your purposes.

In this chapter we have examined delivery as a means to an end rather than an end in itself. It seems sensible to approach personal presentation of speeches by first recognizing that constructively communicative physical behavior arises as controlled but free response to thought and feeling fully experienced. If physical and vocal behaviors are means rather than ends in speaking, a general standard for good delivery is easily found: *Good delivery helps the listener to concentrate upon what is said; it does not attract attention to itself.*

There are, as we have tried to show, general principles of bodily and vocal action which encourage free and full use of the human body in reinforcing thought and feeling. There are also specific behaviors to be learned

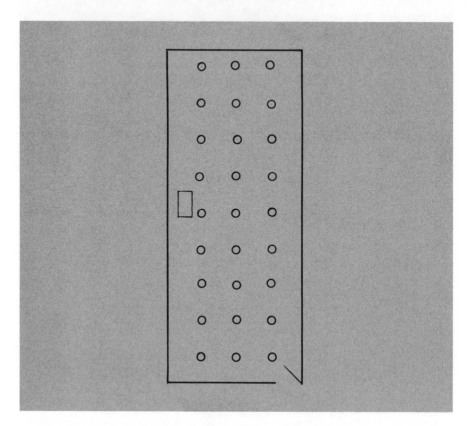

Figure 10–5

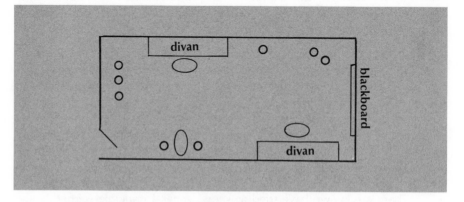

Figure 10–6

if listeners are to empathize favorably with speakers' messages. In essence, however, it is a speaker's attitudes toward his ideas, himself, and his audience that govern the functional value of his delivery. We have offered suggestions concerning constructive use of body and voice, and on reading for public speaking. But our belief is that it is from knowing and reflecting upon the possibilities of communicative action and from private drill to achieve conventional and variable habits that effective delivery ultimately emerges on the platform.

EXERCISES

Written

1. Write a description of the bodily action used by one of the following:
   a. A professor during a lecture.
   b. A classmate delivering a speech.
   c. Your roommate as he goes about his daily activities.
2. Write an analysis of your voice after listening to a recording of it. Comment specifically upon volume, rate, pitch, and quality.
3. Listen to a live speech delivered in person or over television. Write a description of the speaker's delivery with these questions in mind: What did the speaker do to support his ideas visually and vocally? What did he do with his body and voice which detracted from what he was saying?
4. Observe one of your classmates as he delivers a speech and during an informal conversation. Write a comparative account of his use of body and voice in these two situations. Note the similarities and differences in vocal and visual elements.

Oral

1. Make a short speech during which you read aloud from at least three different literary forms: news account, scientific report, fictional prose, sonnet, ballad, essay, or dramatic scene.
2. Prepare and deliver a speech 3 to 6 minutes long in which you explain some procedure requiring much action: how to do a dance, how to perform artificial respiration, how to handle a fencing foil, how to execute wrestling holds, how to direct calisthenics, or some similar subject. (Note: If you feel unduly nervous about speaking to a group, you will find this exercise or something of its kind particularly helpful in reducing your tensions.)
3. If bodily movement is not your "style" in communication, try this exercise. Below are a series of common events that need at least *some* nonverbal communication whatever you say about them. Put the items in some narrative or make an explanation that will allow you to use each idea; then give a brief talk in which you convey the meanings physically as well as by words.
   a. A man was out-of-doors and, for some reason, *he studied the sky.*
   b. *A small* cloud intrigued him. It seemed about the size (choose a size) and it

was *shaped* like this (choose the shape and communicate it verbally and non-verbally).

c. For some reason his thoughts drifted to air travel (perhaps he hears a plane), and he looked toward the horizon *somewhat to his left.*

d. He had a thought of *great importance* (to you, to your audience, or both). Perhaps it was about pollution, how small the world is, or whatever you choose.

e. You would like *to offer us* your own interpretation of this thought.

The italicized ideas are spots at which some kind of movement, if only of eyes, will be essential if you are to observe the speaking conventions of our culture.

4. Explain the "layout" of a supermarket. Tell your listeners, in your own words, that as one enters past the shopping carts into the main display area, the fresh produce will be on one side, the frozen foods will be on the other, the meat department in a far corner, etc. Without being dramatic, try at least to *suggest* by some kind of action and vocal variety the spatial pattern of such a store. (Note: If you need practice in broader physical movement, try this exercise using a large space and *demonstrate* the spatial positions; or use a blackboard drawing if you need experience in using visual aids.)

5. If using your hands in communication seems unusual or awkward, try this exercise. Give a 2-minute talk on "Some Geometric Figures We Couldn't Do Without." You might try describing rectangles of different sizes, an octagon, various shapes of triangle, or others. If you refuse to use a blackboard or other externally derived visual aid, you will discover (a) that you have to describe with hands, arms, and other movements, and (b) that these are quite natural and easy things to do.

6. Assign each of the following sentences to three or four members of your class. Ask each person to say or read his sentence with an emphasis different from that used by the person preceding him, changing the meaning of the sentence each time it is read. Following the readings, discuss the differences in volume, pitch, and rate employed to achieve the differences.

a. Whom do you suppose I saw in class today?

b. Oh yes I'd love to go.

c. You aren't really sure of that are you?

d. I've never seen such food.

e. There are always a lot of men at the movies on Saturday night.

f. It was the most spectacular yet peculiar race you ever saw.

g. There was the book just where I'd left it rain-soaked and falling apart.

h No I simply can't believe that that is so.

i. Whoever heard of a person doing such a thing.

j. Oh my dear what have you done?

CHAPTER
11

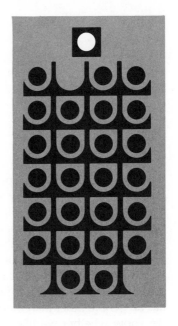

Judging
Public Speech

A liberally educated citizen ought ideally to be able to explain what happens when he is addressed by a speaker. He ought to be able to describe the speech he hears and to explain why and how it contributed to the results that followed. If people could do these things expertly in all cases, judging speeches would be a science, and public speaking would be human engineering. None of us has achieved precision in observing and analyzing public speech, nor are we likely to achieve it soon; but we can do better than we are accustomed to.

Even the highly educated find it difficult to perceive the components of speech as they listen. They find it even more difficult to judge the effect speech has on people other than themselves. As Robert S. Cathcart has said, "Usually we know whether we like a speech, but being able to judge that speech as effective or influential is quite another matter."[1] Those who have carefully studied the theory and practice of speechmaking judge qualities and effects more reliably than those who have not, though the experts are by no means infallible. Like reliable criticism of fiction, poetry, or painting, reliable evaluation of speaking depends greatly on practical and theoretical knowledge of what is possible and impossible. With practical and theoretical knowledge the Ciceronian ideal nears possibility, the "expert and the plain man" see alike, but the expert can give reasons for his judgment.[2]

Criticism is both the way we tell ourselves what is going on and the way we learn how to practice the art with greater insight. We are not likely to reduce speaking or any other art to science, but we still have both need and responsibility to bring as much knowledge as possible to bear when we respond to discourse. To equip us for such informed responses is a general object of all liberal education and a special object of speech courses.

The broad aims of a liberal education are to stimulate you to think in a variety of ways, to increase your ability to judge, to enable you to choose among alternatives, and to prepare you to take a responsible place in the world.

---

1. *Post Communication. Critical Analysis and Evaluation* (Indianapolis: Bobbs-Merrill Company, Inc., 1966), p. 1.
2. See *De Oratore,* trans. H. A. Rackham (Cambridge, Mass.: Harvard University Press, 1948), pp. 157, 159, bk. III, chap. 51.

We have explored theories with you, to enlarge your understanding. We have described procedures and methods to enable you to fill your roles as a speaker and as a listener to speech. As a final matter we invite you to consider how to form useful critical judgments.

We know there are those who believe that students are too young and inexperienced to be critics. But we believe criticism of live speeches is an important and necessary aspect of your study of speaking. You were not prepared to function as critic at the beginning of your first course in speaking, but with some theories at your command you are ready and able to evaluate speeches with regard to those principles at least. Most important, critical activity will benefit you both as a speaker and as a private person.

The audience reactions revealed to you in early talks are valuable. By knowing what your audience thought of your first talks, you can improve your adaptation to the group in later efforts. We are not saying audiences ever remain the same. Having lived a day longer your classroom audience changes each time you meet. Nonetheless, there are some criteria by which they measure effective speaking—criteria which do not change from session to session. Their consistent standards and recurring judgments can teach you much about speech and yourself. Some of these will be discussed here.

Criticism in a classroom ought to be a reciprocal activity. By openly registering your responses to your peers, you will aid immensely in their improvement, just as their frank responses to your speechmaking will provide you with directions for improvement and always with insights into how others judge speaking.

To exercise full responsibility as a critic in your class or elsewhere, you need to develop powers of discrimination and to know the methods and standards for criticism. We say still what Dean Everett L. Hunt said nearly a half century ago:

> . . . we might be better satisfied with the returns from the money and energy spent on rhetorical training if we cared more about producing educated and critical audiences. . . . Critical and analytical study of rhetoric and oratory should not be limited to those who expect to become professional speakers or writers, or to those who expect to teach it; it should be offered to all students who desire to understand the significance of rhetoric in modern life.[3]

Unfortunately, modern education has not met Hunt's challenge.

Whether or not you are invited to criticize spoken or written speech at any juncture in your speech course, you owe it to yourself as a part of your education to develop standards of judgment and critical acuity toward the speeches you will hear, read, or deliver in future days or years. For this you must understand the standards and methods commonly employed in evaluating speeches in the laboratory of the classroom and elsewhere.

---

3. "Editorial: 'From Rhetoric Deliver Us,'" *The Quarterly Journal of Speech,* XIV (April 1928), 266–267.

THE NATURE OF SPEECH CRITICISM

Criticism of any kind is judgment and/or appreciation. To evaluate or criticize implies analysis and comparison and commendation or censure. All reactions to objects, ideas, actions, and persons are critical or noncritical. Assessments or evaluations are criticism. Descriptions, reviews, commentaries, and surveys, unless interpretive, are not. They merely report data.

Criticism is essentially a comparative activity involving discrimination. Whenever we make a judgment or register appreciation, we do so with some standards of perfection in mind. Where we are subjective in our judgments, our standards are likely to be very personal. We may not even be conscious of them. Where we become objective, we tend to become consciously aware of the standards we apply and to identify them in our minds or on paper. Then we know *why* we say what we do. Whichever cast of mind characterizes our criticism, we do use some standards, and our judgments place what we judge somewhere along a continuum of excellence. The speech we appraise is always measured by some standards and found to correspond to them in some degree. It corresponds closely to the standards or it does not. This is the nature of our private judgments—of speech or anything else. Whether our judgments are useful to anyone other than ourselves depends on our capacity to communicate both *standards* and judgments, which is why "objective" criticism is necessary if classmates are to profit from your critical observations.

THE CRITICAL OBJECT

A focus upon some object is the beginning of any type of criticism. The object may be tangible or intangible. It may be material or a combination of materials, an action or an ideal. In aesthetic criticism this object may be a specific painting such as Picasso's "The Lovers"; a pattern of sounds such as Beethoven's Fifth Symphony, interpreted by a great orchestra; or physical action performed by dancers, such as the *pas de deux* from *The Firebird*. Objects for literary criticism are novels, short stories, poems, or essays, usually in the tangible form of printed words on a page. Whatever the kind of criticism, there is some object that exists to be appreciated and/or evaluated and perhaps to be praised or condemned.

A critic who assesses live speaking, speaking as it is delivered, deals with a distinctive critical object. What he examines, appreciates, and judges consists of a combination of sounds and actions symbolizing ideas, existing in time, air, and sight. This object is in constant flight, not static, not arrested. It is unlike some other critical objects. It is not a statue which can be placed on a pedestal and viewed from all sides. It is not a musical score nor a play script which can be consulted. It is not a painting which can be gazed at for hours. It is not print which can be pored over. Speech cannot be taken in fully with either the eye or the ear alone. Ideally, it must be seen and heard — all in the moments of its creation. Like dance, it will not "freeze" for examination, and yet its verbal nature makes it seem analogous to the more stable objects of literary criticism. The contrasts go further. While it is true that a critic viewing a painting takes in first one part, then another, and the critic of music hears sounds in sequence in time, a critic of live speeches faces a more exacting assignment. He must see and hear sequences that have never before occurred in just that way. Usually he will not even have a drama critic's advantage of consulting a script before or after seeing and hearing the object he is to criticize, though occasionally this is possible with very formal speeches.

A speech critic deals with a critical object which usually exists once and only once. Normally there will be no public preview of it, and there may even be no subsequent record. Speeches may be on identical subjects and in identical words, but, still, exact duplication is impossible. The components of the speech situation also constantly shift. In public interviews the interviewee can not foresee what he must next talk about until he receives the interviewer's question. The bits of talk, which may be regarded as small speeches, and which are a part of rap sessions, class discussions, political interchanges on television, and arbitration sessions — all of these are flexible, fluid, and in constant flux. They can never be exactly reproduced in any future place or time. But despite all of this anyone who would evaluate public speech must try to note and account for the ongoing adjustments speakers are or should be making.

To complicate matters further, a speech critic cannot always be present when the speech he needs to evaluate takes place. For example, he may want to criticize oral utterance only after he finds that it was of some importance to society or that it exerted some particular influence. He may not know a press conference was "news" until it is over. In such circumstances he is unable to experience the *real* speech, yet it may still be worthwhile to ask what happened when the speaking took place.

The most advantageous situation for criticism of past talk rarely exists. It is conceivable, though not very likely, that our would-be critic could obtain a video tape or sound motion picture that made all possible observations of visible and audible elements. A tape or film of this sort would come closest to reproducing the real speech, but it cannot reproduce the entire speech situation because it will fail to reveal some three-dimensional, conditioning factors. A video tape or film is simply not as reliable as on-the-spot observation for assessing such factors as environment, history, and audience reactions. In any case, this filmic alternative will seldom be open to you as critic for films are frequently unavailable, and when they are they often contain only portions of major speeches.   Ideally, the would-be critic would make his own filmed record of the critical object and otherwise record background information.

A second kind of critical speech object is some form of electrical transcription of the sounds of the speech.   This form of the speech will not give you the visual aspects of speech, but it does allow some evaluation of vocal performance, and it affords a precise check on texts.   This is important since most printed texts of speeches are inaccurate in details.   In classrooms and outside, critics can often tape speeches and discussions at the time of observation and then use the tapes as checks on the accuracy of their impressions. Under other circumstances, if a critic cannot make his own recording, he can sometimes obtain one through a radio or television station or buy one which has been commercially marketed.   The availability of such recordings is limited, and, of course, recordings of orators who spoke in the early days of sound recording are critical objects of dubious quality.

More often, a critic who was not present when a speech was delivered will have to content himself with some written record: a handwritten manuscript or a printed transcript of some sort.   Fortunately, he may pore over, analyze, outline, and study this kind of record.   He may be able to supplement such a transcript with other written accounts that help him reconstruct the milieu, the occasion, and audience reaction.   He may be able to read the criticisms others wrote after the speech was delivered.   He may, and often does, use the methods of historical, literary, and experimental study to bolster his knowledge and objectify his analysis.   But with all these aids his critical object remains the least satisfactory of those we have thus far discussed, for he must always see and hear with the eyes and ears of others.

The critical objects for critics of spoken discourse, then, are four.   The object may be the live, pulsating, reacted-to utterance of the moment; a video tape or film; an electrical transcription; or a manuscript or printed text.   Any of these critical objects must be approached differently from the objects of other kinds of criticism because they are never "real" until their contexts have been somehow understood.

The purpose of speaking also influences speech criticism.   Public speech seeks to gain immediate or long-range response or both, and it must be judged in the light of its purpose.   It is possible to judge the literary value, the historical significance, and the moral qualities of speaking, but these judgments alone cannot yield full appreciation or analysis of what was said.   They do not produce evaluations recognizing that the primary purpose of speechmaking is practical—or, at least, it is assumed to be by those who hear it.

Wichelns, in his essay entitled "The Literary Criticism of Oratory," says of rhetorical criticism:

> . . . we find that its point of view is patently single.   It is not concerned with permanence, nor yet with beauty [as may be the case in the judgment of literature].   It is concerned with effect.   It regards a speech as a communication to a

specific audience and holds its business to be the analysis and appreciation of the orator's method of imparting his ideas to his hearers.[4]

Wichelns was thinking mainly of criticism as a scholarly activity involving the analysis of speech texts, but what he says also applies to audiences and critics who hear and see speaking in classrooms or outside and to those who read or hear records of speaking. His elaboration of rhetorical criticism bears quotation because he concisely identifies the basic questions all speech critics need to raise in their minds.

> Rhetorical criticism is necessarily analytical. The scheme of a rhetorical study includes the elements of the speaker's personality as a conditioning factor; it includes also the public character of the man—not what he was, but what he was thought to be. It requires a description of the speaker's audience, and of the leading ideas with which he plied his hearers—his topics, the motives to which he appealed, the nature of the proofs he offered. These will reveal his own judgment of human nature in his audiences, and also his judgment on the questions which he discussed. Attention must be paid, too, to the relation of the surviving texts to what was actually uttered: in case the nature of the changes is known, there may be occasion to consider adaptation to two audiences—that which heard and that which read. Nor can rhetorical criticism omit the speaker's mode of arrangement and his mode of expression, nor his habit of preparation and his manner of delivery from the platform; though the last two are perhaps less significant. "Style"—in the sense which corresponds to diction and sentence movement—must receive attention, but only as one among various means that secure for the speaker ready access to the minds of his auditors. Finally, the effect of the discourse on its immediate hearers is not to be ignored, either in the testimony of witnesses, nor in the record of events. And throughout such a study one must conceive of the public man as influencing the men of his own times by the power of his discourse.[5]

As a critic analyzes and evaluates he ought to keep the varied demands of the audience, the material, the situation, and the speaker uppermost in his mind. The assignment—the rhetorical situation—that faced the speaker should be the primary consideration as a critic describes and then sets forth what ought to have been said and how it ought to have been said under the peculiar circumstances which constituted the constraints and opportunities of that situation.

It is also of value to remember what rhetorical criticism is not. Loren D. Reid, in reflecting upon the myopia of young critics, warns:

> Rhetorical criticism is not simply a discussion of the speaker's ideas, . . . not simply a narrative of the circumstances under which a speech is delivered,

4. Herbert A. Wichelns, "The Literary Criticism of Oratory," in *Studies in Rhetoric and Public Speaking in Honor of James Albert Winans* (New York: Century, 1925), p. 209. Reprinted in Donald C. Bryant, ed., *The Rhetorical Idiom* (Ithaca: Cornell University Press, 1958), pp. 1–42.
5. *Ibid.*, pp. 212–213 or pp. 38–39.

. . . not simply a classification or tabulation of rhetorical devices, . . . [and] not primarily an excursion into other fields of learning.[6]

The "perils" Reid enumerates all lead to mere description or too-simple comment on a speech. A preoccupation with any of them will produce something less than significant critical judgments; your colleagues will not be helped much by mere description. Constructive criticism, as we have said, involves evaluation as well as description. And because he evaluates, a critic's values — his point of view — inevitably color his criticism.

CRITICAL POINTS OF VIEW

The Pragmatic Viewpoint

Value systems underlie all our judgments of speaking. Whether we wish to call them critical standards or philosophies, we all hold basic tenets about what is "more" and what is "less" important. These basic views determine the qualities we emphasize in our assessments. Perhaps the most important of the viewpoints which normally shape speech criticism is the pragmatic. This is a view which leads the critic-evaluator to stress the *effects* of the speaking he examines. This emphasis underlies Wichelns's distinction between rhetorical criticism and other kinds of comment about speeches. Weaver, Borchers, and Smith call it applying the "empirical standard."[7] McBurney and Wrage label it "the results theory" of criticism.[8]

If you use this point of view, you will consider speaking an especially practical matter. You ask, "Was the speaking effective? Did it elicit the response sought? Did it achieve the intended result? Did it fulfill its purpose?" In the classroom you are also likely to ask, "Did the speaking fulfill the assignment for which it was designed?"

If you approach criticism entirely pragmatically, you will also tend to measure the success of the speech on the basis of immediate rather than long-range effectiveness. Here is a limitation; you may forget that failure to attain an immediate, visible response does not always mean the speaking was a failure. A speech or general public statement may not elicit immediate response but have effects that operate at some later time. Who can declare that public speech proposing legalized abortion twenty years ago had no influence on those who are now changing state laws? Some of the public forums, broadcast discussions, and even classroom speaking of a generation

---

6. "The Perils of Rhetorical Criticism," *The Quarterly Journal of Speech*, XXX (Dec. 1944), 416–422.
7. See Andrew T. Weaver, Gladys L. Borchers, and Donald K. Smith, *The Teaching of Speech* (Englewood Cliffs, N.J.: Prentice-Hall, 1952), pp. 497–498.
8. See James H. McBurney and Ernest J. Wrage, *The Art of Good Speech* (New York: Prentice-Hall, 1953), pp. 22–24.

ago may have begun to ready the minds of legislators now altering laws of long standing. (Who knows, someone in your speech class may become a legislator. It has happened, as we can testify.) To base your judgment of over-all quality exclusively on immediate response is simply to see too little of the social power of public speech. It is also not entirely fair. The speeches of a political campaigner may be excellent—even ideal for his purposes—but because of extrinsic forces it may be impossible for any speaking to win him an electoral victory.

Of course, we should not dismiss immediate effect. Practically, the speech must get some effect at some time to do its work. Yet, to consider only immediate or even long-range effects will still produce but a partial evaluation, for public speech may have other merits that can make it commendable or deplorable.

The Ethical Viewpoint[9]

A second value system that can underlie judgments of public speech gives special interest to the *intentions* of speakers. If the motives of a speaker are in line with ours and if his intentions are admirable, we may praise him for upholding what we think is the right ethical position. In viewing speech from this vantage point we ask, "Is the speaker honest, sincere, courageous in the beliefs he enunciates? Is he truthful? Is he consistent? Is he on the side of the good?"

These are all appropriate questions which should not be overlooked by any thoughtful critic. As a critic, you probably do not wish to hold up as exemplary, talk that is untrue, biased, or designed to hurt the audience. Lying, cheating, plagiarizing, and speaking with bad intent are, to most of us, reprehensible. We must pause in this sort of judgment, however, to consider that oral discourse may be filled with truths and be based on the soundest motives and still not represent an intelligent or artistic use of the resources of human speech. Who would deny that some clergymen and professors honorably present what they believe to be truth and still prove poor, inadequate preachers and lecturers? And there is also such a thing as wasting time by telling truths to listeners who cannot understand them.

So, we say first that ethical merit, even though highly prized, is no guarantee of quality or even competence in speechmaking. Second, it is very hard most of the time to discover all of a speaker's motives. It is not always possible to declare that he is sincere, honest, acting with good will, or appealing ethically to the feelings of his auditors. Third, and perhaps most serious, it is often impossible to tell just what "truth" is in a given case. Fourth, it is

---

9. This viewpoint, as we discuss it, involves both ethical and truth considerations. McBurney and Wrage see these as separate viewpoints. See *ibid.*, pp. 24–28.

well to bear in mind that ethical standards vary from society to society, group to group, era to era, and age level to age level.   Ethical standards are relative. And the question, "How can we know the 'good'?" is still in dispute among philosophers and men of religion.   This is not to say that we, as critics, can dodge responsibility for making ethical judgments that are plainly and defensibly open to us.   A function of humane education is to aid in the discovery of truths and formulation of a system of values.   Still, even where we can make fair and supportable judgments on the ethical merits of speech, these cannot be the sole standards applied to rhetorical efforts, for then we would praise ineffectiveness and effectiveness alike.   To concentrate on ethical considerations alone tends to close the mind to social effects and to rhetorical skills. Therefore, in our opinion, the ideal viewpoint for a critic is an "artistic" one.

The Artistic Viewpoint

A third value system that can govern criticism esteems artistic excellence.   It inclines a critic toward judging on the basis of the skill with which theories and principles of an art have been applied.   The artistic viewpoint

> . . . holds that speech is an art reducible to principles.   Good speech is constructed on these principles, exhibits these principles to the discerning critic, and may be judged by these principles.   Any speech in any situation for any purpose is good in the degree to which it measures up to or incorporates these principles, and it is poor speech in the degree to which it does not.[10]

A value system emphasizing what is possible within the allowances of art places great weight upon the skill with which the resources of the art have been used.   Such a way of viewing speech is actually eclectic.   It formulates and applies criteria with an eye to both effectiveness and ethical worth.   It calls upon the critic (1) to know the particular methods and possibilities open to speakers given the situations in which they speak; (2) to perceive whether or not these opportunities have been used skillfully and unobtrusively; and (3) to offer judgments that can be defended with clear argument concerning the public worth of the speech as a whole.   To the authors of this book the artistic viewpoint seems most likely to produce socially comprehensive and practically useful speech criticism.

CRITICAL CRITERIA

It is not enough to apply values to public speech.   You must also be prepared to furnish specific judgments of specific choices speakers make.   This entails

---

10. *Ibid.,* pp. 28–29.

accurate, fair description of precisely what the speakers did. Your description need not always involve detailed or intricate observations, but there must be awareness of a speaker's matter and method. Particularly in classroom criticism, where one goal is to teach, it is essential to know what each speaker is trying to accomplish and what the available methods are for accomplishing it. Purpose will determine which aspects of speaking are crucial to success and which are not. You will need to move from awareness of the total speech to specific judgments on how well principles and techniques are applied. The facts of the speech, its purpose, the relevant circumstances, and the strategies and tactics used need to be held in your mind. However, the relative importance of these descriptive data will alter as you move from speech to speech.

Changing the Emphasis in Criticism

Your classmates try to learn from your critical reactions and judgments. So, as you suit your criticism to the learning task of each speaker in your class, it is important to choose consciously what to emphasize in each critique. The aspects of speaking which you choose to evaluate will form a hierarchy in your mind as you approach the task of judging. On one occasion the organization of the speech may be the item at the top of your list, the most important aspect of the speech to be judged. On another, structure will be far down the list. This is particularly true when you are judging classroom speeches. When you have been concentrating on organization and outlining in class, structure may loom as the most important thing to be considered in oral criticism or in the notes you provide for the speakers. In listening to a lecture or to a court plea, structure may be important but not as important as the speaker's choice of topics or arguments or the evidence he uses as support. Structure then moves down from the head of the list of rhetorical resources to be emphasized in criticism to second or third place. In criticizing another speech, you may find yourself discounting both disposition and invention while heavily weighing the speaker's stylistic achievements. You may conclude that the ideas are necessarily familiar ones and that structure was dictated so the speaker had little choice of patterns, given his situation. The topical or chronological patterns may seem to you about the only appropriate ones for this speaker to use. Given such circumstances, you may decide that originality in wordings and use of images were the chief resources open to this speaker. So you move style and delivery and their attendant aspects ahead of structure and invention in your evaluation of this speaker's accomplishments.

Thus, a critic's rankings of criteria shift constantly depending upon the aims of the speaker, his subject matter, and the demands of the situation. You must decide upon your critical hierarchy each time you criticize speech. As you listen or read to describe and evaluate, you must separate the important from the unimportant qualities of discourse.   If you do not, you may end by concentrating on trivial matters to the neglect of items that deserved most attention.

Consideration of ideas and their reasoned structure is often neglected. Among the ways you can assist your colleagues in classroom speaking is by considering with special care what you and the other listeners are *required* to believe if you are to agree with what the speaker is saying.   Here, Professor Toulmin's concept of argument can help.   Toulmin maintains that the persuasiveness of an advocate depends especially upon whether his listeners can and will accept the DATA and the WARRANTS he offers in support of his conclusions (see pages 113–116).   You can assist your colleagues greatly if you will consider *why* you *do* or *do not* accept the DATA and WARRANTS upon which their CLAIMS rest.   Obviously, speaking cannot be persuasive unless those who hear it accept the DATA upon which CLAIMS depend.   Unless "How do you get there?" (from information or DATA to conclusion or CLAIM) is answered satisfactorily for the listeners, you cannot hope to convince them. So, if you disagree with a colleague's CLAIMS, it will be very useful for you to explain whether it is the DATA you doubt or the WARRANTS you question. In other words, "*Why* do I believe?" and "*Why* do I doubt?" are questions you need to answer for a colleague if you are to explain your own critical reactions to his persuasion.   When shift in belief or attitude is a speaker's aim, considering and explaining how you or other listeners look upon the DATA and WARRANTS used can be a particularly rewarding emphasis in your criticism.

You will need to guard against developing fixations, especially about delivery.   For some, voice or bodily action always occupies first place when they listen to the speech of others.   These seem easiest to comment on.   In your critique of classmates a danger sign is present if you always say: "Jim doesn't make any gestures," or "John has too many breaks in fluency," or "George rattled the keys and change in his pocket—most distracting!"   All you have said may be true, but you also must focus on the total speech or its most important aspects for this situation, unless some special agreement within your class has determined that delivery is your only concern.

Detailing the Criteria

Once you decide which matters are most important in criticizing a specific bit of public talk, you will become concerned with other specific judgments. Usually you will start with the broader aspects of the communication and work to the details.   In assessing a unit of speech giving information, for example, you will want first to ask yourself questions about the communication as a unit.   Did it have an identifiable central purpose?   Did it have a recognizable introduction, body, and conclusion? What was the quality of its total impact? Descriptive data so collected become the bases for specific evaluations.

Your criteria will differ chiefly as the formats and focuses of communication differ. You will want on many occasions to ask special questions about speeches or units of speech which constitute communication calculated to give information. You might ask, "Does the audience understand the subject better now that they have heard what was said?" To answer why they do or do not, you may pose questions relating directly to expository techniques: "Was there justification in the subject matter and in the audience's interest for the way this speaker used exposition, description, and narration at various points? Did this speech or unit of talk meet the special demands for good expository speaking by being accurate, clear, and interesting? Were visual aids used or needed to clarify points or were they used for their own sake?"

From these kinds of questions you may turn to specific details which may or may not be exclusively applicable to informative speaking. Here, you will ask such questions as "Did the story of the male student who knitted his own socks and ate light bulbs illustrate originality or peculiarity?" "Were reliable statistics used to show the relationship between monetary support and the quality of higher education? Were they truly representative?" "Were appropriate gestures used to support the idea that public schools are bursting with students? Well coordinated? Definite enough?" "Isn't the word pronounced gri-*mace,* not *grim*-ace?" These and like questions of detail complete your movement: evaluating the speech or unit of communication first as a whole, then as a particular kind of speech, and finally as a communicative effort consisting of detailed strengths and weaknesses.

Criticism sheets used to assess classroom speaking will sometimes assist you in deciding which questions to ask and which questions are most important. The criticism sheet we have designed for use with formal speeches is reproduced below. It provides for both structured and unstructured comment. Aspects of speechmaking that need constant attention, no matter what the kind of speech, are arranged along the left-hand side of the paper with spaces in which quick reactions can be entered while the speech is being delivered. The right half of the sheet provides space for personal notations and for revised, final reactions to the speech. The box in the lower right-hand corner encourages the user to recommend areas for improvement so that the criticism will fulfill the constructive obligations of any critic's task.

We want to emphasize that this criticism sheet is not a "scoring sheet." It simply contains quick-answer items that experienced teachers have to comment on and ask for comment about again and again in speech classes. If you use this or any other criticism sheet, remember what we have just said about shifting your critical criteria to suit different formats and purposes of speaking. You, not a criticism sheet, must decide the relative importance of specific criteria in each speaking situation.

NAME: **SPEECH NO:**
SUBJECT: **DATE:**

SUBJECT AND PURPOSE   *Symbols:*
   Subject worthwhile? _____   X — No
   Purpose delimited? _____   √ — Yes
                                             Grades:
CONTENT AND ORGANIZATION   Papers:
 Introduction   Speech:
   Get attention? _____   For the round:
   Needed information given? _____   Consult Instruc-
   Purpose made clear? _____   tor? _____
 Development
   Organization — soundly planned? _____   _____
    — easily followed? _____
    — transitions effective? _____
    — internal summaries appropriate? _____
   Supporting material — clear? _____
    — interesting? _____
    — convincing? _____
    — visual aids effective? _____
 Conclusion
   Provide a note of finality? _____
   Whole speech in focus? _____

DELIVERY
 Mental Alertness
   Realize each idea as uttered? _____
   Keen sense of communication? _____
 Body
   Eye contact adequate? _____
   Posture acceptable? _____
   Movement meaningful? _____
   Gestures effective? _____
 Voice
   Distinct? _____
   Vocal variety adequate? _____
    Rate? _____ Pitch? _____ Volume? _____
   Fluency adequate? _____

LANGUAGE
   Have good oral qualities? _____
   Convey ideas clearly? _____
   Grammar correct? _____
   Pronunciation correct? _____
   Increase interest and impact? _____   NEXT TIME work especially for:

OVERALL EVALUATION
   Adapted to situation and audience? _____
   Purpose fulfilled? _____
   Make good personal impression? _____
   Interesting? _____

THE CRITICAL ACT

In the Classroom

A good classroom critic, like a good speaker, considers the effects his observations will have on his audience. He aims for and expresses judgments which cast the most light for the largest number. In public evaluations he minimizes his personal preferences and deals minimally with problems of concern only to a particular speaker. He sees himself as a student and teacher of oral discourse. Instead of using class time to comment on one speaker's peculiar vocal habit, he dwells on problems and strengths that are important to all speakers. He concentrates on whatever can be useful to all those he speaks to, and to himself as a student of an art. All faults and strengths are fair game for his criticism but he treats them constructively. In the classroom as elsewhere, matters having general application deserve public comment; basically personal matters are best criticized in private conferences or in tactful notes.

Your education as a speech critic begins in the classroom. To make the most of it, and to give others greatest benefit from your observations and judgments, we suggest you approach classroom criticism in the following ways.

1. *Ready yourself for your critical task by preparing to concentrate on what you will see and hear.* Focus, visually and aurally, upon the speaking that is going on. You must listen intently (see Chapter 2, pages 18–21). Try to rid yourself of distractions from without and within. Exclude all bids for attention except those of the speaker.

2. *Locate your critical criteria consciously.* Decide what you are listening for, what aspects of speech deserve your special consideration because of their importance in *this* speaking situation. In other words, decide which achievements in speaking rank highest in importance at *this* time, for *this* speaker, in *this* situation. By attending to the facets of speechmaking which you are currently studying in class, you will give your criticism purpose. The more specific you can be in defining your own critical purposes, the more specific will be your description and the more useful your evaluation.

Do not try to observe every aspect of the speech at once. You cannot describe and evaluate all the phenomena of speech, so let a deliberately chosen set of critical criteria define the scope of your analysis. Register your reactions accordingly. Scattering your attention over too many items will be of little service to the speaker and will impede the development of your own critical faculties. A speaker is not helped by superficial comments about a dozen things. He will be able to solve only a few artistic problems at any one time. And you will not be helped as a critic, by trying to judge a host of items in haphazard fashion. Aim to substantiate and develop a few major, situationally appropriate critical judgments.

3. *Adopt a constructive attitude.* As you try to detect the choices the speaker has made, consider the alternatives. As you note merits and flaws, ask: "What else might have been done in this situation given the speaker's purpose?" "What specific, constructive suggestions can I offer for this speaker's improvement?" Negative comment, registering only personal impressions without substantiating evidence or affirmative suggestions, will be of little help. To say, "Your speech was poorly organized," or even, "Your economic argument was unsound," does not get to the heart of the matter. It does not get to the "why" of the trouble. It doesn't offer an analysis upon which someone else can build. "You didn't look at your audience," "Your sentences were clumsy," or "You committed several grammatical errors" may be accurate descriptions of speech, but unless they are accompanied by suggestions for correction they are no help. Such comments are critical, but they do not teach. It is probably a good rule not to point out negative features if you cannot suggest remedies.

Starting critical remarks with positive things, with strong points, and proceeding to the less praiseworthy works well. Such an approach is simply good audience adaptation. The speaker will listen to what you say, will know that you are not picking him apart for malicious reasons, and he will be likely to remember to do again those things he did well and to remedy those he did poorly. It has been said, "Only those who have the heart to help have a right to criticize."

4. *Measure the speech against the criteria you are applying.* Set clearly in mind the three basic aspects to be examined: effectiveness, ethical worth, and artistry. Measure what the speaker did against criteria that relate specifically to ideas, proofs, arrangement, style, and delivery. But keep the rhetorical situation uppermost in your mind as you make your educated guesses on the effectiveness, apparent truth, and skill of what the speaker is doing.

As you listen, jot down reminders of your descriptive observations and of the criteria you are applying, then note your judgments along with the most pertinent examples and illustrations. A few notes will do. Do not become a stenographer. You and your colleagues are members of an audience, though you are also critics. You should remember that no speaker can be at his best when trying to address a roomful of bowed heads. Remember, too, that no critic functions effectively without giving himself the opportunity to take in the visual as well as the aural elements of spoken communication.

Your job is to judge the speaking, not the person. Of course, there is never speech without a speaker, but your business is to assess that speaker's *communicated* personality as a force in the speech. Consider how his *ethos* contributes to the speech, not what contributes to your like or dislike for him as a person.

5. *Make a judgment.* This admonition may sound superfluous, but we make it because we have found it is often needed. In too many cases you will be tempted merely to describe what you see and hear. Description is, to be

sure, a first step in fruitful criticism, but not your main business as a critic. Your ultimate function is to deliver a decision—a judgment—based upon the relationship between what you perceive and what you know. To be an effective critic you must avoid straddling the fence. Decide whether the aspect of speech which you are considering is effective or ineffective, true or untrue, adequate or inadequate, skillfully or unskillfully handled, successful or unsuccessful, and why.

6. *Be as specific as possible in formulating your judgments.* Document your criticism with descriptive evidence. Refer directly to the speech, to specific arguments, illustrations, and wordings. Provide examples to back up both favorable and unfavorable evaluations. If you are criticizing style, strive to identify moments during which style was effective and other moments when it was not. Refer to specific sentence structures, phrasings, and images. This will reveal that you have been both perceptive and thorough in arriving at your judgments. It will also be constructively useful to all who hear your criticism. Find segments of the speech illustrating strengths and weaknesses in clarity, liveliness, force, and the like. The more precise you can be about exactly what was done and exactly why it was effective or ineffective, the more worthy of attention your observations will be.

7. *Register your judgment.* When you present your critical assessments orally or in writing, articulate your convictions. Silence during an oral criticism period following a speech or submitting doodlings on a scrap of paper will contribute nothing to the speaker or to your own development as an intelligent, informed critic. Do not feel that you must couch your judgments in rhetorical jargon. Do feel that you must be tactful in wording and frank in your remarks. Clear, direct, precise expression of your position, the data on which it rests, and your suggestions are required.

We have emphasized throughout this book that public speaking does not always take place on the platform. Public interviews draw forth units of talk that function as "speeches"; "debates" in business meetings and other public gatherings evoke "speeches"; segments of uninterrupted talk on broadcast "talk shows" operate on listeners as "speeches"; astronauts' explanations from outer space and rap sessions are all forms of public communication. To understand these "pieces of talk" better you may need to conceptualize them as more formal speeches. If you do, they will often prove amenable to the kind of critical evaluation we have been discussing in this chapter. How well one communicates according to his or her purpose in public interviews and meetings has as much importance as how well one does in platform speaking. Artistic effectiveness is just as desirable off the platform as on. For these reasons we suggest below how you may approach minimally formalized public speech in substantially the same critical spirit you would apply to a formal speech.

Interviews are often conducted so as to allow the interviewee to make short speeches in response to topics opened up by the questioners' queries.

Almost any press conference creates situations in which the interviewee can (and often should) make responses of up to several minutes in length. Those responses can be understood and evaluated if you think of them as short, often one-point, "speeches" occasioned by a rhetorical situation and delivered under circumstances calling for artful invention, disposition, choice of language, and presentation, and, however impromptu, as affecting listeners essentially as other public speeches do. You can approach such responses in an interview, discussion, or public meeting as speech inviting criticism of the same sort as we are considering in this chapter. Essentially the same criteria apply to people who speak uninterruptedly in these circumstances as apply for more formal addresses.

Whenever and wherever you can discern a "major unit of rhetorical discourse," that "talk" is open to criticism as a speech even though it may be embedded in an interview, talk show, coverage of a space venture or, for that matter, conversation with your auto mechanic! If ideas are being developed for an audience of some sort, the criteria of speech criticism apply because artistic excellence in using rhetorical resources becomes possible. Descriptions and evaluations of purpose, applications of situationally suitable criteria, and judgments on how nearly the talk achieved its potential influence are issues whether you undertake to criticize formal or informal public communication.

Evaluating Texts of Discourse

Sometimes as critic your task may be to deal with what remains of discourse — a tape recording or a printed or manuscript record. Perhaps your critical object will be the verbatim transcript of an interview or of the cross-examination of witnesses at a hearing, published in such a source as *The New York Times*. Perhaps it will be the printed version of a formal public lecture published in *Vital Speeches*. The object for analysis and appraisal might even be a chunk of rhetoric on a mimeographed handbill, a quoted paragraph from your school paper, or a partial tape or filmic recording. You will work with all that remains of what someone said as he stood before a group of students in confrontation, as he rapped with a group of students in his office, or as he held forth in a public group discussion somewhere on campus. In such circumstances you will be faced with only the remnants of live, oral utterance. It will be as if an archaeologist gave you only some pieces of a Greek vase and then asked your opinion of the whole. When you find yourself in such a situation your critical procedure will be different from that used to evaluate discourse you can both see and hear.

Most differences in procedure will result from your lack of knowledge about the immediate or historic settings for the discourse, or about the speaker. You will find it necessary to substitute reading for listening or listening for seeing or bits for wholes. You will be taking in words with only the eye *or* ear, not seeing *and* hearing at first hand and completely. Delivery cannot be described fully, if at all. Voice may be judged from a recording, but not bodily action, unless you have access to a sound film. A bit of film may have to serve as "representative." Most judgments on delivery will be far from satisfactory since they must be based on accounts furnished by others who saw and heard what happened or on partial evidence.

In all cases criticism of texts, alone, will be postmortem evaluations. You will substitute "read" for "listen" in the steps for criticism of live communication which we have already given. Your perceptions will be restricted to word symbols since you are denied the stimuli of the real situation.

Tasks in appraising written records of discourse which *must precede* those necessary for evaluating classroom speeches are:

1. *Determine the authenticity of your text.* Ascertaining the genuineness and completeness of the written record before you may not be easy. (See exercise 4 at the end of this chapter.) Unless you are convinced of the trustworthiness of the transcriber and editor of the text, you will have to match the text you use with others, should they be available, in order to produce a reliable one of your own. You will wish to work with the best text obtainable. You must also be sure, insofar as possible, whether what you work with was actually composed and delivered by the speaker himself. Ghost writers are nothing new. They have been employed since the fourth century B.C. at the very least. You ought to know, insofar as possible, to what extent your text was prepared *for* the speaker and to what extent it was prepared *by* him.

2. *Inform yourself of the immediate speech setting.* To make judgments you must know the particulars of the rhetorical situation. You must know when and where the utterance took place, to whom it was directed, and what expectations and constraints controlled the impact of the message. Getting such knowledge calls for the kind of research that will lead you to sources dealing with immediate or distant history. If possible, you ought to know who was present, who saw and heard the discourse. When you know this you ought to interview those who actually witnessed the communication taking place if they are available and willing to talk with you. When you have exhausted these research possibilities, then you will want to turn to accounts that deal specifically with the communication, treating: the circumstances that determined the subject matter; the composition and the delivery; the immediate physical surroundings; and all other immediate influences that operated on the audience which heard the message.

3. *Inform yourself of the milieu.* For a full understanding of rhetorical discourse you often need to have extensive knowledge of the "times" as well as the immediate circumstances. It is often important to know what ideas were in the air, what philosophies prevailed, what historic events had recently occurred, and what were the day-to-day concerns of the people. No one can understand Lincoln's "Second Inaugural Address" without understanding how

the Civil War was going at the time and what visions some Northerners had of "reconstructing" the South.   Nor can one understand the speaking of Senator George McGovern as a candidate for President of the United States in 1972 without understanding what was meant that year by such terms as "open party" and "new politics."   To understand such things you will have to read historical and interpretive accounts of the cultural, economic, religious, political, and moral activities peculiar to the time in which your speech was given.   You will certainly have to acquire a sense of the chronology of events near the time of the speech.

It is true that understanding the milieu of public speech often entails a good deal of historical-sociological investigation, but this effort is frequently imperative if you are to describe and judge speech fairly and on *its* proper terms.   If it was wise rhetorical speech, it was created for and influenced by listeners who were the creatures of their environment.   To know them and thereby know the speech, you must know a good deal about that environment.

4. *Inform yourself about the speaker.*   A study of the speaker will further your understanding of any spoken or printed record of rhetorical discourse.   You will need to acquire information about his reputation, his place in society, his habits of mind and life, his sense of values, and his impact on other people.   To gain such insights you will need to study autobiographical and biographical materials, diaries, memoirs, photographs, and letters.   Your task will be to produce a portrait of the speaker as speaker in your own mind.   To do this you will have to sift through your resource materials to find whatever you can about his speech training, his methods of oral composition, his ways of thinking, and whose influence might have affected his speaking.   You will also need to look for descriptions and evaluations of him as a person.

5. *Read the criticism written by others.*   Turning to see what others have done or how they have treated a discourse of the past will reward you.   The amount of published criticism of oral utterance is usually not great, and you will sometimes find it difficult to locate.   But often there are at least some news articles, essays, headnotes, and journal articles containing criticism of speakers of the past and present.   Often the newspapers published the day after an event will give some appraisal of what was said and of the speaker's performance.   The appraisals may be judicious or superficial, but you are not reading the criticism written by others so that you can imitate them.   Your purpose is to winnow and synthesize all the judgments you can find and then to arrive at your own point of view.

You can see that criticizing oral communication when only a recorded or written text is available is much more difficult than criticizing utterance you can personally witness.   When you hear and see a speaker, you are normally acquainted with the immediate and historical settings because you are a part of them.   You may even know a good deal about the personality who addresses you.   But the job of criticizing speech from a text adds many preliminary tasks to all the other things you do to criticize a live performance.   The object of most of this preliminary research is simply to produce a description—a re-creation of the attendant circumstances. These attempts at re-creation will draw you into many fields of knowledge—history, philosophy, literature, sociology, psychology, religion. It is understandable that some professionals argue that no one is ready to criticize spoken discourse until he has passed considerably beyond a beginning course in speech. You will also see, on the other hand, why other people regard criticism of speeches as particularly appropriate to the process of acquiring a liberal education. We hold the second view and hope that somewhere during your education you will try your hand at making a thoroughgoing criticism of some unit of public speech that occurred outside your classroom.

Evaluating Live Speech outside the Classroom

If your assignment were that just mentioned in the last paragraph, the criticism of a live speech outside the classroom, how might you proceed? Suppose you were asked to do an appraisal of a sermon delivered at your church or synagogue next week or to make an evaluation of a speech by a local political candidate who is currently campaigning. Which of twelve steps discussed in the preceding two sections might you use? Which of the five for examining texts of speeches and the seven for judging classroom speaking might you pursue?

Of those dealing with the printed text, you will probably omit the first step, which concerns textual authenticity, because it is unlikely that a text of the speech will be made available to you. If it is, then, of course, you will want to examine it for originality of idea (perform what is called "higher textual criticism"). Chances are that a text furnished you by the speaker or his agent would be the most reliable. It may be unnecessary to match it against other texts. You will, however, wish to check this text against what the speaker actually says or against a recording of some sort should you have one.

Step 2 will be omitted because you will be in the immediate setting and can make your own notes about it, noticing its impact and the speaker's adaptation to it.

Step 3 will also be unnecessary insofar as research is concerned, though you should take into consideration the news of the day, the philosophical, religious, and political ideas astir in society, and any other events which may affect the rhetorical situation.

Step 4 may, in the case of "live" outside criticism, be undertaken if you wish to supplement your knowledge of the speaker. You will wish to, of course, if you know very little about him and if there is written material on his life and activities. In some instances you will, of course, be able to bypass this step.

You will simply be unable to pursue Step 5 unless you delay your critique until after the speech has been reported in the press, should that be the case, or unless you wish to read what others have written about other speeches given by the speaker.

All of the other steps, the seven usable for classroom criticism, in the order we have given them, will then be appropriate in what some have called the "case method" of criticism—which is the sort you will be engaged in. You can follow the steps as we have given them in the foregoing pages.

The experience of completing the assignment of judging speech in a setting less laboratory-like than the classroom ought to be a rewarding one and may well test all that you have learned in class.

Criticism is judgment and/or appreciation based on informed description. It is essentially comparative. In every art the critical act calls into play full knowledge of the art's resources and potentialities and the capacity to take in or understand the critical object to be examined. When this critical object is public speech, it is necessary to understand what is possible in speaking and how to analyze the constituents of speech.

The form and content of any criticism are largely determined by the creative purposes that brought the object of judgment into being. The purposes dominating the creation of most public utterance are utilitarian, as we have seen. Effect is usually placed above such criteria as permanence or beauty in evaluations of the speaker. Nonetheless, judgments that evaluate only effects are but partial. Ethical and artistic considerations, too, are relevant. We contend that criticism which focuses upon the artistic achievements of speakers—the degrees to which they fully use the resources of their art in seeking utilitarian and ethical effects—produces the most comprehensive and constructive judgments.

In the classroom or out of it, the criticism of speech requires method and wisdom. Criticism, we think, requires (1) concentration on speech as a critical object, (2) conscious identification of relevant data and criteria, (3) constructive attitudes toward the critical process, (4) comparison of observed performance with criteria that define the ideal, (5) formulation of judgments that are specific and cogent, and (6) documented expression of the criticism itself.

EXERCISES

Written

1. Identify in advance some speech which is going to be delivered on some future date in your community. The speech must be one which you can both see and hear. Prepare to criticize this speech by systematically writing down pertinent information about the speaker and his purpose, the audience, and the occasion. Attend the speech. Make notes during its delivery using a body of criteria which you have decided to make the basis of your criticism in consequence of preliminary analysis of speaker, audience, and occasion. Finally, write a balanced evaluation.

2. Select a famous speech from a past era. Obtain the best text of the speech avail-

able. Read background materials on the period, including writings on the prevalent culture, living habits, and beliefs. Also read autobiographical or biographical materials about the speaker. After achieving an understanding of the total situation and of the total speech, choose one of the following topics for detailed, written analysis and criticism:

a. The speaker's rational justifications.

b. The speaker's use of amplifying materials such as example, narration, statistics, definition.

c. The structure of the speech as it relates to the subject matter, the audience, and the occasion.

d. The speaker's style.

e. The authenticity of the text of the speech studied.

3. a. Choose some piece of recorded rhetoric which is not thought of by most people as open to the methods of speech criticism, for example:

(1) The lyrics of a song.

(2) A poem.

(3) A newspaper editorial.

(4) The copy in an advertisement.

(5) A dramatic scene which contains a fairly large segment of uninterrupted discourse.

(6) The copy on a flyer or pamphlet handed to you on the street.

Using the pattern for criticism discussed in this chapter, write a criticism of your critical object.

b. Write several paragraphs in which you explain how you had to modify your pattern of criticism in order to do justice to your critical object.

4. Read Professor Robert W. Smith's "The 'Second' Inaugural Address of Lyndon Baines Johnson: A Definitive Text," *Speech Monographs*, XXXIV (March 1967), 102–108, then do one of the following:

a. Prepare a "definitive text" of any public speech. Defend its "definitiveness" either orally or in writing.

b. Write an essay (or make a speech) evaluating the "reliability" of some speech that exists exclusively in printed form.

Oral

1. Listen intently to a classroom speech assigned to you for evaluation. Keep in mind the requirements set forth in the speaker's assignment or avowed purpose. Take written notes where appropriate. Structure your judgments on the various aspects of the speech as clearly as possible. During the oral criticism period reserved for the speech assigned, deliver a 1- or 2-minute extemporaneous speech working from your notes.

2. Prepare and deliver a speech in which you discuss one of the following:

a. The essential considerations involved in appraising one of the canons of public speaking: invention, disposition, style, delivery, *memoria*.

b. The differences between the procedures for criticizing a live speech and those to be used in criticizing the text of a speech.

c. The distinctions between the critical object in speech criticism and in other arts.

d. The problems involved in arriving at a set of criteria to be applied in judging a particular speech.

APPENDIX

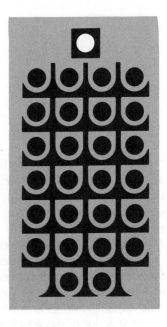

Rhetorical Theory: A Heritage

"What makes speech effective?" has been pondered since the days of the ancient Greeks. Plato (c. 429–347 B.C.) and Aristotle (384–322 B.C.) discussed the nature of man speaking. Famous Romans such as Cicero (106–43 B.C.), a great orator, and Quintilian (c. A.D. 35–100), a great teacher, reorganized and refined what they found in Greek writings on public communication. St. Augustine (A.D. 354–430) and medieval men of learning added to and adapted their inherited bodies of rhetorical theory as they attempted to help men of their times function effectively in new kinds of speech situations. Especially in America and Europe, scholars have continued to search for new insights and fuller understandings in solving the problems of spoken discourse.

It is our purpose in this section to tell you about important thinkers and explain how some of their theories of rhetoric and speech communication have developed. We hope that knowledge of the origins of what is thought today will help you to think and to apply your thinking to the problems you face as a human being with powers of speech.

As a first step we shall identify some important writings which serious scholars of rhetoric and speech have used in arriving at theories of their own. Then, we shall set forth the five major kinds of problems that all communicators face. These problems were first conceptualized by Greeks and Romans some-time before the Christian era, but as creators' problems they remain with all of us. They are the problems of: *Invention* (discovering communicable ideas and their logical aspects); *Disposition* (organizing or structuring ideas); *Style* (finding the right language); *Delivery* (deciding how to present a message); and *Memoria* (command of an entire speech, once planned and composed, a problem our term memory inadequately represents). We shall review ideas about these problems, pointing to those which have attained special importance as Western thought. Ours is not an ample record of how our cultural conceptions of oral communication became what they are. We offer instead a review to show that most questions you will raise as you seek to improve as a speaker are questions others have raised and tried to answer ever since Western man has taken the powers of speech seriously.

LANDMARKS OF RHETORIC

Landmark works on speech and rhetoric in ancient Greece have been of towering influence to the present day. Especially important were Plato's two dialogues, *Gorgias* (c. 387 B.C.) and *Phaedrus* (c. 380 B.C.), and Aristotle's *Art of Rhetoric* (c. 330 B.C.). During the period of the Roman Republic the most influential writings published were *Rhetorica ad Herennium* (c. 82 B.C.), formerly attributed to Cicero,[1] and Cicero's *De Oratore* (55 B.C.). Quintilian's *Institutio Oratoria* (A.D. 93) and "Longinus's" *On the Sublime*[2] belong to the period of the Roman Empire.

St. Augustine's *De Doctrina Christiana* (c. 426) is a work on Christian preaching and stands as the greatest rhetorical study produced during the late Empire-medieval period. Bacon's *The Advancement of Learning* (1605) and its Latin revision *De augmentis scientiarum* (1623) contain the most profound thought touching human communication to emerge during the Renaissance.

Fénelon's *Dialogues on Eloquence* was published in France in 1717 and was influential in France and England in the eighteenth century. This and other works of major importance in the eighteenth and nineteenth centuries can be divided into three groups.

The originators of the "elocutionary movement" in England had vast influence in England and America. Representative writers in this group include: Thomas Sheridan, *A Course of Lectures on Elocution* (1756); Joshua Steele, *Prosodia Rationalis* (1775); and Gilbert Austin, *Chironomia* (1806).

In a rival tradition other writers sought to integrate classical theory and the newly emerging "science of human nature." They include such British writers as George Campbell, *Philosophy of Rhetoric* (1776) and Richard Whately, *Elements of Rhetoric* (1828). Hugh Blair's *Lectures on Rhetoric and Belles Lettres* (1783) stands as the chief example of a third tradition reflecting classical influences filtered through such writers as Fénelon and "Longinus." Blair also reflects a wish to intertwine the arts of rhetoric and poetic.

In the twentieth century several works have had especially wide influence on thought about speech communication. They are James A. Winans, *Public Speaking* (1915); Charles H. Woolbert, *Fundamentals of Speech* (1920); I. A. Richards, *The Philosophy of Rhetoric* (1936); Kenneth Burke, *A Grammar of Motives* (1945) and *A Rhetoric of Motives* (1950); Stephen E. Toulmin, *The Uses of Argument* (1958); and Chaim Perelman and L. Olbrechts-Tyteca, *The New Rhetoric* (1969), originally published as *La nouvelle rhetori-*

---

1. It is now generally agreed that the work is by an unknown author. Its earlier attribution to Cicero added immeasurably to the book's reputation. For an authoritative discussion see Harry Caplan's "Introduction" to *Rhetorica ad Herennium* (Cambridge, Mass.: Harvard University Press, 1954), pp. vii ff.
2. The author and date of this work are also uncertain. Authorities place its date at either the first or third century A.D. and remain in doubt about the real author. See G. M. A. Grube's "Translator's Introduction" to *Longinus on Great Writing* (*On the Sublime*) (New York: The Liberal Arts Press, 1957), pp. vii–xxi.

que: Traité de l'argumentation (1958). These and other works will be briefly discussed on later pages where we shall sketch the development of Western thought about the five major constellations of problems in speechmaking. We provide a bibliography of the most easily obtainable, reliable editions of the works mentioned in the foregoing paragraphs at the end of this appendix.

RHETORICAL INVENTION

That whoever communicates rhetorically must make decisions about *what* to say is a truism that was recognized at the very beginning of Western thought about speaking. Sometime between Aristotle's day and the appearance of early Latin rhetorics, theorists' and teachers' ideas on speakers' problems of discovery came to be grouped under the general heading of *inventio*. Thus the so-called canon of *invention* came into being. The term is actually no more than a topical heading for whatever a rhetorical theorist has to say concerning problems of generating and adapting communicable ideas and whatever other forces can be directly controlled in evoking responses to speech.

Aristotle was the first to see that a speaker "invents" more than just ideas. He argued that there are three major kinds of force or "proof" by which a speaker gains his ends. These are: the intellectual content of his communication, which the Greeks called *logos*[3] — the *content;* the emotional forces in the rhetorical situation, which the Greeks called *pathos;* and the forces emanating from the speaker, which the Greeks called *ethos*. Across twenty-five hundred years this analysis of persuasive forces has never been successfully challenged, though what is involved in the *logos, pathos,* and *ethos* of communications has been understood and misunderstood in a variety of ways. We shall review leading attitudes men have had about how to create and manage these forces, hoping you will gain a better understanding of these power-sources in spoken communication.

Logos: The Content

The earliest attempts we know of to answer "How do I discover what to say?" came from two Sicilians of the fifth century B.C., Corax and Tisias. They were counsellors to citizens who had to plead their own cases in court. The chief advice Corax and Tisias gave inexperienced speakers was that the main thing to prove in court was that what you advocated was more *probably* true than

---

3. All classical scholars agree that there is no single English word that expresses the meaning of this very general Greek term. Quite mistakenly, many twentieth-century rhetoricians have equated *logos* with "logic," but this is far too narrow an understanding of the Greek idea. "'Discourse' and 'reason' are one and the same thing — in Greek they are designated by one and the same word, *logos,*" says John Herman Randall, Jr., in his *Aristotle* (New York: Columbia University Press, 1960), p. 6.

your opponent's contention.[4]   Allegedly these teachings on probability were carried to Athens and promulgated there.

Other views having to do with rhetorical invention included those of Gorgias of Leontini (c. 483–376 B.C.), a leading sophist.   He held that nothing can truly be known to exist, if anything does truly exist men cannot know it, and even if someone could know what exists he could not communicate that knowledge to others.   Invention for Gorgias, then, became a matter of refining the methods of arguing the probabilities of things alleged.

Other sophists (teachers) also wrestled with the problem of how men should think and talk about the uncertain.   Protagoras of Abdera (c. 480–410 B.C.) maintained that even the existence of the Gods was uncertain, that truth was relative, and that man is the measure of all things.   Accordingly he taught that there are two sides to every question and that both ought to be argued.   He had his pupils give speeches of praise and dispraise on such human qualities as friendship, patriotism, and cupidity because he thought that the many standard themes or "commonplaces" which would then emerge were suggestive of ways to develop thoughts approving or disapproving qualities.

A very different tack was taken in the teaching of Prodicus of Ceos (c. 465 B.C.), another sophist.   He taught that to face death courageously was a virtue and he spoke in praise of the ideals of labor, hardihood, and simplicity. Clearly what and how to think were for Prodicus ethical questions as well as scientific ones.   Much the same was true of Plato's view.   He deplored the sophists' teachings.   In *Phaedrus* (see headnote to Chapter 3, page 38) he asserted that a true rhetorician must know his subject completely and also know human psychology well enough to fit his own thought to the particular "soul" he addressed.   Plato seems to have felt that only a true philosopher could know enough to speak the truth.   The inventional problems of philosophers and orators in attempting to speak truly thus become identical.   In solution, Plato recommended the intellectual processes of defining the subject thought or spoken of, then analyzing all the details of the subject implied in its definition.

Aristotle, in dissatisfaction, stated his counterposition concisely:

All teaching and learning that involves the use of reason proceeds from pre-existent knowledge.   This is evident if we consider all the different branches of learning; because both the mathematical sciences and every other art are acquired in this way.   Similarly too with logical arguments, whether syllogistic or inductive; both effect instruction by means of facts already recognized, the former making assumptions as though granted by an intelligent audience, and the latter proving the universal from the self-evident nature of the particular.

---

4. Just what the relationship was between these two men and what they did teach is uncertain, but whatever the facts may have been, later rhetoricians traced their discipline back to Corax and Tisias and to these teachings. See George Kennedy, *The Art of Persuasion in Greece* (Princeton: Princeton University Press, 1963), pp. 58–61.

The means by which rhetorical arguments carry conviction are just the same; for they use either examples, which are a kind of induction, or enthymemes, which are a kind of syllogism.[5]

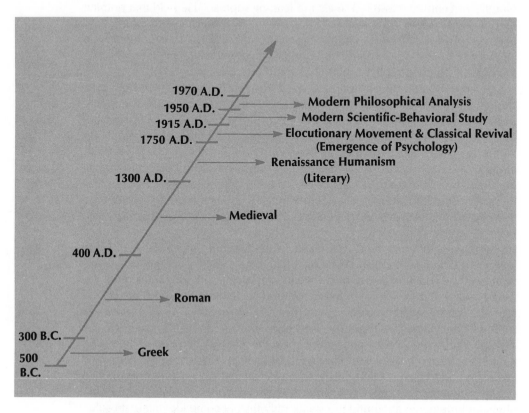

Diagram showing major periods in the development of rhetorical theory.

This statement and its amplifications in such places as Aristotle's *Rhetoric, Topics, Politics, Ethics,* and *Sophistical Refutations* constitute the Western world's most comprehensive conception of human inventional processes. Particularly important is the fact that it recognizes the distinction between thinking and discovering in *scientific logic* (by rigorous induction and deduction) and in *rhetorical communication* (by psychologically oriented induction through *examples,* and by psychologically oriented deductions through *enthymemes*). By calling rhetorical reasoning "example" and "enthymeme" Aristotle was indicating that what an audience knows and wants and can make use of must be the chief content in all rhetorical situations. In scientific discovery and reasoning "absolute" self-evidence, formal logical rigor, and

5. Aristotle, *Posterior Analytics,* trans. Hugh Tredennick (Cambridge, Mass.: Harvard University Press, 1960), p. 25.

judgments of the best thinkers govern intellectual processes—but the knowledge and wants of audiences have no place in such thinking. Aristotle's great contribution to understanding rhetorical invention, then, was to emphasize that though its processes *resemble* those of scientific investigation, these rhetorical processes are different from the scientific because *the audience to be addressed must always guide* the speaker's search for ideas and his creation of chains of reasoning.[6] The differences between logical and rhetorical invention have occupied the theorists and philosophers of rhetoric ever since.

In their love of refining and classifying earlier theory, Romans gave special attention to two questions pertaining to invention: "How does one amplify ideas and themes already discovered?" and "How does one discover which available data ought to be used in pleading a legal case?" Cicero made the contributions of most significance. He re-explored the *topoi* or "topics" the Greeks had referred to as "places" to look when searching for thoughts useful in developing a theme. In his *De Inventione* (confined to legal speaking) and *De Oratore* (his most inclusive book), he showed how lawyers and legislators ought to work their minds in preparing for speaking. He posed four inventional questions about an issue of fact: "Is it?" (Are there any facts?); "What is it?" (What are the facts?); "What is its quality?" (What does it mean?); and "Is this the forum in which to discuss it?" It would not be unfair to say that these four analytical questions were the most significant contribution the Romans made concerning the theory of rhetorical invention.

In the Roman era an unfortunate confusion of Aristotle's distinction between logical and rhetorical invention also occurred. In the centuries of the Roman Empire *all* thinking became increasingly looked upon as *rhetorical* thinking. The probable judgments of an *audience* came to control and constrain virtually every kind of thought. Science, philosophy, and literature naturally deteriorated as what-the-audience-is-*used-to* confined even men's private reflections.

During the Middle Ages and the Renaissance, the confusion of rhetoric with logic, inherited from the Romans, persisted. Until the time of Francis Bacon (1561–1626) leading writers treated "logic" as the method which would work in a debate or disputation. With the distinction between thinking to investigate and thinking to communicate lost, there was no need for a theory of *rhetorical* invention, so "rhetoric" became the art of "dressing" "logical" arguments with ornaments of style and, perhaps, delivery.

There was, however, one powerful idea about the content of communication expressed by St. Augustine in the fifth century A.D. It was influential well into the sixteenth century. This was the thought that a Christian speaker's inventional problems were chiefly problems of *interpreting* sacred works. Once he had abandoned paganism for Christianity, Augustine's original mind

---

6. Further details of Aristotle's contributions to the theory of rhetorical invention are discussed and applied in Chapter 5, Invention: General Tactics.

discerned that his old rhetorical rules for amplifying a theme and analyzing a legal question were irrelevant to his new mission of expounding the Scriptures. Thus was born a new and specialized art of rhetoric called *homiletics* — literally the art of preaching. The notion that the rhetorician's main task is to *interpret* his authority, then organize and make persuasive his interpretations, was uniquely appropriate to religious speaking. But when applied to other communication, the scheme encouraged men of the Middle Ages and the Renaissance to believe that rhetorical invention — if there was any at all — consisted merely of choosing an authority, defending the choice, and interpreting it.

In the sixteenth century two views of rhetorical invention came into open competition. The classical view that inventing for communication was a special process was espoused in England, first by Leonard Cox in *The Arte or Crafte of Rhetoryke* (1530). This was the first book on rhetoric in English, as far as we know. Thomas Wilson's *Arte of Rhetorique* (1553), a book which passed through eight editions, insisted still more strongly on the classical view of rhetorical invention. Cox and Wilson contended that rhetoricians must search the world of popular ideas for the content of their rhetoric. But in France a counter and ultimately more popular view was offered by Petrus Ramus (1515–1572). He was determined to eliminate the confusion of logic and rhetoric inherited from the Middle Ages. Thinking had two aspects, Ramus thought: discovering through reason (invention) and evaluating one's findings (judgment). He denied that the same processes could exist in two "arts," assigned "invention and judgment" to logic, and thus reinforced the medieval notion that the function of rhetoric is simply to "dress" the products of "scientific" thought. Since he made no distinction between *stating* something and *discovering* something, Ramus' concept of logic was naive to the point that it was incapable of generating scientific discovery, nor was there any place in his vision for restudying the known to discover that which was adaptable to an audience. But for a century his was the dominant theory of intellectual activity taught in the schools of Western Europe, in England, and to a lesser extent in the American colonies.

A man of far greater perception than Ramus was Francis Bacon, whose primary interest was in restoring creativity to scientific thought. Threaded through *The Advancement of Learning* and *De augmentis scientiarum* were many new terms and details of an essentially Aristotelian conception of communication and rhetorical invention. Bacon deplored the exclusive stress on style and delivery in the rhetoric of his day and re-explained the distinction between investigating to discover what is true and investigating what is already known to discover what to communicate to a prospective audience.[7]

---

7. Bacon's scattered observations on communication have been organized and synthesized by Karl R. Wallace in his *Francis Bacon on Communication and Rhetoric* (Chapel Hill: The University of North Carolina Press, 1943).

Bacon defined rhetoric as applying reason to the imagination for the better moving of the will. Finding out what to do in order to achieve this end, he thought, required inspecting existing knowledge for its psychological appropriateness for a specific audience. For this process he recommended use of *topoi* — topics not different in kind from Aristotle's *topoi*. Additionally he analyzed kinds of fallacies and predispositions found in popular thinking. His famous Idols of the Tribe, Cave, Marketplace, and Theatre are identifications of the kinds of fallibility men are heir to.

Bacon's reaction against medieval logic and Ramistic rhetoric grew out of his desire to reorder all human knowledge and prepare the way for true scientific investigation. A generation later in France, and then in England, a different reaction developed in opposition to the authoritarian interpretation of rediscovered classical works by Renaissance scholars. A young priest, François Fénelon (1651–1715), for example, undertook to apply the then popular doctrine "follow Nature" to the art of preaching.[8] Drawing especially on St. Augustine, Plato, "Longinus," and frequently upon thoughts found in *The Art of Poetry,* written by his contemporary Nicholas Boileau-Despréaux, Fénelon emphasized the social character of rhetoric and the necessity of adapting even scriptural meanings to the differing intelligences and motivations of audiences. He stressed "instruction" and "making men better" as the proper ends of speaking. He insisted that a right understanding of religious and moral truth, coupled with an awareness of audiences' differences and a determination to be both "natural" and "tasteful," would lead a preacher to discover what to say and how to say it. True knowledge was, of course, lodged in religious sources; rhetorical invention involved intuitively and psychologically adapting that truth to specific congregations. Howell says that Fénelon's was "the earliest statement we have of what may be said to have become the dominant modern attitude toward rhetoric."[9] The statement seems fair for "follow Nature and adapt to your audience" does sum up what most modern rhetorics have advised.

From Bacon's time, the naturalist-literary-religious trend in rhetorical theory paralleled attempts at scientific theory building. In his *Philosophy of Rhetoric* George Campbell (1719–1796) clearly drew upon the writings of Francis Bacon and the eighteenth-century philosopher-psychologist, David Hume. Campbell saw analysis of evidence as the persistent problem in finding truth and estimating probabilities. But once data are obtained, he thought, the object of rhetorical communication becomes to find means of arousing "passions" that will make listeners *want* to accept the speaker's claims. The explanation was unorthodox in its time but not basically inconsistent with much modern psychological thinking. Under this explanation rhetorical

---

8. His *Dialogues on Eloquence* were written while he was a young man but were not published until 1717, after his death.
9. Wilbur Samuel Howell, "Introduction" in Fénelon, *Dialogues on Eloquence,* trans. W. S. Howell (Princeton: Princeton University Press, 1951), p. 46.

invention becomes much as Aristotle proposed: the discovery in the *known* of that which can by rhetorical methods be made desirable to hearers.

Hugh Blair (1718–1800), on the other hand, said almost nothing about the processes of rhetorical invention in his *Lectures on Rhetoric and Belles Lettres*. With Fénelon he believed that art or method could not help. Following nature, following standards of good taste, and thinking about "the viscera of the cause" were his only answers to how to handle content.

Richard Whately (1787–1863) extended some of George Campbell's thoughts and contracted others. Whately wrote only of argumentation in his *Elements of Rhetoric*. Other possible functions of rhetoric such as explaining, impressing, and blaming go undiscussed. Discovering the best strategies for supporting a proposition, given a specific audience and situation, was the main aim in Whately's view of invention. Thus, he omitted much that might have been said, but he did add several especially useful observations. He pointed out, as Aristotle had not, that arguments from example have persuasive force different from arguments by analogy. He was also first to notice that a defender of the *status quo* usually is assigned a lighter "burden of proof" by listeners and hence has a lighter inventional obligation than an arguer who contends for change in what *is*.

With Whately we come to the end of the list of older theorists who tried to cope with how rhetorical communicators invent what they communicate. From the 1820's to the mid-1900's writers have variously said, "Follow nature," or "Dress what 'logic' gives you," or "Think," or "Read what others have said." It has been assumed that rhetorical theory had nothing to tell a communicator until he had by some unfathomable means acquired all that he would say; then it could advise him on how to arrange, style, and deliver the content he had discovered and thought about.

A line of thought in philosophy began to break in upon this complacent view of rhetorical invention in the mid-1900's. A few philosophers in America and abroad pointed forcibly to the fact that formal or scientific logic does not and cannot explain how thought is communicated by such people as lawyers, judges, or even philosophers. The real, not the assumed, *logos* became the object of intensive philosophical speculation. For explanations of how *logos* actually works, some philosophers like Richard McKeon, Stephen Toulmin, Chaim Perelman, L. Olbrechts-Tyteca, Henry Johnstone, Jr., and others turned back to the classical explanation: the *logos* or content in a communication is the product of (1) some degree of logical investigation into what is or seems to be true, (2) a combination of that information with what is already popularly known, and (3) a further adjustment of the content to suit the knowledge and desires of whatever audience the communicator has in mind. That view has come to seem philosophically defensible. Some empirical evidence justifies it. It allows advisers on rhetoric to give speakers and writers more help than is given by telling them to "Follow nature" or "Dress your logic." It is the view we have taken in this book. We believe that *logos* or content of speech has most force if it is discovered and adapted to give it clarifying and persuasive force.

Pathos: The Emotive Force

From earliest recorded time in Western culture it has been recognized that the emotive force of things said has power. Homer dwelt on leaders' powers to sway others by appealing to their feelings. Thucydides attributed a part of Pericles' ability to lead Athens to the fact that he evoked necessary feelings according to his will. But when the Greeks began to think analytically about communication and its effects, many of them became uneasy concerning the "right" uses of emotion. As with so many things, the conclusions drawn by Plato and Aristotle proved representative of kinds of judgment later preserved in Western thought.

Plato granted that a complete rhetorician must understand the nature of human feeling. The reason was: "men of a special sort under the influence of speeches of a particular kind are readily persuaded to take action of a definite sort because of the qualitative correlation that obtains between speech and soul."[10] But Plato was unwilling to grant that everyone should have and exercise this kind of affective power. Accordingly, in his *Republic* he conceived an ideal system in which only philosopher-kings would have full power and only they would decide who should influence the masses intellectually and emotionally and by what means.

Aristotle was uneasy, too; but, as usual, he was pragmatic. In his view all people act because they have desires which reflect the emotional aspects of their natures. All but the most technical communications will thus be responded to emotionally as well as intellectually. Aristotle wished it were otherwise—that men were truly rational beings—but he was convinced that human nature encompassed more than intellect. Somewhat sadly, perhaps, he concluded that *pathos* was bound to be a persuasive force in all rhetoric and that speakers must understand the different kinds of human emotions, what causes them, toward whom they are likely to be directed, and how to arouse them and allay them. This knowledge was an integral part of a speaker's necessary equipment, Aristotle thought, and he devoted most of Book II of his *Rhetoric* to a discussion of these topics. The section is a veritable social psychology of Athenian audiences.

The Romans were no less sensitive to the inevitability of emotional power in communication, but their responses to that fact differed from those

10. Plato, *Phaedrus,* trans. W. C. Helmbold and W. G. Rabinowitz (New York: The Liberal Arts Press, 1956), p. 63.

of the Greeks.   In *Rhetorica ad Herennium,* for example, the author undertakes to tell his pupils exact ways to put emotional qualities into their speaking. Among other things, he tells them how to sound indignant, accusing, and calm. He cautions against being emotional in introductions but calls for emotionality in conclusions.   Many Roman teachers of rhetoric followed this lead, treating emotion as something to be *put into* the content of a speech or its delivery. They treated the emotive power of speech as something a speaker added or subtracted as he composed and delivered his ideas.   The Greek idea that feelings occur not in language but in people, and are to be regulated by speech, was drastically narrowed.

Even Cicero and Quintilian failed to see the full difference between advising speakers how to put *in* "emotional appeals" and advising them how to *understand* the emotions of audiences and how to *adjust* to that reality as purpose required.   However, Cicero, as a statesman, had a further concern with the acknowledged emotional power of content, style, and delivery, and Quintilian followed Cicero's lead.   To Cicero it was important that emotions displayed and emotions aroused be properly Roman, with due gravity, dignity, and decorum always maintained.   Both attitudes toward emotional force in communication, as revealed in Cicero's writings and the *Rhetorica ad Herennium,* had the severe limitation of emphasizing study of the speaker's emotionality and minimizing study of the emotional readinesses of listeners. Ultimately, in the later days of the Roman Empire, it became difficult to distinguish speakers from actors, so strong was concern with how emotions could be portrayed.

St. Augustine, once converted to Christianity, had to rethink the implications of emotions' roles in speaking and in the responses of listeners.   His conclusion was perhaps simplistic, but it was more functional than the conventional Roman views.   One must give information (Christian teaching) *pleasingly,* he said, else it would not be attended to.   But once understanding was achieved, the speaker must arouse strong feelings or there would be no change in the listeners' actual behavior.   It was aroused emotion that caused the will to change.   Augustine's analysis was more lasting than any previous thinker's.   Its main weakness was that it saw teaching, pleasing, and moving emotively as separated functions, but it restored to Western thinking the conception that emotions are present or absent in people, not in messages *per se.*

Logic, grammar, and disputation preoccupied the attention of most commentators in the Middle Ages.   Men like Ramus tended to ignore audiences, and men like Bacon were suspicious of the feeling states of human beings.   It was therefore not until Fénelon that another major rhetorician gave serious attention to the role of emotion in the "proofs" of rhetorical speech. This was natural, for he depended heavily on the writings of St. Augustine and was caught up in the thought of literary men anxious to free themselves from the tyranny of neoclassical rules of communication.   As we have already suggested, Fénelon saw the preacher's function as providing first the "bread" of reasoning to generate understanding, then the "spice" — "everything capable of arousing your [the listener's] sentiments, of making you love demonstrated truth. This is what is called persuasion."[11] Fénelon clung to Augustine's conception that emotion was not involved in understanding but was a different force which moved people to accede to the content of messages. The philosopher, he said, acts only to convince, but the orator must go beyond, using every resource capable of arousing sentiments. Only so will he secure willful adherence to the demonstrated truth.

Here, the Western world's ideas on the role of emotion in rhetorical response stood for more than a century. In the eighteenth century, the scientific spirit in England led David Hume and then George Campbell to re-examine these dimensions of communication. Campbell came to a conclusion that would have troubled Plato, Aristotle, Augustine, and Fénelon:

> If the orator would prove successful, it is necessary that he engage in his service all these different powers of the mind, the imagination, the memory, and the passions. These are not the supplanters of reason, or even rivals in her sway; they are her handmaids, by whose ministry she is enabled to usher truth into the heart and procure there a favourable reception. As handmaids they are liable to be seduced by sophistry in the garb of reason, and sometimes are made ignorantly to lend their aid in the introduction of falsehood. But their service is not on this account to be dispensed with; there is a necessity of employing it, founded on our nature. . . . Nor are those mental powers, of which eloquence so much avails herself . . . perfectly indifferent to good and evil, and only beneficial as they are rightly employed. On the contrary they are by nature . . . more friendly to truth than to falsehood, and more easily retained in the cause of virtue, than in that of vice.[12]

The modern, psychological age appears to have arrived prematurely in Campbell's analysis of the inseparable, inevitable, emotional and logical forces that rhetorical communication expresses and governs. He saw reason and feeling as "handmaids" existing outside the message, but in the audience. He saw the complex response capabilities of humans as challenges to speakers' intelligent, purposeful art. Aristotle might have agreed sadly; Augustine and Fénelon would have found the "handmaid" concept hard to understand; but with Campbell the interrelatedness of the thinking-feeling forces of communication were at last recognized.

The "handmaid" notion remained difficult for those who could not see men as unitary beings. Though he was Hume's personal friend, Hugh Blair never recognized the new psychology's challenge to the old reason-emotion dichotomy, and Whately avoided the issue in a way that was generally followed for the next century. Using different terms, he readopted Augustine's formula. Part I of his *Elements of Rhetoric* was labeled, "Of the Address to the

---

11. *Dialogues,* trans. W. S. Howell, "Second Dialogue," p. 89.
12. George Campbell, *Philosophy of Rhetoric,* ed. Lloyd F. Bitzer (Carbondale: Southern Illinois University Press, 1963), p. 72, bk. I, chap. 8.

Understanding, with a View to Produce Conviction (Including Instruction)."
Part II reasserted (without reference to them) Augustine's and Fénelon's conception of instructing and moving as two separate steps in communication.
Whately entitled his second section "Of the Address to the Will, or Persuas-
sion." It was here that he treated "address to the feelings generally" and
"of the favourable or unfavourable disposition of the hearers or readers toward
the speaker or writer, and his opponent."

In nineteenth- and twentieth-century books on speaking and writing the
"conviction-persuasion" dichotomy persisted almost without challenge until
Charles Henry Woolbert (1877–1929) attacked it in a series of essays published
in the *Quarterly Journal of Speech*, beginning in 1917.[13] Though many would
quarrel with Woolbert's purely behavioristic premises, few psychologically
sophisticated persons today would dispute his basic contention against the
rhetorical tradition that conceived the emotive power of speech as separable
from its intellectual power. Wrote Woolbert:

> . . . the error of the conviction-persuasion, emotion-intellect, thought-action
> duality is found in the fact that we discuss this issue not in terms of what the
> responder actually does, but in terms of what the observer perceives him doing.
> . . . *It is a difference, not between acting and thinking, but between one kind
> of action that happens also to be perceivable movement* ["emotional response"]
> *and another kind of action in which the movement is invisible and unperceivable*
> ["intellectual response"].[14]

In the same essay Woolbert concluded:

> The whole theory of argumentation, conviction, persuasion, the rhetoric of pub-
> lic address, must be rewritten to fit the facts of mind as accepted today; which
> will be tantamount to restating them in terms of stimulus-response, object-subject,
> and environment-attitude.[15]

Speech scholars continue to investigate the functioning of emotive
power in human communication. They have arrived at no final explanation.
But it seems psychologically clear that: (1) the "emotional" power of a communication is not in the communication or its delivery but in the readiness of
listeners to respond both feelingly and reasoningly to particular features of
logos and to the credibility of the messenger; (2) speech can modulate but it
cannot create feelings that are not at least latent in listeners; (3) people do not
feel *or* reason, they reason because they feel and feel because they think they

---

13. From premises of behavioristic psychology Woolbert attacked the notion that respondents to communication experience reasoned and emotive responses as separable processes. His essays included, "Conviction
and Persuasion: Some Considerations of Theory," *Quarterly Journal of Speech*, III (July 1917), 249–264; "The
Place of Logic in a System of Persuasion," *ibid.*, IV (Jan. 1918), 19–39; "Persuasion: Principles and Methods,"
ibid., V (Jan. 1919), 12–25; "Persuasion: Principles and Methods," V (March 1919), 101–119; "Persuasion:
Principles and Methods," *ibid.*, V (May 1919) 212–238. (The journal referred to was published under varying
titles but is indexed under the title given here.)
14. "Conviction and Persuasion: Some Considerations of Theory," *ibid.*, III (July 1917), 258. Italics in the
original.
15. *Ibid.*, p. 264.

have reason for it; (4) human experience in response to speech or any other stimulus is *unitary* — there is always some blend of what the world has come to call, probably mistakenly, "reason and feeling."

In our earlier discussions of invention, disposition, style, delivery, and speech criticism, we have tried to hold to this modern understanding that the emotive power of speech is not devoid of reasonableness nor reasons devoid of appeal to human desire.

Ethos: Credibility of the Source

What creates or diminishes the credibility of a speaker and how perceptions of credibility "prove" or "disprove" in the minds of listeners fascinated the Greeks and Romans and has received more attention than any other single aspect of rhetoric in the twentieth century. These questions seem first to have been raised in connection with the teaching and speaking of the Greek sophists. To some, these men seemed less credible because they took money for teaching and speaking. Some of them insisted rhetoric was an amoral art, and this made all they said seem less believable to their critics. If we can rely on Plato's and Aristotle's pictures of him, Gorgias of Leontini claimed not to care what means he used as long as he achieved his rhetorical ends. In his *Gorgias* Plato condemns both Gorgias and the entire art of rhetoric as dishonest, deploring rhetoric as a mere art of flattery.

Aristotle explored the sources of credibility in rhetoric more deeply than any other of the ancients. He conceptualized all speakers as communicating an *ethos* — a complicated quality of believability or unbelievability comprised of their *seeming* intelligence, personal integrity, and goodwill toward their listeners. Interestingly, modern empirical researchers have identified "expertness" and "trustworthiness" as clear constituents of any communicator's "credibility." Aristotle's idea that "goodwill" is another element listeners watch for has not been confirmed to date, nor is it certain that "dynamism," a quality some experimenters suggest is an aspect of credibility, is responded to by hearers.

We are left to believe, therefore, that there is such a persuasive force as "credibility" or *ethos* in all speaking, that this force either reinforces or undermines what a speaker's content says, and that "intelligence-expertness" and "integrity-trustworthiness" are qualities listeners constantly measure in their minds as they determine whether or not to accept what they hear.

Cicero's conception of the force of *ethos* in speaking was naturally that of an orator, not that of an analyst such as Aristotle. What *ought* a speaker to *be* as well as seem? was the question that interested him. His answer was deeply colored by his love of the Roman Republic and his personal philosophy concerning the duties of men to each other and to the state. Perhaps the clearest statement of what he thought could produce a *proper* identification between speaker and listener is in his philosophical essay, *On Duties:*

> . . . of all the ties that cement us together, there is none stronger or more admirable than that which unites in genuine intimacy good men of like tastes and character; for if we behold even in another that goodness to which I refer so frequently, we are attracted by it and seek the friendship of him who seems to us to possess it. And though every virtue attracts us and makes us love those in whom it appears to us to dwell, yet justice and charitableness exert the most powerful attraction of all. Besides, nothing draws men more closely and affectionately together than the mutual appeal of good character, for when both have the same interests and inclinations, it follows . . . that each loves the other as himself, and . . . many have become one.[16]

It is clear that possessing substantially the virtues Aristotle isolated, plus "like tastes and character," was the source of *ethos* in Cicero's view.

Quintilian attempted to establish the "oughts" of credibility also; however, his method was not descriptive, as was Cicero's, but definitional. In the twelfth book of his *Institutes* Quintilian makes his argument on behalf of Cato's definition: an orator is "a good man, skilled in speaking." The argument is circular and ends with Quintilian contending no more than that if he cannot call a speaker "good" he will deny him the name "orator." Quintilian's difficulty exemplifies how easily one can confuse answers to two quite different questions about a speaker: Do *I* endorse him? Is he credible *to those he addresses?* Like a good many commentators before and after his time, Quintilian gave his answer to the first question, then treated that answer as though it were a statement about the *actual* credibility or *ethos* of the speaker in a specific rhetorical situation. Aristotle's and Cicero's insistence that it is *seeming* qualities which affect response in rhetorical and personal relationships furnishes the classical era's clearest analysis of how the force of *ethos* works in actual speaking.

In *On the Sublime* the author sought the *source* of that credibility that critics said was present in great oratorical works. Ultimately, Longinus thought, there must be evidence of "nobility of soul" or "largeness of conception." Boldness in thinking and feeling, and enthusiasm, seemed to him also discernible in works admired over generations. The uniqueness of Longinus's observations lies in the fact that his is the first great effort to infer critically, from works themselves, what human qualities had contributed to their popularity.

St. Augustine was, of course, concerned chiefly with the credibility of preachers. Their humbleness before God, their love of others, and their knowledge of sacred works were the qualities he most wanted speakers to reveal. He insisted that *display* of "art" was likely to invite either distrust or

---

16. Cicero, *On Duties,* trans. Hubert M. Poteat, in *Brutus, On the Nature of the Gods, On Divination, On Duties* (Chicago: The University of Chicago Press, 1950), p. 485.

ignorant applause from listeners. Either effect would demolish the true function of preaching: teaching, reminding listeners of the truths that were within them. On the whole Augustine's view of *ethos* as a force was like Cicero's, with Christian virtues and duties substituted for virtues Cicero associated with the Roman Republic. For Augustine as for Cicero, if the speaker possessed virtue, it would show through and become a part of his "proof"; if he lacked virtue, this too would show and operate in listeners' minds against even "good" content.

Fénelon's was the next major discussion of *ethos*. On the whole Fénelon's *Dialogues* restated St. Augustine's position, applying that view to seventeenth-century French preaching. But, perhaps reflecting literary theory of the time, Fénelon also contended that things cannot be truly beautiful unless they are true, and he made this idea the basis for severe criticism of showy French preachers who sought to be impressive not for their truth and devotion but for their "artistry." Their choices showed shallowness and self-centeredness, Fénelon insisted, and these qualities must detract even from truths they might utter.

Bacon and Campbell gave little direct attention to the role of *ethos* in communication. Blair followed Cicero and Quintilian and treated the subject unoriginally. He reflected the times in which he lived by emphasizing the importance of "good taste" and acquaintance with all the liberal arts as qualities speakers must show in order to influence the educated. And Blair followed Augustine in insisting that preachers, in particular, must be known to live impeccable lives, else their reputations would undercut their religious messages.

In most respects Whately, too, treated *ethos* traditionally, but he made the important point that having a reputation for eloquence can damage a persuader's *ethos*. Such speakers are apt to be suspected of trying to succeed by "art" rather than by substance. And Whately made Cicero's and Blair's comments on "good taste" more practical by pointing out that tastes vary among audiences. If speakers are to enhance their *ethos,* they must adjust marks of taste to specific audiences, said Whately.

As we have hinted, the functioning of *ethos* or credibility has been a major topic of interest in the twentieth century. Rhetoricians, advertisers, "image makers," journalists, and social psychologists have discussed, studied, and speculated about this force. The literature is too large to summarize here,[17] but on the whole Aristotle's analysis has been confirmed. Practical speakers may operate confidently on his counsels: that *ethos*—listeners' impressions of the speaker himself—is a powerful force in determining the effects of any oral message; that it is important for speakers to *improve on* their reputations for intelligence and trustworthiness *during* speaking; and that

17. The 1971 cumulative index to speech journals lists 45 published papers on the subject without including the many studies reported in journals of other academic fields. See Chapter 5, pp. 117–124 for further discussion of basic findings and their implications.

something resembling goodwill toward listeners or dynamic identification with them deserves to be a perceptible part of any oral communication.

DISPOSITION

Ideas about structuring oral presentations seem to have appeared in the very earliest writings on rhetoric. A lost work attributed to Corax and Tisias apparently taught that a speech ought to have at least three parts: a proem or introduction to win the favor of listening judges, a narration or proof of one's case, and an epilogue or conclusion. In his *Phaedrus* Plato also argued that discourse ought to have three parts, comparable, he said, to the parts of the human body. Introduction, body, and conclusion were to a composition as head, torso, and feet are to a human being.

Aristotle took issue with the older three-part concept. He opened the final section of Book III of his *Rhetoric* by saying earlier speculations on the divisions of speeches had been absurd. A speech has only two *essential* parts, he said: (a) you state your point or case and (b) you prove it. He granted that in most circumstances these essentials needed to be introduced and concluded. In certain kinds of speaking there would be room to narrate a relevant set of circumstances, but these adjustments of the essentials were seen as *special* responses to special speech situations. They were not always needed in effective, satisfying communications.

Some of what Aristotle had to say about rhetorical structure was specifically related to the *types* of speeches commonly composed in his day: the epideictic (or ceremonial), the deliberative (or legislative), and the forensic (or speech for the court). He also gave scattered bits of advice concerning ways claims to *ethos* and variations in style might be necessary in fulfilling the functions of divisions of speeches.

Cicero, Quintilian, and the authors of most Roman school manuals discussed the organization of speeches (especially legal speeches) with great enthusiasm. They detected six divisions in normal speeches: introduction, statement of facts or the "narration," "division" or preview of proofs to be offered, proof, refutation, and conclusion. As is plain from this list, it was in what we would call the "body" of a speech that the Romans thought they found additional, special functions regularly carried out. And the list reflects their special concern with legal speaking. There are, of course, facts of a case to be given or events and conditions to be described as a normal part of presenting the case. Arguments to be developed are often previewed as the pleader asserts what he will and will not try to prove. Once the arguments have been supported, it is also common in courts to refute and try to remove objections before concluding. Roman theory about organization was, then, largely a special theory for "forensic" speaking. Their thinking was highly formalistic in contrast to Aristotle's functionalism, and in most later periods

Roman formalism dominated over Greek functionalism in Western thought about "building" speeches.

Between Roman times and the Renaissance there were few fresh thoughts about the organization of rhetorical works. And when the humanists of the Renaissance rediscovered their ancient heritage, they tended to perceive rhetoric, poetry, and history as all parts of "eloquence" and to conceive the principles of all "eloquence" in poetic terms. When poetry was recognized as different from rhetoric, style remained the principal feature studied in both arts. It is not surprising, therefore, that poetic principles — what we might call principles of literature — influenced theory, teaching, and criticism of rhetoric very deeply during the Renaissance.[18]

Fénelon understandably rejected the rigid, artificial rules of organization inherited from Rome and medieval homiletics. In his *Dialogues* he contends that the organic unity of a communication is destroyed by imposing complicated divisions on subject matter. Fénelon's arguments forecast those of some modern teachers who also feel that speech ought to follow "natural" forms allegedly inherent in subjects. Fenelon made milder claims for another idea sometimes contended for today: that the order in which ideas reach the threshold of a creator's consciousness is a "natural" order for presentation. A problem with both views is that unless considerably enlarged, neither invites adaptation to the specific demands of specific rhetorical situations.

If we except "psychological writers" like Bacon and George Campbell, it is fair to say that from Fenelon's time to the twentieth century most commentators on rhetoric have taken refuge either in rigid "classical (Roman) rules" or in the doctrines of "natural order" we have mentioned in referring to Fénelon. Twentieth-century experiments to discover the effects of formal structures on listeners have produced conflicting results and yielded little reliable advice. One contemporary, empirical scholar accurately says: "Indeed, the original question asked . . . [Should the most important point be presented first or last?] is still unsolved."[19]

We suggest that at least two misunderstandings contribute to the confusion and contradictions in past and present thought about disposition of ideas in oral communication. First, the full subtlety of the best ancient thinking about disposition has been missed by many. As Russell H. Wagner pointed out some years ago:

> The service which will be rendered by a return to "disposition" in rendering *dispositio* and in referring to its classical doctrines will be nugatory indeed, if we do not restore the full meaning behind the term. . . . It is concerned with the principles of disposing (in the sense of using) the materials invented for a speech, in the best possible manner, for the purpose of effecting the end intended by the

---

18. For a full treatment of these developments see Jerold E. Seigal, *Rhetoric and Philosophy in Renaissance Humanism* (Princeton: Princeton University Press, 1968), especially pp. 260–262.

19. Ernest C. Thompson, "Some Effects of Message Structure on Listeners' Comprehension," *Speech Monographs,* XXXIV (March 1967), 50.

speaker in any given situation. The discussion of disposition usually begins by describing the typical form of the speech—the parts or divisions—or it may be altogether organized under those conventional heads. But always, in the best writers, the principle of adaptation to need is uppermost, and the distinction between conventional organization and functional use of material is insistently made. It is this meaning—the functional selection and use of materials for a particular purpose—which must supplant "arrangement" and which, as "disposition," may well be added to our rhetorical terminology in English.[20]

Experience makes it plain, as you will find, that how you "manage" or "dispose" or "marshal" what you say is a problem you cannot solve apart from *what* you choose to say—the products of your rhetorical invention. As we have shown in Chapter 7, there is the further fact that ideas are not maneuverable entirely at your will. To some extent they will impose their own constraints on your organizational choices. This is a fact to which the "natural order" theorists responded rightly if too exclusively. Second, the experience and expectations of listeners determine to some degree how communicated ideas must be structured. One will err at least sometimes if he tries to structure every communication in the same way—strictly according to rule. Introductions, bodies, and conclusions are normally necessary, but not invariably, as Aristotle was first to point out. Certain units do appear in the bodies of legal speeches, but not all audiences are like courtroom audiences. So, there is no reason to suppose statement-division-proof-refutation is a universally desirable sequence of ideas for the body of a talk. Sometimes what hearers receive *first* will impress them most, but in other circumstances and on other subjects what they hear *last* will be best remembered. Efforts to make rules about the parts of a speech or the importance of first and last positions are based on the assumption that what is being said, who is listening, and where, have no influence on how we are to dispose ideas for presentation. As you have seen in Chapters 7 and 8, our advice is that you adopt a middle position between the "natural order" and the "rule seeking" theorists, organizing your communications with an eye to "standard" organizational strategies that work *most* of the time but are not rules, while remaining alert to the *special* organizational demands that subject matter, a specific audience, and a specific rhetorical situation impose upon you.

STYLE

Referring to what we call "style," a Roman or medieval writer or speaker would have said *elocutio*. Yet *we* associate derivatives from *elocutio* (eloquent, elocution, etc.) with aspects of delivery. This semantic shift needs ex-

---

20. Russell H. Wagner, "The Meaning of *Dispositio*," in *Studies in Speech and Drama in Honor of Alexander M. Drummond* (Ithaca, N.Y.: Cornell University Press, 1944), pp. 292–293.

planation before we discuss theories of style and then theories of delivery.

Our word "style" derives from Old French, which in turn derived its term from the Latin *stilus,* the name of the instrument used in writing. Between 1650 and 1750 the word "style" replaced the Latin word *elocutio* as the name for problems associated with language and its use in composition. As *elocutio* and its derivatives ceased to mean "style," the Latin word *pronuntiatio* and its derivatives came into use to designate the peculiarly oral aspects of using language, hence the modern term "pronunciation." The shifts are of some significance to students of oral rhetoric because they reflect the modern tendency to associate "style" with the written word and to emphasize the delivery aspects of the spoken word. We have shown in this book that there is place for more serious thought about oral style than is often given.

Problems of language were among the earliest concerns of Westerners who studied human speech. Among the early sophists, Protagoras of Abdera observed and classified grammatical parts of speech, verb tenses, and moods, founding the concepts of grammar. Gorgias of Leontini is often called the founder of the *art* of prose because he experimented with ways of giving beauty to prose. Prodicus of Ceos was a kind of early semanticist, exploring meanings and the workings of synonyms. Isocrates (436–338 B.C.) rejected Gorgias's excesses, seeking to conceal his verbal art while creating speech that was at once striking but unified. These and others among the early Greeks may be said to have *founded* the study of language as a resource open to conscious use in communication. Even among them, the perennial issues about choice of language arose: What is *correct?* What is *beautiful?* What *works?* As we shall see, it is about the relative importance of these three questions and their answers that theorists of rhetorical style have chiefly differed over the centuries.

Plato was a brilliant, inventive writer, yet he makes Socrates say in the *Phaedrus* that *correct* diction is the leading standard to be applied to style and that writing is of *doubtful* value because it produces forgetfulness. Plato's art rather than his theory has exerted his influence on the development of style in the West. Predictably, Aristotle was more direct.

He began Book III of his *Rhetoric* by asserting that however important argument might be, *how* things are said must be seriously weighed. Clarity and liveliness were the two qualities of speech Aristotle insisted on most strongly, provided appropriateness to the situation was observed. Metaphors, similes, antitheses, realism, and varied rhythms were the speaker's major resources for achieving clarity and liveliness, he thought. Aristotle's answers to what speakers ought to seek through style were relatively simple and decidedly pragmatic. *What works?* and *Why?* were the questions he chose to try to answer.

As they had in exploring the structural patterns of rhetoric, the Romans who studied rhetorical style seemed more interested in identifying possible maneuvers than in finding out what those maneuvers did and why. Probably the trend had been set by post-Aristotelian Greeks; at any rate, the oldest existing Latin treatise on rhetoric defined and illustrated more than sixty figures of speech.   Having finished his lengthy list of verbal forms exemplified, the unknown author concluded:

> I have here carefully collected all the principles of embellishing style.   If, Herennius, you exercise yourself diligently in these, your speaking will possess impressiveness, distinction, and charm.   As a result you will speak like a true orator, and the product of your invention will not be bare and inelegant, nor will it be expressed in commonplace language.[21]

Knowing and inserting known and approved verbal devices would produce the impressive, distinctive, and charming speaker!

Cicero, the orator, was likewise fascinated by the options offered by known, approved forms of verbal manipulation.   He discussed at length the characteristics and uses of "plain," "middle," and "grand" style.   His emphatic belief that there were clearly distinguishable *levels* of style was derived from rhetoricians before him, but he seems to have been oblivious of the fact that plain-middle-grand express impressions *people* have of language, not *data about* that language.   The goals to which he urged speakers to aspire were: correctness (presumably as *he* defined it), clearness (presumably an absolute quality), appropriateness (to the speech of a "proper" Roman citizen), and ornateness (achieved by full use of verbal resources).

The great Roman teacher of rhetoric, Quintilian, was most concerned with the question: What is *correct?*   "Style," he said, "has three kinds of excellence, correctness, ludicity and elegance. . . .   Its faults are likewise threefold, namely the opposites of these excellences."[22]   Much of Quintilian's advice on style is scattered through his work, but he concentrates on this subject in Books VII and IX.   On balance, he is an apostle of formal correctness, though he does not wholly disregard the pragmatic question, "What works and how?"   Where he deals with this latter question, however, his eye is almost exclusively on the courtroom.

"Longinus" is a perplexing Roman figure.   Whenever he may have written and whoever he was, no extant ancient work on rhetoric draws upon his thoughts concerning the relation of language to effect in communication. Parts of his book are lost—several important bits of thought development are missing—but some of his observations read like direct challenges to the traditional formalism of Roman doctrine on style.   For example:

> What then is the sophomoric?   But the answer is evident: it is a kind of thought characteristic of the schools of rhetoric, which, through over-refinement, ends in frigidity.   Men fall into this vice through aiming at what goes beyond the essential, at elaborate artifice, and especially at charm, and drift away into trumpery and affection.[23]

---

21. *Rhetorica ad Herennium,* trans. Harry Caplan, p. 409, bk. IV, p. 69.
22. *Institutio Oratoria,* ed. and trans. H. E. Butler (Cambridge, Mass.: Harvard University Press, 1921), I, 79, bk. I, p. 1.
23. *On the Sublime,* trans. Benedict Einarson (Chicago: Packard and Co., 1945), p. 8, chap. 2.

But "Longinus's" complaints of classical formalism appear to have influenced no one until the French literary critic Boileau "discovered" and translated his work in 1674!

As far as the record shows, then, the classical interest in how language works in practical communication moved from an era of exploration by the sophists through a period of practical experimentation and theorizing, of which Isocrates and Aristotle were part, into a long period in which artifice was increasingly admired. "What is beautiful?" became the primary question. "What is correct?" meant much the same thing.

This view of rhetorical style predominated for centuries. Through the Middle Ages and the Renaissance rhetorical and poetic styles were badly confused. As late as the sixteenth century beauty was lauded as an end of rhetorical style. In about 1510 the Englishman John Lydgate published his *Court of Sapyence,* in which he asserted that the chief purpose of rhetorical language was to give pleasure to the ear. And Stephen Hawes had in 1506 written a work with a similar theme: *The Pastime of Pleasure.* Hawes's book contained an allegorical treatment of the liberal arts in which rhetoric was called the "honied speech" of poets.

Fénelon had nothing to say in his *Dialogues* about the figures of speech that had made up so much of the centuries' lore on style. Instead, he reflected a new perception of what spoken or written words can do for people: words can *portray.* "Prose has its paintings, albeit more moderated [than poetry]. Without them one cannot heat the imagination of a listener or arouse his passions," Fénelon wrote.[24] A theory was emerging that language achieves its effects through visual qualities and should therefore be concrete in order to stimulate the "passions" of hearers and readers, and Fénelon was one of the first to reflect the development.[25]

George Campbell and Hugh Blair both drew on the conception that a major power of language lies in its power to *portray*—to generate experience that approximates sensory experience, but Campbell's development of the idea was the more interesting. Lloyd F. Bitzer says of Campbell that, "Vivacity, or the lively idea, is without doubt the key concept of Campbell's theory of rhetoric—the concept which fixes the character of his theory."[26] Aristotle's idea that liveliness is essential to effective style became the cornerstone of Campbell's theory of communication, now based on the new "science of human nature" and the view that the main function of language is to generate experience as near as possible to experiencing through the senses. Vivacity together with perspicuity (clarity) and nationally reputable grammar and vocabulary were, in Campbell's view, primary forces in effecting rhetoric's ends of enlightening, understanding, pleasing the imagination, moving the

---

24. *Dialogues on Eloquence,* trans. W. S. Howell, p. 93 (Second Dialogue).
25. Gerard A. Hauser discusses these seventeenth- and eighteenth-century developments in his "Empiricism, Description, and the New Rhetoric," *Philosophy and Rhetoric,* V (Winter 1972), 24–44.
26. "Editor's Introduction" to George Campbell, *The Philosophy of Rhetoric,* ed. Lloyd F. Bitzer, p. xxv.

passions, and influencing the will. Expressing indebtedness to Bacon and to David Hume, Campbell brought functionalism back to the theory of how and why language serves the purposes of rhetoric. But Campbell did not hold the field.

Blair's cast was, of course, literary, and he dealt with style at length. Fifteen of his forty-seven lectures were devoted to discussion of the subject and, if we count the four lectures on taste and the four on language, just under half of his famous *Lectures* were devoted directly or indirectly to style. His touchstones for excellence in choice of language were "taste" and "beauty." His definition of style had wide influence in England and America:

> Style is the peculiar manner in which a man expresses his conceptions by means of language. . . . Style has always some reference to an author's manner of thinking. It is a picture of the ideas which rise in his mind, and of the manner in which they arise there. . . . Style is nothing else than that sort of expression which our thoughts most readily assume.[27]

Blair's pronouncements did not yield much insight into *how* language works, but his widely circulated lectures spread the concepts that beauty, good taste, and correctness were the ideal avenues to effective portrayal through words.

Richard Whately's nineteenth-century treatment of style in his *Elements of Rhetoric* was, according to one of his editors, "a dreary rehearsal of time-worn advice about the selection and arrangement of words."[28] It is true there was nothing very new in what Whately had to say about oral style, for he undertook to blend Campbell's and Blair's observations. In doing so, he tended to blunt Campbell's pragmatic view of the rhetorical functions of language by appending to them Blair's and other traditional injunctions that speakers should seek elegance or beauty in utterance.

Whately's mixture of formalism and pragmatism forecast most of what would be said in the nineteenth century about style. A few, but not many, additional thoughts emerged to affect us today. Samuel Taylor Coleridge emphasized in his essay "On Style" (1818) that major stylistic qualities are not translatable from language to language. Alexander Bain's *Manual of English Composition and Rhetoric* (1866, rev. ed. 1872) expanded Blair's "laws of the sentence" and put into formal circulation what we now hear of as "laws of the paragraph." On the whole American teaching of composition, oral and written, followed Bain's insistence that the study of rhetoric (meaning *style*) is the study of managing the words and the structures of language and has little or nothing to do with content or oral presentation *per se*. Nineteenth-century rhetorics in England and America were chiefly rhetorics of style, chiefly of written style, and chiefly of style detached from content. They were what Douglas Ehninger has called "managerial rhetorics," and by the late 1800's

---

27. Hugh Blair, *Lectures on Rhetoric and Belles Lettres*, ed. Harold F. Harding (Carbondale, Ill.: Southern Illinois University Press, 1965), I, 183–184.
28. "Editor's Introduction" to Richard Whately, *Elements of Rhetoric*, ed. Douglas Ehninger (Carbondale, Ill.: Southern Illinois University Press, 1963), p. xxi.

virtually all of Aristotle's, Bacon's, and Campbell's pragmatic inquiries about language had been lost.

In reaction, perhaps, twentieth-century treatments of literary and rhetorical style have often returned to the pragmatic question: "What *works* and *how?*" How words work psychologically and how we arrive at their meanings have been the main focuses of I. A. Richards's studies.[29] Richards's theory that all language is metaphorically symbolic and that to understand language the emotive and referential functions of words must be differentiated constitutes a theory of semantic analysis that has much influence in literary and rhetorical studies today. Word-by-word analysis of literary works and audience-centered criticism reflects "The New Criticism's" indebtedness to Richards. So, too, does the emphasis on metaphor and "image" that is found in a good deal of speech criticism.

Kenneth Burke's studies of rhetorical style have also had major influence on rhetorical and literary criticism. *A Grammar of Motives* and *A Rhetoric of Motives* have been especially influential. *Identification* is Burke's key concept. He sees use of language as a search for interpersonal identification – a search motivated by the divisiveness that seems part of the human condition. Because there is division that separates human beings, they seek to remove it by using language as a public and collective instrument for reducing division. Burke thus provides a fresh interpretation of the rhetorical function of language. He emphasizes the importance and value of man's power to symbolize and sees study of rhetoric as the method of studying symbolic behavior.

Two other theorist-critics who suggest expansions of critical methods by starting from traditional premises about the nature of rhetorical style are Wayne C. Booth and Ross W. Winterowd. In *The Rhetoric of Fiction* (1961) Booth suggests that even in fiction authors *address* their readers to control attention and belief in rhetorical ways, and he analyzes the rhetorical strategies they use for these purposes. Winterowd's *Rhetoric: A Synthesis* (1968) and other of his writings draw upon the thoughts of Kenneth Burke and upon those of grammarians who have developed the theory of "generative grammar." From these, from classical sources, and from the findings of psycholinguistics, Winterowd hopes to evolve better principles of both composition and criticism.

Special concern with the social significance of meanings motivated Alfred Korzybski to write his *Science and Sanity,* published in 1933, and to found a branch of study called General Semantics. His work was the basis for a popular version of the theories of General Semantics, S. I. Hayakawa's *Language in Action* (1941), later revised as *Language in Thought and Action.* Levels of abstraction are illustrated by General Semanticists by an abstraction ladder representing the levels of meaning beyond the denotative. General Semanticists make the special point that people develop problems when they

---

29. For example, *The Meaning of Meaning,* written with C. K. Ogden (1923), and his *The Philosophy of Rhetoric* (1936).

react to words as though the words *were* the things they name. That our language maps of the world are *not* the "territories" of the world is a central lesson taught by this group of students of style.

A still different way of looking at rhetorical style has come from a group of philosophers interested in the branch of philosophy called "theory of argument." Especially important to practical rhetoricians is *The New Rhetoric* by Chaim Perelman and L. Olbrechts-Tyteca. Working from both classical and modern theories of language, these authors demonstrate that in rhetoric words and word forms *argue* as surely as traditional argumentative forms such as inductions, deductions, analogies, and arguments from cause. Reflections of this line of thought will be found in our treatment of figures of speech in Chapter 9, pages 231–240.

Thought about the role of language in rhetoric, including oral rhetoric, has completed something of a circle. "What works and how?" was the question most interesting to some Greek sophists and to Aristotle and it is the question increasingly asked today in Western Europe, England, and the United States. The nineteenth century's "oratory" of beauty and impressiveness is little heard and the standards that bred it seem little valued. The practical student of practical speaking can, we think, congratulate himself that his is an age in which study of the pragmatic uses of language is in vogue. Doing "business," not observing forms for their own sakes, is the thrust in the modern speech classroom—as it was in Aristotle's and Isocrates's schools!

DELIVERY

We have seen how Western thinking about disposition and style vacillated between practical, communicative considerations and the search for formal rules, doctrines of correctness, principles of aesthetic beauty. The same vacillation characterized thought about presentation of public speech. At many periods our forebears seem even to have thought about delivery more than was good for practical communication.

We do not know just when students of speech began to analyze the manners of delivery they thought effective, but it must have been very early. From the time of Theophrastus (c. 370–285 B.C.) we have evidence of writers' analyses of vocal and gestural patterns. In *De Oratore* Cicero repeats a story that goes back at least to Theophrastus,[30] that Demosthenes was once asked what was most important in speaking. He replied, "Delivery." When asked what was next in importance, he answered the same, and to the question of what came third, he repeated, "Delivery." This story, like the legend telling how Demosthenes improved his articulation by speaking with pebbles in his

---

30. George Kennedy, *The Art of Persuasion in Greece*, p. 283.

mouth, indicates that at least practitioners were preoccupied with delivery from the earliest part of the classical period. It was not so with the earliest theorists we know of.

Plato did not mention delivery specifically, though he did say practice would add to a speaker's natural capacities. Aristotle discussed the subject almost grudgingly in a brief passage at the beginning of Book III of his *Rhetoric*. There he said delivery must be attended to as "something we are bound to do." He granted that it was not enough to know what to say; one must know *how* to say it. But he said these things reluctantly, apparently feeling that such matters fell in the province of actors and were therefore vulgar—at least for a theorist to discuss. Similarly, a book by an unknown author who probably wrote in the generation after Aristotle's omitted mention of problems of oral presentation. The work's Latin title is *Rhetorica ad Alexandrum*.

Though concepts about presenting speeches were slighted by the Greek theorists we know, the subject later received detailed attention at Rome. The unknown author of *Rhetorica ad Herennium* showed his penchant for classification, and that he had some fairly detailed works to draw on, when he classified and described vocal qualities under three headings: volume, stability, and flexibility. He endorsed what he called "conversational tone" and identified four variations of it: the dignified, the explicative, the narrative, and the facetious. He then discussed how these tones should be used in the various parts of a speech. He gave little attention to gestures and facial expressions beyond mentioning their importance, and he concluded by confessing he was not sure it was possible to explain the role of delivery in writing. His confession may be a hint that delivery was still the concern of more practitioners and pedagogues than theorists.

Cicero wrote of delivery as a practitioner, naturally enough, though in what he had to say he offered some interesting speculations on the relative importance of various aspects of presentation. His most significant observations appear in *De Oratore*, some being confirmed in his later book *Orator*, a discussion of the "perfect" speaker. Cicero seems to have accepted the emphasis on delivery reflected in the story of Demosthenes to which we have referred. In Cicero's view, dignity and grace were so important in speaking that those with highest mental capacity would lose esteem without these qualities and speakers of only moderate intellect but great skill in delivery would surpass their intellectual betters. He went beyond the author of *Rhetorica ad Herennium* by discussing both vocal and gestural activity, and he followed the earlier author in stressing that qualities of delivery express speakers' emotions and must, therefore, be precisely suited to thoughts being uttered. Words, Cicero said, can move only those who share your language, but all mankind—illiterates and even barbarians—can see and understand physical behavior.

Aristotle's notion that rhetorical presentation and the presentations of actors are alike did not satisfy Cicero. He insisted that gestural patterns in public speaking were markedly different from the patterns appropriate to acting. Accordingly he paused over the place in rhetorical speech for gestures of the hands and arms, for stamping one's foot, and, especially, the emotional expressiveness of the eyes. He thought that of all the facial features, the eyes best expressed a speaker's emotion.

Quintilian's *Institutio* contained a good many descriptions of vocal and gestural behaviors without differing much from what the author of *Rhetorica ad Herennium* and Cicero had said. But Quintilian did make two points worth mentioning here. He insisted that the ideal speech—in court or elsewhere—was one that had been fully written beforehand. And he reveals that at least some Roman teachers thought speaking and singing required the same kinds of vocal resources and management. Not so, said Quintilian, as he pointed out that speakers need "strong and enduring" voices, not "soft and sweet" ones and that singers must strive for perfection in pitch though speakers need worry little about that problem. In general, Quintilian's third chapter of Book XI of the *Institutio* shows that he and presumably other Romans had studied the speech production system of humans with considerable care and were at least beginning analyses of the human voice not unlike those that re-emerged as delivery began to receive scientific attention in the eighteenth century.

On the whole the Romans *described* vocal and gestural behavior, then tried to *prescribe* specific behaviors for specific emotions, parts of speeches, and rhetorical situations. From fuller understanding of the phenomena of presentation, they moved toward more and more "rules." And this tendency to formulate rules was inherited by men of the Middle Ages and the Renaissance as they rediscovered learning through classical works. The special interest in *style,* which marked the resurgence of literary interest during the Renaissance, discouraged thought about oral delivery. Insofar as the subject was important, the issue was: How shall one read aloud? That question was, of course, quite different from the one the Romans had, at least at first, tried to ask: How shall one speak to be understood as thought and feeling demand?

Fénelon gave much more attention to aspects of delivery than others of the Renaissance. In his *Dialogues* he seemed to be trying to fill out, for delivery, Augustine's themes of devotional directness and pastoral adaptation. These St. Augustine had developed at length relative to style, but he had said little about the preacher's delivery. Fénelon addressed the issues directly, condemning the rigid, artificial rules he found too much followed by his contemporaries. The goal in delivery ought to be artlessness rather than mechanical control, said Fénelon. In the spirit of Augustine and in the spirit of emerging literary theories, Fénelon urged all speakers to put their reliance on cultivated, earnest feeling toward listeners; right feeling would "naturally" yield appropriate, reinforcing, vocal and gestural behaviors.

In contrast with Fénelon's doctrines of "naturalness" there grew up less than a century later a new-old body of theory called "elocution." Its concepts were the antitheses of Fénelon's. To a degree the new concepts were "scientific" extensions of the Romans' ambition to *describe,* then *prescribe;* but there was also new driving force in this movement for intensive study of oral presentation. Frederick W. Haberman writes:

> Elocution was an offshoot of rhetorical study. It was an exhaustive and systematic analysis of delivery. The elocutionary movement, which began about 1750, was a response to the demands of the age. This widespread and intense study of delivery was an answer to the eighteenth-century denunciations of oratorical frigidity, to the pressure for professional and educational training in speech, to the new consciousness of the need for standardization of spoken language, to the desire of the people to obtain facility in speaking a language of which they were becoming proud and to demands of those who dealt with democratic movements. The elocutionary movement, however, was more than a simple renaissance of a particular canon of rhetoric. It was rather, a new ordering of an old subject.
>
> This new ordering resulted from the application of the tenets of science and of rationalism to the physiological phenomena of spoken discourse. The new study of delivery was affected by the impact of science or of rationalism in precisely the same way that the study of history, of economics, of poetry, and of prose style was affected.[31]

Three kinds of textbooks came out of the elocutionary movement: thorough, often research-based, works treating voice, rhythm, and gesture; elementary rule books; and collections of useful and elegant extracts for practice. The elocutionists developed systems for observing voice, gesture, and language and means of recording these observations. In these efforts their work resembled that of modern-day students of nonverbal behavior.

As Haberman indicates, the elocutionists worked from scientific-rationalistic premises. They presupposed that man is ruled by natural laws. Nature is a compelling force. It has immutable laws in the physical universe and immutable codes in the social universe. These laws and codes are systematic and can be disregarded only at one's peril. These theorists thought speech and all worldly matters were capable of scientific systematization. So they embarked upon their mission to reduce speaking to system.

The outpouring of elocutionary books and magazines during the last half of the eighteenth and throughout the nineteenth centuries was much too vast to review here, but Haberman has identified four founders of the movement and a note on each will suggest the directions of research and exposition that characterized this movement.[32] Thomas Sheridan (1719–1788) published *Lectures on Elocution* in 1756. In it he examined the individual sounds of speech and the gestural behaviors associated with familiar emotions. Among other things, he was seeking a scientific phonetics with which to

---

31. Frederick W. Haberman, "John Thelwall: His Life, His School, and His Theory of Elocution," *The Quarterly Journal of Speech,* XXXIII (Oct. 1947), p. 294.
32. Frederick W. Haberman, "The Elocutionary Movement in England, 1750–1850" (Unpublished Ph.D. thesis, Cornell University, 1947).

describe pronunciation and a kind of "grammar" of gesture by which to teach "appropriate" and "natural" physical action.   Joshua Steele (1700–1791) devised a system of musical notations by which to describe the management of the voice.   His *Prosodia Rationalis* treated patterns of melody, rhythm, and pitch in speech and music.   John Walker (1732–1807) was an actor turned elocutionist.   He invented a system by which to describe the "natural" interrelations between vocal inflections and grammatical forms.   His chief publication was *Elements of Elocution* (1781).   Finally, James Burgh (1714–1775) expressed the article of faith which Cicero had expressed and which gave the elocutionists much of their driving energy.   In *The Art of Speaking* (1761) Burgh said "nature had given every emotion of mind its proper expression."   The task for the elocutionists, as for some Romans, seemed to be to catalogue those nonverbal, emotional expressions the better to *teach* them "naturally"!

The elocutionary movement, with its research impulse, its enthusiasm for detailed description, and its determination to *prescribe* "natural" behavior in speaking and acting, dominated English and American thought about speech delivery until the beginning of the twentieth century.   In their desire to apply the laws of nature to man's speaking behavior, the elocutionists often produced artificial rules and systems more complex than any Roman had had the tools to produce, but in a number of cases their research efforts became the foundations for such modern sciences as phonetics, vocal acoustics, and some branches of linguistics.   Indeed, a good deal of current research on nonverbal behavior covers ground on which the elocutionists were pioneers.

The classical revivalists who wrote on communication during the period in which elocution burgeoned and flourished insisted on a different way of thinking about speech behavior.   Both Hugh Blair and Richard Whately differed from the elocutionists, but they also differed from one another, and the viewpoint of each has its knowing or unknowing followers today.

Blair's conception of delivery and the aspects he considered important are discussed chiefly in Lecture XXXIII of his *Lectures on Rhetoric and Belles Lettres*.   The lecture is titled "Pronunciation, or Delivery."   Blair saw delivery as vocal and gestural behavior that operates within natural languages understood by all.   Words, he said, are arbitrary symbols of ideas and therefore are not universally understood.   The "natural" symbolizations of voice and gesture are not so confined in meaning.

There are hints that Blair thought what he called "pitches of voice" were naturally and uniquely associated with specific kinds of speaking.   Also, other remarks scattered through his lectures indicate that he thought different styles of delivery were peculiarly suited to different kinds of speech.   In most other respects Blair's comments on delivery were traditional, but his advice to speakers contained subtle, internal contradictions one can also see in discussions of speechmaking today.

Like most writers, Blair urged speakers to let delivery reflect their actual feelings. "Follow nature," he says in effect. On the other hand, he suggests that the secret of effective delivery is thinking one's thought clearly while uttering it. Further, he counsels study of proper models and practice "for many persons are naturally ungraceful." But then: "Whatever is native, even though accompanied with several defects, yet [it] is likely to please; because it shows us a man; because it has the appearance of coming from the heart."[33] Blair seems not to have considered these pieces of advice incompatible, and in this he resembled many moderns who advise speakers to "be natural" but then criticize those speakers' grace and taste.

Richard Whately was more vigorously in reaction against the elocutionists than Blair, but he did not, as some have believed, counsel "following nature" in impulsive, undisciplined ways. What he said of "naturalness" echoed Blair but was more clearly thought out. Whately was strongly critical of all mechanical guides to "natural" or effective presentation, but it is evident that he did not advocate impulsive response to feelings. He did say:

> The practical rule then to be adopted, in conformity with the principles here maintained, is, not only to pay no studied attention to the Voice, but studiously to *withdraw* the thoughts from it, and to dwell as intently as possible on the Sense; trusting to nature to suggest spontaneously the proper emphases and tones.[34]

At a later point Whately added this qualification:

> When however I protest against all artificial systems of Elocution, and all *direct* attention to Delivery, *at the time,* it must not be supposed that a *general* inattention to that point is recommended; or that the most perfect Elocution is to be attained by never thinking at all on the subject; though it may safely be affirmed that even this negative plan would succeed far better than a studied modulation.[35]

It is clear that Whately was recommending that speakers occupy their minds with ideas rather than prescribed behaviors, and in this he was injecting a new thought into Western lore on how people can best express what they mean, vocally and physically. The notion was radical and it required modification, but in the mind of the American James A. Winans, Whately's thought evolved into a balanced, cogent view of what is required mentally for the most "natural" delivery possible in public speech.

Winans's (1872–1956) influence on contemporary theories about practical delivery has been immeasurable since 1915. Contending that Whately's "think-the-thought" doctrine could as easily produce soliloquy as direct, effective, public speech, Winans altered the formula by adding to it. He wrote:

---

33. Lecture XXXIII. *Lectures on Rhetoric and Belles Lettres,* ed. H. F. Harding, II, pp. 222, 224.
34. Richard Whately, *Elements of Rhetoric,* ed. Douglas Ehninger, p. 352.
35. *Ibid.,* pp. 346–347.

> . . . your delivery will have the desired conversational quality when you retain upon the platform these elements of the mental state of live conversation:
>
> 1. Full realization of the content of your words as you utter them, and
>
> 2. A lively sense of communication.[36]

Winans's first point was Whately's; his second the corrective. Winans was convinced that effective delivery depends on *both* awareness of one's thought *and* a strong wish to convey the thought to someone else.

Refining another familiar notion—that effective delivery is somehow related to the "conversational"—Winans also argued for a distinction between "conversational *quality*" and "conversational *style*." Public speech ought to have the *quality* of conversation, Winans insisted, but if it *imitated* the "style" of ordinary, informal conversation it would belie the publicness of the speaker's situation.

To us, at least, Winans seems to have resolved the paradox of centuries: speakers have to *mean* what they say, both vocally and physically, yet they speak with special responsibilities in public settings, and these responsibilities are *not* "natural" for them. Greek rhetorical theory, as we know it, virtually ignored the problem. Romans and elocutionists counselled *learning* "proper" behaviors of "nature." Fénelon and others trusted "nature" and feelings completely, but candor forced the eclectic Blair to admit that some who want to speak are naturally clumsy until they *learn* otherwise. Whately saw the *thought* as the generator of meaningful behavior, but it remained for Winans to emphasize the importance of being *dually* aware—of thought and of the communicative relationship with others in which speakers engage in public speech. Our treatment of delivery in Chapter 10 developed from the Whately-Winans premises.

MEMORIA

Memoria has been called the "lost canon" of rhetoric, presumably meaning that no one pays attention to it any more. The term *memoria* refers to that body of theory and advice that concerns managing and controlling utterance, according to plan, when speaking occurs. The English term "memory" connotes considerably less than the full range of rhetorical problems that confront a speaker who has prepared a speech and now must present it. More than memorizing or recall of a plan is involved. It is for this reason we are using the Latin term, there being no sound equivalent in English.

Speakers face problems involving *memoria* from the outset of speech preparation. They must choose subjects they will *be able to command;* they

---

36. James A. Winans, *Public Speaking* (New York: The Century Co., 1917), p. 31.

must set purposes they *will still understand* when they are speaking; they must build structures and frame outlines and notes they, themselves, *will be able to follow;* they must choose language natural enough to them so they *will be able to command it under pressure;* they must make plans for delivery which they *will be able to execute;* and, of course, they must keep their wits and all their plans about them as they speak. Much more than *memory* is involved, but this has not always been recognized in Western thought about *memoria*.

For much of the classical era *memoria* meant little more than "memory" of one's speech. The earliest writers seem to have felt that the best service they could render speakers was to pass on instructions on memory systems. Thus the story of Simonides of Ceos is repeated in several books on rhetoric. Simonides was a poet. After reading a long, lyric poem at a banquet, he was called from the hall. Moments later, the roof fell in, killing the remaining guests and disfiguring them beyond recognition. But Simonides was able to match the bodies and the names by mentally picturing the former seating arrangement. His alleged success dramatized for others the usefulness of associating ideas with spaces. One could then call up the spatial image and, by association, remember the ideas "put there."

The Simonides story came from Greece, but the Greek theorists we know of did not deal with those problems which the Romans called the problems of *memoria*. The first extended treatment of the subject now known appears in the *Rhetorica ad Herennium*. There *memoria* is called "the guardian of all the parts of rhetoric," but the author seems not to have had a conception of a speech as a *plan* of internally grouped ideas. The story of Simonides is told to illustrate how an "artificial" memory system can help the "natural" memory. In short, this early Roman author seems to have been mainly interested in supplying his pupils with mnemonic devices for jogging their memories, whether the task was to recall words, related ideas, or situations.

Cicero treated *memoria* briefly in *De Oratore* and he emphasized the point that it is possible to store proofs in the mind in *interrelated ways* so they can be recalled as pertinent to specific lines of argument useful in building legal cases and legislative arguments as changes in such rhetorical situations require. For him, the problem was to file away data and ideas in ways that would allow a speaker to recall and use those ideas *adaptively*. The problems of *memoria* were more complex for Cicero than the mere problem of memorizing, though he also gave advice on memorizing.

Quintilian's was the most extensive treatment of *memoria* among the existing ancient writings, but he generally followed Cicero's topics of discussion. Quintilian seems to have seen new dimensions of the subject, however, for he touched upon at least two new points. He observed—and was the first known writer to do so clearly—that paying attention to the (logical?) principles of rhetorical division and composition could be of great value to a speaker trying to command his speech in anticipation of delivering it. "If our composition be what it should, the artistic sequence will serve to guide the memory."[37] Here, the connection between a speaker's *planning* and his capacity to command the whole discourse seems recognized.   A second "new" consideration recognized by Quintilian was that the psychological problems of commanding ideas and language during extemporaneous speaking are different from those faced when a speaker memorizes and delivers a "set" speech.   Once more, Quintilian seems to have been the ancient writer who saw most clearly that Simonides' mnemonic devices could not answer all of an active speaker's problems of self-command.

Except as treated in tracts on preaching, which stressed "division" (preview) as helpful to determining and remembering systems of arrangement for sermons, little was said in rhetorical treatises on rhetoric written during the Middle Ages.   True, Alcuin (c. 735–804) did advise the emperor Charlemagne that a speaker ought to avoid drunkenness if he expected his memory to function effectively![38]   In the main, however, it was not until the appearance of Thomas Wilson's *Arte of Rhetorique* that *memoria* was again discussed even at the level of Roman sophistication.   And since succeeding rhetorics tended to deal with both speaking and writing, the special problems of speakers' *memoria* received limited attention until the twentieth century.[39]

It is in textbooks on speaking published in the twentieth century that speakers' *memoria* problems have been faced with greater penetration than Quintilian's.   James Winans's and Charles Woolbert's early textbooks explained the contributions of the new discipline, psychology, to solving speaker's problems of command during speaking.   Borrowing from pragmatic psychology, Winans pointed to the importance of outlines as mental guides and assurances that speeches would be presented with their planned, "due proportion, emphasis, unity, and coherence."   And, said Winans, outlines also serve as visual images of the soundness and the "logic" of interconnections among ideas; once seen, these interconnections allow speakers to sense their observations as *wholes,* not as series of points.   Woolbert was devoted to a different psychology, behaviorism, so he stressed a different aspect of the theory of *memoria.*   Let speakers *condition* themselves properly, was his major counsel.   Accordingly, he urged that speakers (and readers) first formulate the "perspective" of their material, then concentrate on "details," doing both *orally* — so as to involve their senses of hearing in the acquisition of material — and performing all these functions in imagined or real circumstances as nearly approximating the actual circumstances of speaking as possible.

The psychologies on which Winans and Woolbert depended are partially outmoded today, but as each advance is made in understanding how human

37. *Institutio Oratoria,* trans. H. E. Butler, IV, 235, bk. IV, p. 39.
38. Wilbur S. Howell, *The Rhetoric of Alcuin and Charlemagne* (Princeton: Princeton University Press, 1941), pp. 137, 139.
39. A more detailed discussion of *memoria* as treated in works we are passing over is Wayne E. Hoogestraat's "Memory: The Lost Canon?" *Quarterly Journal of Speech,* XLVI (April 1960), 141–147.

beings *learn,* advances can be made in solving the perennial problems of *memoria* which *public* speakers, especially, face. How we shall best command the whole of our plans during the moments of speaking and adjusting to rhetorical situations is still not fully known; there is much mystery still.[40] But one idea held by both ancients and moderns seems especially valuable: commanding a *visual* plan of ideas and their interconnections—in outline form or other—establishes content and plan in the mind but with sufficient flexibility to allow the adaptive restructuring that public speech so often demands.

We have been concerned with command of material and action throughout this book—with mental and physical command. As we have treated invention, disposition, style, and delivery and the special problems of audience adaptation, we also have treated ways of solving the problems of *command* through consciousness of what one is doing in preparation and through bringing plans into visual, practiced form, the better to assure true *memoria* in the moments of speaking.

CONCLUSION

In the history of Western thought about oral rhetoric only disposition and *memoria* of the five great constellations of communicative problems have missed their hour in the limelight. Neither has ever dominated thought about public speech; invention, style, and delivery have so dominated, not without unfortunate results for balanced, forceful speaking.

The ancient Greeks laid a foundation for the art of public speech, importantly stressing the necessity of transforming thoughts into *communicable* thoughts. Romans refined and amplified, ultimately stultifying the art by excessive formalization in the period of the Roman Empire. Augustine Christianized the Roman lore, but for preaching only. His achievement could not prevent later confusion of rhetoric with poetic or the ultimate absorption of rhetoric into logic. When the residual rhetoric was style, there were some who clung, to the classical tradition in which invention was the key process in speech communication—an emphasis ultimately restored in the twentieth century despite the tempting distractions of "naturalism" and elocution. To the new classical revival, modern psychological and philosophical investigation has added and continues to add to the ways speakers can learn to meet those invariably present problems of speaking: what to say, how to give it form, what language to use, how to present it, and how to keep plans under command.

If there is a practical lesson to be learned from this historical review, it seems to us to be that to neglect *any* or to overvalue *one* or *two* of these sets

---

40. See, for example, Will Bradbury, "The Mystery of Memory," *Life,* LXXI (Nov. 12, 1971), 66–76, and Mark R. Rosenzweig, "Biologists Try to Learn Exactly How We Learn," *The New York Times,* Jan. 12, 1970, p. 72C.

of problems has proved mistaken wherever it has occurred, across more than 2500 years. But when men have thought as hard as they knew how about.*all* of these problems, they have produced thought of historic significance and public speech of great practical and artistic merit. Thus, the classic age of Greece, the era of the Roman Republic, England in the eighteenth century. Fortunately we occupy an age which has the knowledge with which to maintain a like balance and to hope for significant achievement (*not* "oratory") in public speech.

BIBLIOGRAPHY OF LANDMARK WORKS IN RHETORIC[41]

Plato, *Gorgias*. Translated by W. R. Lamb. Cambridge, Mass.: Harvard University Press, 1925.

————, *Phaedrus*. Translated by H. N. Fowler. Cambridge, Mass.: Harvard University Press, 1914.

Aristotle, *The Rhetoric of Aristotle*. Translated and edited by Lane Cooper. New York: Appleton-Century-Crofts, 1932.

Rhetorica ad Herennium. Translated by Harry Caplan. Cambridge, Mass.: Harvard University Press, 1954.

Cicero, *De Oratore*. Translated by E. W. Sutton and H. Rackham. 2 vols. Cambridge, Mass.: Harvard University Press, 1942.

Quintilian, *The Institutio Oratoria of Quintilian*. Translated by H. E. Butler. Cambridge, Mass.: Harvard University Press, 1953.

Longinus, "On the Sublime." Translated by W. Rhys Roberts. In J. H. Smith and E. W. Parks, *The Great Critics*, 3rd ed. New York: W. W. Norton, 1951.

Saint Augustine, *On Christian Doctrine*. Translated by D. W. Robertson, Jr. Indianapolis: The Bobbs-Merrill Co., Inc., 1958.

Bacon, Francis—See Wallace, Karl R., *Francis Bacon on Communication and Rhetoric*. Chapel Hill: The University of North Carolina Press, 1943. (This is a masterful synthesis of Bacon's ideas on rhetoric as found in the works mentioned in this chapter.)

Fénelon, *Dialogues on Eloquence*. Translated by Wilbur S. Howell. Princeton: Princeton University Press, 1951.

Sheridan, Thomas, *A Course of Lectures on Elocution*. London, 1762.

Steele, Joshua, *Prosodia Rationalis*. London, 1779.

Austin, Gilbert, *Chironomia or a Treatise on Rhetorical Delivery*. Edited by Mary Margaret Robb and Lester Thonssen. Carbondale, Ill.: Southern Illinois University Press, 1966.

Campbell, George, *The Philosophy of Rhetoric*. Edited by Lloyd Bitzer. Carbondale, Ill.: Southern Illinois University Press, 1963.

Blair, Hugh, *Lectures on Rhetoric and Belles Lettres*. Edited by Harold F. Harding. Carbondale, Ill.: Southern Illinois University Press, 1965.

---

41. We have listed here the most reliable and most easily obtainable editions at the time of writing. They are listed in chronological order.

Whately, Richard, *Elements of Rhetoric*. Edited by Douglas Ehninger. Carbondale, Ill.: Southern Illinois University Press, 1963.

Winans, James A., *Public Speaking*. New York: Century Company, 1917.

Woolbert, Charles H., *The Fundamentals of Speech: A Behavioristic Study of the Underlying Principles of Speaking and Reading*. New York: Harper & Brothers Publishers, 1920.

Richards, I. A., *The Philosophy of Rhetoric*. New York: Oxford University Press, 1965.

Burke, Kenneth, *A Grammar of Motives* and *A Rhetoric of Motives*. New York: The World Publishing Company, 1962.

Toulmin, Stephen E., *The Uses of Argument*. New York: The Cambridge University Press, 1958.

Perelman, Chaim, and Olbrechts-Tyteca, L., *The New Rhetoric: A Treatise on Argument*. Translated by John Wilkinson and Purcell Weaver. Notre Dame, Ind.: University of Notre Dame Press, 1969.

EXERCISES

Written

1. Write a book review (1500–2000 words) treating the whole or a part of one of the works on rhetorical theory mentioned in this chapter.
2. Write an essay comparing the treatments of one of the rhetorical "canons" (invention, disposition, style, delivery, or *memoria*) in two of the books cited in this chapter. For example, compare Aristotle's theory of oral style with Blair's, or Cicero's theory of delivery with Whately's.
3. Explore some contemporary psychological research on communicative credibility and write a report comparing those findings with Aristotle's speculations (or Cicero's or Quintilian's).

Oral

1. Prepare and deliver a 2- to 3-minute speech introducing a person whose name is mentioned in this chapter. Assume that he is about to deliver a lecture to your class on an aspect of rhetorical theory.
2. After reading in one of the works mentioned in this chapter, make a short report on some aspect of theory that you feel is applicable to speechmaking today.
3. With four or five classmates engage in a discussion on the question, "What is it to be 'natural' in speaking publicly?" When your group has come to a conclusion or unresolvable disagreement, report the results to your class.

Special Index for the Study of Types of Speeches

This index is designed as an aid to students and teachers who wish to structure the study or preparation of speeches around purposes for which speeches are made. The general section of the index identifies treatments of topics pertinent to all or to several purposes. Subsequent sections indicate the portions of this book which relate directly or with special relevance to a specific type of speech.

Index